THE COMPLETE
MAHABHARATA
Santi Parva

THE COMPLETE MAHABHARATA

Volume 8

Santi Parva

Part I
Rajadharmanusasana Parva
Part II
Apaddharmanusasana Parva

Manjulika Dubey and S.B. Pillay

RUPA

Published by
Rupa Publications India Pvt. Ltd 2016
7/16, Ansari Road, Daryaganj
New Delhi 110002

Sales centres:
Allahabad Bengaluru Chennai
Hyderabad Jaipur Kathmandu
Kolkata Mumbai

ISBN: 978-81-291-3751-7

First impression 2016

10 9 8 7 6 5 4 3 2 1

The moral right of the author has been asserted.

Printed at Gopsons Papers Ltd, Noida

In memory of
Padmanabha Vijai Pillai

Contents

PART I

Rajadharmanusasana Parva

CANTO 1

AUM! Bowing down to Narayana and Nara, the foremost of Purushas, and to Devi Saraswati, I invoke the spirit of Jaya!

Vaisampayana said, "After offering oblations of water to all their friends and kinsmen, the sons of Pandu, Vidura, Dhritarashtra, and all the Bhaarata women continue to dwell on the banks of the sacred stream, Bhagirathi. They spend the month of mourning outside the Kuru city. Yudhishtira Dharmaraja performs the water-rites, and many great Rishis arrive to see the monarch. Among them are the island-born Vyasa, Narada, Devala, Devasthana and Kanwa, all accompanied by their best disciples.

Many other Munis, wise and expert in the Vedas, Grihastas and Snatakas, also come to meet the Kuru king. Yudhishtira duly worships the Maharishis and seats them on precious carpets. They accept the worship suitable for this period of mourning and impurity, and thousands of them sit in due order around the king. They offer consolation and comfort to the grieving Yudhishtira, king of kings, whose heart is racked by anguish.

After greeting Vyasa and the Rishis, Narada addresses Yudhishtira, the son of Dharma. 'Through the might of your arms and by the grace of Madhava you have righteously won this whole earth, and by your good fortune you have emerged alive from this dreadful war. Observant as you are of the Kshatriya dharma, do you not rejoice, O son of Pandu? Now that you have killed all your enemies and won this victory, will you not gratify your friends, O Rajan? I hope grief does not still afflict you.'

Yudhishtira replies, 'I have indeed subjugated the whole world, through the might of Krishna's arms, the grace of the Brahmanas and the strength of Bhima and Arjuna. However, this heavy sorrow is always in my heart, that through my greed I have caused this fearsome carnage of my kinsmen.

Having caused the death of Subhadra's precious son, and of the sons of Draupadi, O holy one, this victory appears to me to be a defeat. What will my sister-in-law, Subhadra of Vrishni's race, say to me? What will the people of Dwaraka have to say to Krishna when he returns from here? Again, the thought of Draupadi, who has always been considerate of us, and is now bereaved of her sons and kinsmen, causes me relentless pain.

There is another subject, O Narada, about which I will speak to you. It afflicts me that Kunti kept from us a great and terrible secret: that Karna—strong as ten thousand elephants, Maharatha unrivalled in this world, of leonine pride and gait, of vast intelligence and boundless compassion, whose generosity and liberality were legend—was her son. Born secretly to her, Karna, who kept many high vratas, who was the refuge of the Dhartarashtras, who was sensitive about his honour, whose prowess was irresistible, who was ever ready to repay every injury and always wrathful in battle, who vanquished us in repeated encounters, who was quicksilver in the use of weapons, conversant with every kind of warfare, possessed of great skill and endowed with wonderful valour— was thus, our own brother.

Only while we were offering oblations of water to the dead did Kunti speak of him as the son of Surya. She had placed that glorious infant in a basket made of light wood and committed him to the current of the Ganga. He whom the world regarded as a Suta's child born of Radha was really the first son of Kunti—our eldest brother by blood. Alas, by coveting the kingdom I have caused my brother to be killed. It is this that burns my limbs, like fire a heap of cotton.

Arjuna of the white steeds did not know Karna for a brother. Neither

I nor Bhima, nor the twins, knew him for such. However, he, the great archer, knew we were his brothers. We learnt that our mother Kunti went to him and said, "You are my son! You must make peace with your brothers and join their side in battle."

The illustrious Karna refused. He said to our mother, "I cannot desert Duryodhana! It would be dishonourable, cruel and ungrateful of me. If I yield to your wishes and make peace with Yudhishtira, people will say that I am afraid of Arjuna Swetavahana. After I have vanquished Arjuna and Krishna in battle, I will make peace with Dharma's son."

Kunti said again to her magnificent son, "Fight Arjuna, then, but spare my other four princes."

With folded hands, Karna told his trembling mother, "If I ever hold your four other sons' lives in my hands, I will not kill them. Have no doubt, O Devi, that you will continue to have five sons. If Arjuna kills Karna, you will have five. If, on the other hand, I kill Arjuna, you will still have five—including me!"

Wanting the good of us Pandavas, our mother said to him, "Go then, O Karna, do good to your brothers whose weal you always seek."

And with that, Kunti took his leave and returned home.

Arjuna has slain this hero, a brother by a brother! Neither Kunti nor Karna ever disclosed their secret, O lord. And so did Arjuna kill in battle that greatest of Kshatriya bowmen. Only later, Dvijottama, did I learn that he was my brother. Why, I learnt from Kunti that he was the first-born, the eldest among us. How my hearts burns knowing that I caused my brother's death! If I had both Karna and Arjuna on my side, I could have vanquished Krishna himself.

While the evil sons of Dhritarashtra tormented me in the midst of the Kuru sabha, my suddenly risen anger cooled in a moment at the sight of Karna. During that game of dice, even while listening to Karna's harsh and bitter words, uttered from his desire to please Duryodhana, my wrath cooled at the sight of Karna's feet. It seemed to me that Karna's feet resembled the feet of our mother, Kunti! I reflected on this strange likeness for a long time, but I could not fathom it.

Muni, why did the earth swallow the wheels of his chariot during the battle? Why was my brother cursed? You must tell me. I must hear everything from you, O holy one. You know everything in this world, even the past and the future!'"

CANTO 2

Vaisampayana said, "Thus questioned, the Rishi Narada discloses the manner in which Karna, whom people believed to be a Suta's son, had been cursed.

Narada says, 'It is just as you say, O Bhaarata! Mahabaho, no one could resist either Karna or Arjuna in battle. Listen to me carefully, for what I am about to tell you is unknown even to the gods. Long ago, a question arose about how all the Kshatriyas could be given an opportunity to attain Swarga by dying in battle.

For this, Kunti conceived a child, Karna, in her maidenhood, a son capable of provoking a vast and general war. Endowed with tameless energy, this child came to have the status of a Suta. He acquired the science of weapons from Dronacharya, the foremost descendant of Angirasa's vamsa.

The young man burned with envy seeing the might of Bhimasena, the quickness of Arjuna at archery, your intelligence, Yudhishtira, the humility of the twins, the lifelong friendship between Vasudeva and the Gandivi, and the affection of the people for all of you. Early in life, he had made friends with Duryodhana, partly by accident and partly due to his own nature and the hatred he bore you.

Seeing that Dhananjaya was superior to everyone in the astra shastra, Karna one day approached Drona in private and said to him, "You love us, your pupils, as much as you do your son. I want to acquire the Brahmastra, with all its mantras and the power of withdrawing it, for I want to fight Arjuna. I pray that through your grace all the masters of weaponry will regard me as a Maharatha."

Drona, from partiality for Arjuna, as well as from his knowledge that Karna had evil in him, replied, "Only a Brahmana who has duly observed all his vows, or a Kshatriya who has practised austere penances, may have the Brahmastra, no other man."

Hearing this, Karna paid Drona obeisance, took his leave and went to Parasurama who lived on the Mahendra mountain. Approaching Rama, he bowed and said, "I am a Brahmana of Bhrigu's vamsa."

This pleased Rama and he welcomed him so kindly, and with such honour, that Karna was overjoyed. While living on the Mahendra mountain, which resembled heaven itself, Karna met and mingled with many Gandharvas, Yakshas and Devas, and duly acquired all their astras, becoming a favourite of the celestial ones and the great Asuras and Rakshasas, too.

One day, O Partha, while Surya's son roved alone along the sea-coast near this asrama, armed with bow and sword, he accidentally slew the homa cow of a learned Brahmavadi who was performing his daily Agnihotra puja.

Karna tried repeatedly to pacify the Brahmana saying, "O holy one, I killed your cow unintentionally, forgive me for what I did!"

But, filled with wrath, the Brahmana cursed him, crying, "Base wretch, you deserve to be killed. Let the fruit of this deed be yours, evil one: that while fighting him whom you are always challenging, and for whose sake you strive so much every day, the earth will swallow the wheels of your chariot. And while you are dazed and helpless, your enemy will cut off your head! Leave me now, vile man. Just as you have heedlessly killed my cow, your enemy too will kill you whilst you are distracted!"

Karna still sought to gratify that foremost of Brahmanas by offering him cattle, wealth and precious gems. The Brahmana, however, said, "Nothing can deflect my curse. Go away or remain here, as you please." Hanging his head in sorrow, Karna returned apprehensively to Rama, pondering what had happened.'"

CANTO 3

"Narada continues, 'Parasurama, tiger of Bhrigu's race, was well pleased with the might of Karna's arms, his affection for him, his self-restraint, and his attention to the needs of his guru. Rama of great tapasya joyfully taught his tapasvi sishya everything about the Brahmastra, along with the mantras for loosing and withdrawing it.

Having acquired this knowledge, and endowed with wonderful prowess, Karna devoted himself with great enthusiasm to the science of weapons, spending his days happily in Bhrigu's asrama. One day, while roaming with Karna in the vicinity of his hermitage, Rama suddenly felt exhausted by the rigorous fasts he had kept. The son of Jamadagni affectionately and familiarly set his head down on Karna's lap and slept soundly.

While his guru was sleeping, a large and frightful insect, which lived on phlegm and fat and flesh and blood, and whose bite was agonizing, dug its teeth into Karna's thigh. Afraid of waking his guru, Karna could neither pluck out and fling away nor kill that insect. O Bhaarata, though it pierced deep into his thigh with its fangs, the son of Surya allowed it to have its way, lest his acharya should awake.

Karna bore the intolerable pain with heroic patience, and continued to hold Bhargava Rama's head on his lap, without making the slightest movement. When finally Karna's blood flowed onto the face of Rama of great tejas, the Bhargava awoke and said in some alarm, "Alas, I have been sullied! What have you done? Tell me the truth without fear!"

Karna told him about the insect's bite and Parasurama beheld the creature, which resembled a minute boar with eight feet, vicious teeth and needle-like bristles. Called Alarka, its limbs had shrunk with fear. As soon as the mighty-armed son of Jamadagni cast his eyes upon it, the creature gave up its life, melting into the very blood which it had drawn.

Then in the sky they saw a Rakshasa of terrible form, dark in hue, with a red neck, who could assume any form at will. Staying upon the clouds, his object fulfilled, the Rakshasa, with folded hands, addressed Rama, "O Mahatapasvin, you have rescued me from the hell I was in. Blessed are you! I adore you. You have saved me!"

Rama asked him, "Who are you, and why did you fall into hell? Tell me."

The Rakshasa said, "Once I was a great Asura called Dansa. In the Krita yuga, O sire, I was of the same age as Bhrigu. I ravished that sage's beloved wife, and in anger your ancestor cursed me, 'Subsisting on urine, fat and phlegm, you will lead a hellish life!' I fell down onto the earth in the form of a hideous insect.'

I asked him, 'When, O Brahmana, will this curse end?'

Bhrigu replied, 'This curse will end through Rama of my race.' Since then I have been living the life of an unclean soul. Righteous one, you have rescued me from that sinful life."

With these words, the great Rakshasa bowed to Rama and vanished. Now Rama turned in wrath on Karna: "Fool, no Brahmana could endure such agony. Your patience is that of a Kshatriya. Tell me the real truth about yourself and who you are."

Karna, fearing a curse and wanting to mollify his master, replied, "O Bhargava, know me for a Sutaputra. People call me Radheya Karna, the son of Radha. I came here in all humility, only from a desire to acquire your astras from you. A revered guru in the Vedas and other branches of knowledge is like one's father, and it was for this that I told you that I was a Brahmana, one of your own varna."

To the unhappy and trembling Karna, prostrate with folded hands upon the earth, Jamadagnya, smiling though his anger, said, "Since you are not a Brahmana and have been false, and since you came here from your greed for weapons, O wretch, know that when you are engaged in battle with a warrior equal to yourself, and death is upon you, this Brahmastra will fade from your memory, and will not appear at your bidding. However, on earth, no Kshatriya will be your equal in battle. Go now! This is no place for a liar like you."

Humbly taking his dismissal, Karna came away. Arriving then before Duryodhana, he said, "I have mastered all the astras!"'"

CANTO 4

"Narada says, 'Having thus obtained weapons from Parasurama of Bhrigu's race, Karna began to pass his days pleasurably in the company of Duryodhana.

About this time, Chitrangada, the ruler of the country of the Kalingas, held a swayamvara for his daughter in his opulent capital city of Rajapura. Hundreds of kings travelled there to try and win the hand of the princess. Hearing of the contest, Duryodhana too went to the city in his golden chariot, taking Karna with him.

Among those assembled were Sisupala, Jarasandha, Bhishmaka, Vakra, Kapotaroman, Nila, Rukmi of great prowess, Sringa the ruler of the kingdom of women, Asoka, Satadhanwan and the heroic king of the Bhojas. Besides these, O Yudhishtira, many others from the countries of the south, many master warriors of the Mlechcha tribes, and many rulers from the east and the north also came there. With their manly, glowing bodies, adorned with splendid golden angadas, all of them were like tigers.

After the kings had all taken their seats, the maiden princess, accompanied by her nursemaid and a guard of eunuchs, entered the arena. As she circled the arena, the names of each of the kings present were recited to her as she approached each one.

When the fair princess passed over Duryodhana, the son of Dhritarashtra of Kuru's vamsa could not brook her rejection. Disregarding all the kings, he commanded the princess to stop. Intoxicated with the pride of power, and relying upon Bhishma and Drona, Duryodhana abducted the young woman, forcing her into his chariot. Karna, great hero, riding his own chariot, armed with a sword, clad in mail, and with his fingers cased in leather fingerlets, rode just behind Duryodhana.

There was an uproar among the kings, all of whom gathered ready for battle. They shouted "Put on your mail! Let the chariots be made ready!"

Enraged, they pursued Karna and Duryodhana, showering arrows down on them like masses of clouds pouring rain upon two hills. Karna kept cutting down all their bows and arrows with sure, single shafts of his own. Some of the Kshatriyas became bowless; some rushed on, bows in hand; some were on the point of shooting their arrows, and some flew after the two, armed with spears and maces.

The dexterous Karna, foremost of all bowmen, crushed them all. He killed many of their charioteers until, vanquished, those lords of the earth turned away crestfallen from the battle. Protected by Karna, Duryodhana forged on with a joyful heart, bringing the princess home with him to Hastinapura.'"

CANTO 5

"Narada continues, 'Hearing of Karna's legendary might, the king of the Magadhas, Jarasandha, challenged him to single combat. A fierce battle took place between them and both masters of the devastras attacked each other with diverse unearthly missiles. Finally, when they had exhausted their arrows, broken their bows and swords and lost their chariots, the two Mahayoddhas fought with bare hands.

Karna quickly prevailed and could have severed into two his antagonist's body, once united by Jara. Finding himself in mortal danger, Jarasandha gladly made peace with Karna: "Enough! I submit."

Out of friendship he then gifted Karna the town of Malini. Until then, Karna, tiger among men and scourge of all foes, had been king only of the Angas, but from then onwards, the Parantapa began to rule over Champa too, which, as you know, had the approval of Duryodhana.

Thus Karna became famed on earth for the valour of his arms. When, for your sake, Indra, king of the Devas, tricked him with divya maya and begged him for the kundala and kavacha with which he was born, Karna gave away those precious talismans that safeguarded his life. Once Karna had been deprived of his earrings and divested of his natural armour, Arjuna was able to kill him in Krishna's presence.

A Brahmana's curse; the curse of the illustrious Parasurama; the boon granted to Kunti; the illusion with which Indra deceived him; his humiliation by Bhishma, who mockingly called him an ardharatha, half a chariot-warrior, at the naming of Rathas and Atirathas; the undermining of his confidence by the sharp-tongued Salya; Krishna's strategy; and lastly, the devastras which Arjuna had received from Rudra, Indra, Yama, Varuna, Kubera, Drona and the illustrious Kripa: for these many reasons the wielder of the Gandiva succeeded in killing Vikartana's magnificent son, Karna, resplendent as Surya himself.

Ah, your brother had been cursed and beguiled by many. Yet, because he has fallen in battle you should not grieve for him, Naravyaghra!'"

CANTO 6

Vaisampayana said, "Having said these words, the Devarishi Narada falls silent. Filled with sorrow, Rajarishi Yudhishtira plunges into deep dejection. Seeing him sighing like a snake, unmanned by sorrow and sobbing, Kunti, herself quite deranged with grief, tries to console him.

She says gravely and gently, 'Mahabaho, Yudhishtira, it does not become you to mourn like this. You of great wisdom, kill this sorrow of yours, and listen to me. Before the war, I told Karna that you are his brother. Surya Deva also appeared to him in a dream and again in my presence, and counselled him like a well-wisher solicitous of his good. But neither Surya nor I could change his mind or sway his loyalty away from Duryodhana. It was fate that made him your inveterate enemy, bent upon doing you all harm and I, too, gave up trying to reason with him.'

Yudhishtira is like a smouldering fire, overcome with anxiety and despair, to think of his dead sons, grandsons, kinsmen and friends, and most of all of Karna. Tears burning his eyes, he says to his mother, 'This great tragedy has overtaken us because you kept your secret from me!'

Then, in his terrible sorrow, that mighty king of dharma of blazing tejas, curses all the women of the world: 'From now on, no woman will succeed in keeping a secret!'

Again, the king thinks of his slain sons and grandsons and other kinsmen and friends and is plunged in intolerable woe. The wisest of kings resembles a fire covered with smoke, as despair overpowers him."

CANTO 7

Vaisampayana said, "With a troubled and sorrowful heart, Dharmatma Yudhishtira begins to grieve for the mighty Maharatha, Karna.

Sighing repeatedly, he says to his brother, 'O Arjuna, had we been beggars in the cities of the Vrishnis and the Andhakas, this miserable end would not be ours that we have achieved by exterminating our kinsmen. Our enemies, the Kurus, have attained Swarga by purifying themselves in battle, while we who are guilty of slaughtering our kinsmen have lost all the purusharthas, and have no right to the fruits of dharma.

A curse on the famous might, valour and wrath of Kshatriyas! It is on account of these that tragedy has overtaken us. Blessed are forgiveness, self-restraint, purity, renunciation and humility, abstention from causing injury, and truthfulness of speech on all occasions, such as Rishis and Munis practise. Full of pride and arrogance, we have fallen into this plight from greed, recklessness and a desire to enjoy the fruits of power.

Looking at our kinsmen slain on the field of battle, such is our grief that not even sovereignty over the three worlds will make us happy. Alas, for worldly reasons we sinfully slew those noble lords who did not deserve to die at our hands; we are alive, but deprived of friends and stripped of the very meaning of life. Like a pack of dogs fighting over a piece of meat, we have been overtaken by a great disaster. And that piece of meat means nothing to us. It is fit to be thrown away.

They who have been slain did not deserve to die, not for the sake of mountains of gold or all the horses and kine in the entire world. Filled with envy and greed, and swayed by anger and pleasure, all of them are now dead and gone to Yamaloka.

Fathers practise asceticism and brahmacharya, truth and renunciation, in the hope of getting sons blessed with every kind of prosperity. So, too, with fasts, sacrifices, vows, sacred rites and auspicious ceremonies, mothers conceive and carry their offspring, anxiously hoping for a safe delivery and wondering, "Will they be born safely, grow in might and be honoured on earth? Will they be able to give us happiness in this world and the next?"

Alas, those mothers have had to abandon all their expectations now that their sons, glorying in youth and resplendent with ornaments, have been slain. Without having enjoyed the pleasures of this world, without having paid the debts they owed to their parents and to the gods, they have gone to Yamaloka. Alas, O my mother, those kings have been slain at just the time when their parents expected to reap the fruits of their might and wealth.

They were always governed by envy and greed for earthly pleasures, and slaves to rage and desire. Because of their evil deeds, they could never enjoy the fruits of victory. I believe that all the Panchalas and the Kurus that have fallen in this battle, those slain as well as those who slew them, have perished without reaching Swarga as they should have in the normal course. The people regard us as the cause of the destruction of the world, although it was the sons of Dhritarashtra who were actually responsible. Duryodhana was always cunning, always evil and deceitful. Although we never offended him, he always treated us perfidiously. Yet, we have not vanquished them, nor have they vanquished us. The Dhartarashtras could not enjoy this earth, their costly gemstones and well-filled treasury, or their vast territories, women or music. They did not heed the counsels of ministers, their friends and men learned in the scriptures. Their hatred for us consumed them and denied them happiness and contentment. Seeing our prosperity, Duryodhana became envious, growing pale and emaciated, and Sakuni reported this to King Dhritarashtra. As a doting father, Dhritarashtra tolerated his vile policy, disregarding the advice of Vidura and Ganga's noble son Bhishma to restrain his wicked and covetous son Duryodhana, who was entirely governed by his passions. The king has met with destruction, just like me.

Beyond doubt, Suyodhana has tarnished his blazing fame by causing the death of his brothers and bringing terrible grief to his parents. What other Kshatriya would use such language against his kinsmen as he did, in the presence of Panchali? Because of our evil star, Duryodhana, our very race has perished. We have killed those whom we should not have slain, and thereby incurred the censure of the world. Having installed this sinner as king, Dhritarashtra grieves today. We have slain our heroic foes and taken their possessions and kingdom. It has pacified our anger but, ah, my grief stupefies me!

O Dhananjaya, we can only make amends by auspicious deeds, by confessing to all that we have sinned, by repentance, by alms-giving, by penances, by journeys to tirthas after renouncing everything, by constant meditation on the shastras. Of all these, the Srutis aver that he who practises renunciation escapes from birth and death, and attains Brahman. So, O Arjuna, with your leave, I will go to the forest, casting off all worldly attachments, adopting mauna, and practising Gyana Yoga, the path of wisdom.

The Srutis declare, and I have seen with my eyes, that a man with worldly desires can never find any kind of punya. I have myself committed this sin which, as the Srutis have said, causes the cycle of samsara. Abandoning my entire kingdom, and my worldy possessions, I shall go to the forest, escaping from the ties of the world, freed from grief and attachment.

I beg you, O Kurusthama, rule this earth, to which you have restored peace, and which you have divested of all evil, for I have no need for kingdom or for pleasure.'

Having said these words, Yudhishtira stops. His younger brother Arjuna then addresses him in the following words."

CANTO 8

Vaisampayana said, "Like one unwilling to forgive an insult, the tejasvin Arjuna, betraying some fierceness but smiling the while, says gravely, 'It grieves me to see the distress that urges you to abandon this great prosperity which you have gained after such a superhuman victory. Having killed your enemies, and having conquered the world legitimately through adherence to your svadharma, why should you abandon everything through fickleness of heart?

Where on earth has an impotent or an irresolute man ever acquired sovereignty? Why then did you, in blind rage, kill all the kings of the world? He who aspires to live like a sannyasi will not want to enjoy the good things of the world. Poor and stripped of his wealth, he can never win fame or acquire sons and possess great and noble animals. O king, if you abandon this vast kingdom and live like a wretched mendicant, what will the world say of you?

Why do you want to renounce your wealth and power, and lead the life of a sadhu; you, born a king? Having conquered the whole world, do you really wish from folly to live in the forest, abandoning all things of artha and kama?

If you take vanavasa, in your absence evil men will destroy yagnas, and the stain of that desecration will certainly be yours. King Nahusha, having committed many base sins in a state of poverty, gave up his mendicancy and proclaimed that poverty is for vanaprasthas.

Making no provision for the morrow is a practice for Rishis, as you know. Kshatriya dharma depends entirely on wealth, and one who robs another of wealth, robs him of his dharma as well. Who among us, O king, would forgive such robbery if it is practised against him? A poor man, even if he is only an onlooker, is falsely accused of a crime. Poverty is a sin and it is wrong for you to applaud it.

The fallen man, O king, also grieves like a poor man. I do not see the difference between them. All kinds of punya and karma flow from the possession of great wealth, all religious performances, all pleasures, and Swarga itself! Without wealth, a man cannot find the means of sustaining existence. The karma of a man of small wit, a fool who allows himself to be stripped of his wealth, is dried up like shallow streams in the summer. He who has wealth has friends and relatives, and we regard him as a worthy and accomplished man in the world. On the other hand, if a man without wealth wants to achieve any purpose, he meets with failure.

Wealth attracts wealth, as tame elephants entice wild ones into captivity. Religious acts, pleasures, joy, courage, wrath, learning and dignity, all these proceed from wealth, O king! From wealth one acquires family honour, and increases one's religious merit. He who is without wealth has neither this world, nor the next, O best of men. He cannot perform deeds of dharma, for these spring from wealth like rivers from a mountain.

He who has few possessions in terms of horses and cows, servants and guests is truly leaner than an emaciated man. Judge truly, O king, by the conduct of the Devas and the Danavas who forever wish to slaughter their kinsmen, the Asuras. If one did not regard as righteous the appropriation of wealth belonging to others, how would kings practise their dharma on this earth?

The sages have in the Vedas laid down this injunction: that kings should live reciting the three Vedas every day, seek to acquire wealth, and carefully perform sacrifices with the wealth thus acquired.

When the gods have obtained footing in Swarga and won their

prosperity through great battles, what fault can there be in such strife? The Devas act in this way, and the eternal precepts of the Vedas sanction it.

To learn, teach, sacrifice and assist at others' yagnas, these are our principal duties. The wealth that kings plunder becomes the means of their prosperity, and that has never been obtained without some injury to others. The reason why kings conquer this world is to acquire riches, and that appropriated wealth becomes as much theirs as the riches claimed by sons of their sires. The Rajarishis who have gone to Swarga have declared this to be the royal dharma, for, like water flowing forth from a replete reservoir, wealth runs in every direction from the treasuries of kings.

This earth which once belonged to king Dilipa, Nahusha, Ambarisha and Mandhatri, now belongs to you! You should perform a great yagna, O Rajan, making generous gifts of every kind, spending a vast quantity of the earth's produce, or else the sins of this kingdom will be upon you. The subjects whose king performs an Asvamedha yagna with bountiful gifts, all become purified of sin and sanctified by attending the ablutions at the end of the yagna.

Vishwarupa Mahadeva, in a great sacrifice requiring libations of all kinds of flesh, poured all creatures as sacrificial offerings into the fire and then his own self. Eternal is this auspicious path, for one can never destroy its fruits. This is the great path called Dasaratha, and if you abandon it, O Rajan, what other course will you take?'"

CANTO 9

"Yudhishtira says, 'For a little while, O Arjuna, if you were to concentrate your attention and fix your mind and inner hearing on your antaratma, you would approve of what I am about to say. Abandoning all worldly possessions and pleasures, I will follow the path of dharma—but I will not tread the path that you recommend. Regardless of whether you ask me or not, I will show you the only path that is auspicious and that one should walk.

Renouncing the pleasures and activities of the world of men, I will perform mahatapasya, living on fruit and roots in the forest and wandering with the animals that have their home there. Performing yagnas, pouring libations into the sacred fire at the proper times, morning and evening, I will reduce my body through starvation and, with matted hair, covering myself with skins, enduring cold, wind, heat, hunger, thirst and toil, I will emaciate myself with tapasya as laid down in our shastras.

I will daily listen to the clear strains of the free and joyful birds and animals living in the forest, charming to the heart and the ear. I will enjoy the fragrance of flower-laden trees and creepers, and the varied fruits that grow in the forest. I will spend my time in the company of its many excellent sannyasis. I will not do the slightest injury to any living creature anywhere.

Leading a reclusive life and devoting myself to contemplation, I will live upon ripe and unripe fruits and gratify the Pitris and the Devas with offerings of wild fruits, spring water and grateful hymns. Observing in this way the austere regulations of a forest life, I will pass my days calmly awaiting death or, living alone in silence, with my head shaved clean. I will obtain my food by begging fruit each day of only one tree.

Smearing my body with ashes, and finding shelter in abandoned houses, or lying at the foot of trees, I will cast off all things, dear or hateful. Aloof from both grief and joy, regarding with equanimity censure and applause, hope and affliction, and prevailing over all the works of maya, I will live in detachment: following mauna vrata, assuming the outward form of a blind and deaf idiot, living in contentment and deriving happiness from my own soul. Without doing the least injury to any of the four kinds of moving and unmoving creatures, I will behave equally towards all, be they conscious of dharma or merely following the dictates of their senses.

I will not jeer or frown at anybody and, restraining all my senses, always be of cheerful aspect. Asking no one for directions, I will journey along any path that I happen to meet, taking no note of the country or the points of the compass or looking behind me, divesting myself of desire and anger, turning my gaze inwards and casting off pride of soul and body.

Nature always walks ahead; thus, food and drink will somehow come. I will not think of those pairs of opposites that stand in the way of such a life. If I fail to find pure food in a small measure in one house, I will go to other homes. I shall go to seven houses in succession to satisfy my hunger. When the smoke from a house no longer issues forth, its hearth-fires having been extinguished; when husking-rods have been kept aside, and all the inmates have eaten; when mendicants and guests cease to wander, I will go and beg for alms at two, three or five houses at the most.

I will wander over the earth having broken the bonds of desire and, preserving equanimity in success and failure, become a tapasvin, and behave as one who is neither fond of life nor at the point of death: viewing both with equal indifference.

If a man strikes off one of my arms, and another smears the other arm with sandal-wood paste, I will not wish either evil to the one nor good to the other. The only acts I perform will be to open and shut my eyes and take as much food and drink as will barely sustain life in my body. Without ever being attached to action, and always restraining the functions of the senses, I will give up all desires and cleanse the soul of every impurity. Freed from all attachments and tearing off all bonds, I will live free as the wind and enjoy everlasting contentment.

Impelled by desire, and from ignorance, I have committed great sins. Many grihastas performing both auspicious and inauspicious acts are yoked to the wheel of karma, maintaining their wives, children and kinsmen, all bound to them in relations of cause and effect. When they die they take upon themselves all the effects of their sins, for none but the actual doer is burdened with the consequences of his deeds. Bound by karma, men come into this ever-turning wheel of life, are born again and again, and, being born, meet their fellow men.

He is sure to find happiness who abandons the worldly course of life, which is really a fleeting illusion, though it seems eternal, and is afflicted by birth, death, decrepitude, disease and pain. When the very Devas and great Rishis, who understand the law of karma, fall down from heaven or from their positions of eminence, who would wish to have even heavenly prosperity? Insignificant kings, having found success through diverse means, often slay another king through some contrivance.

Through reflection this nectar of wisdom has come to me and, having attained it, I want to find a permanent, eternal and unchangeable place for myself. By adopting this fearless path of life, I will make an end to this physical frame that is subject to birth, death, decrepitude, disease and pain.'"

CANTO 10

"Bhimasena says, 'Your understanding, Rajan, has become blind to the truth, like that of a foolish and hollow chanter of the Vedas. If you criticize the dharma of kings and want to lead a life of idleness, O Bharatarishabha, you had no reason to destroy the Dhartarashtras.

Do we not find in the Kshatriyas forgiveness and compassion, pity and mercy? If we had known that this was your intention, we would have never taken up arms or slain a single man. We would have subsisted on alms until death took us, and this terrible war between the rulers of the earth would have never been fought.

The learned have said that this mobile and immobile world is the object of enjoyment for the strong, and that the Kshatriya's duty is to eliminate all who stand in the way of the one assuming the sovereignty of the earth. Accordingly, we killed all those who stood as enemies of our kingdom, so that by adherence to our dharma we now rule this earth. Govern it righteously, O Yudhisthtira.

To refuse the kingdom now is to be like the man who, having dug a well, stops his work before finding water and comes up covered in mud; or, like the man who, having climbed up a tall tree and taken the honey, dies before tasting it. It is to be like one who, having set out on a long journey, turns back in despair short of his destination; or like one who, having slain all his enemies, O Pandava, falls by his own hand. It is to be like the hungry man who, having obtained food, refuses to eat it, or like a man under the influence of kama who, having obtained a woman reciprocating his passion, refuses to take her.

We follow you, O king of feeble understanding, because you are our eldest brother, and you have made us objects of censure. We are all maharathas, accomplished in knowledge and endowed with great energy, yet we are obedient to the words of a eunuch, as though we were entirely helpless. We are the refuge of the helpless but, when the people see us like this, they will think we are impotent.

Consider what I say. The shastras decree that only in times of distress should aged and weak kings, or those defeated by enemies, adopt a life of renunciation. Men of wisdom, therefore, will not applaud renunciation as the dharma of a Kshatriya but regard that course of life as a loss of virtue.

How can the true Kshatriyas condemn these duties? Indeed, if these obligations be blameworthy, why should Ishwara not be censured? It is only the poor and non-believers who support this interpretation of the Vedas, that a Kshatriya should take sannyasa. In reality, a Kshatriya who adopts the life of a sannyasi fails to support life by his prowess and exertions, and thereby fails in his dharma.

Only that man who cannot support his sons and grandsons and worship the Devas, Rishis, Atithis and Pitris, can happily lead the life of a solitary hermit in the forest. Just as the deer, boars and birds, though they lead a forest life, cannot attain heaven, able Kshatriyas who fail to exert their power cannot attain Swarga by becoming sannyasis. There are other ways for them to seek religious merit.

If anyone were to gain success from renunciation, then mountains and trees would surely have it, for are all Brahmacharins who lead such lives, injuring no one and remaining always aloof from worldliness. If it be the truth that a man's success depends upon his own lot in life and not upon that of others, then, as a Kshatriya, you should take yourself to a life of action.

If they who only fill their own stomachs could attain success, then all aquatic creatures would be successful, for they have no one to support but themselves. Look, the world moves on, with every creature in it employed in karma proper to its nature. And so, you must adopt a life of action, for the man of inaction can never prosper.'"

CANTO 11

"Arjuna says, 'In this regard, O Bharatarishabha, an itihasa is told of a discourse between certain sannyasis and Sakra. A number of well-born Brahmana youths, foolish and immature, abandoning their homes, left for vanavasa. Thinking that this would be a virtuous path, these rich youths wanted to live as Brahmacharins, and abandoned their brothers and parents. It so happened that Indra felt pity for them and, assuming the form of a golden bird, the holy Sakra addressed them, saying, "Men who perform yagnas and share the leftover sacrificial food acquire great punya and their lives are praiseworthy. Having accomplished their purushartha, these virtuous men attain the highest end."

The Rishis said, "Look, this bird lauds those who subsist upon the leftovers (avasesha) of yagnas, and tells us this because we live upon such leftovers."

The bird replied, "I do not praise you. You are filthy and impure, and living on refuse renders you vile, for you do not subsist upon the remnants of sacrifice."

The Rishis said, "We regard this course of our life to be blessed. Tell us, O bird, what is good for us. Your words inspire us."

The bird said, "If you do not lose faith in me by fighting against your better selves, I will advise you on what is true and beneficial."

The Rishis said, "We will listen to your words, for the different paths are all known to you, O Dharmatman, and we are ready to obey your commands. Instruct us."

The bird said, "Among quadrupeds, the cow is the foremost; among metals, gold; among words, mantras; and among those who walk on two legs, Brahmanas. These mantras regulate all the rites of a Brahmana's life, beginning with those concerning gyana and the period after it, and ending with those concerning death and cremation. The Vedic rites are his foremost sacrifice and his path to Swarga. If it were not so, how could those in quest of heaven find what they seek through mantras?

He who, in this world, worships his soul, firmly regarding it to be a particular Deva, gains success consistent with the nature of that God. The seasons measured by fortnights lead to the sun, the moon, or the stars. Depending upon the action, these three kinds of success, are desired by every man.

The grihasta's life is superior and sacred and is called the domain for the cultivation of success. What paths do these men take that are against action? Foolish and destitute, they incur sin because they live by abandoning the eternal paths of the Devas, Rishis and Brahmanas and taking instead to the paths disapproved of by the Srutis.

There is a law in the mantras which says, 'O Sacrificer, perform the sacrifice represented by gifts of valuable things. I will give you happiness in the form of sons, kine and Swarga!' To live thus in accordance with the shastras is said to be the highest tapas of the tapasvin. And so you should perform yagnas and tapasya in the form of gifts. The due performance of these eternal duties—the worship of the Devas, the study of the Vedas, the gratification of the Pitris, and respectful services to the gurus—are called mahatapasya.

By performing these arduous penances, the Devas have obtained the highest glory and power. And I tell you to bear the burden of the duties of the grihasta. Without doubt, tapasya is the foremost of all things and is the root of all creatures; however, it is to be practised by leading the life of a grihasta, upon which everything depends.

They who eat the leftovers of feasts, after duly apportioning the food morning and evening among kinsmen, attain ends that are hard indeed to achieve. They are called eaters of the remnants of feasts who eat after having served Sadasyas, Devas, Rishis and kinsmen.

Thus, those who observe their svadharma, who keep difficult vratas and are truthful in speech become objects of great respect in the world, with their own faith exceptionally strengthened. Free from pride, these achievers of the most strenuous feats go to Swarga and live for endless time in the realms of Sakra."'

Arjuna continues 'Hearing those words, beneficial and full of righteousness, those Rishis abandoned the path of renunciation, saying, "There is nothing in it," and became grihastas. Therefore, O Dharmarajan, calling to your aid that same ananta gyana, rule the wide world that is now free of your enemies.'"

CANTO 12

Vaisampayana said, "Hearing these words of Arjuna, O Parantapa, the mighty-armed and broad-chested Nakula, bronzed of skin, wise and moderate in speech, looked at the king, the foremost of all dharma purushas, and spoke, appealing to his brother's heart.

Nakula said, 'The very gods have established their fires in the region called Visakha-yupa, O Rajan, so you know that the Devas themselves depend upon the fruits of action. The Pitris that support life by dispensing rain on earth even to all disbelievers, by observing the laws of Ishwara as declared in the Vedas, are engaged in karma. Those who reject the declaration of the Vedas recommending action are godless, while the man who follows the path of the Devas attains, O Bhaarata, the highest realms of heaven.

The grihasta's life, all men acquainted with Vedic truths say, is superior to all the other modes of life. Knowing this, the man who restrains his soul, O Rajan, and gives away his righteously acquired wealth in yagnas to Brahmanas well versed in the Vedas is regarded as the true renouncer. However, he who disregards the life of a grihasta, the source of much happiness, and attempts to leap to the next asrama of life, that of a sannyasi, moves in darkness.

The man who roves the world homeless, O Kaunteya, a mendicant who has the foot of a tree for his shelter, who observes the mauna vrata, never cooks for himself, and seeks to restrain all the functions of his senses, is actually a man who has given up the vows of a sannyasi. The Brahmana who, disregarding anger and joy, and especially deceit, employs all his time in the study of the Vedas, is actually turning away from the observance of the vows of a sannyasi.

The four different varnasramas were at one time weighed in the balance. The wise have said that when grihasta was placed on one side of the scale, it required the three others to be placed on the other to counterbalance it. Observing the result of this examination, and seeing further that domesticity alone contains both heaven and pleasure, grihastasrama became the way of the greatest Rishis and the refuge of all men conversant with the ways of the world.

Therefore, O Bharatarishabha, he who adopts the way of the grihasta, thinking it to be his duty, and relinquishing all desire for the fruits thereof, is a real sannyasi, and not the man of clouded understanding who goes into the vana abandoning his home and its surroundings. A man who, in the garb of dharma, fails to vanquish his desires even as a vanaprastha, is bound by grim Yama with his deadly noose round the sinner's neck.

The karma that is performed from vanity is said to be unproductive, while the karma done from a spirit of renunciation always bears abundant fruit. Tranquillity, self-restraint, fortitude, truth, purity, simplicity, sacrifice, perseverance and righteousness are regarded as virtues recommended by the greatest Rishis. The deeds of a grihasta, it is said, are intended for Pitris, Devas and Sadasyas.

In this varnasrama alone, O Rajan, are the three-fold aims of dharma, artha and kama to be attained. The renouncer who unswervingly adheres to this mode of life, in which one is free to perform all karma, does not encounter ruin either here or hereafter.

The sinless Ishwara created living beings with the intention that they would adore him through yagnas, which include generous gifts. Creepers, trees, leaf-shedding herbs, animals that are clean and ghrita were created to be the ingredients of the yagna. For a grihasta, the performance of a yagna is fraught with impediments. That is why this asrama is said to be exceedingly difficult, well-nigh unattainable. Grihastas who possess wealth and corn and animals but do not perform yagnas earn eternal sin, O Rajan.

Amongst Rishis, there are some that regard the study of the Vedas to be a sacrifice, and others that regard dhyana to be a great sacrifice which they perform in their minds. O Rajan, the very gods covet the companionship of a regenerate man who, as a result of treading the path of dhyana, has become equal to Brahman.

By refusing to spend for yagnas the diverse kinds of wealth that you have taken from your enemies, you are only displaying your want of faith. I have never seen a king in the observance of grihastasrama renounce his wealth in any way but the Rajasuya, the Aswamedha, and other kinds of great sacrifices. Like Sakra, the king of the Devas, O Rajan, perform these other sacrifices that are praised by the Brahmanas.

The king through whose heedlessness subjects are plundered by robbers, and who does not offer protection to those whom he is called upon to rule, is said to be the very embodiment of the demon Kali. If, without giving away horses, kine and female slaves, elephants adorned with trappings, and villages, populous lands, fields, and houses to Brahmanas, we take vanavasa with our hearts harbouring unfriendly feeling towards relatives, we will become such Kalis among Kshatriyas. Kshatriyas who do not practise charity and give protection to others incur great sin. Sorrow is their portion hereafter, not bliss.

If, O lord, you take to a wandering life without performing mahayagnas and the due rites in honour of your deceased ancestors, without bathing in sacred tirthas, you will meet with destruction like a small cloud separated from a mass and shredded by the winds. You will fall away from both worlds and have to be born as a Pisacha.

A man becomes a true sannyasi by casting off every internal and external attachment, not merely by abandoning his home to live in the forest. A Brahmana who lives observing these laws in which there are no impediments does not fall from this or the other world. Observing one's svadharma, duties respected by the ancients and practised by the best of men, who would grieve for having slain prosperous enemies in war, like Sakra razing the armies of the Daityas?

Having observed the Kshatriya dharma and subjugated the world through your prowess, O Rajan, and having made gifts to those who know the Vedas, you can go to realms higher than heaven. It does not become you, O Kaunteya, to indulge in grief.'"

CANTO 13

"Sahadeva says, 'O Bhaarata, one does not attain felicity by renouncing all external objects, or by discarding mental attachments. Let our enemies enjoy the religious merit and happiness that come to one who has cast off worldly things but whose mind still covets them! On the other hand, let our friends enjoy the religious merit and happiness that come to him who rules the earth, having relinquished all internal attachments.

The word *mama*—mine—is Yama, Death's self; while the opposite, *na-mama*—not mine—is eternal Brahman's. Brahman and Yama, O Rajan, entering invisibly into every soul, cause all creatures to act. If this entity that is called Atman is never subject to destruction, then destroying the bodies of living men cannot make one guilty of murder. If, on the other hand, the Atman and the body of a being are born or destroyed together, then the rites and deeds prescribed by the shastras would be futile.

Therefore, driving away all doubts about the immortality of the Atman, the man of intelligence should adopt that path which the men of dharma of ancient times have ever trodden. Life is certainly fruitless for a king who, having acquired the entire earth with its mobile and immobile creatures, does not enjoy it. As for the vanaprastha who lives upon wild fruits and roots, but whose attachment to things of the earth has not ceased, such a one, O king, lives within the jaws of death.

Look, O Bhaarata, the hearts and the outward forms of all creatures are but manifestations of yourself. They who look upon all creatures as their own selves escape the great fear of destruction. You are my father and my protector; you are my brother, my elder and guru. So, O lord of the earth, forgive these confused and sorrowful utterances of a grief-stricken one, which I have spoken out of my love for you.'"

CANTO 14

Vaisampayana said, "When Kunti's son, Yudhishtira Dharmaraja, remains silent after listening to his brothers tell these truths of the Vedas, the noble, beautiful and large-eyed Draupadi speaks to that bull among kings, seated like the leader of a herd of elephants in the midst of his brothers, themselves like so many lions and tigers.

Expecting loving regard always from her husbands, especially from Yudhishtira, she is always treated with affection and indulgence by the king. Conversant with her wifely duties and observant of them in practice, this wide-hipped princess, casting her eyes on her lord, wanting his attention, speaks in pointed but sweet words.

'O Kaunteya, your brothers dry their palates with laments like the chataka bird, but you do not make them happy. Gladden with seemly words the hearts of your brothers who are like great tuskers in musth, these heroes who have drunk the cup of misery. Why, O king, while living beside the Dwaita lake, did you reassure your brothers who were with you, suffering cold, wind and sun?

Why did you say to them, "Rushing into battle for victory, we will kill Duryodhana and enjoy the earth that can grant every wish. Depriving great Maharathas of their chariots, slaying huge elephants, and strewing the field of battle with the bodies of great warriors, horsemen and heroes, you, Parantapas, will perform mahayagnas of diverse kinds with gifts in profusion. All these sufferings of exile in the forest will end in happiness."

Having once said these words to your brothers, O foremost of all men of dharma, why do you now dismay us with this new resolve? Just as there can be no fish in a dry swamp, no eunuch can ever have children or enjoy wealth. A Kshatriya, or a ruler without the power to punish, can neither shine nor enjoy the earth, nor can his subjects ever have happiness.

Friendship for all creatures, charity, study of the Vedas, penances—these constitute the duties of a Brahmana and not of a Kshatriya, O best of kings! Restraining the evil, cherishing the honest and never retreating from battle—these are the highest duties of kings. He is said to be conversant with dharma in whom both forgiveness and anger exist, giving and taking, terrors and fearlessness, and chastisement and reward. It was not through study, or gift, or sannyasa that you have acquired the earth. You have vanquished and slain the force of the enemy, ready to burst upon you with all its might, an army abounding with elephants, horses and chariots, strong with three kinds of strength, and protected by Drona, Karna, Aswatthaman and Kripa!

This is why I ask you to enjoy the earth. Once, O king, you conquered the realm called Jambu, with all her populous kingdoms, as well as Kraunchadwipa to the west of the great Meru, equal to Jambudwipa, Sakadwipa to the east of the great Meru, equal to Kraunchadwipa, Bhadraswa on the north of the great Meru, equal to Sakadwipa, O Purushavyaghra!

You even penetrated the ocean and captured other realms, islands surrounded by the sea and containing many densely peopled provinces. O Bhaarata, having achieved such immeasurable feats, and having obtained through them the adoration of the Brahmanas, how is it that your soul is not gratified? Seeing your brothers, O Bhaarata, these heroes swelling with strength and resembling bulls or mighty elephants in musth, why don't you speak words to them that will bring joy to their hearts?

All of you are like Devas, able to resist any foe and able to scorch your enemies. Had only one of you become my husband, my happiness would have been immense, O Naravyaghra. What can I say when all five of you are my husbands and care for me as the five senses inspire the physical frame? The words of my mother-in-law, who has great knowledge and great foresight, cannot be untrue. "O princess of Panchala," she said to me, "Yudhishtira will always keep you happy."

I see, O Dharmaraja, that having slain thousands of powerful kings, you are about to render this achievement futile through your folly. They whose eldest brother has lost his mind now all have to follow him in madness. Through your madness, O king, all the Pandavas are about to lose their minds.

Had your brothers been in their senses, O Rajan, they would have imprisoned you with all unbelievers and taken upon themselves the sovereignty of the earth. One who from dullness of intellect does as you now want to do, can never succeed in winning prosperity. The man who treads the path of madness should be treated with incense and kohl, with drugs infused through the nose, and with other medicaments.

O best of the Bhaaratas, I am the worst of all my sex, since I want to live on even though I am bereaved of my children. You should not disregard my words or those of your brothers who are trying to dissuade you from your deranged purpose. Indeed, by abandoning all the earth, you urge adversity and danger upon yourself.

Shine, O Rajan, like those two great kings, Mandhatri and Ambarisha, admired in their time by all the lords of earth. Protecting your subjects righteously, govern Bhumi Devi, this Goddess Earth, with her mountains and forests and islands. Do not become downcast, O king; worship the gods with many sacrifices, fight your enemies and make gifts of wealth, apparel and other objects of enjoyment to Brahmanas, O best of all kings.'"

CANTO 15

Vaisampayana said, "Hearing these words of Yajnasena's daughter, Arjuna speaks once more, showing proper regard for his mighty-armed eldest brother of unfading glory.

Arjuna says, 'The man armed with the rod of punishment, the Neeti danda, governs and protects all his subjects with it. This authority is awake when everything else is asleep. For this reason, the wise have characterized the rod of chastisement to be dharma itself. It protects dharma and artha. It is identified with purusharthas, and protects grain and wealth. Knowing this, O learned one, take up the rod of punishment and observe the course of the world.

One class of sinful men desist from doing evil through fear of the danda in the king's hands, another from fear of Yama's danda, another from fear of the next world and yet another from fear of society. Thus, O Rajan, in this world, everything depends on the punitive danda, and there is a class of men for whom the only restraining force from devouring one another is that rod. If it did not protect people, they would have sunk into the darkness of hell.

The wise thus named the rod of chastisement, because it restrains the ungovernable and punishes the wicked. One should punish Brahmanas by oral censure; Kshatriyas, by giving them only as much food as necessary to support life; Vaisyas, by the imposition of fines and forfeitures of property, while for Sudras there is no punishment.

Under the name of danda we have established laws in the world to keep men aware of their duties and for the protection of property. Wherever dark-skinned and red-eyed punishment stands ready to tackle every offender, and the king is a Dharmaraja, the subjects never forget themselves. The Brahmacharin and the grihasta, the rishi and the sannyasi, all walk in their respective ways through fear of punishment alone.

He who is without the restraint of fear never performs a sacrifice or gives anything away, never adheres to any commitment or covenant. Without achieving the most difficult feats and without killing, as a fisherman kills fish, no man can obtain great prosperity. Without bloodshed, no man has been able to achieve fame in this world or acquire wealth or subjects.

By the killing of Vritra, Indra himself became the Great. Men offer their worship much more to those of the gods who are given to taking life. Rudra, Skanda, Sakra, Agni, Varuna, Kaala, Mrityu, Vayu, Kubera, Surya, the Vasus, the Maruts, the Sadhyas, and the Viswadevas, O Bhaarata, are all death-dealers. Humbled by their prowess, everybody bends to these gods, never to Brahma, Dhatri or Pushan.

Only a few men who are noble of disposition worship gods who are self-restrained, peaceful and equally disposed towards all creatures. I do not perceive any creature in this world that supports life without doing any injury to others. Animals live upon animals, the stronger upon the weaker. The mongoose devours mice; the cat devours the mongoose; the dog devours the cat; the dog again is devoured by the spotted leopard. Behold, all things in turn are devoured by Yama, the Destroyer, when he comes! The gods have wrought this universe, moving and motionless, as food for living creatures, and the true gyani is never confused by this.

It is appropriate for you, O Maharajan, to be what you were born to be. Only a foolish Kshatriya, restraining anger and joy, takes refuge in the vana. The very sannyasis cannot support their lives without killing creatures. In water, on earth, and in fruits, swarm innumerable creatures, and it is not true that one does not kill them.

What higher dharma is there than supporting one's life? There are many creatures so minute that their existence can only be guessed at, and the mere falling of one's eyelids destroys them. There are men who, subduing anger and pride, take to an ascetic course of life and, leaving village and towns, become hermits in the forest. Arriving there, they become confused and adopt the grihasta's life once more.

One sees other grihasthas tilling the soil, uprooting herbs, felling trees, killing birds and animals, performing yagnas, and finally attaining Swarga. O Kaunteya, I have no doubt that the deeds of all creatures are crowned with success only when the policy of punishment is properly applied. If one were to abolish punishment from the world, all creatures would soon be destroyed.

Like fish in the water, stronger animals prey on the weaker. Remember the truth declared long ago by Brahma himself that punishment, properly applied, sustains all beings. Look, the very fires, when almost extinguished, blaze up again, in fright, when blown upon. Such is the fear of force or discipline. If there were no danda, the good could not be distinguished from the bad, the whole world would be enveloped in darkness and all things would be plunged in chaos.

Even those who are breakers of laws, who are atheists and scoff at the Vedas, become disposed to observe laws and restrictions from fear of punishment. Everyone in this world is kept straight by fear of danda. A man who is by nature pure and righteous is scarce.

Yielding to fear of punishment, man becomes disposed to observe rules and restraints. Danda was ordained by the Creator himself for protecting dharma and artha, for the happiness of all the four orders, and for making them righteous and humble. If punishment could not inspire fear, then ravens and beasts of prey would have devoured all other animals, men and the sacrificial ghrita.

If discipline did not uphold and protect, nobody would have studied the Vedas, nobody would have milked a cow, and no maiden would have married. If discipline and fear of punishment did not uphold and protect, destruction and chaos would have set in on every side, all barriers would have been swept away, and the very idea of property would have disappeared. People could then never duly perform annual sacrifices with large gifts, and no one, to whatever mode of life he might belong, would observe the duties of their particular varnasrama declared in the shastras, no one would have succeeded in acquiring knowledge.

Even if yoked, camels, oxen, horses, mules or donkeys, would not draw chariots and carriages, without the application of the danda; on danda depend all creatures. The learned, therefore, say that punishment is the root of everything, and upon it rests this world and the heaven that men desire.

Wherever enemy-destroying punishment is well applied, no sin, no deception and no evil is seen. If the danda of punishment is not upraised, the dog will lick the sacrificial butter and the crow will fly away with the first yagna offering.

Whether through dharma or adharma, this kingdom is now ours, and our duty is to abandon grief, to enjoy it and perform yagnas. Men who are fortunate, living with their beloved wives and children, eat good food, wear rich attire, and cheerfully acquire virtue. All our karma, without doubt, is dependent on wealth, which is again dependent on danda.

Understand, therefore, the importance of discipline. One declares duties only for the maintenance of the relations of the world. There are two things here: abstention from injury, and injury prompted by dharma; the second, being superior as dharma, may be done without fault.

There is no deed that is wholly meritorious, nor any that is wholly evil, since in all karma something exists of both right and wrong. Animals are castrated, their horns cut off, and they are made to bear burdens, tethered and beaten.

In this samsara of no substance, this cruel world, rotten with sin and full of pain, O Rajan, maintain the ancient customs of men. Perform yagnas, give alms, protect your subjects, and practise dharma. Slay your enemies, O Kaunteya, and protect your friends. Do not be sorrowful, Rajan, while killing your enemies, for you will not incur the slightest sin. He who takes up a weapon to cut down an armed foe advancing against him, does not incur the sin of murder, for it is the fury of the advancing enemy that provokes the wrath of the slayer.

The inner soul of every creature can never be slain. When the Atman is incapable of being slain, how then can one be slain by another? As a man enters a new house, even so creatures enter successive bodies, abandoning forms that are worn out, acquiring new forms. Those who can see the truth view death as being this repeated transformation.'"

CANTO 16

Vaisampayana said, "After Arjuna's speech, Bhimasena, passionate and energetic, mustering all his patience, says to his eldest brother, 'O Rajan, you know all about dharma, nothing is unknown to you. We always try to emulate your conduct, but alas, we cannot.

I tried to restrain myself from saying anything. But my anguish compels me to speak. Listen to me, O ruler of men. Because of your confusion, everything we have is in danger, and we are made unhappy and weak. How is it that you, the ruler of the world, familiar with every branch of knowledge, have let sorrow cloud your understanding like a coward?

You know the paths of dharma and adharma of the world, as well as the future and the present. So, O puissant one, I will tell you why you should assume sovereignty. Listen to me.

There are two kinds of diseases, physical and mental, each linked to the other, and neither of them exists independently. Mental sickness springs from physical ailment, the physical from the mental: this is the truth. He who feels regret because of past physical or mental grief finds yet more sorrow in sorrow, and suffers twice over.

Cold, heat and wind are the three attributes of the body, and their existence in harmony is the sign of good health. If one of the three prevails over the rest, there are remedies laid down for it. Cold checks heat, and heat checks cold.

Sattva, rajas and tamas are the three attributes of the mind. The existence of these three in harmony is the sign of mental health. If one of these prevails over the rest, there are remedies prescribed.

Grief checks joy, and joy checks grief; one man living in the present, enjoying bliss, wants to remember his past sorrows, while another, living in present sorrow, wants to recollect his past happiness. You, however, were never made sad by misfortune or glad by fortune. So, you should not use your memory now to make yourself sad during times of bliss, or glad during times of sorrow. Perhaps Destiny is all-powerful, or perhaps it is because of your nature that you are so afflicted.

But how is it that you do not remember the sight of Draupadi being dragged before the sabha barely clad while in her period, or our expulsion from Hastinapura and our vanavasa wearing deerskins and living in the great forests?

Why have you forgotten the woes inflicted on us by Jatasura, the battle with Chitrasena, and what we suffered at the hands of the Sindhu king; how Kichaka kicked Draupadi during our ajnatavasa? Parantapa, another fierce battle, like that which you fought against Bhishma and Drona, now lies before you, but this one will have to be fought with your mind alone, without arrows, friends, relatives or kinsmen.

If you give up your life before winning this battle, you will have to be reborn to fight these same enemies again. So, fight that battle this very day, O Bharatarishabha. Disregard the concerns of your body, use your own ability, identify your mind's foe and conquer it. I cannot imagine what your condition will be if you do not succeed in this battle; whereas, by winning it, you will attain the great end of life. Apply your intellect to this, ascertain the right and the wrong paths, follow the course that your father did before you, and rule your kingdom with dharma.

By good fortune, the sinful Duryodhana and all his followers are dead, and Draupadi has braided her hair again. With due ceremonies and lavish gifts, perform the Aswamedha yagna. The tejasvin Krishna and we are your servants, O son of Pritha!'"

CANTO 17

"Yudhishtira says, 'Discontentment, heedless attachment to earthly goods, the absence of tranquillity, power, folly, vanity and anxiety: all these affect you, and so you covet sovereignty, O Bhima. Try to be happy freed from desire, prevailing over joy and grief and attaining tranquillity. The peerless king who will rule this unbounded earth will nevertheless have but one stomach. Why then do you applaud this course of life?

One's desires, O Bharatarishabha, cannot be fulfilled in a day, or in many months. Desire can never be gratified, cannot, indeed, be exhausted in the course of one's whole life. Fire, when fed with fuel, blazes forth; otherwise, it is extinguished. So you should extinguish with a little food the fire in your stomach when it appears. He who is ignorant seeks endless food for his belly. Conquer your stomach first and you will then be able to conquer the earth.

Once you conquer and win the earth, it will be for your permanent good. You applaud desires and enjoyments and prosperity, but those who have renounced all enjoyments and have reduced their bodies through penance, attain regions of supreme happiness. The acquisition and preservation of a kingdom involves both dharma and adharma. The desire for them exists in you. Free yourself from your great burdens, and adopt renunciation.

To appease his hunger, the tiger slaughters many other animals.

From greed, other weaker beasts, scavengers, live off the tiger's prey. If kings practise renunciation while enjoying worldly possessions and pleasures, they can never have contentment, and a loss of understanding is noticeable in them. However, those who subsist on leaves of trees, or use two stones only or their teeth for husking their grain, or live upon water or air alone, succeed in conquering Naraka. Between the king who rules this unbounded earth, and the man who regards equally stone pebbles and gold, it is the latter who attains his purusharthas, not the former.

So, depend upon that which is the eternal refuge of joy both here and hereafter, and stop wishing and hoping and being attached to your wants. Those who have given up desire and enjoyment never grieve, while you yearn for pleasures to come, and mourn them as they go. It is only after discarding desire and its gratification that you will succeed in liberating yourself from hypocrisy.

There are two well-known paths for us: the path of the Pitris and the path of the Devas. They who perform yagnas take the Pitri-patha, while those who are for moksha, go by the path of the gods. Casting off their bodies, the great Rishis attain realms that are above the power of Yama; they do this through brahmacharya, tapasya and the study of the Vedas.

The knowing call worldly enjoyments bonds, bandhana, as well as karma. Liberated from those two sins—bondage and action—man attains the highest end. One has heard of Janaka, freed from the duality of opposites, liberated from desire and enjoyment, observant of the religion of moksha, singing a verse: "My treasures are immense, yet I have nothing! If fire again destroys the whole of Mithila and reduces it to ashes, nothing of mine will be burnt!"

Like a man on the hill-top looking down upon men on the plain below, he who has ascended to the summit of gyana sees people pining for things that do not call for grief. He who, casting his eyes on visible things, really sees them, is said to have true vision and understanding, because of the knowledge he has gained of unknown and incomprehensible things.

Men who know the words of sages are cleansed souls, and those who have attained a state of Brahman, succeed in obtaining great honour. When one understands that creatures of infinite diversity are all one and the same, and that they spring from the same essence, one attains Brahman.

Those who reach this highest condition attain the supreme and blissful end, not they who are without gyana, or who are of small and narrow minds, or are bereft of understanding, or are without tapasya. Indeed, everything rests on the trained understanding!'"

CANTO 18

Vaisampayana said, "When Yudhishtira falls silent, Arjuna, moved by what the king said, and afire with sorrow and grief, once more addresses his eldest brother. 'People tell this old story, O Bhaarata, about the discourse between the ruler of the Videhas and his queen. It relates to the words which his grief-stricken spouse said to her lord when, abandoning his kingdom, he resolved to lead the life of a sannyasi. Casting off wealth, children, wives and precious possessions of various kinds, the established path for acquiring religious merit and the sacred agni itself, King Janaka shaved his head and put on the garb of a sannyasi.

His wife found him without wealth, observing the vows of a mendicant, resolved to abstain from inflicting any kind of injury on others. Free from vanity of every kind, he was prepared to subsist upon a handful of barley fallen from the stalk and obtained by gathering the grains from crevices in the field.

Approaching her lord at a time when no one was with him, the queen, endowed with great strength of mind, fearlessly and in anger uttered to him these words full of reason: "Why have you adopted the life of a sannyasi, abandoning your kingdom full of wealth and corn? A handful of fallen barley cannot be proper for you. Your resolution does not suit your karma, O Rajan, for you are abandoning your great kingdom but coveting instead a handful of grain. With this handful of barley, how will you gratify your athithis, the Devas, Rishis and Pitris? Your labour is pointless. Alas, abandoned by all of them, you intend to lead the life of a wandering mendicant, O king, having cast off all action!

Until now, you were the supporter of thousands of Brahmanas versed in the three Vedas, and of many others besides. How can you now want to beg them for your own food, renouncing your blazing prosperity, and looking around like a dog for its meagre pickings? Today, your mother has lost a son and your wife, the princess of Kosala, is a widow. These helpless Kshatriyas, expectant of fruit and religious merit, depend upon you, and have all their hopes set on you. By killing their hope, to what regions will you go, O king, especially when moksha is uncertain and creatures are dependent on karma? Sinful as you are, you have neither this world nor the other, for you wish to live abandoning your wife.

Why do you lead a life of a sannyasi, abstaining from your karma, abandoning garlands and perfumes and ornaments and robes of different kinds? Once you were a large and sacred lake for all creatures, a mighty tree worthy of adoration and granting its shelter to all. Alas, how can you wait upon and worship others? If even an elephant desists from all work, packs of carnivores and innumerable worms would devour it. What then can be said of you in this state?

How can your heart be set on a mode of life which recommends an earthen pot and a triple-headed stick, forces one to abandon his very clothes and permits the acceptance of only a handful of barley? You say that your kingdom and a handful of barley are the same to you; why then do you abandon the first? If, again, a handful of barley becomes an object of attachment with you, then your original resolution of renouncing everything fails.

If you live up to your resolution of renouncing everything, what am I to you and you to me, and what is your grace to me? If you want to be happy, then rule this earth! Those who wish for happiness, but are poor, destitute and abandoned by friends, may adopt renunciation. But he who imitates such men by giving up palatial mansions, beds and chariots, robes and ornaments, does so improperly indeed! One always accepts gifts made by others, another always gives gifts. You know the difference between the two, but who, indeed, of these two should be considered the superior? If a gift be made to one who always accepts gifts, or is proud, that gift becomes useless, like clarified butter poured upon a forest fire. As a fire, O Rajan, never dies till it has consumed all that has been cast into it, even so a beggar can never be silenced until he receives alms.

In this world, the food that is given by a charitable man is the sure support of the pious. If, therefore, the king does not give food, where will the pious go who seek salvation? Those who have food in their houses are grihastas, and they support sannyasis. Since life flows from food, the giver of food is the giver of life. Leaving the life of a grihasta, the sannyasis depend upon the very varna from where they come. By doing so, these self-restrained men acquire and enjoy fame and power.

A man does not become a sannyasi by merely renouncing his possessions, or adopting a life dependent on charity. Only he who renounces the possessions and pleasures of the world with a sincere mind is a true sannyasi. Unattached at heart, though attached in outward appearance, standing aloof from the world, having broken all his bonds, and regarding friend and foe equally, such a man, O king, is regarded to be free!

Having shaved their heads clean and putting on the ochre robe, men may be seen to adopt vanaprastha, but in fact they are bound by many ties and ever on the lookout for useless wealth. Those who, after casting off the three Vedas, their natural occupations and their children, adopt a life of mendicancy by taking up the triple-headed crutch and the brown robe, are really fools.

Understand, O Rajan, that without having shed anger and other faults, adopting the ochre robe is only to earn sustenance. Those with clean-shaven heads who have set up the banner of virtue have just this objective in life. Therefore, O king, keeping your passions under control, do you win regions of bliss hereafter by supporting the truly pious amongst men of matted locks or clean-shaven heads, naked or clad in rags, skins or ochre robes. Who is there more virtuous than he who maintains his sacred fire, who performs sacrifices with gifts of animals and dakshina, and who practises charity day and night?"'

Arjuna continues, 'We regard King Janaka to be a gyani in this world. Even he became confused, in this matter of the meaning of dharma. Do not yield to bewilderment! This is the way that those who practise charity observe the duties of grihasta. By abstaining from violence of all kinds, by casting off desire and wrath, by being engaged in protecting all creatures, by observing the excellent dharma of dana and, lastly, by cherishing superiors and the elderly, we will succeed in attaining the regions of happiness to which we aspire. By duly gratifying gods, guests, and all creatures, by worshipping Brahmanas, and by truthfulness of speech, we will certainly attain realms of bliss.'"

CANTO 19

"Yudhishtira says, 'I am conversant with both the Vedas and the scriptures that lead to the attainment of Brahman. In the Vedas there are principles of both kinds—those that instill action and those that teach renunciation of karma. The shastras are confusing but I know their well-reasoned conclusions and the truth that is in the mantras. You know only weapons and the ways of Kshatriyas, and do not truly understand the meaning of the scriptures.

If you knew your dharma, you would understand that even one with the clearest insight into the meaning of the scriptures and the truths of religion, should not address such words to me. However, whatever you said out of brotherly love was proper. I am thankful to you for that, O Arjuna!

No one in the three worlds is equal to you in all the ways of battle and in the diverse skills of the way of karma. You can surely speak of the subtleties connected with these subjects, nuances that are impenetrable to others. But, O Dhananjaya, it is not fitting for you to doubt my intelligence. You know the science of war, but you have never waited upon the aged and do not know the decisions arrived at by those who have studied the subject both in brief and at length. Even intelligent men seeking salvation arrive at the conclusion that between tapasya while living in the world, sannyasa and the knowledge of Brahman, the second is superior to the first, and the third to the second.

To think that there is nothing superior to wealth is an error, and I will convince you of it, so that wealth may not again appear to you in that light. One sees all men of dharma devoted to sannyasa and the study of the Vedas. Since they have the merit of tapasya, the Rishis have many eternal regions reserved for them. Others possessed of tranquillity of soul, having no enemies, and dwelling in the vana, have gained Swarga through tapasya and study of the Vedas. By restraining desire for worldly possessions, and casting off that darkness born of folly, pious men go northward by luminous paths to the realms kept for practisers of tyaga.

The lunar regions, the path of the south that leads to regions of light, are kept for men devoted to action. Those who are subject to samsara, to birth and death, attain these. However, the end which those who desire salvation have before their eyes is indescribable. Yoga is the best means for attaining it.

I cannot explain it easily to you. The gyanis live, reflecting on the scriptures from a desire to identify what is unreal. But they are often led astray in the belief that the object of their search exists in this and that. Having mastered the Vedas, the Aranyakas, and the other scriptures, they miss the Real, like men failing to find solid timber in an uprooted banana plant.

Some of them, disbelieving in its unity, regard the Atman that dwells in this physical frame, consisting of the five elements, to be possessed of the attributes of desire and aversion and others. Incapable of being seen by the eye, exceedingly subtle and inexpressible through words, the Atman revolves in a round of re-births among the creatures of the earth, keeping before it that which is the root of karma.

Having made the Atman, which is the spring of every kind of blessedness, advance towards itself, having restrained all desires of the mind, and having cast off all kinds of action, one may become perfectly independent and happy. When such a path trodden by the righteous exists and it is attainable through gyana why, O Arjuna, do you laud wealth which is full of every kind of calamity?

Men of olden times who were conversant with the shastras, who were always engaged in distributing gifts, sacrifice and action, were of this opinion, O Bhaarata! There are some fools who, accomplished in the science of debate, deny the existence of the Atman, based on the strength of their convictions of a previous life. It is very difficult to make them accept this truth about final emancipation and moksha.

Those wicked men, though possessed of great learning, travel all over the world making empty speeches in assemblies and courts, and deprecating the true doctrine of Mukti. O Partha, who else will succeed in understanding that which we do not understand? Indeed, since these men cannot understand the true meaning of the scriptures, they cannot know those wise and pious men who are truly great and who know the shastras deeply.

O son of Kunti, men who know the truth obtain Brahman through asceticism and intelligence, and great happiness by renunciation.'"

CANTO 20

Vaisampayana said, "After Yudhishtira stops, the great Rishi Devasthana says eloquently and reasonably to the king, 'Phalguna told you that there is nothing superior to wealth. I will discuss this subject with you. Listen to me with undivided attention.

O Ajatasatru, you have righteously won the earth. Having won her, it does not become you, O king, to abandon her without cause. Four asramas of life are indicated in the Vedas, which you will duly pass through, one after another. At present, you should perform great sacrifices with lavish gifts. Among the very Rishis, some engage themselves in the tapasya represented by Vedic study, and some in that presented by gyana. O Bhaarata, you must know that action possesses these very sannyasis.

The Vaikhanasas preach that the man who does not seek wealth is superior to him that seeks it. I believe that he who follows this principle makes a grave mistake. Men collect diverse things for performing yagnas, simply because the Vedas require it. Tainted by his lack of understanding, he who gives away wealth to the undeserving, rather than to the deserving, does not know that he incurs the very sin of killing an unborn.

The exercise of the dharma of daana after discerning the deserving from the undeserving is not easy. The Supreme Ordainer created wealth for sacrifice, and created man to husband this wealth, and to perform sacrifice. For this reason the whole of one's wealth should be applied to yagnas. Pleasure would be a natural consequence.

Possessed of prodigious energy, Indra, by performing diverse yagnas with lavish gifts, surpassed all the Devas. Becoming their king, he shines in Swarga. Everything should be applied to sacrifices.

Clad in deer-skin, the high-souled Mahadeva, having poured his own self as a religious offering in the yagna called Sarva, became the first among the gods and, surpassing all creatures in the universe, shines in radiant glory.

King Marutta, the son of Avikshit, with his enormous wealth vanquished Sakra himself, the lord of the Devas. In the great sacrifice he performed, all the vessels were of gold, and Sree herself came to it. You have heard that the great king Harischandra, having performed yagnas, earned great merit and great happiness. Though a mortal man, he vanquished Sakra with his wealth. For this reason everything should be applied to sacrifice.'"

CANTO 21

"Devasthana says, 'Let me tell you in this context an old story about the sermon Brihaspati gave Indra at his request.

Brihaspati said, "Contentment is the highest heaven, the highest bliss, and there is nothing higher than it. When a man withdraws from all his desires, like a tortoise drawing in all it limbs, the natural splendour of his Soul soon shows itself. When one does not fear any creature or frighten any creature, when one conquers one's desire and aversion, then they say one sees one's Soul. When one seeks to injure nobody and cherishes no desire, in word and thought, they say one attains Brahman."

Thus, O Kuntiputra, men obtain corresponding fruits, whatever religion they follow. Awaken yourself to this thought, O Bhaarata! Some praise quietude, others action, while there are others who extol contemplation, and others again who advocate both quiescence and action.

Some praise sacrifice, others, renunciation; some praise charity, others, acceptance; and some, abandoning everything, live in silent meditation. Some praise sovereignty and the cherishing of subjects, after enslaving and killing foes, while some are for passing their days in seclusion. Observing all this, the learned conclude that only that religion which consists in not injuring any creature is worthy of the approval of the righteous. Abstention from injury, truthfulness of speech, justice, compassion, self-restraint, having children by one's own wives, good nature, modesty, patience—the practice of all these is the best religion, as told by Swayambhuva Manu himself. O son of Kunti, observe this dharma with care.

The Kshatriya who, conversant with the truths of Rajadharma, the royal dharma, takes sovereignty upon himself, restraining his soul at all times, regarding as equal that which is dear and that which is not, and subsisting upon the remains of sacrificial feasts, who restrains the wicked and cherishes the righteous, who obliges his subjects to tread the path of virtue and who himself treads that path, who at last hands over his crown to his son and retires to the forest as a sannyasi, to subsist on the produce of the wilderness and to live according to the laws of the Vedas, having cast off all idleness, is sure to obtain the most excellent fruits in both this world and the next, for he conducts himself in conformity with the well-known duties of kings.

The Moksha of which you speak is exceedingly difficult to gain, and its pursuit involves countless difficulties. Those who observe their svadharma and practise charity and ascetic penances, who are compassionate, free from desire and anger, and who engage in ruling their subjects with righteousness, protecting cows and Brahmanas, attain a lofty end. The Rudras with the Vasus, the Adityas, the Sadhyas and hosts of kings adopt this dharma, O Parantapa, and by practising it with care, they reach Swarga.'"

CANTO 22

Vaisampayana said, "After this, Arjuna once more says to his eldest brother, King Yudhishtira, of unfading glory but of doleful heart, 'O Vidheyajala, having through the practice of Kshatriya dharma obtained sovereignty that is so difficult to acquire, and having conquered all your enemies, why do you burn in grief?

Rajan, for Kshatriyas, death in battle is regarded as more meritorious than the performance of all the diverse sacrifices. The shastras that lay down the dharma of Kshatriyas declare that tapasya and renunciation are the dharma of Brahmanas. Even this is the law for the two varnas in the next world. Indeed, O powerful one, death in battle is for Kshatriyas; their dharma is exceedingly fierce and always connected with the use of weapons, and the shastras decree that when the time comes, they should perish by weapons in the battlefield.

The life of even a Brahmana, O king, who lives in the observance of the Kshatriya dharma, cannot be faulted, for Kshatriyas also spring from Brahmanas. Neither renunciation, nor sacrifice, nor penances, nor dependence on the wealth of others is for Kshatriyas. You, Bharatarishabha, know all your duties and, as a wise king skilled in all karma, can distinguish what is right and what is wrong. Cast off this gloom brought about by repentance, and with a strong will, prepare yourself for action!

The heart, especially of a Kshatriya, is as hard as the vajra. Through the exercise of the Kshatriya dharma, you have vanquished your enemies and acquired an empire, which is now peaceful. Now conquer your soul, O ruler of men, engage yourself in the performance of sacrifices and in the practice of charity.

Indra himself, though a Brahmana, became a Kshatriya in his actions and battled with his sinful kinsfolk, eight hundred and ten times. His actions were commendable and worthy of praise, and as a result, he became the king of the Devas. Perform sacrifices with lavish gifts, just as Indra did, O Rajan, and liberate yourself from your fever.

Do not, Bharatarishabha, grieve like this for what is past. The slain men have attained Swarga, purified by weapons in accordance to the laws of the Kshatriya dharma. That which has happened, had to happen, and Destiny, O Purushavyaghra, cannot be resisted.'"

CANTO 23

Vaisampayana said, "Thus addressed by the wavy-haired Arjuna, Yudhishtira remains silent. Then the island-born Vyasa says, 'The words of Arjuna, O amiable Yudhishtira, are true. The highest dharma, as declared by the scriptures, depends on the dharma of a grihasta. You know all your duties, so practise the dharma of grihasta that is prescribed for you.

A life of retirement in the forest, casting off garhapatya, is not for you. The Devas, Pitris, athithis and dasas, all depend for their sustenance upon a man leading the life of a grihasta; you should support all of them, O lord of the earth! Men leading domestic lives support birds and animals and various other creatures; so is grihasta superior to all the other asramas, and is the most difficult of all the four stages of life.

Live this most difficult life of a grihasta then, O Kaunteya, as you know all the Vedas well and have earned great ascetic merit. You must bear like an ox the burden of your ancestral kingdom, O Rajan.

To obtain success Brahmanas should strive to the best of their ability after tapasya, tyaga, kshama, gyana, sannyasa, keeping the senses under control, dhyana, living in solitude, contentment and knowledge of Brahman.

Let me now remind you of the duties of Kshatriyas, which you already know. As we are told, sacrifice, learning, exertion, ambition, wielding the danda, fierceness, protection of subjects, knowledge of the

Vedas, practice of all kinds of penance, goodness of conduct, acquisition of wealth, and gifts to deserving persons—it is these, well performed and acquired by Kshatriyas, that secure for them both this world and the next.

Amongst these, O son of Kunti, wielding the rod of punishment is the foremost. Strength must always abide in a Kshatriya, and upon strength depends punishment. These duties that I have mentioned are, O king, the principal ones for Kshatriyas and contribute greatly to their success.

Brihaspati, in this connection, sang this verse: "Like a snake devouring a mouse, the earth devours a king who prefers peace and a Brahmana who prefers the life of a grihasta."

One again hears that only by wielding the rod of chastisement did the Rajarishi Sudyumna find the highest success, like Daksha himself, the son of Prachetas.'

Yudhishtira then asks, 'O holy one, by what deeds did Sudyumna, the lord of the earth, obtain the highest success? I want to hear the story of this king.'

Vyasa replies, 'There were two brothers—Sankha and Likhita, of high austerities. The brothers had separate houses, both of which were beautiful. Situated on the bank of the Bahuda river, these dwellings were always adorned with trees laden with flowers and fruits. One day, Likhita visited his brother Sankha when he was not at home. Arriving at the hermitage of his brother, Likhita plucked many ripe fruits and began to eat them without any qualms of conscience. While he was still eating, Sankha returned home.

Sankha asked his brother, "From where have you plucked these fruits, and why are you eating them?"

Approaching his elder brother and greeting him, Likhita smilingly replied, "I have plucked them from here."

Filled with great rage, Sankha told him, "You have committed theft by taking these fruits without permission. Go to the king and confess what you have done. Tell him that you have committed an offence by taking what was not given to you and, let him, observing his Kshatriya dharma, punish you as a thief."

The highly blessed Likhita of rigid vows, at the command of his brother, went to King Sudyumna. Hearing from his gate-keepers that Likhita had come, Sudyumna, with his counsellors, received the sage. Meeting him, the king said to that noble one conversant with dharma, "Tell me, O revered one, the reason for your visit. You may consider it done!"

The Rishi said to Sudyumna, "Promise first that you will grant what I ask. And you must keep your word. O bull among men, I ate some fruits that my elder brother had not given me. Do you, O Rajan, punish me for it without delay."

Sudyumna answered, "If the king be regarded as competent to wield the rod of danda, he should be regarded as equally competent to pardon. O Anuvrata, consider yourself pardoned. Tell me now what other wishes you have, and I will certainly do what you want."

Vyasa continues, 'Thus honoured by the high-souled king, the Maharishi Likhita did not ask any other favour. Then the ruler of the earth commanded that both his hands be cut off and, after bearing the punishment, the Rishi went away. Returning to his brother Sankha, Likhita, in great affection, said, "You must now pardon this wretch, whom you have punished as he deserved."

Sankha said, "I am not angry with you, nor have you injured me, O foremost of all persons, O true knower of dharma. Your virtue, however, had suffered a setback. I have rescued you from that plight. Go without delay to the Bahuda river, gratify the Devas, the Rishis and the Pitris with offerings of water, and never again set your heart on paapa."

Obeying Sankha, Likhita performed his rites in the sacred stream and was about to begin the water-rite when two hands, like two lotuses in beauty, appeared at the extremities of his stumps. Filled with wonder, he came back to his brother and showed him the two hands. Sankha explained, "I accomplished this through my tapasya, so do not be surprised. Providence has been the instrument here."

Likhita then asked, "O you of great splendour, when such was the power of your tapasya, why did you not purify me at first?"

Sankha replied, "I could not do otherwise, for I am not your punisher. The king who punished you has himself been purified, like you, along with the Pitris!"

Vyasa continues, 'This king, O eldest son of Pandu, became renowned for this deed and gained the highest success, like the lord Daksha himself! Even this is the dharma of Kshatriyas, the ruling of subjects. Any other path, O monarch, would be regarded as a wrong one for them. Do not give way to grief. O best of all men, conversant with dharma, listen to the beneficial words of your brother. Wielding the danda, O Rajan, is the duty of kings, not shaving the head!'"

CANTO 24

Vaisampayana said, "Once more the great sage Krishna-Dwaipayana tells Ajatasatru, the son of Kunti, 'Let these great Maharathas of abundant energy of mind, your brothers, O Yudhishtira, obtain the wishes that they cherished during your vanavasa. Rule the earth, O son of Pritha, like another Yayati, the son of Nahusha.

Misery was yours while you lived in the forest as ascetics. That misery has ended, O Purushavyaghra. Enjoy happiness, therefore, for some years. Then, O Bhaarata, having earned and enjoyed dharma, artha and kama for a goodly period with your brothers, you may seek vanavasa.

Be freed first from the debt you owe to sannyasis, to the Pitris, and to the Devas. Later, O son of Kunti, you can practise all the other asramas that follow the grihasta. Perform the yagnas of Sarvamedha and Aswamedha, O Rajan, and you will attain Swarga hereafter. Include your brothers also in great yagnas, with plentiful gifts for Brahmanas, and you will acquire great fame.

There is a saying, O Naravyaghra, to which you should hearken, for by living according to it, Kuruttama, you will not swerve from dharma. Only those men, Yudhishtira, who act like robbers are able to influence kings to follow the career of war and victory. The king who, guided by considerations of place and time and moved by an understanding of the scriptures, pardons even a number of robbers, incurs no paapa. The king who, realizing his tribute of a sixth, fails to protect his kingdom, acquires a fourth part of the sins of his kingdom.

Listen to how a king will not deviate from dharma. By violating the scriptures one incurs sin, while by obeying them one may live fearlessly. Guided by an understanding based upon the scriptures and disregarding lust and anger, the king who behaves impartially, like a father towards all his subjects, never incurs sin, O you of great splendour! If, due to misfortune, a king fails to do his duty, such failure will not be called a transgression. By force and policy the king should put down his enemies. He must not suffer sin to be perpetrated in his kingdom but should cause dharma to be practised.

Brave and honourable men who are virtuous, erudite Brahmanas who have mastered Vedic texts and rites, and men of wealth, should especially be protected. In judging legal suits and in carrying out religious activities, only the most learned men should be employed.

A prudent king will never repose his confidence upon one individual, however accomplished. The king who does not protect his subjects, whose passions are ungovernable, who is full of vanity, who is arrogant and malicious, is a culpable and tyrannical king. If his subjects perish from want of protection and the gods punish them, if robbers ruin them, the sin of all this besmirches the king himself. There is no sin, O Yudhishtira, in undertaking a task wholeheartedly, after full deliberation and consultation with capable advisors. Our tasks fail or succeed through destiny. If the king makes an effort, sin would not touch him.

I will tell you, O tiger among kings, the story of an ancient monarch called Hayagriva, heroic and of unstained deeds, who was defeated and killed after having himself slain a large number of enemies in battle, while he had no follower by his side. He did all that was necessary to keep his enemies in check and to protect all his subjects. Hayagriva acquired great fame from the battles he fought. Grievously injured by robbers whom he boldly faced, the Mahatman Hayagriva, ever attentive to his dharma, lost his life in battle and, having achieved the object of his life, now enjoys great bliss in Swarga.

The bow was his sacrificial stake and the bowstring was the rope to bind victims. Arrows constituted the smaller ladle and the sword the large one, and blood was the clarified butter that he poured onto the sacrifice of battle. His chariot was the altar, the wrath he felt in battle was the fire, and the four excellent steeds yoked to his ratha were the four Hotris.

Having poured upon that sacrificial fire first his enemies as offerings, and then his own life-breath at the completion of the sacrifice, this bold lion among kings, Hayagriva, was freed from sin, and now sports in Devaloka. The high-souled and self-renouncing Hayagriva of potent mind, the performer of yagnas, protected his kingdom through good governance and intelligence, and filled all the worlds with his fame. He received merit from the performance of sacrifices and every kind of punya connected with human affairs. He wielded the danda, the rod of punishment, and ruled the earth with vigour and without pride. For this the virtuous Hayagriva, practising renunciation actuated by his faith, and full of gratitude, left this world and won the regions that are reserved for the intelligent and the wise, for those that follow the approved customs and conduct and are always prepared to die in battle.

Having studied the Vedas as well as other scriptures, having ruled his kingdom ably and caused all the four varnas to adhere to their respective dharmas, Hayagriva now rejoices in Devaloka. Having won many battles, cherished his subjects, drunk the soma rasa in sacrifices and gratified the foremost of Brahmanas with gifts, and having judiciously wielded the rod of chastisement over those under his sway, this king, at last, casting away his life in battle, dwells happily in heaven.

His life was worthy of every praise, and learned and honest men extol it. Crowned with success, this Mahatman, a king of virtuous deeds, won Swarga and acquired the realms reserved for great heroes.'"

CANTO 25

Vaisampayana said, "Hearing the words of the island-born Rishi and seeing Dhananjaya angry, Yudhishtira, the son of Kunti, salutes Vyasa and says, 'This earthly sovereignty and its enjoyment fail to give any joy to my heart. On the other hand, this poignant grief at the loss of my kinsmen is eating away its core. Hearing the lamentations of these women who have lost their heroic husbands and children, I fail to find peace, O sage!'"

Vaisampayana continued, "Thus addressed, the virtuous Vyasa, foremost of all men conversant with Yoga, possessed of great wisdom and intimately acquainted with the Vedas, says to Yudhisthira, 'No man can acquire anything by his own actions, neither through sacrifices and worship, nor by giving anything to a fellow man. Man acquires everything in the course of Time, as intended by Brahma. If Time is unfavourable, men cannot by mere intelligence or study of the scriptures acquire any earthly possession, while sometimes an ignorant fool succeeds in winning wealth. Time is the effective way for the accomplishment of all karma.

During times of adversity, neither science, nor prayers, nor medicaments, yield any result. In times of prosperity, however, those very things, properly applied, become successful and bear fruit. By Time the winds blow violently, the clouds become rain-charged, tanks become adorned with lotuses of different kinds, and trees in the forest become decked with flowers. By Time nights become dark or lit, and the moon becomes full. If the Time has not come, trees do not bear flowers and fruits, the currents of rivers do not gather force, and birds, snakes, deer, elephants and other animals never become excited.

If the Time has not come, women do not conceive. It is with Time that winter and summer and the monsoon come. If the Time for it has not come, no one is born and no one dies; the infant does not acquire power of speech and the child does not grow to youth. It is with Time that the seed sown puts forth its sprouts.

If the Time has not come, the sun does not appear above the horizon nor does it repair to the Asta hills; the moon does not wax or wane, nor the ocean, with its high billows, rise and ebb. In this connection one remembers the old story told, O Yudhishtira, by King Senajit in grief. The irresistible course of Time affects all mortals; all earthly things, ripened by Time, come to perish.

Some men, O king, slay others, and others again slay the slayers. This is the language of the world. In reality, no one slays and no one is slain: it is only a matter of perception. The truth is that, as ordained, the birth and death of all creatures must come to pass and are a result of their very nature.

Upon the loss of one's wealth or the death of one's wife, son or father, one cries out saying "Alas, what grief!" and dwelling upon this sorrow always enhances it. Why do you, like a foolish man, indulge in grief? Why do you grieve for them who are beyond grief? Indulgence increases grief, just as fear grows if one yields to it.

This body, or anything on this earth, is not mine, for the things of this earth belong as much to others as to me. The wise, seeing this, do not allow themselves to be deluded, for there are thousands of causes for sorrow, and hundreds of causes for joy. These daily affect the ignorant, but not the wise. These, in course of time become objects of affection or aversion and, appearing as bliss or sorrow, revolve as if on a wheel and affect all living creatures. There is only sorrow in this world but no happiness, and it is for this reason that only sorrow is felt.

Indeed, sorrow springs from the affliction called desire, and happiness springs from the affliction called sorrow. Sorrow comes after happiness, and happiness after sorrow, and one does not always suffer sorrow or always enjoy happiness. Happiness always ends in sorrow, and sometimes proceeds from sorrow itself. He, therefore, who desires eternal happiness, must abandon both. Since sorrow must arise upon the cessation of happiness, and happiness upon the conclusion of sorrow, one should cast off like a snake-bitten limb that from which one experiences sorrow or heart-burning, that which it nurtures or which is the root of one's anxiety.

Be it happiness or sorrow, be it agreeable or disagreeable, whatever comes should be borne with an unaffected heart. O agreeable one, if you abstain in even a slight measure from doing what is pleasing to your wives and children, you will then know who is whose, and for what reason. Those who are very stupid or those who are masters of their souls enjoy happiness here, while those who occupy an intermediate place suffer misery. This, O Yudhishtira, is what was said by Senajit of great wisdom, the king who knew what is good and bad in this world, with dharma, and with happiness and misery.

A man can never be happy if other people's sorrows affect him. There is no end to grief, and it arises from happiness itself. Happiness and misery, prosperity and adversity, gain and loss, death and life, in their turn, affect all creatures. For this reason the wise man with an unagitated soul will neither be elated with joy nor be depressed with sorrow. To engage in battle is the yagna for a king; a due observance of the science of punishment is his yoga; and the gift of wealth in sacrifices, in the form of dakshina, is his renunciation. All these should be regarded as acts that sanctify him.

By governing the kingdom with intelligence and policy, casting off pride, performing sacrifices, and looking at everything and all persons with kindness and impartiality, a high-souled king sports in Devaloka after death. By winning wars, protecting his kingdom, drinking the soma rasa, improving the lot of his subjects, judiciously wielding the danda, and casting off his body at last in battle, a king enjoys happiness in Swarga.

Having studied all the Vedas and the other scriptures, having protected the kingdom and caused all four varnas to adhere to their respective duties, a king becomes sanctified and finally finds and dwells in Swarga. He is the best of kings whose conduct is applauded by the inhabitants of cities and country, counsellors and friends even after his death.'"

CANTO 26

Vaisampayana said, "Now the noble Yudhishtira reasons with Arjuna, saying, 'You think, O Partha, that there is nothing superior to wealth, and that the poor man can neither have heaven, nor happiness, nor the fulfillment of his wishes. This is not true, for we see many men crowned with success through sacrifice in the shape of Vedic study, while many sages have with tapasya acquired Swarga.

O Dhananjaya, the gods regard as Brahmanas those who observe the practices of the Rishis by adopting brahmacharya, and who become knowers of dharma. O son of Pandu, you should always regard as truly virtuous those Rishis devoted to the study of the Vedas and those devoted to the pursuit of true knowledge.

All our actions depend upon those who devote themselves to the acquisition of gyana. O Bhaarata, we know this to be the opinion of the Vaikhanasas, and that the Ajas, the Prishnis, the Sikatas, the Arunas, and the Kitavas have all gone to heaven through the merit of Vedic study. O Dhananjaya, the Vedas prescribe that it is through battle, by studying the scriptures, by sacrifices, and by the restraint of passion, all arduous duties, that one goes to heaven by Dakshinayana, the southern path of the sun, which, as I told you, belongs to such men. Those who devote themselves to Yoga travel by Uttarayana, the northern path, to eternal and bright regions.

Of the two, those conversant with the Puranas laud the northern path.

You should know that one acquires heaven through serenity, and that from tranquillity springs great happiness. There is nothing higher than serenity. For the Yogin who has controlled anger and joy, contentment is his triumph. In this connection, one quotes the discourse by Yayati. Listening to this discourse, one may succeed in withdrawing all desires, like a tortoise drawing all his limbs into his shell.

When one does not fear anything, and no one and nothing is afraid of one, when one cherishes no desire, when one bears no hate, then one attains the state of Brahman. When one does not sin against any creature, in act, thought or word, one attains Brahman. When one has controlled one's pride and folly, and has withdrawn oneself from all attachments, it is then that the pious man of shining soul becomes fit for attaining salvation and the annihilation of separate existence.

Listen now to me with concentrated attention, O son of Pritha. Some desire virtue, some good conduct, and some wealth. One may desire wealth as a means for acquiring virtue, but it would be better to abandon such desires, since there are many hazards attached to wealth and consequently, to the religious deeds that one performs with wealth, as we have seen with our own eyes. You must understand that he who desires wealth will find it very difficult to abandon it later. Good deeds are very rare in those who amass riches, for wealth can never be acquired without injuring others and, when obtained, it brings numerous troubles.

A man of narrow heart, and without remorse, tempted by even a little wealth, will commit acts of aggression towards others, unconscious all the while of the sin of Brahmahatya that he incurs by his karma. After acquiring wealth with so much difficulty, such men will burn with grief if they have to give a portion of it to their servants, grief equal to what they would feel if they were actually robbed by thieves. If one does not part with one's wealth, disgrace becomes one's lot, while he who has no wealth never becomes the subject of censure.

Withdrawn from all attachments, such a man can become happy in all respects by supporting life upon what little he may obtain as alms. The acquisition of wealth cannot give anyone happiness. In this connection those who know the ancient scriptures recite certain verses relating to sacrifices.

The Creator created wealth for the sake of sacrifices, and created man for protecting that wealth and performing yagnas. For this, all wealth should be applied to yagnas, and it is not proper to spend it for the gratification of desire or enjoyment.

Understand, O son of Kunti, you that are the foremost of all wealthy persons, that the Creator confers wealth upon mortals for the sake of yagnas. It is for this that the wise think that wealth does not belong to anybody on earth. One should perform yagnas with it and give it away with a trustful heart. One should gift away what one has acquired, and not waste or spend it in gratifying one's desires or for enjoyment. What use is there in amassing more and more wealth when such proper objects exist on which to spend it?

Men of little understanding who give away wealth to those who have swerved from the duties of their order, have to subsist hereafter for a hundred years on excrement and dirt. Men give to the undeserving and not to the deserving, unable to discriminate between the two. For this reason the practice of the virtue of charity is difficult, and even when acquired, these two faults connected with wealth remain.'"

CANTO 27

"Yudhishtira says, 'Grief does not forsake my wretched self as a result of the deaths in battle of young Abhimanyu, the sons of Draupadi, Dhrishtadyumna, Virata, King Drupada, Vasusena who knew dharma well, the royal Dhrishtaketu, and of numerous other kings hailing from diverse lands. I am a slayer of kinsmen, inordinately covetous of kingdom and an exterminator of my own race.

Alas, I have cut down in battle, through lust of sovereignty, this Ganga's son upon whose breast and limbs I used to play as a boy. It lacerated my heart to see Sikhandin assailing our grandfather, a lion among men, to see him trembling and reeling from Partha's shafts like thunderbolts, and to watch his tall form, pierced all over with blazing arrows, turn weak like an aged lion. It stunned me to see this destroyer of hostile chariots collapse like a mountain summit and fall in his own ratha with his face turned towards the east.

This Kurusthama who, bow and shafts in hand, waged a fierce battle for many days with Rama himself of Bhrigu's line, on the field sanctified by Kuru, this son of Ganga, this hero who, at Varanasi, in order to take brides for Hastinapura, challenged to battle on a single ratha the assembled Kshatriyas of the world, and who burnt that irresistible and foremost of kings, Ugrayudha, with the energy of his weapons—alas, I caused this Kshatriya to be slain in battle.

This hero, knowing full well that Sikhandin, prince of Panchala, was his nemesis, nevertheless refrained from killing him with his arrows. Alas, Arjuna slew that magnanimous warrior. O best of sages, my heart burned at that moment when I saw our Pitamaha stretched out on the earth and covered in blood. Alas, for lust of a kingdom, I am now the slayer of reverend elders, a perfect fool for causing the death of one who protected and nurtured us when we were children. All for the sake of a sovereignty that will last but a few days.

I approached our guru, the great archer Drona, adored by all the kings, and gave him false news of the death of his son. The memory of this sears my limbs. The Acharya said to me, "Tell me truly, O king, whether my son still lives." Expecting truth from me, the Brahmana asked me of all others but I lied to him, though silently, saying the word 'elephant'. I am culpable for coveting the kingdom and murdering my revered elders, for, throwing off the mantle of truth which everyone believed me to wear, I told my guru on the battlefield that we had killed Aswatthaman when, in fact, we had only slain an elephant of that name.

To what hell will I go, having perpetrated such ignominious deeds? I also caused my eldest brother Karna to be slain, that awesome warrior who never retreated from battle. Who is there more sinful than I? Through greed I caused the adolescent Abhimanyu, that Kshatriya who resembled a lion born in the hills, to break into the chakra vyuha that Drona himself protected. I am like one guilty of infanticide. Since then I have not been able to look in the face Arjuna or the lotus-eyed Krishna. I grieve also for Draupadi, bereft of her five sons like the earth bereft of her five mountains. I am a great offender, a great sinner and a destroyer of the earth.

Without rising from this seat that I now occupy, I will starve myself to death. I, the killer of my guru and exterminator of my race, will sit here in the observance of the Praya vrata, in order that I may not be reborn in any of the other order of beings. I will forgo food and drink and, without moving from this place, O great ascetic, I will dry up my precious life-breaths. I beg you humbly to grant me leave to do this and thereafter go wherever you please. Let everyone grant me leave to cast off this body of mine.'"

Vaisampayana continued, "Restraining Pritha's son, who uttered these words stricken by sorrow on account of his kinsmen's deaths, Vyasa, the best of Rishis, says to him, 'This cannot be! It does not become you, O monarch, to indulge in such an excess of grief. I will repeat what I have said earlier. All this is Destiny, O mighty one. Without doubt, all creatures that are born display at first a combination of diverse materials and forces which at the end, dissolve. Like bubbles in the water they rise and disappear.

All things held together are sure to crumble, and all things that rise must fall. Union ends in dissolution, and life ends in death. Idleness, though temporarily agreeable, ends in misery and skilfull labour, though temporarily distressing, ends in happiness. Affluence, prosperity, modesty, contentment and fame dwell in labour and skill, not in idleness.

Friends are not competent to bestow happiness, nor foes competent to inflict misery. Similarly, wisdom does not bring wealth, nor does wealth bring happiness. Since the Maker has created you, O son of Kunti, to engage yourself in karma, and success springs from karma, it is not fitting for you to avoid karma, O king.'"

CANTO 28

Vaisampayana said, "Vyasa then dispels the grief of the eldest son of Pandu who, burning with sorrow on account of the slaughter of his kinsmen, has resolved to kill himself.

Vyasa says, 'O Purushavyaghra, let me tell you the old story known as Asma's discourse. Listen to it, O Yudhishtira! Janaka, the ruler of the Videhas, once filled with sorrow and grief, questioned a wise Brahmana named Asma to alleviate his anguish.

Janaka asked, "How should a man who wishes his own good behave upon occasions such as the accession and destruction of both kinsmen and wealth?"

Asma replied, "Immediately after the formation of a man's body, joys and grief attach themselves to it. Either of the two can overtake the man, and whichever does, quickly robs him of his reason like the wind driving away gathering clouds.

In times of prosperity, one thinks, 'I am of high birth! I can do whatever I like! I am not an ordinary man!' His mind becomes soaked with such triple vanity. Addicted to earthly enjoyments, he begins to waste the wealth accumulated by his ancestors. Impoverished in the course of time, he regards it as laudable even to appropriate what belongs to others. Like a hunter piercing a deer with his shafts, the king then punishes this wicked robber of the possessions of others, this transgressor of law and rule. Such men scarcely live beyond twenty or thirty years, and never attain a full human span of a hundred years.

Carefully observing the behaviour of all creatures, a king should, by the exercise of his intelligence, apply remedies to allay the great sorrows of his subjects. The causes of all mental sorrow are two—delusion of the mind and accumulation of suffering; no third cause exists. All these diverse sorrows, and those arising from attachment to worldly pleasures that overtake man, are as follows.

Age and Death, like a pair of wolves, devour all creatures, strong or weak, short or tall. No man can escape decay and death, not even the conqueror of the entire earth circled by the sea. Whether it is happiness or sorrow that comes upon creatures, it should be enjoyed or borne without elation or dejection, since there is no method of escape. The evils of life, O king, can overtake one in early, middle or old age. They can never be avoided, while the sources of bliss that one covets never come. The absence of what is agreeable, the presence of what is disagreeable, good and evil, bliss and sorrow, follow Destiny. The birth of creatures and their death, their gain and loss, are all pre-ordained.

Even as scent, colour, taste and touch spring naturally, happiness and misery arise from what is pre-ordained. Fine seats, beds and vehicles, luxuries, drinks and food, come and go in the course of time. Even physicians fall ill, the strong become weak, and they who enjoy prosperity lose all and become indigent. The course of Time is indeed marvellous. High birth, health, beauty, prosperity and objects of enjoyment, all are gained through Destiny. The poor, although they may not desire it, have many children, while one sees the affluent to be childless. Astonishing is the course of Destiny. The evils caused by disease, fire, water, weapons, hunger, poison, fever, falls from high places and death overtake a man according to the Destiny under which he is born.

One sees that in this world somebody without sinning suffers diverse ills, while another, having sinned, is not weighed down by calamity. One in the enjoyment of wealth perishes in his youth, while one who is poor drags on existence for a hundred years, worn down by decrepitude. One born to an ignoble race may have a very long life, while one sprung from a noble line may perish as quickly as an insect. In this world, it is common for people in affluent circumstances to have no appetite, while the poor can digest chips of wood.

Impelled by destiny, the man with an evil soul, discontented with his condition, commits sins, saying, "I am the doer," which he regards as being all for his good. The wise censure hunting, dice, women, wine, fighting, but we see many men possessed of extensive knowledge of the scriptures to be addicted to them. Objects, whether coveted or otherwise, come upon creatures as a result of Time's course, for one can trace no other cause. Who makes and who supports air, space, fire, moon, sun, day, night, the luminous bodies in the firmament, rivers and mountains? Cold, heat and rain come one after another in the course of Time. Just so is the case with the happiness and misery of mankind.

Neither medicines nor mantras can rescue the man assailed by age or overtaken by death. Just as two logs of wood floating on the great ocean come together and separate again, creatures come together and, when the time comes, part. Time acts equally towards men who are rich and enjoy the pleasures of song and dance in the company of women, and towards helpless men who live upon food that others give them.

In this world one contracts a thousand kinds of relationships, such as mother and father, son and wife. In reality, however, whose are they and whose are we? No one can belong to us, nor can we belong to another. Our union here with wives and kinsfolk and well-wishers is like that of travellers at a road-side inn.

Where am I? Where shall go? Who am I? How did I come here? For what and for whom do I grieve? Reflecting on these questions, one obtains tranquillity. Life and its conditions are constantly revolving like a wheel, and the companionship of those who are dear is transitory. The union with brother, mother, father and friend is like that of ways-farers at a sarai.

Men of knowledge perceive the unseen next world, as if with physical eyes. Without disregarding the scriptures, one desirous of knowledge should have faith. One possessed of knowledge should perform the rites laid down in respect of the Pitris and the Devas, practise all religious duties, perform sacrifices, judiciously pursue dharma, artha and kama.

Alas, no one understands that the world is sinking on the ocean of Time that is immensely deep and infested with the great crocodiles called decrepitude and death. We see many physicians become themselves afflicted, with all the members of their families, although they have carefully studied the science of medicine. Taking bitter and diverse kinds of oily medicaments no more allows them to escape death than the continents can escape being submerged in the ocean.

We see age overcoming men well-versed in the arts of chemistry, notwithstanding chemical compounds applied judiciously, even like elephants breaking down trees. So, too, we see men of tapasya, devoted to study of the Vedas, practising charity, and frequently performing sacrifices, fail to escape decrepitude and death. For all creatures that have taken birth, neither years, nor months, nor fortnights, nor days, nor nights that have once passed, ever return. In due course, man, whose existence is transitory, is forced inevitably by Time onto this broad path that every creature perforce has to tread.

Whether the body springs from the creature or the creature springs from the body, one's union with wives and friends is truly like that of transients at a wayfarers' lodgings. No one can obtain a lasting companionship with another. One cannot obtain such companionship with one's own body: how then can it be had with anyone else? Where, O king, is your father today, and where your grandfather? You do not see them, O sinless one, and they do not see you!

No person can see either heaven or hell. The scriptures, however, are the eyes of the virtuous. Frame your conduct, O king, according to the scriptures. With pure heart, one should first practise the vow of brahmacharya, then have children, and then perform sacrifices, to pay the debt one owes to the manes, the gods and men.

A wise man, after having first kept the vow of brahmacharya, should perform yagnas and have children and, after casting off all anxieties of his heart, should pay court to heaven, this world, and his own soul. The king bent upon the practice of dharma, who strives judiciously to acquire Heaven and earth, and who takes only his share of earthly goods, wins a reputation that spreads over all the worlds and among all creatures, mobile and immobile."

The ruler of the Videhas, of clear understanding, having heard these wise words, became free from grief and, taking Asma's leave, returned to his home. O Yudhishtira of unfading glory, cast off your sorrow and rise up. You are equal to Sakra himself. Suffer your soul to be happy: you have won the earth in the exercise of Kshatriya dharma, so enjoy her, O son of Kunti. Do not disregard my words.'"

CANTO 29

Vaisampayana said, "Yudhishtira Dharmaputra, best of kings, remains silent. Pandu's son Arjuna says to Krishna, 'This Parantapa, Dharma's son, burns with grief on account of his slaughtered kinsfolk. Comfort him again, O Madhava. All of us have fallen into great danger. You, Mahabaho, must dispel his grief.'"

Vaisampayana continued, "The lotus-eyed Govinda of eternal glory turns his face towards the king. Yudhishtira cannot possibly disregard Kesava, for from their earliest years Govinda was dearer to him than even Arjuna.

Taking the king's hand, smeared with sandalwood-paste and looking like a column of marble, the mighty-armed Saurin begins to speak, gladdening the hearts of all who listen to him. His face, adorned with beautiful teeth and eyes, glows like a full-blown lotus at sunrise.

Vasudeva says, 'Do not, Purushavyaghra, indulge in grief that emaciates your body. Those slain in this battle cannot be brought back. These Kshatriyas, O king, who have fallen in this great war are like objects in one's dreams that vanish when one awakes. All of them were heroes and ornaments of battle.

We vanquished them while they rushed at us, their enemies. They were all slain facing us, none had wounds in their backs from fleeing battle. They all fought with heroes and, after having cast off their life-breath in the great war, ascended into heaven, sanctified by weapons.

It is not right to grieve for them. All of them, cleaving to the Kshatriya dharma, possessed of valour, perfectly conversant with the Vedas and their angas, have attained the blissful end reserved for heroes. Set aside your grief for them after hearing the stories of ancient days about the high-souled lords of the earth who departed from this world.

There is an old story about the discourse of Narada with Srinjaya who was grief-stricken at the death of his son. Narada said, "You, I and all creatures, O Srinjaya, are subject to happiness and misery, and will have to die. Then what cause is there for sorrow? Listen to me with attention as I recite the great blessedness of some ancient kings. Listening to the story of these noble lords of the earth, you will cast off your grief and abate your sorrow.

As I recite their charming and delightful tales to you in detail, the malignant stars will be propitiated and the span of your life will increase.

We hear, O Srinjaya, that there was a king of the name of Marutta who was the son of Avikshit, and that even he fell prey to death. The gods, with Indra and Varuna and Brihaspati at their head, came to the sacrifice, called Viswasrij, performed by this great monarch. Challenging Sakra, the lord of the Devas, Marutta vanquished him in battle.

From a desire to earn Indra's favour, the learned Brihaspati had refused to officiate at Marutta's sacrifice. Thereupon Samvarta, the younger brother of Brihaspati, acceded to the king's request to be his chief Ritvik. During the rule of Marutta the earth yielded crops without being tilled and was embellished with diverse kinds of ornaments. At the sacrifice of this king, the Viswadevas sat as courtiers, the Maruts were the distributors of food and gifts and the high-souled Sadhyas were also present.

During this sacrifice of Marutta, the Maruts drank soma. The sacrificial gifts the king made surpassed in value those ever made by the Devas, the Gandharvas and all men. When even Marutta, O Srinjaya, who surpassed you in religious merit, knowledge, renunciation and affluence, and who was purer than your son, fell prey to death, do not grieve for your son.

We hear, O Srinjaya, of another king named Suhotra, the son of

Atithi, who too, fell a prey to death. During his rule, Maghavat showered gold for one whole year upon his kingdom. Obtaining this king for her lord, the earth became in reality, and not merely in name, Vasumati.

Indra showered upon the rivers, during the sway of this sovereign, golden tortoises, crabs, alligators, sharks and porpoises. Beholding these golden fish, sharks and tortoises in hundreds and thousands, Atithi's son became filled with wonder. Collecting the vast wealth of gold that covered the earth, Suhotra performed a sacrifice at Kurujangala and gave it away to Brahmanas.

When this King Suhotra, O Srinjaya, who surpassed you in the four attributes of tapasya, gyana, vairagya and dhana, and who was purer than your son, fell prey to death, do not grieve for your dead son. Your son never performed a sacrifice and never made gifts. Knowing this, pacify your mind and do not give away to grief.

We also hear, O Srinjaya, that Brihadratha, the king of the Angas, fell prey to death. He gave away a hundred thousand horses and a hundred thousand maidens, adorned with golden ornaments, as dakshina at a yagna that he performed. A hundred thousand elephants also of the best breed he gave away as gifts at another yagna that he performed.

He also gave away as sacrificial charity a hundred million bulls, adorned with golden chains, accompanied by untold thousands of cows. While the king of Anga performed his sacrifice by the hill called Vishnupada, Indra became intoxicated with the soma he drank, and the Brahmanas with the gifts they received.

During the yagnas, O monarch, numbering hundreds, that this king performed in the days of old, the gifts he made far surpassed those ever made by the Devas, the Gandharvas and Manavas. No other man born, or that will ever be born, will give away so much wealth as did the king of the Angas during the seven sacrifices he performed, each of which was marked by the consecration of soma.

When, O Srinjaya, this Brihadratha, who was your superior in the four attributes and who was purer than your son, also fell prey to death, do not grieve for your dead son.

We hear also, O Srinjaya, that Sibi, the son of Usinara, fell prey to death. This king swayed the whole earth as one does the leather shield in his hand. Riding on a single chariot that proved victorious in every battle, King Sibi subjugated every other monarch and caused the earth to resound with the rattle of his wheels.

Usinara's son Sibi gave away in a sacrifice all the cows and horses he had, both domesticated and wild. The Creator himself thought that no one among the kings of the past or the future had or would have the ability to bear the burden, as this Usinara's son Sibi did, that foremost of kings, that hero who possessed skill equal to that of Indra. Do not, therefore, grieve for your son who never performed any sacrifice or made any gift when indeed, Sibi, who was far superior to you in the four attributes and who was purer than your son, fell prey to death.

We hear, O Srinjaya, that the high-souled Bharata also, the son of Dushyanta and Sakuntala, who had a vast and well-filled treasury, fell prey to death. Devoting three hundred horses to the gods on the banks of the Yamuna, twenty on the banks of the Saraswati, and fourteen on the banks of the Ganga, that king of great tejas, of the olden days, performed a thousand Aswamedhas and a hundred Rajasuyas.

None among the kings of the earth can match the great deeds of Bharata, just as no man can, by the might of his arms, soar into the sky. Erecting numerous sacrificial altars, he gave away innumerable horses and untold wealth to the Rishi Kanwa. When even he, O Srinjaya, who was far superior to you in the four attributes and who was purer than your son, fell prey to death, do not grieve for your dead son.

We hear, O Srinjaya, that Rama, the son of Dasaratha, also fell prey to death. He always cherished his subjects as if they were his own sons. In his dominions there were no widows and no one who was helpless. Indeed, in ruling his kingdom Rama was always like his father Dasaratha. The clouds, yielding showers seasonably, caused crops to grow in plenitude. During his rule, food was always abundant in his kingdom. No death occurred by drowning or by fire.

As long as Rama ruled, there was no fear in his kingdom of any disease. Every man lived for a thousand years, blessed with a thousand children. During Ramarajya, all men were whole and all men had their wishes fulfilled. When even the women did not quarrel, then what can be said of the men? During his rule his subjects were virtuous, contented, their desires satisfied, fearless, free and wedded to the vow of truth.

The trees bore flowers and fruit perennially, and met with no injury. Every cow yielded milk filling a drona to the brim. Having dwelt in the observance of severe tapasya for fourteen years in the forest, Rama performed ten Aswamedhas of great splendour to which he invited everyone. Young and dark, handsome, with reddened eyes, he looked like the leader of an elephant herd, with great and mighty arms stretching down to his knees and with shoulders like those of a lion.

Ascending the throne of Ayodhya, he ruled for ten thousand and ten hundred years. When Rama, O Srinjaya, who excelled you by far in the four principal attributes and who was purer than your son, fell prey to death, do not grieve for your dead son.

We hear, O Srinjaya, that King Bhagiratha also died. During one of the sacrifices of this king, intoxicated with the soma he had drunk, Indra, the adorable chastiser of Paka and king of the Devas, put forth the might of his arms and vanquished many thousands of Asuras.

At one of the sacrifices he performed, King Bhagiratha gave away a million maidens adorned with ornaments of gold. Each of these maidens sat on a chariot attached to four pedigreed steeds. With each chariot were a hundred elephants, all of the finest breed and decked with chains of gold. Behind each elephant were a thousand horses, and behind each one a thousand cows and behind each cow a thousand goats and sheep.

The river-goddess Ganga, earlier known as Bhagirathi, sat upon the lap of this king who dwelt near her stream, and since then came to be called Urvasi, 'one who sits on the lap'. The triple-coursed Ganga had agreed to be the daughter of Bhagiratha of Ikshvaku's race, the monarch always engaged in the performance of sacrifices with gifts in profusion to Brahmanas.

When he, O Srinjaya, who transcended you in respect of the four principal attributes and who was purer than your son, fell prey to death, do not grieve for your son.

We hear, O Srinjaya, that the Mahatman Dilipa also fell prey to death. The Brahmanas love to recite his innumerable deeds. During one of his great sacrifices this king, with his heart fully assenting, gave away the entire earth, abounding with wealth, to the Brahmanas. At each sacrifice performed by him, the chief priest received as sacrificial fee a thousand elephants made of gold.

At one of his yagnas, the stake set up for slaughtering the victims was made of gold and exceedingly beautiful. Discharging the duties assigned to them, the gods having Sakra for their lord, used to seek the protection of this king. Upon this shining golden stake, decked with a ring, six thousand Devas and Gandharvas danced in joy, and Viswavasu himself in their midst played a raga on his vina. Such was Viswavasu's music that every creature, whatever he might be, thought that the great Gandharva was playing to him alone.

No other monarch could imitate this achievement of King Dilipa. The elephants of this king, intoxicated and adorned with trappings of gold, would be found lying down on the roads. The men who succeeded in obtaining even a sight of the Rajarishi Dilipa, went to heaven, as he was ever truthful in speech and his bow could withstand a hundred foes equal in energy to a hundred Anantas.

These three sounds never ceased in Dilipa's abode—the chanting of the Vedas, the twanging of bows, and cries of 'Let it be given!' When he, O Srinjaya, who transcended you in the four principal attributes and who was purer than your son, fell prey to death, do not grieve for your dead son.

Yuvanaswa's son Mandhatri also, O Sanjaya, we hear, fell prey to death. The Maruts extracted this child from his father's stomach through one side. Sprung from a quantity of clarified butter sanctified by mantras that had by mistake been quaffed by his father instead of his mother, Mandhatri had been gestated in the belly of Yuvanaswa.

This most prosperous king, Mandhatri, conquered the three worlds. Seeing this child of celestial beauty lying on the lap of his father, the gods asked one another, 'From whom shall this child suckle?'

Then Indra came forward, saying, 'He shall have it even from me!' The chief of the deities therefore named the child Mandhatri. For the nourishment of that great child, the finger of Indra, placed in his mouth, began to yield a jet of milk. Sucking Indra's finger, he grew into a powerful youth in a hundred days. In twelve days he looked like one of twelve years.

The whole earth in one day came under the sway of this high-souled, virtuous and brave king who resembled Indra himself for his prowess in battle. He vanquished King Angada, Marutta, Asita, Gaya and Brihadratha of the Angas. When Mandhatri fought in battle with Angada, the gods thought that the firmament was breaking apart with the twanging of his bow, and the whole earth from where Surya rises to where he sets was his field.

Having performed a hundred Aswamedhas and a hundred Rajasuyas, he gave the Brahmanas many Rohita fish. These fish were each ten yojanas in length and one in breadth. The other varnas divided among themselves those that remained after gratifying the Brahmanas.

When he, O Srinjaya, who transcended you in the four principal attributes and who was purer than your son, fell prey to death, do not grieve for your dead son.

We hear, O Srinjaya, that Yayati, the son of Nahusha, also fell prey to death.

Having subjugated the whole world with its seas, he journeyed through it, decking it with successive sacrificial altars; with throws of a heavy piece of wood, he measured the intervals between the altars. Indeed, he reached the very shores of the sea as he went performing great sacrifices on those altars along his way.

Having performed a thousand yagnas and a hundred Vajapeyas, he gratified the foremost of Brahmanas with three mountains of gold. Having slain many Daityas and Danavas in battle, Nahusha's son Yayati divided the earth among his children. At last, discarding his other sons, headed by Yadu and Drahyu, he installed his youngest son Puru on his throne and then entered the forest with his wife.

When he, O Srinjaya, who far surpassed you in the four principal attributes and who was purer than your son, fell prey to death, do not grieve for your dead son.

We hear, O Srinjaya, that Ambarisha also, the son of Nabhaga, fell a prey to death. The subjects regarded this protector of the world and foremost of kings as the embodiment of dharma.

During one of his sacrifices, this sovereign assigned to the Brahmanas, to wait upon them, a million kings who had themselves performed thousands of sacrifices each. Men of piety praised Ambarisha, the son of Nabhaga, saying that such feats had never been achieved before, nor would their like be achieved in the future. These hundreds upon hundreds and thousands upon thousands of kings, that had at the command of Ambarisha waited at his sacrifices upon the presiding Brahmanas, became, through Ambarisha's punya, crowned with the fruits of the Aswamedha and followed their lord by the southern-path to regions of brightness and bliss.

When he, O Srinjaya, who far surpassed you in the four principal attributes and who was purer than your son, fell prey to death, do not grieve for your dead child.

We hear, O Srinjaya, that Sasabindu also, the son of Chitrasena, fell prey to death. This Rajarishi had a hundred thousand wives, and a million consorts, and sons by them, all of whom used to wear golden armour and were excellent bowmen. Each of these princes married a hundred princesses, and each princess brought a hundred elephants as her dower. With each of these elephants were a hundred chariots. With each chariot were a hundred steeds, all of good breed and all decked with trappings of gold. With each steed were a hundred cattle, and with each cow were a hundred sheep and goats.

This countless wealth Sasabindu gave away, at a horse-sacrifice, to the Brahmanas. When he, O Srinjaya, who far surpassed you in the four principal attributes and who was purer than your son, fell prey to death, do not grieve for your dead child.

We hear, O Srinjaya, that Gaya also, the son of Amurtarayas, fell a prey to death. For a hundred years, this king subsisted upon the remains of sacrificial food. Pleased with such devotion, Agni wanted to give him boons. The boons solicited by Gaya were, 'Let my wealth be inexhaustible, even if I give endlessly. Let my regard for dharma exist for ever. Let my heart take pleasure in Truth forever, through your grace, O consumer of sacrificial offerings.'

We hear that King Gaya obtained all these wishes from Agni. On days of the new moon, on those of the full moon, and on every fourth month, for a thousand years, Gaya repeatedly performed the Aswamedha. During this period he gave away a hundred thousand cattle and hundreds of mules to Brahmanas at the completion of every sacrifice.

This bull among men gratified the Devas with soma, the Brahmanas with wealth, the Pitris with Swadha, and the women with the satisfaction of all their wishes. During his great Horse-sacrifice, Gaya caused a golden ground to be made, measuring a hundred cubits in length and fifty in breadth, and gave it away as the sacrificial fee. This foremost of men, Gaya, the son of Amurtarayas, gave away as many cows as there are grains of sand in the Ganga river.

When he, O Srinjaya, who far surpassed you in the four principal attributes, and who was purer than your son, fell prey to death, do not grieve for your dead son.

We hear, O Srinjaya, that Sankriti's son Rantideva also fell a prey to death. Having undergone the austerest of penances and worshipped Sakra with great reverence, he solicited these boons from him: 'Let us have abundant food and numerous guests. Let not my faith sustain any diminution, and let me not have to ask anyone for anything.'

The animals, both domesticated and wild, slaughtered at his sacrifice, used to come of their own accord to the high-souled Rantideva of rigid vows and great fame. The secretions that flowed from the skins of the animals slaughtered in his sacrifices produced a mighty and celebrated river which to this day is known by the name of Charmanwati. King Rantideva would make gifts to the Brahmanas in an extensive enclosure.

When the king said, 'I give you a hundred nishkas!' the Brahmanas rejected what was offered. When, however, the king would say, 'I give a thousand nishkas!' they accepted. All the vessels and plates in Rantideva's palace, all the jugs and pots, the pans, plates and cups, were of gold. On nights when guests lived in Rantideva's abode, twenty-thousand and one hundred cattle had to be slaughtered. Yet even on such occasions, the cooks, decked in earrings, used to boast to those who sat down to eat: 'There is abundant soup, take as much as you wish; but we do not have as much meat today as we used to.'

When he, O Srinjaya, who far surpassed you in the four principal attributes and who was purer than your son, fell prey to death, do not grieve for your dead son.

We hear, O Srinjaya, that the high-souled Sagara also fell a prey to death. He was of Ikshvaku's race, a tiger among men, and of superhuman prowess. Sixty-thousand sons used to walk behind him, like ten thousand stars waiting upon the moon in the cloudless firmament of autumn. His sway extended over the whole of this earth. He gratified the gods by performing a thousand Horse-sacrifices. He gave away to deserving Brahmanas palatial mansions with columns and other parts made of gold, containing costly beds and bevies of beautiful women with eyes like lotus petals, and diverse other kinds of precious objects. At his command, the Brahmanas divided these gifts among themselves.

Through anger this king caused the earth to be excavated, whereupon she came to have the ocean on her bosom, and for this, the ocean has come to be named Sagara after him. When he, O Srinjaya, who far surpassed you in the four principal attributes and who was purer than your son, fell prey to death, do not grieve for your dead son.

We hear, O Srinjaya, that king Prithu, the son of Vena, also fell prey to death. The great Rishis, assembling together in the great forest, installed him in the sovereignty of the earth. And because it was thought that he would advance all mankind, he was called Prithu, the advancer.

And because he protected people from injuries—Kshata, he was called a Kshatriya.

Seeing Prithu, the son of Vena, all the creatures of the earth exclaimed, 'We are now attached to him!' From this circumstance of the devotion of all creatures to him, he came to be called a Raja—one who can inspire attachment. The earth, during his sway, yielded crops without being tilled, every leaf that the trees had bore honey, and every cow yielded a large jugful of milk. All men were healthy, all their wishes granted. They had no fear of any kind. They used to live as they pleased, in fields or in houses.

When Prithu wanted to go over the sea, the waters became solid. The rivers also never swelled up when he had to cross them but remained perfectly calm. The flag on his chariot moved unobstructed everywhere. King Prithu, during one of his grand Aswamedha Yagnas, gave away to the Brahmanas twenty-one mountains of gold, each measuring three nalwas. When he, O Srinjaya, who far surpassed you in the four principal attributes and who was purer than your son, fell prey to death, do not grieve for your dead son.

What, O Srinjaya, are you reflecting in silence? It seems, O king, that you do not hear my words. If you have not heard them, then my discourse has been a fruitless rhapsody, like medicine or a diet to a person on the point of death."

Srinjaya said, "I am listening O Narada, to your discourse of excellent import and perfumed like a garland of flowers, this discourse upon the conduct of Rajarishis of wondrous deeds and great fame that can certainly dispel grief. Your discourse, O Maharishi, has not been a fruitless rhapsody. The very sight of you has freed me from grief. Like one never replete from drinking nectar, I am not satiated with your words. If you of true vision, O lord, can show grace towards this man burning with grief on account of the death of his son, then this son, through your grace, is sure to be revived and to rejoin me once more in this life."

Narada said, "I will give back your son bereft of life named Suvarnashthivin, whom Parvata gave you. Splendid as gold, this child shall live a thousand years."'"

CANTO 30

"Yudhishtira asks, 'How did the son of Srinjaya become Suvarnashthivin? Why did Parvata give Srinjaya this child and why did he die? When the lives of all men in those days extended for a thousand years, why did Srinjaya's son die in infancy? Or was he Suvarnashthivin, gold-secreter, only in name? How did he come to be so? I want to know all.'

Krishna replies, 'I will tell you, O king, the facts as they happened. There are two Rishis, the foremost ones in the world, named Narada and Parvata. Narada is the maternal uncle and Parvata is his sister's son. With cheerful hearts, the uncle Narada and the nephew Parvata, in the olden days, left heaven to ramble across the earth and to taste clarified butter and rice.

Both of them, possessed of great ascetic merit, wandered over the earth, subsisting on food eaten by men. Filled with joy and entertaining great affection for each other, they entered into a compact that whatever desire, good or bad, one of them entertained, he would disclose it to the other and, in the event of one of them doing otherwise, he would be subject to the other's curse.

Agreeing to this understanding, these two great Rishis, adored by all the worlds, went to King Srinjaya, the son of Sitya, and told him, "For your benefit, both of us will stay with you for a few days. O lord of the world, attend to all our wants."

The king, saying "So be it!" set himself to attend upon them hospitably. One day, the joyful Srinjaya introduced to these illustrious ascetics his fair daughter, saying, "This is my daughter Sukumari, and she will wait upon you both. Bright as the filament of the lotus, she is beautiful and of faultless limbs, accomplished and of sweet manners."

"Very well," said the Rishis in reply, upon which the king instructed his daughter, "My child, attend upon these two Brahmanas as you would attend upon the gods or your father."

Saying, "Tathaastu," the virtuous Sukumari began to attend upon them in obedience to her father's behest. Her dutiful services and her unrivalled beauty very soon charmed Narada, and he began to cherish a tender flame towards her. This sentiment began to grow in the heart of the illustrious saint like the moon gradually waxing on the accession of the lit fortnight.

However, overwhelmed by shame, Narada could not disclose this growing ardour to his sister's son, the high-souled Parvata. Through his ascetic power, and also by Narada's behaviour, Parvata understood all. Inflamed with rage, he resolved to curse his love-afflicted uncle.

He said, "Having made a compact with me that whatever desire, good or bad, is cherished by either of us will be disclosed to the other, you have violated it. These were your own words. O Brahmana! I will curse you for this. You did not tell me that the charms of the maiden Sukumari have pierced your heart! You are a Brahmacharin, my guru, a Muni and a Brahmana. Yet you have broken the compact you made with me. I am angry and I will curse even you. Listen to me. This Sukumari will, without doubt, become your wife. From the time of your marriage, however, O Great One, both she and all men will see you as an ape, for your true features will disappear and you will have a monkey's face!"

Hearing this, Narada, filled with wrath, cursed his nephew Parvata in return, "Although you have ascetic merit and brahmacharya and truth and self-restraint, and although you are ever devoted to dharma, you will yet not be able to return to Swarga."

Thus in rage they cursed each other like two infuriated elephants.

From that time the high-souled Parvata began to wander over the earth, respected as he deserved, O Bhaarata, for his own tejas. Narada, the greatest of Brahmanas, obtained with due rites the hand of Srinjaya's daughter, the faultless Sukumari.

But the princess saw Narada exactly as the curse had said. Indeed, just after the priests recited the last of the wedding mantras, Sukumari saw the celestial Rishi with the face of an ape. She, however, did not disregard her husband; on the contrary, she dedicated her love to him. Indeed, the princess, chaste as she was, devoted herself entirely to her lord and did not in her heart desire anyone else for a husband, even among the Devas, Munis and Yakshas.

One day, the illustrious Parvata, in the course of his wanderings, entered a solitary forest, and saw Narada there. Saluting him, Parvata said, "Show your grace to me, O mighty one, by allowing me to return to heaven." Seeing the unhappy Parvata kneeling before him with folded hands, Narada felt sorry and told him, "You cursed me first, saying, 'Be an ape!' After which, I cursed you from anger, saying, 'From this day you will not live in heaven!' It was not right of you to curse me, since you are like a son to me."

The two sages then freed each other from their curses. Seeing her husband possessed of celestial form and blazing with beauty, Sukumari fled from him, thinking him to be somebody other than her lord. Seeing the beautiful princess flying from Narada, Parvata said to her, "This is indeed your husband. He is the illustrious and powerful Rishi Narada, the foremost of virtuous men. He is your husband of one soul with you. Do not have any doubt about this."

Assured in diverse ways by the high Parvata and informed also of the curse, the princess regained her equanimity. Then Parvata ascended to heaven and Narada returned to his home.'

Krishna continues, 'The illustrious Rishi Narada, who himself played a part in this matter, is here, O best of men. If you ask him he will tell you everything that happened.'"

CANTO 31

Vaisampayana said, "The royal son of Pandu then asks Narada, 'Holy one, I want to hear of the birth of the child whose excreta were gold.' Narada Muni begins to narrate everything about the child of the golden secretions.

Narada says, 'It is exactly as Kesava has said. Since you asked me I will now tell you the remaining part of this story. My sister's son, the Maharishi Parvata, and I once came to stay with Srinjaya, foremost of all victorious kings. He honoured us with all ceremony and gratified our every wish when we lived with him.

After the season of rain had passed, and when the time came for our own departure, Parvata raised this important and appropriate point with me: "We have dwelt in the abode of this king for some time, O Brahmana, and have been greatly honoured by him. Think of what we should give him in return."

I then told Parvata of blessed aspect, "Nephew, this concern becomes you, O you of great power, and all this depends upon you. Through your blessings let the king be made happy and let him obtain his wishes. Or, if you choose, let him be crowned with success through the ascetic merits of both of us."

At this, having summoned King Srinjaya, Parvata said to him, "You have gratified us exceedingly, Rajan, with your sincere hospitality. Think of a gift you would like. Let it be such that it may not imply enmity to the gods or destruction to men. Accept then, O king, a boon, for we think you deserve one."

Srinjaya replied, "If I have satisfied you both, then I have gained my object, for this is itself my greatest gain and I regard this as the realization of all my desires."

Parvata once again said, "Ask us, Rajan, for the fulfillment of that wish which you have cherished in your heart for a long time."

Srinjaya answered, "I desire a son who will be heroic and possessed of great energy, firm in his vows and of long life, highly blessed and possessed of splendour equal to that of Indra himself."

Parvata said, "Your desire will be fulfilled, but your child will not be long-lived, for your wish for such a son is also for prevailing over Indra. Your son will be known by the name of Suvarnashthivin. He will have splendour like Indra, but take care to protect him always from that Deva."

Hearing these words of Parvata Mahatman, Srinjaya began to beg the Rishis to change his boon, saying, "Let my son be long-lived, O Muni, through your tapasya."

Parvata remained silent, being partial to Indra. Seeing the king very sad I told him, "Think of me, O king, in your distress and I promise to come when you do. Do not grieve, O lord of earth! I will give you back your beloved child, even if he is dead, in his living form."

With that, both of us left his presence to go our different ways, and Srinjaya to his palace. In due course, the Rajarishi Srinjaya became the father of a son of great ability who blazed with tejas. The child grew up like a large lotus in a lake, and became Suvarnashthivin in reality as in name.

This extraordinary child, O Kuruttama, soon became widely known over the world. Indra also came to know that he was the fruit of Parvata's boon. Fearing humiliation at the hands of the child when he grew up, the slayer of Bala and Vritra began to watch closely for any lapses by the prince.

He commanded his Vajra, standing before him in embodied form,

"Go, powerful one, and, assuming the form of a tiger, kill this prince. When grown up, this child of Srinjaya may, as Parvata prophesied, humiliate me through his achievements." The Vajra, razer of hostile towns, began from that day to continually watch for any lapse from the prince.

Meanwhile, Srinjaya was filled with joy having got a child whose splendour resembled that of Indra himself. The king, accompanied by his wives, and the other women of his household, began living in the midst of a forest. One day, on the shores of the Bhagirathi, the boy, accompanied by his nurse, was playing, running about here and there. Though only five years of age, his prowess, even then, resembled that of a mighty elephant.

While playing, the child met a powerful tiger that came upon him suddenly. The infant prince trembled violently as the tiger attacked him, and fell lifeless on the earth. His nursemaid gave vent to loud cries of grief.

Having slain the prince, the tiger, through Indra's powers of maya, vanished. Hearing the screams of the nurse, the king ran to the spot in great anxiety, and saw his son drained of blood, lying dead on the ground like the moon fallen from the firmament. Taking the boy covered with blood up onto his lap, the grief-stricken king began to lament piteously. The royal women rushed wailing to King Srinjaya.

The king thought of me with concentrated attention. Knowing that the king was thinking of me, I appeared before him. Stricken as the king was, I told him all those stories, Rajan, that this hero of Yadu's race has already related to you. With Indra's leave, I brought Srinjaya's child back to life.

That which is ordained must come to pass, it is impossible that it should be otherwise. After this, Prince Suvarnashthivin of great fame and energy began to delight the hearts of his parents. Of great prowess, he ascended the throne after his father's death, and ruled for one thousand and one hundred years. He worshipped the gods with many great sacrifices distinguished by lavish gifts. Possessed of great splendour, he gratified the Devas and the Pitris.

He had many sons, all of whom multiplied the race, and after many years he met with a natural death. O best of men, dispel this grief born in your heart, as Kesava and Vyasa of austere penances have counselled you to. Rise up, Rajan, and bear the burden of this your ancestral kingdom; perform high and great sacrifices so that you may obtain hereafter whatever regions you desire!'"

CANTO 32

Vaisampayana said, "To king Yudhishtira, who still remained speechless and plunged in grief, the island-born Maharishi Vyasa, knower of dharma, says again, 'O you of eyes like lotus petals, the protection of subjects is the dharma of kings. Those who are always observant of dharma regard it to be all-powerful. Do, therefore, O Rajan, walk in the steps of your ancestors.

For Brahmanas, tapasya is a duty, as laid down by the eternal law of the Vedas. Tapasya, therefore, Bharatarishabha, constitutes the eternal duty of Brahmanas.

A Kshatriya is the protector of all in respect of their dharma. The man who, obsessed by earthly possessions, breaks wholesome restraints and offends social harmony must be punished with a strong hand. Such a brutish man who seeks to offend authority, be he an attendant, a son or even a sage, should by every means be chastised, or even killed, along with all men of similar sinful natures.

The king who conducts himself in any other manner incurs sin. He who does not protect dharma when someone disregards it is himself a transgressor of righteousness. The Kauravas were transgressors of dharma and you have slain them along with their followers. Since you have been observant of your svadharma, why then, Pandava, do you indulge in such grief?

The king must kill those who deserve death, make gifts to persons deserving of charity, and protect his subjects according to the law.'

Yudhishtira says, 'I do not doubt the words that fall from your lips, O Mahatapasvin! Everything concerning niti and dharma is well known to you. I have, however, for the sake of kingdom, caused numbers to be slain. These savage and bloody deeds, O Brahmana, consume me!'

Vyasa asks, 'Is the Paramatman the doer, or is man the doer? Is everything the result of chance in this world, or are the fruits that we enjoy or suffer the results of karma? If man is responsible for all karma, good or bad, being urged to do so by Brahman, the Supreme Being, then the fruits of these acts should be for Brahman himself. If a man cuts down a tree in forest with an axe, it is he who incurs the sin, not the axe.

Or, if one says that the axe being only the material cause, the consequence of the deed should attach to the animate agent and not to the inanimate tool, then the sin may be said to belong to the man who made the axe—but this can scarcely be true. If it is not reasonable, Kaunteya, that one man should incur the consequence of a thing done by another, then you should ascribe all responsibility to the Supreme Being.

If, again, man is himself the agent of all his actions, virtuous and sinful, then there is no Supreme Agent, and so, whatever you have done cannot bring evil consequences upon you. No one, O king, can ever turn away from what is destined. If, again, destiny be the result of the deeds of former lives, then no sin can be attached to one in this life, just as the sin of cutting down a tree cannot touch the maker of the axe.

If you think it is only chance that acts in the world, then such a vast war of destruction would never have happened, nor ever will. If you need to ascertain what is good and what is evil in the world, attend to the shastras. These scriptures have laid down that kings should stand with the danda uplifted in their hands. I think, Bhaarata, that karma, good and bad, continually revolves here as a wheel, and men obtain the fruits of their actions, good or evil.

One sinful deed proceeds from another. Therefore, Purushavyaghra, avoid all evil actions and do not set your heart upon grief. You should adhere to the duties, even if reproachable, of your own order. This self-destruction, Rajan, is not commendable in you. Atonements have been ordained for evil acts. He who is alive can perform them, but he who dies fails in their performance. Therefore, O Rajan, without laying down your life, perform these expiatory rites. If you do not perform them, you may have to repent in the next world.'"

CANTO 33

"Yudhishtira says, 'Sons and grandsons, brothers and fathers, fathers-in-law, acharyas, maternal uncles and grandfathers, many noble Kshatriyas, many relatives by marriage, friends, companions, sisters' sons, and kinsmen have fallen O grandfather, and many great men coming from diverse countries. I alone have caused all of them to be slain, from my desire for kingdom. Having slain many heroic kings devoted to dharma, all of whom had drunk soma during sacrifices, what end will I attain, O wisest of all sages?

My body is on fire, thinking that the earth is bereft of the many prosperous lions among kings who were enjoying great prosperity. Having witnessed this slaughter of kinsmen and millions of other men, I burn with grief, grandfather!

Oh, what will be the plight of those best of women deprived of their sons, of husbands, and of brothers? Reproaching the Pandavas and the Vrishnis as cruel murderers, these gaunt-faced women, plunged in grief, will throw themselves on the earth and, through sorrow, will cast off their life-breath, and go to the halls of Yama, O best of Brahmanas. I have no doubt of this!

The course of dharma is subtle, and it is plain that we will be stained with guilt for the deaths of these women. Having killed our kinsmen and friends and committed an inexpiable sin, we will fall into hell with our heads downwards.

So, O best of men, we will waste our limbs with the austerest of tapasyas. Tell me, O Pitamaha, what asrama of life I should adopt?'"

Vaisampayana continued, "Hearing these words of Yudhishtira, the island-born Rishi, having reflected keenly for some time, says, 'Remember the dharma of a Kshatriya, O Rajan, and do not give way to grief. All these Kshatriyas have fallen while engaged in performing their svadharma of pursuing greater prosperity and greater fame on earth, O Bharatarishabha. These great men, all of whom were mortal, have perished through the influence of Kaala, inexorable Time.

You were not their slayer, nor Bhima, nor Arjuna, nor the twins. It is Time that took away their lives according to the inviolable law of change. Kaala has neither mother, nor father, nor anybody to whom he is disposed to show any favour. He is the witness of the actions of all creatures, and it is he who has taken them away. This battle, O Bharatarishabha, was only an event that he created. He causes creatures to be slain through other creatures, and this is how he demonstrates his irresistible power.

Understand that Kaala in his dealings with creatures is dependent upon the bonds of action and is the witness of all karma, good and bad. It is Time that brings about the fruits of our deeds, whether bliss or sorrow. Think, O Mahabaho, of the deeds of these Kshatriyas who have fallen. Their karma was the cause of their destruction, and for that they perished.

Think also of your own karma, of adhering to vows with a calm soul, and also of how the Supreme Ordainer has forced you to do your karma—the slaughter of so many men. Just as a weapon made by a smith or carpenter is under the control of the one that handles it, and moves as he moves it, this universe, controlled by actions done in Time, moves as those actions move it.

Seeing that the births and deaths of creatures take place without any assignable cause and in perfect wantonness, grief and joy are entirely needless. Although this entanglement of your heart is a mere delusion, still, if it pleases you, O king, perform expiatory rites to purify yourself of your so-called sin.

It is heard, O Kaunteya, that the Devas and the Asuras, covetous of prosperity, fought each other. The Asuras were the elder, and the gods the younger, brothers. Fierce was the battle between them, lasting for thirty-two thousand years. Making the earth one vast sea of blood, the Devas slew the Daityas and gained possession of Swarga.

Having obtained possession of the earth, a large number of Brahmanas, conversant with the Vedas, armed themselves, and stupefied with pride, sided with the Danavas and helped them in the fight. They were known by the name of Salavrika and numbered eighty-eight thousand. But the Devas slew all of them. So these evil men who desire the extinction of dharma and who were promoting adharma deserved to be slain, just as the gods did the ferocious demons.

If by slaying a single individual a family can be saved, or, if by slaying a single family the whole kingdom can be saved, such an act of killing will not be a transgression. Sin, O king, sometimes assumes the form of virtue, and virtue sometimes assumes the form of sin. However, they who are learned know which is which.

Therefore, console yourself, O son of Pandu, for you are well versed in the shastras. You, O Bhaarata, have only followed the path that the gods formerly trod. Men like you never reach hell. Comfort your brothers and all your friends, O Parantapa.

He who deliberately sins and feels no shame, but continues transgressing as before, is called in the shastras a great sinner. There is no atonement for him, and his offences know no diminution. You are born into a noble race. Forced by the faults of others, you have most unwillingly fought this war and, having done so, you repent.

The great yagna, the Aswamedha, is the expiation for you. Make preparations for this sacrifice, O monarch, and you will be freed from your sins.

The divine chastiser of Paka, having vanquished his foes with the help of the Maruts, gradually performed a hundred sacrifices and became Satakratu. Freed from stain, possessed of Devaloka and having obtained many realms of bliss and prosperity, Sakra, surrounded by the Maruts, shines in beauty, and illumines all the quarters with his splendour. The Apsaras adore the lord of Sachi in the heavens. The Rishis and the other gods all worship him with reverence.

You have won the earth through your prowess. You have vanquished all the kings, O sinless one; through your power, go with your friends to their kingdom, O king, and install their brothers, sons or grandsons on their thrones. Behave with kindness towards even the children in the womb, make your subjects glad, and rule the earth. Install on their thrones the daughters of those who have no sons. Women are fond of pleasure and power, and they will cast off their sorrows and become happy. Having comforted the whole empire in this way, O Bhaarata, please the gods with an Aswamedha yagna as the virtuous Indra did in earlier days.

It is not proper for us to grieve for the noble Kshatriyas who have fallen in battle. Struck by the power of the Destroyer, they have perished while observing their swadharma. You have discharged the duties of a Kshatriya and gained the earth without any thorn left in it.

Observe your swadharma, O Kaunteya, for then you will be able to enjoy happiness in the other world, O Bhaarata.'"

CANTOS 34–35

"Yudhishtira says, 'When does it become necessary for a man to perform penance? And what must he do to be freed from sin? Tell me, O Pitamaha.'

Vyasa says, 'If a man neglects to do what the Supreme Ordainer has ordained for him, or if he does what is forbidden to him, or if he behaves deceitfully, he is compelled to perform atonement rites.

The Brahmachari who forgets a vow; who rises from bed after sunrise, or goes to bed while the sun is setting; one who has rotten nails or black teeth; one whose younger brother weds first, or who weds before his elder brother; one who is guilty of killing a Brahmana; who speaks ill of others; who weds a younger sister before the older sister is married or weds an older sister after having married a younger one; who kills a Muni; who imparts knowledge of the Vedas to a person unworthy of it, or does not impart knowledge to one who is worthy of it; who takes many lives; who sells flesh; who has abandoned his sacred fire; who sells his knowledge of the Vedas; who slays his guru or a woman; who is born into a sinful family; who slaughters an animal wilfully; who sets fire to a dwelling house; who lives by deceit, or acts in opposition to his guru; one who has violated an agreement—they are all guilty of sins requiring expiation.

I will now mention other actions that are prohibited by both the world and the Vedas. Listen to me attentively.

The rejection of one's svadharma; the practice of the dharma of others; helping at the sacrifice or the religious rites of one unworthy of such assistance; eating food that is forbidden; deserting one that craves protection; neglecting to maintain servants and dependants; selling salt and sweet and other similar substances; killing birds and animals; refusing, though competent, to procreate upon a soliciting woman; omitting to present daily gifts grass to cows and the like, or to give dakshina; humiliating a Brahmana—these are all actions that those conversant with dharma have proscribed.

The son who quarrels with his father, the man who violates the bed of his guru, one who neglects to produce offspring with his wedded wife, are all sinful, O Naravyaghra. I have now told you, in brief and in detail, those actions and omissions by which a man becomes liable to perform expiation. Listen now to the circumstances under which men, even after committing these deeds, do not become stained with sin.

If a Brahmana well acquainted with the Vedas takes up arms and rushes at you in battle in order to kill you, you can take his life. By such an act the slayer does not become guilty of Brahmahatya. There is a mantra in the Vedas, O Kaunteya, which lays this down, and I am telling you only of those practices that are sanctioned by the authority of the Vedas.

One who kills a Brahmana who has renounced his own dharma and who advances, weapon in hand, with intent to kill, does not truly become the slayer of a Brahmana. In such a case it is the anger of the slayer that proceeds against the wrath of the slain.

By drinking alcoholic stimulants, in ignorance or upon the advice of a virtuous physician when his life is at peril, a man should have the regenerating ceremonies performed once more in his case. All that I have told you about the eating of forbidden food can be cleansed by these expiatory rites.

Sexual congress with the guru's wife at the preceptor's command does not stain the disciple. The Rishi Uddalaka had his son Swetaketu begotten by a disciple. Sin does not stain one who commits theft for the sake of his acharya in a season of distress. One who takes to theft for his own enjoyment, however, becomes tarnished.

A man is not defiled by stealing from other than Brahmanas in a season of distress and for the sake of one's guru. Sin leaves untouched only one who steals under such circumstances without appropriating any portion to himself. A falsehood can be spoken for saving one's own life or that of another, for the sake of one's guru, for gratifying a woman, or for bringing about a marriage.

One's vow of brahmacharya is not broken by having dreams that cause him to ejaculate. In such cases, the expiation laid down consists in the pouring of libations of clarified butter onto the sacred fire. If an elder brother dies or has renounced the world, the younger brother does not incur sin by marrying his brother's wife. Solicited by a woman, one does not lose virtue through intimacy with her.

One should not kill or cause an animal to be slain, except in a sacrifice. Through the kindness manifested towards animals by the Creator himself in his laws they have become sacred, and fit for sacrifice. By making a gift in ignorance to an undeserving Brahmana one does not incur sin. The omission of charity towards a deserving man through ignorance does not lead to sin. By casting off an adulterous wife one does not incur sin, for by this, the woman herself can be purged while the husband avoids sin.

One who knows the true use of the soma juice, does not incur sin by selling it. By dismissing a servant who is incompetent to render service, sin will not touch you. I have now told you those actions by which one does not incur sin. I will now tell you how to do penance, in detail.'"

CANTO 36

"Vyasa says 'Through penance, religious rites, and gifts, O Bhaarata, a man can wash away his sins if he does not commit them again. By subsisting like a sannyasi upon one meal a day procured by begging, by doing all his work himself without a servant, by begging with a human skull in one hand and a khatvanga in another, by becoming a Brahmacharin and always ready for hard work, by casting off all malice, by sleeping on bare ground, by announcing his offence to the world—by doing all this for full twelve years, a man can cleanse himself from the sin of Brahmahatya, having slain a Brahmana.

By dying at the hands of a warrior of one's own will and on the advice of men learned in the shastras, or by throwing oneself down three times, head downwards, into a blazing fire, or by walking a hundred yojanas, all the while reciting the Vedas, or by giving away one's entire property to a Brahmana conversant with the Vedas, or at least so much as would secure to him a livelihood, or a house properly furnished, and by protecting cattle and Brahmanas, one can be cleansed of Brahmahatya, the sin of having slain a Brahmana.

Again, by living upon the scantiest food every day for six years, a man can be cleansed of this sin. By observing a more rigorous vow with regard to food one can be purified in three years. By living upon one meal a month, one can be cleansed in just a year. By observing, again, an absolute fast, one can be purified within a very short time.

There is no doubt, again, that an Aswamedha yagna purifies a man. Men guilty of having slain a Brahmana who succeed in taking the avabhrita snana, the final bath at the completion of the sacrifice, are washed clean of all their sins. This is an injunction of great authority in the Srutis. One becomes cleansed of the sin of having killed a Brahmana, and indeed of all one's sins, by dying in a battle undertaken for the sake of a Brahmana, or by giving away a hundred thousand cattle to those deserving of gifts.

One becomes cleansed of all one's sins by giving away twenty-five thousand Kapila cows, all of which have calved, or at the point of death by giving away a thousand cows with calves to poor but deserving persons.

The man, O king, who gives away a hundred steeds of the Kamboja breed to deserving Brahmanas, becomes freed from sin. The man, O Bharata, who gives to just one man all that he asks for, and who, having given it, does not speak of it to anyone, is freed from sin.

If a person who has once drunk alcohol drinks as expiation hot liquor, he sanctifies himself both here and hereafter. One frees oneself of all sins by jumping off the summit of a mountain or entering a blazing fire, or by going on an everlasting journey after renouncing the world. By performing the sacrifice laid down by Brihaspati, a Brahmana who drinks can succeed in attaining to Brahmaloka. Brahma himself has said that if a man, after having drunk, becomes humble, makes a gift of land and abstains from liquor ever after, he becomes sanctified and cleansed.

The man who has violated his acharya's bed should lie on a heated sheet of iron and, having cut off his manhood, should take sannyasa with eyes always turned upwards. By casting off one's body, one becomes purified of all evil acts.

Women become cleansed of all their sins by leading a regulated life for one year. The man who observes a very arduous vow, or gives away the whole of his wealth, or perishes in a battle fought for the sake of his guru, is purified of all his sins. One who lies to his guru or acts in opposition to him, becomes cleansed of that sin by doing something agreeable to his preceptor.

One who has deviated from the vow of Brahmacharya can be exorcised of the sin by wearing the hide of a cow for six months and observing the penances laid down in the case of the slaughter of a Brahmana. One who is guilty of adultery, or of theft, can become clean by observing rigid vratas for a year. When one steals another's property, one should, by every means in his power, return the value of the stolen property and thereby be washed clean of the sin of theft.

The younger brother who has married before the marriage of the elder brother, and the elder brother whose younger brother has married before him, becomes pure by observing a severe vow, sincerely, for twelve nights. The younger brother, however, should marry again for rescuing his deceased ancestors. By such a second marriage, the first wife becomes cleansed and her husband himself will not incur sin by marrying her.

Men who know the scriptures declare that women may be cleansed of even the greatest sins by observing the vow of chaturmasya, all the while living upon scant and sattvik food. Men conversant with the shastras do not take into account the sins that women commit in their hearts. Whatever be their sins of this description, their menstrual course renders them clean, like a metal plate scoured with ash.

Plates made of the alloy of brass and copper made impure by a Sudra eating from them, or a vessel of the same metal that a cow has sniffed at, or that a Brahmana's Gandusha gargle has made unclean, can be cleansed by means of the ten purifying substances.

The shastras have laid down that a Brahmana should acquire and practise the full measure of dharma, and a Kshatriya should acquire and practise a measure of dharma less by a fourth part. So, a Vaisya should acquire a measure a quarter less than a Kshatriya's and a Sudra a fourth less than a Vaisya's. The heaviness or lightness of sins for purposes of expiation of each of the four varnas should be determined upon this principle.

Having killed a bird or an animal, or cut down living trees, a man should make known his sin and fast for three nights. For indulging in intercourse with one with whom it is prohibited, the expiation is to wander in wet clothes and to sleep on a bed of ashes. These, O king, are the atonements for sinful deeds, according to precedent, reason, the shastras and the laws.

A Brahmana can be cleansed of all his sins by reciting the Gayatri in a sacred place, while living upon frugal fare, casting off malice, abandoning anger and hate, remaining unmoved by praise and blame, and abstaining from speech. He should during the day-time be under the shelter of the sky and should lie down there even at night. Thrice during the day, and thrice during the night, he should plunge with his clothes into a stream or lake and perform his ablutions. Observing these rigid vows, he should abstain from speech with women, Sudras and sinners. By observing such regulations a Brahmana is purified of all sins that he unconsciously commits.

A man obtains in the other world the fruits, good or bad, of his karma which the elements witness. Be it punya or be it paapa, according to the true measure that one acquires of either, one enjoys or suffers the consequences even in this world. Through gyana, tapasya and by dharma, one enhances one's happiness even here, or one can enhance one's misery by committing sins. One should, therefore, always do what is righteous and abstain altogether from deeds that are not.

I have now indicated how the sins that I have mentioned can be expiated. There is atonement for every sin except those that we call Mahapatakas or the most heinous sins.

As regards sins in respect of unclean food, improper speech and the like, they are of two kinds: those that one commits consciously and those committed unconsciously. All sins that one commits consciously are grave, while those that one commits unconsciously are trivial or light. There is expiation for both.

Indeed the observance of the above rules can wash away all sin. However, God lays down these laws only for believers and those who have faith in Him. They are not for atheists or those who have no faith, or those in whom pride and malice predominate. A man who wishes for prosperity both here and in the hereafter, O Purushavyaghra, should adopt righteous behaviour, listen to the counsels of righteous men and observe the dharma that the shastras have ordained for him.

So, for the reasons I have already given, O Rajan, you will be cleansed of all your sins, for you have slain your foes while discharging your dharma as a king and for the protection of your life and inheritance. However, if you still regard yourself as sinful, perform expiation. Do not cast away your life out of grief, in a manner unbecoming of a wise man.'"

Vaisampayana continued, "Thus addressed by the holy Rishi, Yudhishtira Dharmaraja, having reflected for a short while, says these words to the Muni."

CANTO 37

"Yudhishtira says, 'Tell me, O Pitamaha, what food is clean and what unclean, what gifts are praiseworthy, and who should be considered deserving or undeserving of them.'

Vyasa says, 'Let me relate to you the old discussion between the Rishis and Manu, the lord of creation. In the Krita yuga, an assembly of Rishis of high austerities approached the great and powerful Prajapati Manu while he was seated at his ease, and requested him to engage in a discourse on dharma, asking, "What food should be eaten, who is to be regarded as a person deserving gifts, what gifts should be made, how should a person study, and what penances should one perform, how and what deeds should be done and what deeds should not? O lord of creation, tell us everything about all this."

Thus addressed, the divine and swayambhuva Manu told them, "Listen to me as I explain the dharma in brief as well as in detail. The shastras have laid down that the following deeds and places are expiatory in lands in which they are not prohibited—silent recitation of sacred mantras, homa, fasts, knowledge of the self, sacred rivers and regions inhabited by men devoted to pious deeds.

Some mountains also are purifying, as also the eating of gold and bathing in water in which one has dipped gems and precious stones. Tirtha yatra, and eating sanctified butter will also, without doubt, speedily purify a man.

No man would ever be called wise if he is proud and, if he wishes to be long-lived, he should for three nights drink hot water as a tapasya for being proud. Refusal to take what is not given, charity, the study of scriptures, tapasya, abstention from injury, truth, freedom from anger, and worship of the gods by means of yagnas, are the characteristics of dharma.

That which is virtue may, according to time and place, become sin; thus, the appropriation of what belongs to others, untruth, and injury and killing, may under special circumstances, become virtues. Men capable of judging deeds consider them to be of two kinds—virtuous and sinful. From the worldly and the Vedic points of view again, punya and paapa are good or bad according to their consequences.

Virtue and sin, everything a man may or may not do, would be either action or inaction. Inaction, abstention from Vedic rites and adoption of a life of contemplation leads to freedom from rebirth while the consequences of action, the practice of Vedic rites, result in repeated death and rebirth.

From the worldly point of view, deeds that are evil lead to evil and those that are good fetch beneficial consequences. Therefore, punya and paapa are to be distinguished by the good and the evil character of their consequences.

Deeds that are apparently evil, when undertaken from considerations connected with the Devas, the shastras, life itself, and the means by which life is sustained, produce consequences that are good. When an action is undertaken from the expectation, however doubtful, that it will produce harm to some one in the future, or when an action is done whose consequence is visibly harmful, the shastras command penance.

When a deed is done from anger or clouded judgment, then expiation should be performed by inflicting pain on the body, guided by precedent, the shastras and reason. When, again, anything is done in order to please or displease the mind, the sin arising from it may be cleansed by sanctified food and recitation of mantras. The king who lays aside the danda in a particular instance should fast for one night. The priest who abstains from advising the king to inflict punishment in a particular case, should fast for three nights as expiation. The man who from grief attempts to commit suicide with weapons, should fast for three nights.

There is no expiation for those who cast off the duties and practices of their order and class, country and family, and who abandon their very religion. When an occasion for doubt arises respecting what should be done, what ten persons versed in Vedic scriptures or three of those who frequently recite them may pronounce, should be regarded as the injunction of the shastras.

The bull, earth, little ants, worms generated in dirt and poison, should not be eaten by Brahmanas. They should not also eat fish that have no scales, and four-footed aquatic creratures like frogs and others, except the tortoise. Water-fowls called Bhasas, ducks, Suparnas, Chakravakas, diving ducks, cranes, crows, shags, vultures, hawks and owls. Also all four-footed animals that are carnivorous and that have sharp, long teeth, birds and animals with two teeth and those with four, the milk of the sheep, the she-ass, the she-camel, the newly-calved cow, woman and deer, should not be ingested by a Brahmana.

Besides this, food cooked by a woman who has recently given birth to a child, or food cooked by an unknown person should not be taken, nor should the milk of a cow that has recently calved. If a Brahmana takes food that a Kshatriya has cooked, it diminishes his tejas; if he takes the food provided by a Sudra, it dims his Brahmanic lustre; and if he takes the food provided by a goldsmith or a woman who has neither husband nor children, it lessens the span of his life. The food provided by a money-lender is equivalent to dirt, while that provided by a woman living by prostitution is equivalent to semen. The food provided by men who tolerate the infidelity of their wives, and by men whose spouses rule them, is also forbidden.

A Brahmana should not accept food given by a man selected for receiving gifts at a certain stage of a sacrifice; by one who does not enjoy his wealth or make any gifts; by one who sells soma, or who is a shoe-maker; by an unchaste woman, by a washerman, by a physician, by persons serving as watchmen, by a multitude of persons, by one who is pointed at by a whole village, by one deriving his income from dancing girls, by men married before their elder brothers, by professional singers and bards or by gamblers. He should refuse food which is brought with the left hand or which is stale, or mixed with alcohol, or has been already tasted, or that remains after a feast.

A Brahmana should not eat cakes, sugarcane, pot-herbs or rice boiled in sugared milk, if they have lost their taste, or fried barley powder and other kinds of fried grain mixed with curds if they are stale. Brahmanas leading a grihasta's life should not take rice boiled in sugared milk, food mixed with the tila seed, meat and cakes that one has not dedicated to the gods. He should take his food after first gratifying the Devas, Rishis, Athitis, Pitris and household deities.

By living thus in his own house, a grihasta becomes like a Bhikshu who has renounced the world. A man of such conduct, living with his wives in domesticity, earns great religious merit. No one should make a gift for the sake of acquiring fame, or from fear of censure and the like, or to a benefactor.

A virtuous man would not give gifts to persons living by singing and dancing, to professional jesters, to a person who is intoxicated, to one who is insane, to a thief, to a slanderer, to an idiot, to an albino, to one who has a defective limb, to a dwarf, to an evil man, to one born in a low and evil family, or to one who has not been sanctified by the observance of vows.

No gift should be made to a Brahmana who has no knowledge of the Vedas, but only to a Srotriya. An improper gift and an improper acceptance produce evil consequences to both the giver and the receiver. Just as a man who seeks to cross the ocean with the help of a rock or a mass of catechu sinks along with his support, so too do the giver and the acceptor both sink together.

Just as a fire covered with wet fuel does not blaze up, the acceptor of a gift who is remiss in penance, study and piety, cannot confer any benefit upon the giver. Just as water in a human skull and milk in a bag made of dog-skin become unclean due to the uncleaness of the vessels in which they are kept, the Vedas too become fruitless in a man who is not of good conduct.

A man may give from compassion to a low Brahmana who is without mantras and vows, who is ignorant of the shastras and who harbours envy. One may, from compassion, give to a man who is poor or afflicted or ill. But he should not give in the belief that he would derive any spiritual benefit from it, or that he would earn any religious merit by it. There is no doubt that a gift made to Brahmana who is without knowledge of the Vedas becomes perfectly fruitless.

A Brahmana who has not studied the Vedas is like an elephant made of wood or an antelope made of leather, as all three are nothing but names. A Brahmana without mantras is like a eunuch with women, or a cow with another cow, or a featherless bird, all in vain. A gift to a Brahmana devoid of learning is like a grain without a kernel, a well without water, or offerings poured on ashes.

An unlearned Brahmana is an enemy to all and the destroyer of the food that is offered to the Devas and Pitris. A gift made to him goes for nothing, and is like a gift to a robber. He can never succeed in acquiring regions of bliss hereafter. I have now told you in brief, O Yudhishtira, all that Manu said on that occasion. All should listen to this great conversation O Bharatarishabha.""'

CANTO 38

"Yudhishtira says, 'O Maharishi, I wish to hear in detail what the dharma of kings is, and the dharma of all the four varnas. I wish also to hear, O great Brahmana, what conduct one should adopt in times of distress, and how one can subdue the world by treading the path of dharma. This discourse on atonement, dealing at the same time with the subject of fasts, excites great curiosity, and fills me with joy. The practice of punya and the discharge of Rajadharma are always inconsistent with each other. My mind is constantly confused thinking of how to reconcile the two.'

Then Vyasa, the maharishi who is the greatest master of the Vedas, looks at the Devarishi Narada and says, 'If you wish to hear of dharma in detail, ask Bhishma Pitamaha, Mahabaho. A profound knower of dharma and possessed of universal knowledge, the son of Bhagirathi will remove all your doubts on the difficult subject of duty.

The Devi, the celestial river of three courses, gave birth to him. He saw with his mortal eyes all the Devas with Indra at their head. Having gratified with his dutiful services the Devarishis with Brihaspati at their head, he acquired a knowledge of the dharma of kings, with its interpretations, from Usanas and Brihaspati who is the guru of all the celestial ones.

Having practised rigid vows, that Mahabaho acquired knowledge of all the Vedas and Vedangas from Vasishtha and from Chyavana of

Bhrigu's race. In his youth he studied under the eldest-born son of the Pitamaha, Sanatkumara of blazing splendour, knower of the deepest truths of mental and spiritual science. He learnt the duties in full of the Yatis from the lips of Markandeya, and obtained all weapons from Rama and Sakra.

Although he was born among human beings, his death is yet under his own control and will only come when he wills it. We hear that although childless, he has many realms of bliss hereafter. Maharishis of great merit were always his courtiers. Nothing in the world of objects that should be known is unknown to him. Profoundly knowledgeable about all duties and acquainted with all the subtle truths of morality, he will also discourse with you upon these. Go to him before he abandons his prana.'

Thus addressed, Kaunteya of great wisdom says to Satyavati's son Vyasa, 'Having caused a great and horrible slaughter of kinsmen, I have become an offender against all and a destroyer of the earth. Having caused Bhishma himself, that warrior who always fought fairly, to be slain by deceit, how shall I approach him to ask him about dharma?'

Moved by the desire to benefit all the four varnas, the noble and mighty-armed Krishna, lord of the Yaduvamsa race, again addresses the great king. 'It does not become you to show such obstinacy in grief. O best of kings, do what the holy Vyasa has said. The Brahmanas and your brothers of great tejas stand before you, Mahabaho, imploring you like men beseeching the deity of the clouds at the close of summer.

The unslain remnant of the assembled kings, and the people belonging to all the four orders of your kingdom of Kurujangala, O king, are here. For the sake of doing what is agreeable to these noble Brahmanas, in obedience to the command of Vyasa of immeasurable tejas, O Parantapa, and at our request, we who are your well-wishers and Draupadi's, do what we ask you, and what is beneficial to the world.'

Yudhishtira of eyes like lotus petals rises from his seat for the good of the whole world. The Naravyaghra of great fame, entreated by Krishna himself, by the island-born Vyasa, by Devasthana, by Jishnu, and many others, casts off his grief and anxiety. Fully aware of the declarations of the Srutis, with the science that treats the interpretation of these declarations and with all that men usually hear and all that deserves to be heard, the son of Pandu finds peace of mind and resolves upon what he should do next.

Surrounded by all of them, like the moon by the stars, and placing Dhritarashtra at the head of the train, Yudhishtira sets out for the city after offering worship to the Devas and thousands of Brahmanas. He ascends a new white chariot covered with blankets and deerskins, to which are yoked sixteen white bullocks with auspicious marks, sanctified with Vedic mantras. Hymned by poets and bards, the king mounts the chariot, like Soma ascending his own ambrosial vehicle. His brother Bhima, of awesome powers, takes the reins. Arjuna holds a white sovereign parasol of great radiance over his head, as beautiful as a white cloud decked with stars. The two heroic sons of Madri, Nakula and Sahadeva, take up two yak-tails, white as the rays of the moon and adorned with gems, with which to fan the king.

Having ascended the chariot, the five brothers decked with ornaments, O Rajan, look like the five elements that permeate all things and beings. Riding another white ratha yoked to steeds fleet as thought, Yuyutsu follows behind the eldest son of Pandu.

Upon his own brilliant chariot of gold, yoked to Saibya and Sugriva, Krishna with Satyaki follows the Kurus. The eldest uncle of Pritha's son, O Bhaarata, accompanied by Gandhari, goes at the head of the train, upon a palanquin borne on the shoulders of men. The other women of the Kuru household, including Kunti and Krishna, journey in exquisite palanquins, headed by Vidura. Behind, follow a large number of chariots and elephants decked with ornaments, and foot-soldiers and horses.

The Dharmaputra travels towards Hastinapura accompanied by sweet-voiced balladeers and bards singing the king's praises. The progress of King Yudhishtira is majestic and beautiful, O Mahabhaho, beyond anything seen like it before on earth. During the regal progress of Pritha's son, the city and its streets are adorned with happy citizens who have come out to honour the king. Teeming with robust and cheerful men, the streets resound with the hum of innumerable voices. The highway along which the king passes is festooned with flowers and innumerable banners. The streets of the city are perfumed with incense, covered with powdered perfumes and flowers and fragrant plants, and adorned with garlands and wreaths. New metal jars, brimming with water, are kept at the door of every house, and groups of the loveliest young women gather there.

Accompanied by his friends, the son of Pandu, praised in speeches, enters the city through its profusely adorned gate."

CANTO 39

Vaisampayana said, "When the Pandavas enter the city, thousands and thousands of the citizens come out to watch them. The richly adorned squares and streets, swelling each moment with the crowds, are like the surge of ocean waves at the rise of the moon. The great mansions, Bhaarata, that stand on either side, decked with every ornament and full of women, seem to shake with their weight. With soft and modest voices they praise Yudhishtira, Bhima, Arjuna and the two sons of Madri, saying, 'You are worthy of all praise, blessed princess of Panchala, who waits by the side of these great men even as Gautami did by the side of the seven Rishis. Your karma and vows have borne fruit, O Princess Krishnaa!'

O Rajan, the women praise her in this manner, and as a result of these praises, and their talk among one another, and the shouts of joy by the men, the city is filled with a reverberant uproar. After passing through the streets in a stately manner, Yudhishtira enters the beautiful palace of the Kurus adorned with all manner of ornaments.

The people of the city and the provinces, approaching the palace, praise him: 'Through good fortune you have vanquished your enemies, Parantapa, and recovered your kingdom through virtue and energy. Be our king for a hundred years, and protect your people virtuously as Indra protects the inhabitants of heaven!'

Thus praised and blessed at the palace-gate, and accepting the benedictions of the Brahmanas from every side, the king, graced with victory and the blessings of the people, enters the palace that resembles Indra's own, and descends from his chariot. Entering the apartments, the blessed Yudhishtira worships the household gods, the kuladevas, with jewels, perfumes and garlands. He then comes out and sees a number of Brahmanas waiting with auspicious offerings in their hands, to pronounce blessings on him. Surrounded by them he appears like the full moon in the midst of the stars. Accompanied by his priest Dhaumya and his eldest uncle, he joyfully worships these Brahmanas with due rites, and gifts of sweets, gems, gold in profusion, cows, robes and other diverse things that they desire.

Then loud shouts of 'This is a blessed day!' fill the heavens, O Bhaarata. Sweet to the ear, the sacred sound is gratifying to the friends and well-wishers of the Pandavas. The king also hears these sounds, loud and clear like the calls of a flock of swans. He listens to these men familiar with the Vedas, whose speech is meaningful and rich with melodious words. Then, O Rajan, there is a roll of drums and a delightful fanfare of triumphal conches.

A little while later, when the Brahmanas become silent, a Rakshasa named Charvaka, who has disguised himself as a Brahmana, speaks. He is a friend of Duryodhana and stands there in the garb of a sannyasi. With a rosary, a tuft of hair on his head, and the triple staff in his hand, he stands proudly and fearlessly in the midst of all these Brahmanas, all devoted to penances and vows, who have come there in their thousands to bless the king. Charvaka the Rakshasa, wanting to do evil to the noble Pandavas, without consulting these Brahmanas, now tells the king, 'All these Brahmanas, making me their spokesman, say "Shame on you! You are an evil king. You are a slayer of kinsmen. What have you gained, O son of Kunti, by having exterminated your race? For having also slain your elders and guru it is proper for you to cast away your life."'

Hearing these words of that evil one, the Brahmanas present are deeply agitated and beak into a furious uproar. And all of them, including Yudhishtira, O Rajan, become speechless with shame and anxiety.

Yudhishtira says, 'I bow down to you and beg you humbly, to bear with me. It does not become you to shout at me. I will soon lay down my life.'

Then all the Brahmanas, O Rajan, cry loudly, 'These are not our words! Prosperity to you, O Rajan!'

These maharishis, all with knowledge of the Vedas and understanding rendered clear by tapasya, then penetrate the disguise of the speaker with their spiritual insight and declare, 'This is the Rakshasa Charvaka, Duryodhana's friend disguised as a sannyasi, who seeks the good of his dead friend. We have not, O Dharmatman, joined him in what he says. Let your anxiety be dispelled and let prosperity be with you and your brothers.'

The Brahmanas, insensate with rage, then utter the deadly sound '*Hunn*'. Cleansed of all sins, they censure the sinful Rakshasa and slay him there with the very humkara. Consumed by the tejas of these Brahmavadis, Charvaka falls dead like a tree with all its roots and sprouts blasted by Vajra, the thunder of Indra. The Brahmanas go away, duly worshipped, having gladdened the king with their blessings. The royal son of Pandu and all his friends feel great happiness come over them."

CANTO 40

Vaisampayana said, "Now Devaki's son Krishna, Janardana of universal knowledge, says to King Yudhishtira and his brothers, 'For me, in this world, Brahmanas are always to be worshipped. They are Devas on earth who have poison in their speech, but are exceedingly easy to gratify.

Once, in the Krita yuga, O Rajan, a Rakshasa named Charvaka performed austere tapasya for many years in Badari, Mahabaho. Brahma repeatedly told him to ask for boons. Finally, the Rakshasa asked for a vara that he should be freed from fear of any being in the universe. The Prajapati granted the boon, subject to the condition that he should be careful to not offend Brahmanas.

Having obtained the boon, the sinful and mighty Rakshasa, violent and powerful, began to harrass the Devas. Persecuted by the might of the Rakshasa, the Devas went to Brahma, for help to kill Charvaka.

Brahma told them, "I have already arranged to bring about the Rakshasa's death. There will be a king named Duryodhana among men, who will become the friend of this devil. Bound by affection for him, the Rakshasa will insult some holy Brahmanas. Stung by the wrong, the Brahmanas, whose power reposes in speech, will curse him in anger and he will die."

It is that Rakshasa Charvaka, O Rajan, who lies there dead, slain by the chant of the Brahmanas. Do not, Bharatarishabha, give way to sorrow. Your kinsmen, who perished in the observance of Kshatriya dharma, have all gone to Swarga. Attend to your duties now, and do not grieve. Kill your enemies, protect your subjects, and worship the Brahmanas.'"

CANTO 41

Vaisampayana said, "Yudhishtira, free from grief and the fever in his heart, sits down with his face turned eastwards, on a magnificent throne made of gold. On another blazing golden seat facing him sit the two Parantapas, Satyaki and Krishna. On either side of the king, Bhima and Arjuna sit on two other resplendent jewel-encrusted thrones. Pritha sits with Sahadeva and Nakula on a white throne of ivory decked with gold. Sudharman, Vidura, Dhaumya and the Kuru king Dhritarashtra, sit separately on other thrones that blaze with the radiance of fire. Yuyutsu, Sanjaya and the famed Gandhari, all sit around King Dhritarashtra.

Dharmaraja Yudhishtira first touches the beautiful white flowers, swastikas, vessels full of earth, gold, silver and gems placed before him. Then, led by the priest Dhaumya, his subjects approach him, bringing with them auspicious offerings: sacred earth, gold, many kinds of jewels and other things necessary for the performance of the coronation rites. There are golden pots brimming with water, copper, silver and earthen jars, flowers, fried paddy, Kusa grass, cow's milk, sacrificial fuel of the wood of Sami, Pippala and Palasa, honey, clarified butter, sacrificial ladles made of Udumbara, and conches adorned with gold.

At the behest of Krishna, the priest Dhaumya constructs an altar according to the appropriate rules, gradually inclining towards the east and the north. He seats Yudhishtira with Krishnaa, the daughter of

Drupada, on the resplendent throne called Sarvatobhadra, glowing golden, with feet covered with tiger-skin. He pours offerings of ghrita onto the sacred fire, chanting the proper mantras.

Yudhishtira, rising from his seat, takes up the sanctified conch and pours the water it contains over his head. Again at the behest of Krishna, the Rajarishi Dhritarashtra and all the people do the same. The son of Pandu, thus bathed with the sanctified water of the conch, looks radiantly handsome. The beating of panavas, anakas and other drums follows, as King Yudhishtira the Just accepts the gifts his subjects offer him. As is his wont, he in turn bestows gifts lavishly on his people. He gives a thousand nishkas to the Brahmanas, all endowed with wisdom and gentle conduct from their study of the Vedas, and they chant special blessings over him.

Happy with their gifts, the Brahmanas wish him prosperity and victory and, with voices melodious as those of swans, praise him, saying, 'Yudhishtira Mahabaho, by good fortune victory is yours, son of Pandu, and you have recovered your position through your prowess. By good fortune the wielder of Gandiva, Bhimasena, yourself, O Rajan, and the two sons of Madri, are all here with us, having slain your enemies and escaped alive from a war which caused the death of so many heroes. O Bhaarata! Do attend without delay to those karmas that you should perform next.'

Thus these pious men worship king Yudhishtira and his brothers and friends, and install him on the throne of a vast kingdom, O Bhaarata!"

CANTO 42

Vaisampayana said, "Hearing these words of encouragement and support from his subjects, Yudhishtira says to them, 'Truly blessed are the sons of Pandu, whose merits, true or false, the best of Brahmanas assembled together enumerate. Without doubt, we have gained your favour, since you so freely attribute all these qualities to us.

However, King Dhritarashtra is our father and our lord and, if you wish to please me, obey him always and do what he likes. I live for him alone, having killed all my kinsmen, and my dharma is to always serve him punctiliously. If you, like my friends, think I am deserving of your favour, I beg you all to behave towards Dhritarashtra as you used to before. He is our lord and the whole world, along with the Pandavas, belongs to him. You should always bear this in mind.'

He then dismisses the citizens and the people of the provinces, and appoints his puissant brother Bhimasena as Yuvaraja, the most intelligent Vidura as chief advisor and, to oversee the six-fold needs of the state, the mature and accomplished Sanjaya as director and supervisor of finances. He appoints Nakula to keep the register of the military forces, to give the soldiers food and payment and to supervise other affairs of the army. He appoints Phalguna to defend the kingdom against hostile forces and to punish evil-doers, and Dhaumya, that best of priests, to attend daily to the Brahmanas of the kingdom, all rites in honour of the Devas and other religious duties. Sahadeva's duty is to always remain by Yudhishtira's side to protect him in all circumstances. The king also cheerfully employs others as he considers suitable.

Dharmarajan Yudhishtira commands Vidura and Yuyutsu, 'You should always do everything that my royal father Dhritarashtra wishes with alacrity and attention and, after taking his permission, whatever needs to be done in respect of the citizens and the people of the provinces in your respective capacities.'"

CANTO 43

Vaisampayana said, "After this, the noble King Yudhishtira orders the Sraddha rites of each of his kinsmen slain in battle to be performed. King Dhritarashtra, for the good of his sons in the other world, gives away to the Brahmanas rich food, kine, vast wealth and many beautiful and costly gem-stones.

Yudhishtira and Draupadi distribute wealth for the sake of Drona, the great Karna, Dhrishtadyumna, Abhimanyu, the Rakshasa Ghatotkacha, son of Hidimba, Virata, and other well-wishers who had served the Pandavas loyally, as well as for Drupada and the five sons of Draupadi. For the benefit of each of them, the king gratifies thousands of Brahmanas with gifts of gold, jewels, cows and clothes.

He performs the Sraddha rite for the good of those in the next world, of all the kings who had died in battle without leaving kinsmen or friends behind. Further, for the souls of all his friends, he constructs halls for dispensing food, places for the distribution of water, and tanks to be dug in their names. Thus paying off the debt he owes them and avoiding censure in this world, the king is happy and continues to protect his people religiously.

He shows due honour, as before, to Dhritarashtra, Gandhari, Vidura, to all the great Kauravas and all his officials. Full of kindness, the Kuru king honours and protects all the women who lost their heroic husbands and sons in the war. With great compassion, he extends his favour to the destitute, the blind and the helpless by giving them food, clothes and shelter. Free from enemies and having conquered the whole world, Yudhishtira begins to live a life of happiness."

CANTO 44

Vaisampayana said, "Having got back the kingdom, and after his coronation, the wise King Yudhishtira, with folded hands, says to the lotus-eyed Krishna of Dasarha's vamsa, 'O Madhava, through your grace, guidance, might, intelligence and prowess, I have won back my ancestral kingdom. I bow to you again and again, O Parantapa! You are the one and only Being, refuge of all worshippers, whom even the Rishis and Munis adore with innumerable names.

Salutations to you, O Prajapati, Creator of the Universe! You are the Atman of the Universe, which has sprung from you. You are Vishnu, you are Jishnu, you are Hari, you are Krishna, you are Vaikunta, and you are the best of all beings. As said in the Puranas, you have taken birth seven times in the womb of Aditi. It was you who took birth in the womb of Prishni.

The learned say that you are the three yugas. All your achievements are sacred. You are the lord of our senses. You are the great Lord worshipped in yagnas. You are called the Parama Hamsa. You are three-eyed Sambhu. You are One, though known as Vibhu and Damodara. You are the great Boar, you are Fire, you are the sun, you have the bull as your emblem on your banner, and you have Garuda also as your device.

You are, Parantapa, the Being who pervades every form in the universe, of irresistible power. You are the best of all things, you are fierce, you are the Senapati in battle, you are the Truth, you are the giver of food, and you are Guha the celestial Senapati. Unfading, you cause your enemies to fade and waste away.

You are the Brahmana of pure blood, as well as those who have sprung from mixed blood. You are great. You walk high, you are the mountains, and you are called Vrishadarbha and Vrishakapi. You are the Ocean, you are without attributes, you are the three peaks of Trikuta, you have three abodes, and you take human forms on earth, descending from Swarga.

You are the Emperor, you are Virat, and you are Swarat. You are the Lord of the Devas, and you are the cause for the birth of the universe. You are Almighty, you are existence in every form, and yet you are formless. You are Krishna, you are fire. You are the Creator, you are the father of the celestial physicians, you are the sage Kapila, and you are the Vamana. You are the Sacrifice embodied, you are Dhruva, you are Garuda, and you are Yajnasena.

You are Sikhandin, you are Nahusha, and you are Babhru. You are the constellation Punarvasu stretched across the sky. You are tawny in hue, you are the sacrifice known as Uktha, you are Sushena, you are the drum which resounds through all space. Light is the track of your chariot-wheels. You are the lotus of Prosperity, you are the cloud called Pushkara, and you are decked with garlands. You are opulent, you are powerful, you are the most subtle, and it is you whom the Vedas describe.

You are the Ocean, great receptacle of waters, you are Brahma, you are the sacred refuge, and you know the abodes of all. You are called Hiranyagarbha, you are the sacred mantras Swadha and Swaha, and you are Kesava. You are the cause of the birth of all, and you are its dissolution. In the beginning it is you who created the universe. It is under your control, O Creator! Salutations to you, wielder of the Saringa, the Sudarshana and the Kaumodaki!'

Thus praised in song by Yudhishtira Dharmatma in the midst of the Kuru sabha, the lotus-eyed Krishna is pleased. In turn, the greatest of the Yadavas then lauds the eldest son of Pandu with his own words of praise."

CANTO 45

Vaisampayana said, "The king dismisses all his subjects, and they return to their homes. Comforting his brothers, Yudhishtira, blazing in splendour, says to the awesome Bhima, Arjuna and the twins, 'In the Great War, our enemies have lacerated your bodies with different kinds of weapons and you are exhausted, as grief and anger have scorched your hearts. Through my fault, you, Bharatarishabhas, have suffered the privations and miseries of vanavasa like common men. In delight and ease now enjoy your victory. Meet me in the morning after you have rested and regained your strength.'

Then Mahabaho Bhima Vrikodara, like Maghavat entering his own beautiful temple, enters the grand palace that Yudhishtira has assigned to him with the approval of Dhritarashtra, the palace of Duryodhana, consisting of many large mansions and spacious chambers adorned with gemstones of diverse kinds, and thronged with servants, male and female.

The peerless Arjuna, at the command of the king, is given the palace of Dusasana, in no way inferior to Duryodhana's, consisting of many magnificent edifices, with a gateway of gold, abounding in wealth and full of attendants and servitors, both men and women.

The palace of Durmarshana, superior even to that of Dusasana, ornamented with gold and every kind of gem, looks like Kubera's own mansion. King Yudhishtira gladly gives this to the sensitive Nakula, whom the ordeals of vanavasa had affected the most.

The best of palaces, which once belonged to Durmukha, is embellished with gold and contains a plenitude of beds and beautiful women with eyes like lotus-petals. The king gives this to Sahadeva, who was always considerate to him. Sahadeva is as delighted as the Lord of Treasures was upon obtaining Kailasa.

Yuyutsu, Vidura and Sanjaya, O Rajan, and Sudharman and Dhaumya return to the abodes they owned earlier.

Like a tiger entering his cave in the hills, the Purushavyaghra Saurin, accompanied by Satyaki, enters the palace of Arjuna. Feasting on meat and drink kept ready for them, the princes pass the night happily. Awakening in the morning with rested and satisfied hearts, they present themselves before Yudhishtira."

CANTO 46

Janamejaya said, "You must tell me, O learned Brahmana, what Mahabaho Yudhishtira does after he regains his kingdom and also, O Rishi, what the heroic Hrishikesa, the supreme master of the three worlds, does after the war."

Vaisampayana said, "Listen to me, O Rajan, as I narrate in detail what the Pandavas, led by Vasudeva, do after the war. Having won back his kingdom, Kunti's son Yudhishtira enjoins each of the four varnas to perform their respective svadharma. Pandu's eldest son gives a thousand noble Brahmanas of the Snataka order a thousand nishkas each. He then gratifies the servants who are dependent on him and the guests who visited him, including men who are undeserving and those who have heterodox views, by fulfilling their wishes.

He gives his priest Dhaumya kine in thousands and great wealth, gold, silver and robes of diverse kinds. Towards Kripa, O Rajan, he behaves in the way one should towards one's acharya. Observing his vows, he continues to honour Vidura greatly. This most charitable king gratifies everyone with gifts of food, drink, fine robes of diverse kinds, beds and seats. Having restored peace to his kingdom, he pays due honour to Yuyutsu and Dhritarashtra. Placing his kingdom at the disposal of Dhritarashtra, Gandhari and Vidura, Yudhishtira continues to pass his days in peace.

After gratifying everyone, including the common citizens,

O Bharatarishabha, Yudhishtira comes with folded palms into Vasudeva's presence where he sees Krishna, of the hue of a blue cloud, seated on a large throne adorned with gold and gems. Wearing yellow robes of silk and decked with celestial ornaments, Krishna blazes with splendour like a jewel set in gold and, with the crimson Kaustubha ruby adorning his chest, he looks like the Udaya mountain that adorns the rising sun. No metaphor in the three worlds can remotely describe his beauty.

Approaching Him who is Vishnu incarnate, Yudhishtira sweetly and smilingly asks, 'O most intelligent one, have you passed the night happily? You of unfading glory, are all your faculties in their full vigour, and is your understanding luminous? We have got back our kingdom and the earth has come under our sway. Refuge of the three worlds, O you of the Three Steps, through your grace we are victorious and have won great fame without violating our svadharma!'

To Parantapa Yudhishtira who addresses him in this strain, the divine Krishna does not say a word, for he is in deep meditation."

CANTO 47

"Yudhishtira says, 'How wonderful is this, O you of immeasurable valour, that you are rapt in dhyana! O great refuge of the universe, is all right with the three worlds? When you withdraw yourself from the world into turiya, the fourth state, O bull among men, I am filled with wonder. You still the five life-breaths that move within the body and you focus your senses within your mind.

O Govinda, you concentrate both speech and mind within your understanding, and withdraw your senses into your Atman. Your body hair stands erect, your mind and understanding are both still, and you are as immobile now, O Madhava, as a wooden post. O illustrious Devadeva, you are as still as the flame of a lamp in a windless place, as unmoving as a stone.

I beg you as a favour to tell me the cause of your dhyana and dispel my doubts, unless it is a secret that I cannot share. You are the Creator and you are the Destroyer, you are destructible and you are indestructible. You are without beginning and you are without end, you are the first and the greatest of Beings. O Dharmatman, tell me the cause of your Yogic abstraction. I, your devoted worshipper, bow my head to you and ask your favour.'

Thus addressed, the illustrious younger brother of Vasava, recalling his mind, understanding and senses to their mundane sphere, says with a gentle smile, 'That Purushavyaghra Bhishma, who lies now on a bed of arrows and who is like a fire about to be extinguished, is thinking of me. So my mind was turned on him, the twang of whose bowstring and the sound of whose palms being clapped together Indra himself was unable to bear.

I was thinking of him who, having vanquished in a trice all the assembled kings at the Swayamvara of the daughters of the king of Kasi, abducted the three princesses to marry his brother Vichitravirya. I was thinking of him who fought for twenty-three days with Parasurama himself, and whom even Rama of Bhrigu's race was unable to overcome. Collecting all his senses and concentrating his mind through his understanding, he sought my refuge. It was for this that I turned my mind upon him.

I was thinking of him whom Ganga conceived and brought forth, and whom Vasishtha took as a disciple. I was thinking of that hero of powerful energy and great intellect who possesses knowledge of all the celestial weapons and of the four Vedas with all their branches. O son of Pandu, I was thinking of him who is the favourite disciple of Parasurama, son of Jamadagni, and who is the greatest of all men who know dharma; of him, Bharatarishabha, who knows the Past, the Future, and the Present.

When that Naravyaghra, as a result of his achievements, ascends to Swarga, O son of Pritha, the earth will seem a moonless night. Therefore, Yudhishtira, humbly approach Ganga's son, the mighty Bhishma, and question him about what you wish to learn. Ask him, O lord of the earth, about the four branches of knowledge, about the sacrifices and rites laid down for the four varnas, about the four modes of life, and about all kingly duties. When Bhishma, that Kurusthama, disappears from the world, every kind of knowledge will be lost with him. This is why I urge you to go to him now.'

Hearing Krishna's precious advice, the righteous Yudhishtira, his voice choked with tears, answers Janardana, 'What you say, O Madhava, about the eminence of Bhishma is perfectly true and I have not the slightest doubt about it. Indeed, I have heard from noble Brahmanas of the holiness and the greatness of the illustrious Bhishma.

You, Parantapa, are the Creator of all the worlds and there can be no doubt about what you say. If your heart be inclined to show grace, O Madhava, then let us go together to Bhishma, with you leading us. When the divine Surya turns towards the north, Bhishma will leave this world for those regions of bliss that he has won. Before this transpires, that Kurusthama deserves to see you. If you grant my prayer, Bhishma will have a glimpse of you, the first of the gods, destructible and indestructible. Indeed, O Lord, you are the infinite receptacle of Brahman.'"

Vaisampayana continued, "Hearing these words of King Yudhishtira the Just, Krishna says to Satyaki who is sitting beside him, 'Let my chariot be yoked.' Satyaki quickly leaves Krishna's presence and, going out, commands Daruka, 'Let Krishna's chariot be made ready.'

Daruka swiftly yokes Krishna's ratha, the best of chariots, shining with gold, decked with emeralds, moon-gems, sun-gems, and furnished with golden wheels. Fleet as the wind, set with fantastic jewels, it is as beautiful as the morning sun. It has a radiant standard of Garuda flying, and is festooned with numerous other bright banners. It has yoked to it in trappings of gold, the best of steeds, swift as thought—Sugriva and Saibya, and two others. Having harnessed it, Daruka comes and, with folded hands, tells Krishna that his ratha awaits."

CANTO 48

Janamejaya said, "How did the grandsire of the Bhaaratas who lay on a bed of arrows cast off his body, and what kind of Yoga did he adopt for this?'

Vaisampayana said, "Listen, O king, with pure heart and concentrated attention, to how the Mahatman Bhishma cast off his body. As soon as the sun, passing the solstitial point, entered Uttarayana, his northerly course, Bhishma, with the power of dhyana, caused his atman to enter his Atman. Surrounded by many of the foremost of Brahmanas, that hero, his body pierced with innumerable arrows, blazed forth in lustrous beauty like Surya himself with his innumerable rays. Surrounded by Veda Vyasa, by the Devarishi Narada, by Devasthana, by Asmaka, Sumantu, by Jaimini, by the high-souled Paila, by Sandilya, by Devarata, by Maitreya of great intellect, by Asita and Vasishtha and the high-souled Kausika, by Harita and Lomasa and Atri's son of genius, by Brihaspati and Sukra and the Maharishi Chyavana, by Sanatkumara and Kapila and Valmiki and Tumburu and Kuru, by Maudgalya and Rama of Bhrigu's vamsa, and the great Muni Trinabindu, by Pippalada and Vayu and Samvarta and Pulaha and Katha, by Kasyapa and Pulastya and Kratu and Daksha and Parasara, by Marichi and Angiras and Kasmya and Gautama and the sage Galava, by Dhaumya and Vibhanda and Mandavya and Dhaumra and Krishnanubhautika, by Uluka, that foremost of Brahmanas, and the mighty Markandeya, by Bhaskari and Purana and Krishna and Suta, surrounded by these and many other highly blessed powerful sages, and possessed of faith and self-restraint and tranquility of mind, the Kuru hero looked like the moon in the midst of the planets and the stars.

Stretched out on his bed of arrows, that Naravyaghra, Bhishma, with pure heart and palms joined, set his mind, thought and actions on Krishna. With a cheerful and strong voice he hymned the praises of the slayer of Madhu, the Master of Yoga with the lotus in his navel, the Lord of the universe, called Vishnu and Jishnu. With joined hands, that foremost of eloquent men, the puissant Bhishma of perfectly virtuous soul, praises Janardana.

Bhishma says, 'O Krishna, O foremost of Beings, be you pleased with these words that I utter, in brief and in detail, from my desire to hymn your praises. You are pure and purity's self. You transcend all. You are what people say to be THAT. You are the Supreme Lord. With my whole heart I seek your refuge, O universal Soul and Lord of all creatures!

You are without beginning and without end. You are the highest of the high and Brahman. Neither the Devas nor the Rishis know you. The divine Creator, called Narayana or Hari, alone knows you. Through Narayana, the Rishis, the Siddhas, the great Nagas, the Devas, and the celestial Rishis know a little of you. You are the highest of the high and know no deterioration. The Devas, the Danavas, the Gandharvas, the Yakshas, the Pannagas do not know who you are and whence you came. All the worlds and all created things live in you and enter you when the dissolution comes. Like gems strung together on a thread, all things that have attributes reside in you, the Supreme Lord. Having the universe for your work and for your limbs, this universe consisting of mind and matter resides in your eternal and all-pervading soul like a multitude of flowers strung together by a strong thread.

You are called Hari, of a thousand heads, a thousand feet, a thousand eyes, a thousand arms, a thousand crowns and a thousand faces of great splendour. You are called Narayana, divinity, and the refuge of the universe. You are the subtlest of the subtle, grossest of the gross, the heaviest of the heavy and the highest of the high. In the Vaks, the

Anuvaks, the Nishads, and Upanishads, You are regarded as the Supreme Being of irresistible force. In the Samans also, whose declarations are always true, you are regarded as Truth's self.

You are of quadruple soul. You are displayed in only the understanding of all creatures. You are the Lord of those that are bound to you in faith. O God, you are adored by the faithful with four excellent, high, and secret names. Penances are ever present in you. Performed by other creatures to gratify you, penances live in your form. You are the Universal Soul. You are of universal knowledge. You are the universe. You are omniscient. You are the Creator of all.

Like a couple of kindling sticks generating a blazing fire, you have been born of the divine Devaki and Vasudeva for the protection of dharma on earth. For eternal salvation, the devout worshipper, with mind withdrawn from all else and casting off all desires, beholds you, O Govinda, that are the Primal Soul, in his own soul. You transcend Surya in glory. You are beyond the ken of the senses and the understanding. O Lord of all creatures, I place myself in your hands. In the Puranas you have been spoken of as Purusha. On occasions of the commencement of yugas, you are said to be Brahma, while on occasions of universal dissolution you are spoken of as Sankarshana. Adorable you are, and therefore I worship you.

Though one, you have yet been born in innumerable forms. You have your passions under perfect control. Your devout worshippers, faithfully performing the rites laid down in the scriptures, sacrifice to you, O granter of every wish! You are called the sheath within which the universe lies. All created things live in you. Like swans and ducks swimming on the water, all the worlds that we see float in you. You are Truth. You are One and undecaying. You are Brahman, you are That which is beyond Mind and Matter.

You are without beginning, middle or end. Neither the Devas nor the Rishis know you. The Devas, the Asuras, the Gandharvas, the Siddhas, the Rishis and the great Uragas always worship you with concentrated souls. You are the great panacea for all sorrow. You are without birth and death. You are divine. You are self-created. You are eternal. You are invisible and beyond ken. You are called Hari and Narayana, O puissant one. The Vedas declare you to be the Creator of the universe and the Lord of everything that exists in it. You are its Supreme protector. You know no deterioration and you are that which is called the highest. You are of the complexion of gold. You are the slayer of Asuras. Though One, Aditi brought you forth in twelve forms.

Salutations to you that are the soul of the sun! Salutations to you in your form of Soma, said to be the chief of all the regenerate ones, who gratifies with nectar the Devas in the lighted fortnight and the Pitris in the dark fortnight. You are the One Being of transcendent effulgence dwelling on the other side of dense darkness. Knowing you, one ceases to have any fear of death. Salutations to you in that form which is an object of knowledge!

In the grand Uktha sacrifice, the Brahmanas adore you as the great Rik. In the great fire-sacrifice, they sing of you as the chief Adhvaryu. You are the soul of the Vedas. The Riks, the Yajus and the Samans are your abode. You are the five kinds of sanctified libations used in sacrifices. Salutations to you!

You are the seven mantras used in the Vedas. Salutations to you in your form of Sacrifice! Libations are poured on the Homa fire to the accompaniment of the seventeen monosyllabic sounds. You are the soul of the Homa. Salutations to you! You are that Purusha of whom the Vedas sing. Your name is Yajus. The Vedic metres are your limbs. The sacrifices laid down in the three Vedas are your three heads. The great sacrifice called Rathantara is your voice, expressive of gratification. Salutation to you in your form of sacred hymns!

You are the Rishi that appeared during the Mahayagna, lasting for a thousand years, performed by the creators of the universe. You are the great swan with wings of gold. Salutations to you in your form of the Swan! The Mulas, the roots with all kinds of affixes and suffixes are your limbs. The Sandhis are your joints. The consonants and the vowels are your ornaments. The Vedas have declared you to be the divine word.

Salutations to you in your form of the Word!

Assuming the form of the Boar, Varaha whose limbs were constituted by sacrifice, you raised up the submerged earth for the benefit of the three worlds. Salutations to you in your form of infinite prowess! You sleep in Yoga on your serpent bed shaded by the thousand hoods of Anantasesha. Salutations to you in your form of Sleep!

You build the bridge for the good to cross the sea of samsara with Truth, with those means by which Mukti can be obtained, and with the means by which the senses may be controlled. Salutations to you in your form of Truth!

Men practising diverse creeds, actuated by desire for diverse fruits, worship you with diverse rites. Salutations to you in your form of Creed!

From you all things have sprung. It is you that excite with desire all embodied creatures. Salutations to you in your form of Excitement! The great Rishis seek your unmanifest self within the manifest. Called Kshetrajna, you sit in Kshetra. Salutations to you in your form of Kshetra! You are always conscious and present in the self, and the Sankhyas still describe you as existing in the three states of wakefulness, dream and sound sleep. They further speak of you as possessed of sixteen attributes and representing the number seventeen. Salutations to your form as conceived by the Sankhyas! Casting off sleep, restraining breath, withdrawn into their own selves, Yogins of restrained senses behold you as eternal light. Salutations to you in your form of Yoga! Peaceful sannyasins, freed from fear of rebirth by the destruction of all their sins and merits, find you in liberation. Salutations to you in your form of Emancipation!

At the end of a thousand yugas, you assume the form of a blazing fire and consume all creatures. Salutations to you in your form of Fierceness! Having consumed all creatures and making the universe one vast expanse of water, you sleep on the waters in the form of a child. Salutations to you in your form as Maya! From the navel of the Self-born with eyes like lotus leaves, springs a lotus, on which is established this universe. Salutations to you in your form as Lotus!

You have a thousand heads. You pervade everything. You are of immeasurable soul. You have subjugated the four kinds of desire that are as vast as the four oceans. Salutations to you in your form of Yoga-nidra!

The clouds are in the hair of your head. The rivers flow in the several joints of your limbs. The four oceans are in your belly. Salutations to you in your form of Water! Birth and the change represented by death spring from you. All things, again, at the universal dissolution dissolve away in you. Salutations to your form as Cause! You sleep not in the night. You rest not by day. You observe the good and the evil actions of all. Salutations to you in your form of universal Witness! There is nothing, no deed, which you cannot do. You are, again, ever ready to accomplish actions that are righteous. Salutations to you in your form of Work, the form which is called Vaikuntha! In wrath you exterminated in battle twenty-one times the Kshatriyas who had trampled virtue and authority under their feet. Salutations to you in your form of Cruelty!

Dividing yourself into five portions you have become the five vital breaths that act within everybody and cause every living creature to move. Salutations to you in your form of Air! You appear in every yuga in the forms called month and season and half-year and year, and are the cause of both creation and dissolution. Salutations to you in your form of Time!

Brahmanas are your mouth, Kshatriyas are your two arms, Vaisyas are your stomach and thighs, and Sudras live in your feet. Salutations to you in your form of Caste!

Fire constitutes your mouth. The heavens are the crown of your head. The sky is your navel. The earth is your feet. The sun is your eye. The points of the compass are your ears. Salutations to you in your form of the Worlds! You are superior to Time. You are superior to Sacrifice. You are higher than the highest. Yourself without origin, you are the origin of the universe. Salutations to you in your form of the Universe! Men of the world, according to the attributes ascribed to you by the Vaiseshikas, regard you as the Protector of the world. Salutations to you in your form of Protector!

Assuming the forms of food, drink and fuel, you increase the humours and the life-breaths of creatures and uphold their existence. Salutations to you in your form of Life! To support the life-breaths you eat the four kinds of food. Assuming also the form of Agni within the belly, you digest that food. Salutations to you in your form of assimilating Heat!

Assuming the form of half-man and half-lion, Narasimha with tawny eyes and tawny mane, with teeth and claws for your weapons, you took the life of Hiranyakashyapu, the king of the Asuras. Salutations to you in your form of swelling Might! Neither the Devas, nor the Gandharvas, nor the Daityas, nor the Danavas, know you truly. Salutations to your form of exceeding Subtlety!

Assuming the form of the handsome, illustrious and puissant Ananta in the Patalas, you support the world. Salutations to your form of Might! You stupefy all creatures by the bonds of affection and love for the continuance of the creation. Salutations to you in your form of Stupefaction! Regarding that knowledge which is conversant with the five elements to be the true Self-knowledge, people approach you through knowledge! Salutations to you in your form of Knowledge! Your body is immeasurable. Your intellect and eyes encompass everything. You are infinite, being beyond all measures. Salutations to you in your form of Immensity!

You assumed the form of a recluse with a head of matted locks, a staff in your hand, a long belly and a begging bowl for your quiver. Salutations to you in your form of Brahma! You bear the trident, you are the lord of the celestials, you have three eyes, and you are high-souled. Your body is always smeared with ashes, and your linga is always turned upwards. Salutations to you in your form of Rudra! The half-moon forms the ornament of your brow. You have snakes for the sacred thread circling your neck. You are armed with Pinaka and Trisula. Salutations to your form of Fierceness!

You are the soul of all creatures. You are the Creator and the Destroyer of all. You are without wrath, without enmity, without affection. Salutations to you in your form of Peace! Everything is in you. Everything is from you. You are Everything, Everywhere. You are ever the All. Salutations to you in your form of Everything! Salutations to you whose work is the universe, to you that are the soul of the universe, to you from whom has sprung the universe, to you that are the dissolution of all things, to you that are beyond the five elements that constitute all things!

Salutations to you that are the three worlds, to you that are above the three worlds! Salutations to you that are all the directions! You are all and you are the one receptacle of all. Salutations to you, O divine Lord, O Vishnu, and O eternal origin of all the worlds! You, O Hrishikesa, are the Creator, You are the Destroyer, and you are invincible. I cannot behold that heavenly form in which you are displayed in the Past, Present, and the Future. I can, however, behold truly your eternal form as manifest in your works.

You have filled heaven with your head, and the earth with your feet; with your prowess you have filled the three worlds. You are Eternal and you pervade everything in the universe. The directions are your arms, the sun is your eye, and prowess is your vital fluid. You are the lord of all creatures. You stand, shutting up the seven paths of the Wind whose energy is immeasurable. They are freed from all fears that worship you, O Govinda of unfading prowess, you that are clad in yellow robes of the colour of the Atasi flower. Even one genuflection to you, O Krishna, is equal to the completion of ten Horse-sacrifices. The man who has performed ten Horse-sacrifices is not freed from the obligation of rebirth. The man who bows to Krishna, however, escapes rebirth. They who have Krishna for their vow, they who think of Krishna in the night and upon rising from sleep, may be said to have Krishna for their body. Those people after death enter Krishna's self, even as libations of clarified butter sanctified with mantras enter the blazing fire.

Salutations to you that dispel the fear of hell, to you, O Vishnu, that are a boat unto those that flounder amid the waves of the ocean of worldly life! Salutations to you, O God, that are the Brahmana's self, to you that are the benefactor of Brahmanas and kine, to you that are the benefactor of the universe, to you that are Krishna and Govinda! The two syllables Ha-ri constitute the monetary stock of those that sojourn through the wilderness of life, and the medicine that effectively cures all worldly predilections, besides being the means to alleviate sorrow and grief.

As truth is full of Vishnu, as the universe is full of Vishnu, as everything is full of Vishnu, so let my soul be full of Vishnu, and my sins be destroyed! I seek your protection, devoted to you, desirous of finding a happy end, O you of eyes like lotus petals. O best of gods, think of what will be for my good! Yourself without origin, O Vishnu, you are the origin of Knowledge and Penance. Thus are you praised! O Janardana, thus worshipped by me in the Sacrifice constituted by speech, be gratified with me, O God. The Vedas are devoted to Narayana. Penances are devoted to Narayana. The gods are devoted to Narayana. All is forever Narayana!'"

Vaisampayana continued, "Having uttered these words, Bhishma, with mind concentrated upon Krishna, says, 'Salutations to Krishna!' and bows to him. Learning through his Yoga prowess of the devotion of Bhishma, Madhava, otherwise called Hari, entering his body, bestows upon him heavenly knowledge compassing the Past, the Present, and the Future, and then leaves. When Bhishma falls silent, those utterers of Brahman, the Brahmavadis that sat around him, with voices choked with tears, adored that high-souled great Lord of the Kurus in excellent speech. Those foremost of Brahmanas uttered the praises of Krishna also, that first of Beings, and continued in soft voices to laud Bhishma.

Learning of the devotion of Bhishma for him, that foremost of Beings Krishna climbs into his chariot. Kesava and Satyaki ride on one car. On another go those two illustrious Kshatriyas, Yudhishtira and Dhananjaya. Bhimasena and the twins ride on a third, while those bulls among men, Kripa and Yuyutsu, and that Parantapa, Sanjaya of the Suta varna, all ride their own rathas, each of which looks like a town. All of them, riding together, cause the earth to tremble with the rumble of their chariot-wheels.

Krishna, foremost of men, as he goes, cheerfully listens to the praises sung by the Brahmanas along the way. The slayer of Kesi with a glad heart salutes the people lining the streets with joined hands and bowed heads."

CANTO 49

Vaisampayana said, "Krishna, Yudhishtira and all their men, led by Kripa, along with the four Pandavas in their rathas like fortified cities decked with standards and banners, fly to Kurukshetra on their swift horses. They descend on the field where millions of noble Kshatriyas have cast away their lives, and which is now covered with hair, marrow and bones and with hillocks formed of the bodies and bones of elephants and horses, scattered with human heads and skulls like conch-shells. With thousands of funeral pyres and with armour and weapons lying in heaps, the vast plain looks like the drinking garden of the Destroyer himself, used and recently abandoned. The Maharathas travel quickly, viewing the battlefield haunted by throngs of Pisachas and Rakshasas.

On the way, the mighty-armed Kesava, delighter of all the Yadavas, speaks to Yudhishtira about the prowess of Jamadagni's son, Parasurama, 'There, at a distance, O Kaunteya, are the five lakes of Rama, where he offered oblations of Kshatriya blood to the souls of his ancestors! It was there that the mighty Rama, having freed the earth of Kshatriyas twenty-one times, finally ceased his grisly task.'

Yudhishtira says, 'I have great doubts about what you say about Rama having extirpated the Kshatriyas twenty-one times. When Parasurama burnt the very Kshatriya seed, O Yadurishabha, how was it that the Kshatriya varna revived, how did the illustrious one exterminate the

Kshatriya again and again, and how came it to rise yet again? In frightful chariot encounters he slew millions of Kshatriyas, and the earth was strewn with the corpses of warriors. For what reason did Dharmatman Parasurama Bhargava extirpate the Kshatriyas, O tiger among the Yadus? Clear my doubts, O you of Vrishni's race, for you know all things.'"

Vaisampayana said, "The bird-bannered hero, puissant elder brother of Baladeva, then narrates in full everything that happened on earth and how it was again peopled with Kshatriyas."

CANTO 50

"Vasudeva says, 'Listen, O son of Kunti, to the story of Parasurama's birth, his vitality, and prowess, as I learnt it from some great Rishis. Listen to the tale of how Jamadagni's son slew millions of Kshatriyas and repeatedly slaughtered those who sprang up again in the different royal houses of Bharatavarsha.

Jadu had a son named Rajas, whose son King Balakaswa had an upright and virtuous son named Kusika. Resembling the thousand-eyed Indra on earth, Kusika underwent many maha-tapasyas in order to petition the Lord of the three worlds for a son. Seeing him engaged in the severest tapasyas and well able to father a son, the thousand-eyed Purandara himself inspired the king with his force. The great Lord of the three worlds, Indra, tamer of Paka, was himself born as Kusika's son, O Rajan, and was named Gadhi.

Gadhi had a daughter called Satyavati. The powerful Gadhi gave her as wife to Richika, a descendant of Bhrigu. Richika was pleased with her for the purity of her character. He cooked a sacrificial payasa of milk and rice for Gadhi to obtain a son.

Calling his wife, Richika said, "You must take this portion of the sanctified payasa for yourself, and your mother must have this other portion. A son will be born to her who will blaze with tejas and be a bull among Kshatriyas. Invincible to Kshatriyas on earth, he will be the slayer of the greatest of them. As for you, O blessed Satyavati, your portion of the food will give you a very wise son, an embodiment of tranquillity, a Mahatapasvin, and the best of Brahmanas."

Having said these words to his wife, the blessed Richika of Bhrigu's vamsa set his heart on tapasya, and left for the vana. About the same time, King Gadhi, who was on a pilgrimage to the holy tirthas, arrived with his queen at the asrama of Richika. Seeing them, Satyavati fetched the two portions of the sanctified payasa, and told her mother what her husband had said. But, in her eagerness and haste, O son of Kunti, the queen-mother mistakenly gave the portion intended for herself to her daughter, and ate the portion intended for Satyavati. Thus, Satyavati, her body blazing with lustre, conceived a child of terrible form, born to become the exterminator of the race of Kshatriyas.

Seeing a Brahmana child lying within her womb Richika, that tiger among the Bhrigus, said to his wife Satyavati of divine beauty, "Your mother has deceived you by substituting the sanctified payasas, O blessed lady. Your son will become a man of cruel deeds and vindictive heart. Your brother, born of your mother, will be a Brahmana devoted to maha-tapasya. Into the sanctified food intended for you I placed the seed of the supreme and universal Brahman, while into that intended for your mother I mixed all the essence of Kshatriya energy. Now, O Satyavati, that which I had intended will not happen. Your mother will have a Brahmana child, while to you will be born a son who will become a Kshatriya."

Hearing this, the blessed Satyavati prostrated herself and, setting her head at his feet said, trembling, "It does not become you, O holy one, to tell me that my son will be a wretch among Brahmanas."

Richika replied, "I did not intend this for you, Satyavati. You have conceived a son of fierce deeds only because of the substitution of the payasas." Satyavati pleaded, "Maharishi, when you can create other worlds if you wish, why not a child? It is only right to give me a son who will be righteous and devoted to peace."

Richika said, "When I have never lied, even in jest, how can I lie about such a solemn matter as preparing sanctified food with Vedic mantras, after lighting a holy fire? Destiny ordained it, I have ascertained that through my tapasya. All the descendants of your father will be possessed of Brahmanic dharma."

Satyavati then said, "Mahatapasvin, let our grandson be like that, but let me have a son of tranquil pursuits."

Richika said, "O you of the fairest complexion, there is no distinction between a son and a grandson. It will be as you wish. Tathaastu!"

Then Satyavati gave birth to Jamadagni, a son in Bhrigu's race who was of regulated vows and devoted to tapasya and other tranquil pursuits. Kusika's son Gadhi had a son named Viswamitra. Possessed of every attribute of a Brahmana, this son, though born a Kshatriya, was equal to a Brahmana.

Richika's son Jamadagni, ocean of penances, later had a son of fierce deeds who mastered the shastras, including the science of arms. Like a fire, this son was Parasurama, exterminator of the Kshatriyas. Having gratified Mahadeva on the mountains of Gandhamadana, he begged weapons of the Great Deva, especially his axe of fierce power. With that unrivalled weapon of fiery splendour and irresistible sharpness, he became invincible and without peer on earth.

Meanwhile, the mighty son of Kritaviryarjuna of the Kshatriya varna, ruler of the Haihayas, endowed with great tejas, most virtuous in conduct, and possessed of a thousand arms through the grace of the great Rishi Dattatreya, had subjugated the whole world in battle, the earth with her mountains and seven islands. He became a powerful Rajadhiraja and finally gave away the earth to Brahmanas at an Aswamedha yagna.

Once, asked by the hungry god of fire Agni, this Arjuna, the thousand-armed, gave alms to the deity. Springing from the point of his shafts, the fierce Agni consumed what was offered, and incinerated villages, towns, kingdoms and hamlets of cowherds. Then with the help of the powerful Kritavirya, Agni consumed mountains and great forests.

With the help of the king of the Haihayas, the god of fire made the wind to blaze forth as flames, and to burn the uninhabited but delightful asrama of the noble Apava. Possessed of great tejas himself,

Apava, seeing his hermitage consumed by the powerful Kshatriya, cursed him in wrath, O Mahabaho, saying, "Since you have burnt my beautiful wood, O arrogant Arjuna, Parasurama will cut off your thousand arms."

The charitable and brave Arjuna, always devoted to peace and considerate towards Brahmanas, who granted protection to all varnas, did not take the curse of Mahatman Apava seriously. Nevertheless, as a result of that curse, his powerful sons, always haughty and cruel, became the indirect cause of his death. These princes, O Bharatarishabha, seized and brought away the calf of Jamadagni's homa cow, without the knowledge of Kritavirya of the Haihayas, which resulted in a dispute between the noble Jamadagni and the Haihayas. Jamadagni's son, the powerful Rama, filled with wrath, hewed off the thousand arms of Arjuna and brought back his father's calf, which was wandering within the inner compound of the king's palace.

The foolish sons of Arjuna raided the asrama of the high-souled Jamadagni and struck off the Rishi's head with the points of their lances while the celebrated Parasurama was out fetching sacred fuel and grass. Inflamed with anger at the death of his father and burning for vengeance, Rama took up arms and vowed to free the earth of the very race of Kshatriyas. That tiger among the Bhrigus slaughtered all the sons and grandsons of Kritavirya. Massacring thousands of Haihayas in rage, he drenched the earth with blood and indeed stripped Bhumi of all her Kshatriyas. Filled then with remorse, he retired into the forest.

When some thousands of years had passed, the mighty Rama, wrathful by nature, had imputations of cowardice cast upon him by the grandson of Viswamitra and son of Raibya, a Maharishi called Paravasu. Raibya began saying in public, "O Rama, were not those righteous men, Pratardana and others, who were assembled at a yagna at the time of Yayati's fall, Kshatriyas by birth? Your vows, O Rama, are empty boasts among all people! You have taken to the mountains out of fear of Kshatriya heroes."

Parasurama, hearing these words of Paravasu, once more took up arms, and once more strewed the earth with thousands of Kshatriya corpses. However, some hundreds of Kshatriyas, whom he spared, multiplied in time and became mighty kings on earth. So Rama once again slaughtered them, not sparing even their offspring. Indeed, the earth was strewn again with the bodies of Kshatriya children, slain by Parasurama as soon as they were born.

Some Kshatriya women, however, succeeded in protecting their children from Rama's wrath. Having made the earth destitute of Kshatriyas twenty-one times, the powerful Bhargava, Parasurama, at the completion of an Aswamedha yagna, gave away the earth as a sacrificial gift to Kasyapa. In order to save the remaining Kshatriyas, Kasyapa pointed with his hand that still held the sacrificial ladle, and said, "O Maharishi, go to the shores of the southern ocean. It is not right, Rama, for you to dwell within my dominion." At these words, the Ocean instantly created for Jamadagni's son Parasurama, on his further shore, a realm called Surparaka.

Having accepted the earth as gift, O Rajan, Kasyapa gave it away to the Brahmanas of the world and entered the great forest. Then headstrong Sudras and Vaisyas began to ravish the wives of Brahmanas, O Bharatarishabha. When anarchy sets in on earth, the weak are oppressed by the strong, and no man is master of his own property. Unprotected by virtuous Kshatriyas, and oppressed by evil men, Bhumi started rapidly sinking to the lowest depths. Seeing this, Maharishi Kasyapa held her on his lap—his uru; thus is the earth known as Urvi. The Devi Bhumi gratified Kasyapa and begged him for a king for her protection.

Bhudevi said, "I have concealed a few important Kshatriyas among the women, O Muni. They were born in the race of Haihayas. Let them, O Rishi, protect me. There is one raised among the bears in the Rikshavat mountains, Viduratha's son, and he is of Puru's race. The powerful Parasara, ever engaged in yagnas, through compassion has protected the son of Saudasa. Though born in one of the regenerate orders, yet like a Sudra he serves the Rishi and for that has been named Sarvakarman.

Another is the strong son of Sibi, named Gopati, reared in the forest among kine. Let him, O sage, protect me. Let Pratardana's mighty son

Vatsa, raised among calves in a cowpen, protect me. The sage Gautama has concealed and protected Dadhivahana's grandson and Diviratha's son on the banks of the Ganga, where wolves and the mountains of Gridhrakuta have sheltered him. His name is Brihadratha, and he is endowed with tremendous energy and many great qualities.

The Ocean has protected and nurtured many Kshatriyas belonging to the Marutta vamsa, equal in strength to the lord of Maruts. We hear of these children of the Kshatriya varna dwelling in different places among artisans and goldsmiths. If they protect me I will surely be safe gain. Rama of great prowess has slain their fathers and grandfathers for my sake. It is my duty, O Maharishi, to see that someone duly performs their funeral rites. I do not wish that my present rulers protect me, for they are all sinful. O Maharishi, I beg you to do what will enable me to live as before."

Kasyapa sought out the powerful Kshatriyas whom the Devi had named, and installed them as kings to protect her. The Kshatriya races that now exist are the progeny of those princes. This is the answer to your question, O son of Pandu, of what happened long ago.'"

Vaisampayana continued, "Conversing thus with Yudhishtira, the greatest Dharmatman, the noble Yadava hero rides in his fleet chariot, illumining all the points of the compass like divine Surya himself."

CANTO 51

Vaisampayana said, "King Yudhishtira, hearing of these feats of Parasurama, is filled with wonder and says to Janardana, 'O you of Vrishni's race, the prowess of the Dharmatman Rama, who in wrath freed the earth of Kshatriyas, is like that of Sakra himself. The fear of Parasurama has caused the scions of Kshatriyas to be raised in secrecy by the Ocean, kine, leopards, bears and apes. Worthy of every praise is this world of men, and fortunate are they who dwell in it, where a Brahmana has accomplished so awesome and dharmic a feat!'

Concluding their conversation, Krishna and Yudhishtira come to where the mighty son of Ganga lies on his bed of arrows, resembling in splendour the evening sun engulfed by its own rays. Many Rishis surround the Kurupravira, like the Devas of Swarga surrounding Indra of a hundred yagnas. The place where he lies, on the banks of the Oghavati river, is most sacred. Seeing him from a distance, Krishna, Dharma's royal son Yudhishtira, the four other Pandavas and the rest, led by Saradwat alight from their rathas and, controlling their restless minds and concentrating all their senses, approach the great Rishis.

Saluting the Maharishis headed by Vyasa, Govinda, Satyaki and the others approach the Ganga's son, and sit around him. Seeing Bhishma like a fire about to die out, Kesava addresses him sombrely.

Krishna says, 'Is your mind now as clear as before? I hope your understanding is not clouded, O greatest of eloquent men. I hope your limbs do not feel the pain of the arrows. The body becomes weak from mental affliction too. As a result of the boon granted to you by your father, the righteous Santanu, your time of death depends on your own will, O puissant hero. I myself do not have the punya through which you obtained this boon. When the minutest pin inserted in the body produces pain, what need then be said, O Rajan, of the hundreds of arrows that have pierced you? Surely, pain does not afflict you. You know enough, Bhaarata, to instruct the very Devas about the birth and death of living creatures. O you of great gyana, you know everything of the past, the future and the present, as well as about death and the rewards of dharma, for you are an ocean of dharma and karma.

When you were a powerful ruler and, though sound of body, perfectly healthy and surrounded by female companions, I saw you cleave perfectly to brahmacharya. We have never heard of anyone else in the three worlds other than you, O Santanu's heroic son Bhishma of great tejas, who is so devoted to dharma, your sole pursuit, that, lying on a bed of arrows and at the point of death, you still have mastery over your own death through the power of your tapasya.

We have never heard of anyone as devoted as you to truth, to tapasya, to giving dakshina and dana, to the performances of yagnas, to the astra shastra, to the Vedas, to defending men seeking protection; of one who is so harmless to all, so pure in behaviour, so self-restrained, so bent upon the good of all creatures, and also as great a Maharathi as you. I have no doubt that, from a single ratha, you can vanquish the Devas, Gandharvas, Asuras, Yakshas and Rakshasas.

The Brahmanas always speak of you, Mahabaho Bhishma, as the ninth of the Vasus. Through your virtues, however, you have surpassed them all and are equal to Vasava himself. I know, O best of men, that you are celebrated for your prowess even among the gods. Among men on earth, we have never seen or heard of another possessed of such attributes as you, O greatest of men. You have surpassed the Devas themselves. With your power of tapasya you can create a universe of mobile and immobile creatures. Though your dharma and righteous deeds, you have acquired many blessed realms. Dispel now the grief of Pandu's eldest son, who burns with sorrow on account of the slaughter of his kinsmen.

You know well the dharma of the four varnas, and the four varnasramas. O son of Ganga, you know everything in the four branches of knowledge, in the four Hotras, and also the eternal dharma in Yoga and Sankhya philosophy, the duties of the four varnas and the dharma consistent with their declared practices—all these, O Bhaarata, along with their interpretations. The dharma that has been laid down for those who spring from an intermingling of the four varnas, for particular countries, tribes and families, and what the Vedas and wise men declare, are well known to you. The Itihasas and the Puranas are all known to you. The shastras' treatment of dharma and practice is all in your mind.

None other than you, O bull among men, can remove the doubts that may arise in respect of these subjects of knowledge that one studies in the world. With your intelligence, O prince of men, rid Yudhishtira of his sorrow. Men possessed of such great and varied knowledge live just to comfort clouded minds.'"

Vaisampayana said, "Hearing what Krishna says, Bhishma, raising his head a little, says with folded hands, 'Salutations to you, O divine Krishna! You are the origin and the dissolution of all the worlds. You are the Creator and the Destroyer. You, O Hrishikesa, cannot be vanquished by anyone. The universe is your handiwork. You are the soul of the universe and the universe has sprung from you. Salutations to you! You are the end of all created things. You are above the five elements. Salutations to you who are the three worlds and also beyond the three worlds!

O Lord of Yogins, salutations to you who are the refuge of everything! O Best of beings, what you say about me has enabled me to behold your divine attributes as manifest in the three worlds. Govinda, I also see your eternal form. You stand barring the seven paths of the Wind of immeasurable energy. The sky is your head, and the earth your feet. The points of the compass are your two arms, the sun is your eye, and Sakra constitutes your prowess. Attired in yellow robes that resemble the hue of the atasi flower, you appear to us like a cloud charged with flashes of lightning. O best of Devas, think of what would be good for this insignificant self which is devoted to you, which seeks your protection, and which desires to find a blissful end.'

Krishna says, 'O bull among men, since your devotion to me is so great, I have shown my Virata Rupa to you. I do not, O greatest of kings, display this form of mine to anyone who is not entirely devoted to me, or to a devotee who is not sincere, or, who does not have a disciplined heart. You are devoted to me and always follow the path of dharma. Of pure heart, you are always self-restrained and ever observant of tapasya and of charity. It is because of your tapasya that you are able to see me.

The regions from where there is no return are ready for you, O Bhishma. Fifty-six days still remain for you to live in this world O Kurusthama. You will then cast off your body and obtain the blessed reward of your karma. The Devas and Vasus, all in their fiery splendour, riding on their vimanas, await you invisibly until the moment the sun enters his northerly course. Subject to universal time, when the divine Surya turns to his Uttarayana, you, O greatest of men, will go to those realms from where no man of knowledge ever returns to this earth!

O Bhishma, when you leave this world, all true Knowledge will perish with you. It is for this that these men, assembled together, have approached you—to listen to your discourses on dharma. Do you, then, speak of dharma and Yoga to Yudhishtira, who is firm in truth but whose grief at the slaughter of his kinsmen has clouded his understanding. With your advice dispel his grief!'"

CANTO 52

Vaisampayana said, "Hearing these words of Krishna about dharma and artha, Bhishma answers him, 'Master of all the worlds, Mahabaho, Siva, Narayana, O you of unfading glory, I am filled with joy to hear you speak. But, Master of Speech, what words of instruction can I utter in your presence, especially when you have dealt with all of them? Whatever in either world is done, or should be done, proceeds from you, Deva! Only he who is competent to speak on the subject of Swarga in the presence of the Lord of the gods himself can discourse on dharma, kama, artha and moksha in your presence.

O slayer of Madhu, the pain of my arrow-wounds sorely agitates my mind; my limbs are weak, my understanding clouded. O Govinda, these shafts, like poison or fire, afflict me so that I no longer have the power of utterance. My strength is abandoning me and my life-breath is hurrying to leave me.

The very vitals of my body are afire. My understanding is hazy and my speech, from weakness, is becoming indistinct. How then can I venture to speak? Krishna, be gratified with me. I will say nothing, Mahabaho. Pardon my unwillingness. The very master of speech, Brihaspati, would hesitate to speak in your presence.

I can no longer distinguish the points of the compass, or the sky from the earth. Through your tejas, Madhava, I am barely alive. Do you, therefore, speak for the good of Yudhishtira Dharmaraja, for you are the author of all laws. O Krishna, in the presence of you, the eternal Creator of the universe, how can someone like me discourse on such subjects, a mere disciple in the presence of the acharya?'

Vasudeva says, 'Your words are worthy of you, Kurusthama, you who are endowed with consummate tejas, Mahatman of great patience who has grasped every subject. As for the pain of your arrow-wounds, receive this boon that I grant you, Bhishma, O powerful one, of my grace.

Discomfort, stupefaction, burning, pain, hunger and thirst will not overcome you, O son of Ganga! Your perceptions and memory, sinless one, will not be clouded and your understanding will not fail you. Your mind, Bhishma, undarkened by passion, will remain subject to the radiance of goodness, like the moon emerging from clouds. Your understanding will penetrate whatever subject you think of connected with karma, dharma or artha. Purushavyaghra, obtaining preternatural vision, you will succeed in seeing the four varnas of created things. With your powers of perception, Bhishma, all things in creation that you summon to mind will be as clear to you as fish in a limpid stream!'

Then the assembled Maharishis, with Vyasa among them, worship Krishna with hymns from the Riks, the Yajuses and the Samans. A heavenly shower of flowers of every season falls on the spot where Krishna sits, with Ganga's son and the son of Pandu. Celestial instruments of every kind play in the firmament, and the chorus of Apsaras begins to sing.

No evil and no portent of any evil can be seen here. A pure, auspicious breeze springs up, laden with every kind of fragrance. All the points of the compass become clear and quiet and all animals and birds begin to rove in peace. Soon, like a fire at the extremity of a great vana, the divine Surya of a thousand rays descends to the west. The Rishis then rise and salute Janardana, Bhishma and Yudhishtira. Upon this, Kesava and the sons of Pandu, along with Satyaki, Sanjaya and Saradwata's son Kripa, bow in reverence to the sages. Devoted to the practice of dharma, these Rishis, thus venerated by Kesava and others, return to their respective abodes, saying, 'We will return tomorrow.'

Krishna and the Pandavas, saluting Bhishma and circumambulating him, get into their handsome rathas. The heroes depart, accompanied by a host of chariots decked with golden kuvaras, mettlesome elephants looking like mountains, steeds fleet as Garudas and foot-soldiers armed with bows and other weapons. At great speed, the army travels in two divisions, one in the van and the other in the rear of the princes. The scene resembles the two currents of the great Narmada at the point where it is divided by the Rikshavat mountains straddling it.

Gladdening the great host, the divine Chandramas rises before it in the firmament to moisten anew the terrestrial herbs and plants whose juices the sun had sucked up. Then Krishna, that bull of Yadu's race, and the sons of Pandu, entering the Kuru city whose splendour resembles that of the city of Indra itself, return to their respective mansions like tired lions seeking their caves."

CANTO 53

Vaisampayana said, "Madhava retires to bed and sleeps contentedly. Awaking when only half a yaama remains to usher in the day, he commences his meditation. Fixing all his senses, he meditates on the eternal Brahma.

Then a group of sweet-voiced men, versed in Stotras and the Puranas, begin to recite the praises of Vasudeva, the lord of all creatures and Creator of the universe. Others begin to chant melodious hymns, marking the beat by clapping their hands, while minstrels raise their voices in song. Thousands blow conch-shells and beat drums. The spacious mansion of Krishna, resounding with the delightful strains of vinas, panavas and bamboo flutes, seems to be laughing with music. In the palace of King Yudhishtira, too, are heard songs, musical instruments and harmonious voices expressing auspicious wishes.

Krishna performs his ablutions. Joining his hands, the Mahabaho of unfading glory silently recites his secret mantras and, kindling a fire, pours into it libations of clarified butter. Giving away a thousand cattle to a thousand Brahmanas accomplished in mastery of the four Vedas, he causes them to shower blessings upon him.

Then, touching diverse auspicious articles and viewing himself ceremonially in a clear mirror, Krishna says to Satyaki, 'Go, O descendant of Sini, to Yudhishtira's abode and ascertain whether that king of great tejas is ready to visit Bhishma.'

Satyaki hastens to the royal son of Pandu and says, 'The best of Krishna's chariots is ready, Rajan, for Janardana to go to see Ganga's son Bhishma. O Dharmarajan of great splendour, he awaits you. You must decide what to do now.'

Dharma's son Yudhishtira says, 'Arjuna, let my best chariot be made ready. Soldiers will not accompany us today, and we will go forth alone. We should not vex the greatest Dharmatman, Bhishma, with a large gathering. Since from today Ganga's son will speak of things that are great mysteries, O son of Kunti, let the guards stay back.'

Arjuna leaves and returns with the best chariot harnessed. Yudhishtira, the twins, Bhima and Arjuna, like the five elements, then go towards Krishna's abode. While the noble Pandavas are on their way, the sagacious Krishna, accompanied by the grandson of Sini, mounts his ratha. Exchanging salutions with one another from their chariots and enquiring whether the night had passed contentedly, they ride without stopping on their chariots which rumble like clouds. Daruka urges on Krishna's steeds—Balahaka, Meghapushpa, Saibya and Sugriva. Endowed with great strength and speed, they fly ahead, marking the earth with their hooves and devouring the very skies.

Traversing the sacred field of Kuru, the princes reach the spot where the powerful Bhishma lies on his bed of arrows, surrounded by the great Rishis, like Brahma himself in the midst of Devas. Krishna, Yudhishtira, Bhima, Arjuna, the twins and Satyaki alight from their chariots and salute the Rishis by raising their right hands.

Yudhishtira, like Vasava walking towards Brahma, approaches Bhishma, surrounded by the Rishis like the moon thronged by stars. Overcome by apprehension, he timidly casts his eyes on the Mahabaho lying on his bed of arrows like the sun fallen from the sky."

CANTO 54

Janamejaya said, "Tell me, O Maharishi, what discourse results in that meeting after the battle, between the son of Santanu and Ganga, named Devavrata or Bhishma of unclouded glory, the Dharmatman of immense tejas lying on a hero's bed, firmly cleaving to truth, his passions under complete control, and the sons of Pandu sitting around him."

Vaisampayana replied, "Many Rishis and Siddhas, led by Narada, arrive at the spot where Bhishma lies on his bed of arrows. The surviving kings assembled by Yudhishtira—Dhritarashtra, Krishna, Bhima, Arjuna and the twins—approach Bhishma Pitamaha, who resembles the sun fallen from the sky, and lament for him.

Then Narada of godlike aspect, after reflecting for a short while, addresses the Pandavas and the surviving kings: 'The time, I think, has come for you to question Bhishma on dharma and artha, for he is like the sun on the point of setting, about to leave us. He is soon to give over his life's breath. All of you should therefore ask him to speak to you. He is acquainted with the varied dharma of all the four varnas. Old in years, he will attain high regions of bliss after abandoning his body. Request him immediately to clear the doubts that exist in your minds.'

The princes approach Bhishma, but are unable to ask him anything and gaze mutely at one another till Yudhishtira, addressing Krishna, says, 'There is none but you who can question the Pitamaha, O greatest of

Yadu's race. You are the highest among us all and know every duty and usage. Do you, Madhava, therefore speak first.'

Illustrious Kesava, of undimmed glory, approaching the unconquerable Bhishma, asks him, 'Have you, O best of kings, passed the night happily? Has your understanding become clear? Does your knowledge, sinless one, shine in you with inward light? I hope your heart no longer feels pain, and your mind is no longer agitated.'

Bhishma answers, 'Through your grace, Vasudeva, the burning, stupefaction, fatigue, exhaustion, illness and pain I felt have all left me in a single day. O you of incomparable splendour, because of your boon I see as clearly as a fruit placed in my hands all the past, future and present. All the dharma declared in the Vedas, all those laid down in the Vedantas, the dharma that virtuous men of learning have declared, I see clearly and remember, O you of unfading glory!

I also know, Janardana, the duties and practices prevailing in different countries and among particular tribes and families. Everything relating to the four varnas of life has come back to my memory. I am also acquainted with the dharma of kingship. I will say whatever should be said at the right time, Krishna, as by your grace I have acquired a blessed understanding. Strengthened by meditating on you, I feel as if I have become a young man again. Your favour has made me competent to hold a discourse on what is beneficial for the world. Why do you not yourself speak to Pandu's son on all that is good, O holy one? Please explain this, O Madhava!'

Vasudeva says, 'Recognize, Kurusthama, that I am the root of fame and of everything that leads to good. All things, good or bad, proceed from me. Who on earth will be surprised if the moon is said to be of cool rays? Similarly, I who have a full measure of fame already, can scarcely add to it by being described as the most illustrious one. It is your fame that I am resolved to enhance, and it is for this that I have inspired you with such prescience.

O Bhishma, lord of the earth, as long as the earth lasts will your fame travel with undiminished lustre through all the worlds. Whatever you say to the inquiring son of Pandu will be regarded everywhere to be as authoritative as the declarations of the Vedas. He who conducts himself according to your dictates here will obtain henceforth the reward of every meritorious action.

A man's achievements live as long as his prestige lasts in the world. For this reason, Bhishma, I have imparted to you divine understanding, so that your glory will be enhanced on earth. The surviving kings are sitting around you, eager to listen to your discourses on dharma and karma. Speak to them, O Bhaarata!

You are ripe in years and your life is consistent with the laws of the Srutis. You know well the duties of kings and every other aspect of dharma. No one has ever observed any transgression in you, from your very birth onwards. All the kings know that you have knowledge of all the sciences of dharma and karma. Like a father to his sons, advise them about the sanatana dharma.

You have always worshipped the Rishis and the Devas. You must talk about these in detail to men who wish to listen to your discourse on dharma and karma. A learned man should oblige, especially when asked by men of dharma. The Rishis have declared this a duty, O powerful one, and if you do not speak on these subjects, you will incur sin. Therefore, when your sons and grandsons ask you, O learned one, about the eternal duties of men, you must satisfy them, Bharatarishabha.'"

CANTO 55

Vaisampayana said, "Thus envigorated, Bhishma says, 'I will discourse on dharma. By your grace O Govinda, since you are the eternal atman of every being, my speech and mind have become steady. Let the Dharmatman Yudhishtira question me about dharma and karma, and I will be happy to speak on the subject.

Let the son of Pandu question me, the Rajarishi whose birth filled all the Vrishnis with joy, and who has no equal among all the Kurus, among all dharmatman and among men of great fame.

Let Yudhishtira Brahmacharya, who has intelligence, self-restraint, forgiveness, righteousness, mental vigour and energy, question me.

Let Yudhishtira, who by his good offices always honours his relatives, guests, servants and others who are dependent on him, ask me questions.

Let Yudhishtira, in whom are truth, charity, asceticism, heroism, peacefulness, cleverness and fearlessness, ask me questions.

Let Yudhishtira the Dharmatman, whom kama, artha or fear can never influence to commit sin, ask me questions.

Let the son of Pandu, who is ever devoted to truth, forgiveness, knowledge and cordiality, and who always makes gifts to the righteous, ask me questions.

Let Yudhishtira, who is always engaged in tapasya, the study of the Vedas and the practice of dharma and duty; who is ever tranquil and who has heard all the mysteries, ask me questions.'

Krishna says to Bhishma, 'King Yudhishtira the Just, overcome with mortification at having caused a great slaughter, and fearing your curse, dares not come near you. Having pierced with arrows those who deserved his veneration, those who were devoted to him, his acharyas, relatives, kinsmen and those worthy of his highest regard, he cannot pluck up the courage to approach you.'

Bhishma says, 'O Krishna, just as the dharma of the Brahmanas consists of practising charity, study and tapasya, the dharma of Kshatriyas is to kill or die in battle. A Kshatriya should slay all who engage with him in unjust battle—fathers, grandfathers, brothers, gurus, relatives and kinsmen. This is his declared dharma.

That Kshatriya who kills in battle his very acharyas if they happen to be sinful, covetous and disregardful of restraints and vows, O Kesava, is only doing his duty.

That Kshatriya who slays in battle the man who from covetousness disregards the eternal strictures of virtue, knows his duty.

That Kshatriya knows his duty who in battle makes the earth a lake of blood, with the hair of slain warriors like grass and straw floating on it, dead elephants for its rocks and banners for trees on its banks. A Kshatriya, when challenged, should always fight a battle, since a combat for dharma leads him to both Swarga and fame on earth, as Manu has said.'

Hearing Bhishma speak thus, Dharma's son Yudhishtira, with great humility, approaches the Kurupravira and stands in his range of vision. He falls at the feet of Bhishma, who in return gladdens him with words of affection, lovingly nuzzling his head, and asks him to take a seat, saying, Do not fear, Kurusthama! Ask me anything, O child, without any anxiety.'"

CANTO 56

Vaisampayana said, "Bowing to Hrishikesha, saluting Bhishma and taking the permission of all the seniors assembled there, Yudhishtira begins to question his Pitamaha.

Yudhishtira says, 'Men with knowledge of dharma and niti say that Rajadharma constitutes the highest science of dharma. I, too, think that the burden of these duties is exceedingly onerous. Tell us about the dharma of kings in detail, Pitamaha.

Rajadharma is the refuge of the whole world and, with artha and kama, is dependent on kingly duties. It is also clear that the practices that lead to moksha are equally dependent on them. Just as reins control the horse, the ankush or iron hook the elephant, Rajadharma is what keeps the world restrained and in check. If one does not grasp the dharma observed by Rajarishis, chaos will ensue on earth, and all will become confusion and anarchy.

As the rising sun dispels inauspicious darkness, so does Rajadharma prevent every kind of evil in this world. Therefore, O Pitamaha, for my sake, discuss the subject of this dharma first, for you are the greatest of all men that know dharma. O Parantapa, Vasudeva has declared you the wisest of men and so all of us expect to learn the highest knowledge from you.'

Bhishma says, 'Bowing to Dharma who is Supreme, Krishna who is entirely Brahman and to the Brahmanas, I will discourse on the eternal duties of men. Listen to me, Yudhishtira, with concentration, while I describe in precise detail the whole range of Rajadharma and other responsibilities that you wish to understand.

Firstly, O Kurusthama, the king, from a desire to please his subjects, should wait humbly upon the Devas and the Brahmanas, always abiding by the law. By worshipping them, the king pays off his debt to dharma and niti and receives the respect of his subjects.

You should always act promptly, Yudhishtira, for without timely action, mere destiny can never accomplish the objects cherished by kings. Effort and destiny are equal in their operation. Of the two, I regard action to be the superior, for destiny is contingent upon effort. Do not indulge in grief if what has begun at first ends disastrously, for you should then exert yourself on the same task with redoubled diligence. This is the great duty of kings.

There is nothing that contributes so much to the success of kings as Satya. The king devoted to Truth finds happiness both here and after death. For Rishis too, O Rajan, Truth is their greatest wealth. Similarly, there is nothing that inspires as much confidence in kings as Satya. The monarch who is possessed of every accomplishment and good conduct, who is self-restrained, humble and follows his dharma, who has his passions under control, who is personable and liberal, never loses prosperity.

By administering justice, by attending to three principles—concealment of his own weaknesses, discovery of the weaknesses of enemies and keeping his own counsel—and by the observance of straightforward conduct, the king obtains prosperity, O Kurusthama. If he is mild, everybody disregards him. On the other hand, if he becomes fierce, his subjects are troubled. Therefore, observe both kinds of policy.

Never punish the Brahmanas, for the Brahmana is the greatest of men on earth. The Dharmatman Manu sang two slokas in respect of your duties, which you should always bear in mind: "Fire has sprung from water, the Kshatriya from the Brahmana and iron from stone. The three—fire, Kshatriya and iron—can exert their force on every other thing, but when they come into contact with their respective progenitors, their force is neutralized." When iron strikes stone, or fire combats water, or a Kshatriya cherishes enmity towards a Brahmana, all three become weak.

This being so, O Rajan, you will see that the Brahmanas are worthy of homage. Those who are the best among the Brahmanas are Devas on earth. Duly revered, they uphold the Vedas and the yagnas. But those who want to gain such honour but are impediments to the three worlds, Purushavyaghra, should always be subdued by the might of your arms.

Listen with concentrated attention to the two slokas sung by the great Rishi Usanas, in the olden days. "The righteous Kshatriya, mindful of his dharma, should punish a Brahmana, even though he may be the very master of the Vedas, if he rushes to do battle with an uplifted weapon." The Kshatriya who upholds dharma when someone transgresses it, does not thereby become a sinner, for the rage of the assailant justifies the wrath of the punisher. Subject to these restrictions, you should protect the Brahmanas. If they become offenders, you should exile them from your dominions. But even when they deserve punishment, you should show them compassion.

No corporal punishment is for them. If a Brahmana is guilty of Brahmahatya, or of violating the bed of his acharyas or other revered seniors, or of causing miscarriage, or of treason against the king, his punishment should be banishment from your dominions. Those who show respect towards the Brahmanas should be favoured with offices in the state.

No treasure is more valuable to kings than the selection and keeping of servants. Among the six kinds of citadels cited in the shastras, the ready service and love of subjects is the most impregnable. Therefore, the wise king should always show compassion towards the four varnas of his subjects. The king who is a Dharmatman and truthful will succeed in gratifying his people.

However, you must not always forgive everybody, for the king who is mild is regarded like an elephant that is no longer bellicose. In the shastras, Brihaspati has composed a sloka which was applicable to this in ancient times. Listen as I recite it: "If the king happens to be always forgiving, the lowest of men prevail over him, like the man who sits on the head of the elephant he guides."

The king, therefore, should not always be lenient, nor should he always be fierce. He should be like the vernal sun—neither cold, nor hot enough to produce sweat. He should judge friends and foes by the direct evidence of the senses, by conjecture, by comparisons and by the canons of the shastras, O Rajan.

O you of great kindness, avoid all those evil practices that are called Vyasanas. While it is not essential for you never to indulge in them, do not be attached to them, for everyone prevails over one who is addicted to these.

A king who has no love for his people fills them with anxiety. The king should always conduct himself towards his subjects as a mother towards her unborn child—as one who, for the good of her child, relinquishes those things that she herself most treasures.

For the sake of what will benefit his people, Kurusthama, a righteous king's behaviour towards them should always be as towards a cherished elder.

You should always be determined, O son of Pandu. The king who is possessed of fortitude and who is known to inflict punishment on wrong-doers has no cause of fear.

You should not indulge in jests with your servants, O foremost of speakers. Rajan, observe the drawbacks of such indulgence. If the master mingles too freely with them, they begin to disregard him and, forgetting their status, overstep that of the master. Ordered to do a job, they hesitate. They divulge the master's secrets. They ask for things that should not be asked for, and take the food intended for the master. They go to the extent of manifesting annoyance and seeking to outshine the master. They even seek to dominate the king by accepting bribes, practising deceit and obstructing state business. They cause the state to rot through abuses by falsification and forgeries.

They make love with the female guards of the palace and dress in the same style as their master. They become shameless enough to indulge in belching and the like, and expectorating in the very presence of their master. They do not fear to speak of him with levity before others. If the king becomes mild and disposed to jest, his servants, disregarding him, ride on horses and elephants and chariots as good as his. His counsellors, assembled in court, openly say to their sovereign, "This is beyond your capacity. This is a wrong course."

If the king becomes angry, they laugh. They are not contented even when favours are bestowed upon them, though they may express satisfaction for other reasons. They disclose the secret counsels of their master and talk about his evil deeds. Without the least anxiety, they annul the king's commands. If the king's jewels, or food, or the necessaries of his bath, or cosmetics are not forthcoming, the servants show no concern, even in his presence. Instead of taking what is rightfully theirs, they appropriate what belongs to the king. They wish to sport with him as with a bird tied with a string, always giving people to understand that he is very intimate with them and loves them dearly. If the king is easy-going and disposed to jest, O Yudhishtira, these and many other evils spring from his demeanour.'"

CANTO 57

"Bhishma says, 'The king, O Yudhishtira, should always be ready for action. That ruler who, like a woman, is unfitted for exertion is not worthy of praise. In this connection, the holy Sanas quotes a sloka. Listen with attention, as I recite it to you: "Like a snake swallowing mice, the earth swallows these two—the king averse to battle, and the Brahmana excessively attached to wives and children." You should always bear this in mind, O Purushavyaghra.

Make peace with those enemies with whom you should make peace according to the laws, and wage war with whom you should wage war. Whether it is your guru or your friend, you should slay those who act inimically towards any of the seven limbs of your kingdom—the king, army, counsellors, friends, treasury, territory and forts.

There is an ancient sloka about the duty of kings, sung by King Marutta, which is in concord with Brihaspati's opinion. According to the shastras, there is punishment for even the acharya if he becomes haughty and disregardful of what should be done and what should not, and if he transgresses all restraints.

Jadu's wise son, King Sagara, out of benevolence towards his people, exiled his own eldest son Asamanjas. Asamanjas used to drown children in the Sarayu, for which his father repudiated him and sent him into exile. The Rishi Uddalaka cast off his favourite son Swetaketu, a mahatapasvin in his later years, because he used to deceive Brahmanas, after inviting them with promises of entertainment.

The eternal dharma of kings is the happiness of their subjects, observance of truth and sincerity of conduct. The king should not covet the riches of others, but rather, over time, distribute wealth. If he is proficient, truthful in speech and forgiving in temper, prosperity will always attend him. With his soul cleansed of vices, the king should be able to govern his anger, and all his decisions should be in conformity with the shastras. He should always pursue dharma, artha, kama and moksha judiciously, but conceal his counsel in respect of these.

No greater evil can befall the king than the disclosure of his counsel. Kings should protect the four varnas in the discharge of their dharma. It is their perpetual duty to prevent a confusion of dharmas in respect of the varnas. The king should not repose confidence in those other than his own servants, nor full confidence even in them.

He should, by his own judgement, use to advantage the merits and defects of the six essential requisites of sovereignty—peace with a stronger foe, war with one of equal strength, invading the dominions of one who is weaker, halting, seeking protection if weak in one's own citadel and sowing dissension among the chief officers of the enemy. The king who studies the lapses of his foes judiciously, pursues dharma, artha and kama, who sets clever spies to ascertain secrets and to wean away the officers of his enemies by gifts of wealth, deserves commendation.

The king should administer justice like Yama and amass wealth like Kubera. He should observe the merits and defects of his acquisitions and losses, as well as those of his own dominions. He should feed those who have not been fed and enquire after those who have been fed. He should be of sweet speech and speak with a smiling, not sour, countenance. He should always attend to his elders and repress procrastination. He should never covet what belongs to others, and should be careful to follow dharma in his conduct. He should never take wealth from dharmatmans but, instead, seize the wealth of those who do not follow dharma and give it to those who do.

The king should himself be skilful in taking strong action, but should also practise kindness. He should have his mind under control. He should dress magnificently, give gifts when required, have regular meals and be of good conduct. The king who desires prosperity should always have in his service men who are brave, devoted, incapable of being deceived by enemies, healthy, well-behaved, well-born and connected with families of impeccable conduct. They should be respectable, never insult others, possess knowledge of all the sciences, be familiar with the world and its affairs, be unmindful of the future, always do their duties honestly and remain as steadfast as mountains.

There should be no difference between the king and them as regards the objects of enjoyment. The only distinction should consist in his sphere of influence and his power of passing orders. His demeanour towards them, before or after, should be the same. The king who behaves in this way never comes to grief.

His own servants and relatives soon eliminate the crooked and covetous king who suspects everybody and who taxes his subjects heavily. The king who follows dharma and sets about attracting the hearts of his people never succumbs when enemies attack him. Even if overcome, he soon regains his position.

If the king is not wrathful, not addicted to evil ways and not severe in his punishments, if he keeps his passions under control, he becomes an object of confidence to all, as the Himavat mountain is to all creatures.

He is the best of kings who is wise, charitable, personable, prompt in action, ready to take advantage of the lapses of foes, who knows what is bad for each of the four varnas of his subjects, who has his anger under control and is not short-tempered or vindictive, who is high-minded and engages in yagnas and other religious rites, who is not given to boasting and who vigorously accomplishes all work that he commences.

He is the best of kings in whose dominions men live fearlessly, like sons in the house of their father. He is the best of kings whose subjects do not have to hide their wealth and who know what is good and bad for them.

He is a king indeed whose subjects are engaged in their respective svadharmas and do not fear to die in the line of duty, whose people, duly protected, are of peaceful behaviour, docile, tractable, unwilling to be drawn into disputes, and inclined to liberality.

That king earns eternal merit in whose dominions there is no wickedness, dissimulation, deception and envy.

That king truly deserves to rule who honours knowledge, who is devoted to the shastras and the good of his people, who treads in the path of dharma and is liberal.

That king deserves to rule whose spies, counsels and deeds, accomplished and unaccomplished, remain unknown to his enemies.

O Bhaarata, Usanas of Bhrigu's race, sang the following verse in olden days in the narrative called Ramacharita, on the subject of Rajadharma: "One should first select a king in whose dominions one would prefer to live, only then seek a wife and acquire wealth. If there is no king, what will become of wife and acquisitions?"

There is no dharma more obligatory for those who seek to rule than the protection of subjects. The shelter the king grants to his subjects upholds the world.

Manu, the son of Prachetas, sang two verses respecting the duties of kings. Listen to them with attention: "These six men should be avoided like a leaky boat on the sea: an acharya who does not speak, a priest who has not studied the shastras, a king who does not ensure protection, a wife who says what is disagreeable, a cowherd who prefers to rove within the village and a barber who longs to go to the the vana.""

CANTO 58

"Bhishma says, 'Security of subjects, Yudhishtira, is the very essence of kingly duties. The divine Brihaspati does not applaud any duty as much as this one. The Mahatapasvi Kavi Usanas, the thousand-eyed Indra, Manu, the son of Prachetas, the divine Bharadwaja and the sage Gaurasiras, all devoted to Brahman and Brahmavadis, have composed treatises on the dharma of kings. All of them praise the duty of protection in respect of kings.

Yudhishtira, of eyes like lotus leaves and complexion of copper, listen to how you can fulfill the duty of safeguarding your subjects: by giving them their just dues without haughtiness, collecting taxes with consideration, never taking anything from them capriciously and without cause, selecting honest men for discharging administrative functions, seeking the good of the people, employing spies and servants, producing discord and disunion among the enemy by fair or unfair means; it requires adroitness in transacting business, heroism and truthfulness.

It also consists in inflicting corporal punishment and fines justly, never abandoning the honest, granting employment and shelter to men of respectable birth, storing what should be retained and keeping company with intelligent men.

It always includes the comfort of your troops, Yudhishtira, supervision of the people, steadiness in the transaction of business, filling of the treasury, absence of blind confidence in the guards of the city, fostering disloyalty among the citizens of a hostile town, supporting friends and allies living in the midst of the enemy's country, distrusting and strictly watching the servants and officers of the state, personally observing the city, comforting the enemy with assurances, steadily observing the dictates of policy, remaining ready for action, never disregarding an enemy, and eliminating those who are evil.

Brihaspati has said that readiness for action is the root of Rajadharma. Listen to the verses he sang: "Amrita was obtained by toil, the Asuras were slain by effort, Indra himself obtained sovereignty in Swarga and on Bhumi by exerting himself. The hero of work is superior to the hero of speech. The heroes of speech gratify and worship the heroes of work."

An intelligent king who does not exert himself is like a snake without poison, always overcome by his enemies. A king, however strong, should not disregard an enemy, however weak. A spark can kindle a conflagration, and a particle of poison can kill. With only one kind of force, an enemy from within a fort can hold off the whole country of even a powerful and prosperous king.

The secret utterances of the king, the amassing of troops for seizing victory, the crooked purposes in his heart for accomplishing particular objects, and the wrong deeds he does or intends to do, should be concealed by putting on an appearance of frankness. He should act righteously in order to rule over his people. Men of crooked minds cannot bear the burden of an extensive empire. A ruler who is mild cannot acquire superior rank, which depends upon hard work.

A kingdom coveted by all like meat can never be protected by candour and simplicity. Therefore, Yudhishtira, a king should always conduct himself with both frankness and crookedness. If in protecting his subjects a king falls into danger, he earns great merit. This is what the conduct of kings should be. I have now told you only a portion of the duties of kings. Tell me, Kurusthama, what else you wish to know.'

The illustrious Vyasa, Devasthana, Aswa, Vasudeva, Kripa, Satyaki and Sanjaya, all happy and with faces resembling full-blown flowers, exclaim, 'Excellent! Excellent!' and hymn the praises of Bhishma Purushavyaghra.

Then Yudhishtira, with a sorrowful heart and in tears, gently touches Bhishma's feet and says, 'Pitamaha, tomorrow I will ask questions about which I have doubts, for today the sun, having sucked the moisture out of all terrestrial objects, is about to set.'

Kesava, Kripa, Yudhishtira and others, saluting the Brahmanas assembled there and circumambulating Ganga's great son, cheerfully climb into their chariots. All of them, strict observers of vows, then bathe in the current of the Drishadwati. They offer oblations of water to their ancestors, silently reciting the sacred mantras. After performing the evening pujas, these Parantapas enter the city of Hastinapura."

CANTO 59

Vaisampayana said, "Rising from their beds the next day and performing the morning pujas according to the shastras, the Pandavas and the Yadavas set out on their chariots, which resemble fortified towns, for the place where Bhishma lies. They ride to Kurukshetra, approach the sinless Bhishma and enquire whether the best of maharathas had passed the night happily. They then salute all the Rishis and, getting their blessings in return, the princes take their seats around Bhishma.

Then the Dharmarajan, Yudhishtira, after paying respects to Bhishma, says with joined hands, 'Tell me O Bhaarata, when did the word Rajan—King—begin to be used on earth?

Parantapa, why does one man—the king, with hands, arms and neck like others, with understanding and senses like others, with a back, mouth, stomach, bones, marrow, flesh, blood and semen similar to those of the rest of the world, inhaling and exhaling like others, with life-breath and body like other men, resembling others in birth and death, subject to the same kinds of joy and grief, in fact, similar to all others in all attributes of humanity, come to govern the rest of the world containing many other men possessing equal intelligence and bravery?

Since when has one man ruled the wide world, teeming with brave, powerful and high-born men of dharma? Why do all men try to win his favour? Why is it that when this one man is delighted, the whole world is delighted, and if this one man is troubled, the whole world is troubled? I want to hear this in detail, Bharatarishabha! O greatest of speakers, tell me fully, for there must be a serious reason for all this, since we see that the whole world bows down to a single man as to a Deva.'

Bhishma says, 'With concentrated attention on every detail, listen to how sovereignty first began in the Krita yuga. At first, there was no sovereignty, no king, no punishment and no punisher. All men used to protect one another righteously. However, with time they found this task to be irksome. Uncertainty began to assail their hearts; their perceptions became clouded and their virtue began to decline.

When this happened, they became covetous. Because men sought to possess objects they did not own, another passion called greed seized them. When they became subject to kama, another passion, krodha or anger, soon tainted them. Once subject to wrath, they lost all consideration of what they should do and what they should not. Unrestrained sexual indulgence set in. Men began to speak as they pleased. All distinctions disappeared between clean and unclean food, between virtue and vice. When this confusion set in amongst men, the Vedas disappeared.

Upon the disappearance of the Vedas, dharma was lost. When both the Vedas and dharma were lost, the Devas were filled with dread. Overcome with fear, they sought the protection of Brahma.

Having gratified the divine Grandfather of the universe, the Devas sorrowfully said to him with folded hands, "O Devadeva, greed and error have crept into the eternal Vedas in the world of men, and we are terror-stricken. Through the loss of the Vedas, men have lost dharma too, because of which we fear that we ourselves are about to descend to the level of humans.

Men used to pour libations and feed us, while we used to pour rain downwards. But with the cessation of all pious pujas among men, great distress threatens us. O Pitamaha, think of what will benefit us, so that the universe which your power created will not be destroyed."

Thus addressed, the Swayambhuva and divine Lord said to them, "I will think of what should be done for the good to all. Best of Devas, let your fears be dispelled!"

Brahma then composed by his own intelligence a treatise consisting of a hundred thousand chapters. He treated in it three subjects, dharma, artha and kama, and designated it as the triune aggregate. He treated a fourth subject called moksha with opposite meaning and attributes. In it he dealt with the attributes of sattwa, rajas and tamas and a fourth—nishkama karma, the practice of dharma without hope of bliss or reward in this or the other world, which will lead to moksha, liberation.

He included another triple aggregate connected with punishment—conversation, growth and destruction—and in yet another an aggregate of six consisting of the hearts of men, place, time, means, overt deeds, alliances and causes. In it, Bharatarishabha, he laid down the religious rites prescribed in the three Vedas, knowledge and the actions necessary for the support of life—agriculture, trade and commerce, and the very extensive branch of learning called punitive legislation.

The treatise also dealt fully with the attributes of princes, behaviour towards counsellors, spies, secret agents envoys and agents of other kinds, of conciliation, fomenting discord, gifts and punishment, with toleration as the fifth one. He described in detail deliberation of all kinds, counsels for producing dissension, the errors of deliberation, the results of the success or failure of counsels, treaties of three kinds: bad, average and good, made through fear, good offices and gifts of wealth.

In it he also described in detail the four appropriate times for making journeys, three kinds of victory that one secures—righteously, by wealth, or by deceitful means, and also the three types of qualities—bad, average and good—of counsellors, kingdom, fort, army and treasury.

The treatise dealt in detail with the eight kinds of open punishment and the eight kinds of secret punishment. Chariots, elephants, horses, foot-soldiers, conscripted labourers and crews, the paid attendants of armies, guides taken from the country which is the theatre of war: these are the eight instruments, O Kauravya, of open punishment or forces acting openly.

The work also mentioned the three kinds of things—apparel, food and incantations—the use and administration of moveable and immoveable poisons, and delineated enemies, allies and neutrals.

Brahma discussed in the work, the diverse features of roads to be taken, depending on astrological configurations, the attributes of the soil on which to encamp, protection of oneself, superintendence of the construction of chariots and other machinery of war and their use, methods for protecting and improving men, elephants, chariots and horses, various kinds of battle formations, strategies and manoeuvres in war, planetary conjunctions foreboding evil and natural calamities such as earthquakes.

He wrote of skilful methods of warfare and retreat, knowledge of weapons and their proper upkeep, disorders of troops and how to be rid of them, the means of inspiring the army with joy and confidence, of diseases, times of distress and danger, of how to guide the army in battle, the methods of sounding alarms and notifying orders, how to cause fear in the enemy by display of standards, the diverse methods of afflicting the enemy's kingdom by means of robbers, fierce wild tribes, fire-raisers, poisoners and forgers.

He discussed how to produce disunion among the chief officers of hostile armies by cutting down crops and plants, destroying the efficiency of the enemy's elephants by sounding alarms, and honouring those among the enemy's subjects who are well disposed towards the invader.

The work discussed the growth, harmony and waste of the seven essential requisites of sovereignty: the capacity for projected works, the means of accomplishing them, the methods of extending the kingdom, the means of winning over men dwelling in the enemy's territory, the punishment and destruction of those who are strong, the exact administration of justice, the extermination of evil, wrestling, shooting, discharging weapons, the methods of making gifts and of storing requisite provisions and diverse matters.

Brahma wrote on the subject of feeding the hungry and supervising those whom one has fed, gifts of wealth in season, freedom from the vices called Vyasanas, the attributes of kings, the qualifications of military officers, the sources of the aggregate of three and its merits and demerits, diverse kinds of evil intents, the behaviour of dependents, suspicion against all, the avoidance of negligence, the acquisition of coveted objects, the improvement of objects already acquired and the gifting of them to deserving men, and the expenditure of wealth for religious purposes, for acquiring objects of desire and for dispelling danger and distress.

In the work, O Kurusthama, the Swayambhuva mentions the four kinds of vices which the learned say are born of kama—hunting, gambling, drinking and sexual indulgence—and the six kinds of vices born of anger—rudeness of speech, fierceness, severity of chastisement, infliction of pain, frustrating one's own objects and suicide.

The treatise describes diverse kinds of machines and their action. It deals with devastation of the enemy's territories, attacks upon enemies, the destruction and removal of landmarks, the cutting down of large trees to deprive the enemy and his subjects of their refreshing shade, the siege of forts, the supervision of agriculture and other useful operations, the storage of necessaries, the robes and attire for troops and the best means of manufacturing them, and the characteristics and uses of panavas, anakas, conches and drums.

The work duly deals, Yudhishtira, with the six kinds of articles—gems, animals, lands, robes, female slaves and gold—and the means of acquiring them for oneself or destroying them to injure the enemy, pacifying newly acquired territories, honouring the good, cultivating friendship with the learned, knowing the rules in respect of gifts and religious rites such as homa, and ceremonial touching of auspicious articles.

The work deals with how to pay attention to beautifying the body and the seventy-two actions laid down in medical works for the protection, exercise and improvement of the body, the manner of preparing and using food, piety of behaviour, the attainment of prosperity by following one path, truthfulness and sweetness in speech, observance of activities undertaken on festive occasions, social gatherings within and beyond the household, the open and secret actions of men in all places of meeting, the constant supervision of men's conduct, the immunity of Brahmanas from punishment, the reasonable infliction of punishment, and honours paid to dependents in consideration of kinship and merit. It also deals with the protection of subjects and the means of extending the kingdom, the counsels that a king who lives in the midst of a dozen kings should pursue in respect of the four kinds of enemies, the four kinds of allies and the four kinds of neutrals, and the practices of particular countries, tribes and families.

The work covers the subjects of dharma, artha, kama and moksha and lays down the desire for diverse kinds of wealth and the diverse means of its acquisition, the system of agriculture and other activities that form the chief source of revenue, various methods of producing and applying illusions and how one can render stagnant water foul. It describes the way, O Naravyaghra, by which men can be prevented from deviating from the path of dharma and honesty.

Having composed this highly beneficial treatise, the divine Lord cheerfully said to the deities led by Indra, "For the good of the world and for establishing dharma, artha and kama, I have composed this tract representing the very essense of speech. Assisted by punishment and dealing with rewards and punishments, this science will operate among men and will protect the world. Moreover, because men are led to the acquisition of the objects of their existence by punishment, which in fact leads or governs everything, this science will be known in the three worlds as Dandaneeti—the science of punishment.

Containing the essence of all the attributes of the six gunas, this science will always be highly regarded by all noble men. I have dealt in it with dharma, artha, kama and moksha."

After this, the lord of Uma—the divine and multiform Siva of large eyes, the source of all blessings, first studied and mastered it. However, in view of the gradual decrease of the life-span of human beings, the divine Siva abridged this great shastra that Brahma had compiled. Mahatapasvin Indra, devoted to Brahma, received the abridged version called Vaisalakasha, consisting of ten thousand lessons.

The divine Indra abridged it further into a treatise consisting of five thousand lessons and called it Vahudantaka. Later the powerful and intelligent Brihaspati further abridged the work into a treatise consisting of three thousand lessons and called it Barhaspatya.

Finally, the famous and immeasurably wise acharya of Yoga-Kavi reduced it further into a work of a thousand lessons.

Thus did the Maharishis abridge the work for the benefit of the world, in view of the shortening life-span of men and their general decline. The gods, then, approaching the lord of creatures, Vishnu, said to him, "Indicate, O Deva, the one among mortals who deserves to have superiority over the rest."

The divine and powerful Narayana, reflecting a little, by an order of his will created a son to be born of his energy, named Virajas. However, the highly blessed Virajas did not desire sovereignty over the earth, as he was inclined to the life of a sannyasi. Virajas had a son named Krittimat who also renounced pleasure and enjoyment. Krittimat's son Kardama also practised severe tapasya, but his son Ananga was pious, a protector of living things, and fully conversant with the Dandaneeti.

Ananga had a son named Ativala, well versed in policy. However, after inheriting an extensive empire at the demise of his father, he became the slave of his passions. Mrityu had a daughter born of his mind, named Sunita, who was celebrated throughout the three worlds. She was married to Ativala and gave birth to a son named Vena. Vena, a slave of wrath and malice, became vicious and sinful in his conduct towards all creatures.

The Rishis, Brahmavadis, slew him with weapons of blades of Kusa infused with their mantras. They pierced the right thigh of Vena and from that thigh emerged a short-limbed man resembling a charred brand, with bloodshot eyes and black hair.

These Brahmavadis said to him, "Nishida, sit here!" From him have sprung the Nishadas—those evil tribes that have the hills and the forests for their abode, and the hundreds and thousands of others called Mlechchhas, who live in the Vindhya mountains.

The great Rishis then pierced the right arm of Vena, from where sprang a man who was a second Indra in form. Clad in mail, armed with swords, bows and arrows and adept in the science of weapons, he knew the Vedas and their branches thoroughly. He knew all the laws of the Dandaneeti, O Rajan, in their embodied forms.

The son of Vena then, with joined hands, said to these Maharishis, "I have attained an understanding that is keen and conforms to dharma. Instruct me in what I should do with it. I will accomplish without hesitation any task that you indicate."

The Devas and the Rishis who were present there said to Vena's son, "Fearlessly accomplish all those tasks in which dharma resides. Disregard what is dear and what is not, look upon all men with an equal eye. Cast away kama, krodha, lobha and distinction and always follow the dictates of dharma, punishing with your own hands the man, whoever he may be, who deviates from the path of duty. Swear that you will in thought, word and deed, always maintain the religion of the Vedas on earth. Pledge that you will courageously maintain the dharma laid down in the Vedas with the aid of the Dandaneeti, and will never act capriciously. O mighty one, acknowledge that Brahmanas are exempt from punishment, and vow also that you will protect the world from an intermixture of the castes."

Thus addressed, Vena's son Prithu replied to the assembled deities headed by the Rishis, "I will always worship those bulls among men, the greatly blessed Brahmanas."

These Brahmavadis then said to him, "Tathaastu! Let it be so!"

Then Sukra, the vast receptacle of Brahman, became his priest. The Balakhilyas became his counsellors and the Saraswatas his companions. The great and illustrious Rishi Garga became his astrologer.

Men believe the high declaration of the Srutis that Prithu is the eighth from Vishnu. Before that, two men named Suta and Magadha were born, who became his bards and eulogists. Gratified, Prithu, the royal son of powerful Vena, gave to Suta the land lying on the sea-coast and to Magadha the country since known as Magadha.

We hear that the surface of the earth was once very uneven. It was Prithu who levelled it. In every Manvantara, the earth becomes uneven. Vena's son moved the rocky masses lying all around, O Rajan, with the horn of his bow. By this the hills and mountains became lofty.

Then Vishnu, the Devas of Indra, the Rishis, the Regents of the world and the Brahmanas assembled for the coronation of Prithu as the king of the world.

The earth herself, in her embodied form, came to him with a tribute of gems and jewels. Varuna, the lord of rivers, Himavat, the king of mountains and Sakra bestowed upon him inexhaustible wealth. The great Meru, the mountain of gold, gave him enormous masses of the precious metal. Divine Kubera, the lord of Yakshas and Rakshasas, gave him wealth, borne on the shoulders of human beings, enough to gratify the needs of dharma, artha and kama.

Millions of horses, chariots, elephants and men, O son of Pandu, sprang to life as soon as Vena's son Prithu thought of them.

Due to the protection promised by Prithu, neither old age, nor famine, nor calamity, nor disease on earth burdened mankind, nor fear of reptiles or thieves, or from any other quarter. When Prithu went to the sea, its water became solidified. The mountains gave him passage, and his standard was obstructed nowhere. He drew from the earth, like a milcher from a cow, seventeen kinds of crops for the food of Yakshas, Rakshasas, Nagas and other beings. That noble king caused all men to regard dharma as the best of all things and, because he gratified all the people, he was called Rajan, King; and because he also healed the wounds of Brahmanas, he earned the name of Kshatriya; and because the earth during his reign became celebrated for the practice of dharma, she came to be called Prithvi.

The eternal Vishnu himself, Bhaarata, confirmed his power, telling him, "No one, O Rajan, shall transcend you." As a result of the tapasya Prithu performed, the divine Vishnu entered his body. It is for this reason that the entire universe offers worship to Prithu and he is numbered among the gods.

Rajan, your kingdom should always be protected by the science of punishment, the Dandaneeti. By careful observation made through the movements of your spies, you must also ensure its safety in such a way that no one will be able to injure it. All good deeds, Rajan, lead to the benefit of the king. The conduct of a king should be regulated by his own intelligence and also by the opportunities and means that offer themselves. What cause can there be for the multitude to live in obedience to one, save the divinity of the king?

At that time, a golden lotus emerged from Vishnu's brow and the goddess Sree was born of the lotus. She became the spouse of sagacious Dharma. Sree and Dharma had a son Artha and all three, Dharma, Artha and Sree, became established in sovereignty.

Upon the exhaustion of his punya, a man comes down from heaven to earth and takes birth as a king who knows the science of danda. Such a man is endowed with greatness and is really an amsa of Vishnu on earth. He acquires great acumen and obtains superiority over others. The Devas establish him, so no one can transcend him. It is for this reason that everybody acts in obedience to such a one, and that the world cannot command him. Good actions, Rajan, engender good. It is for this that the multitude obeys the king's commands, though he belongs to the same world and is possessed of similar limbs and organs as all men.

He who once beheld Prithu's amiable face became submissive to him, esteeming him as handsome, wealthy and highly favoured. It is because of the might of his sceptre that the practice of dharma and just behaviour became so visible on earth and Bhumi was overspread with virtue.

Yudhishtira, Brahma's treatise contained the histories of all past events, the origin of the Maharishis, the holy waters, the planets, stars and astronomy, the duties in respect of the four varnas of life, the four kinds of Homa, the characteristics of the four orders of men and the four branches of learning. Whatever objects there are on earth he included in it: the Itihasas, the Vedas, the science of Nyaya, tapasyas, gyana, abstention from injury to all beings, truth, falsehood and mahadharma. He fully described in it reverence towards the elderly, gifts, purity of behaviour, alacrity in exertion and compassion towards all men. There is no doubt in this. Since that time, O Rajan, the learned began to say that there is no difference between a Deva and a Rajan.

I have now told you everything about the greatness of kings. What subject, O king of the Bhaaratas, shall I speak of next?'"

CANTO 60

Vaisampayana said, "After this, Yudhishtira salutes his Pitamaha Bhishma, the son of Ganga, attentively with joined hands and asks again, 'What are the general duties of the four varnas and the special duties of each varna? What mode of life should each varna adopt?

What duties are especially called Rajadharma? By what means does a kingdom grow, and what are the means by which the king himself advances? How also, O Bharatarishabha, do the citizens and the servants of the king progress? What sorts of forts, treasuries, punishments, allies, counsellors, priests and acharyas, should a king avoid? Whom should the king trust in different kinds of distress and danger? From what evils should the king guard himself firmly? Tell me all this, O Pitamaha!'

Bhishma says, 'I make my obeisance to dharma, who is great, and to Krishna who is Brahman. Having bowed also to the Brahmanas assembled here, I will discuss duties that are ananta—eternal. Suppression of anger, truthfulness of speech, justice, forgiveness, legitimate fatherhood, purity of conduct, avoidance of quarrels, simplicity and care for dependants— these nine duties belong equally to all the four varnas.

I will now tell you the responsibilities which belong exclusively to Brahmanas. Self-restraint, O Rajan, the shastras declare to be the first duty of Brahmanas. Study of the Vedas and patience in undergoing tapasya are also their responsibility. By carrying out these two, they accomplish all the dharma laid down for them. If, while engaged in the observance of his svadharma, and without doing anything improper, a peaceful, learned Brahmana acquires wealth, he should marry, procreate, practise charity and perform yagnas.

The wise declare that wealth thus obtained should be enjoyed by distributing it among deserving men and relatives. By his study of the Vedas, the Brahmana accomplishes all the pious work laid down for him. Whether or not he achieves anything else, if he devotes himself to the study of the Vedas, he becomes known as a Brahmana or friend of all creatures.

I will also tell you, Bhaarata, the dharma of a Kshatriya. A Kshatriya should give, not beg, should himself perform yagnas, but not officiate as a priest in the yagnas of others. He should never teach the Vedas but study them with the help of a Brahmana acharya. He should protect the people by exerting himself always to destroy robbers and evil-doers, and should demonstrate his prowess in battle.

Those among Kshatriya rulers who perform great yagnas, who are gyanis of the Vedas and who gain victory in battle, become foremost among those who acquire blessed realms in the hereafter through their punya. Men who know the ancient shastras do not applaud the warrior who returns unscathed from battle but, rather, declare him to be a paltry Kshatriya.

There is no higher duty for a Kshatriya than the suppression of brigands. Gifts, study and sacrifices bring prosperity to kings. Therefore, a king who desires to acquire punya should engage in battle. The king should ensure not only that all his subjects observe their respective duties, but also that they follow the dictates of dharma. If he only protects his subjects, whether or not he does anything else, he is considered to be one who has accomplished all meritorious deeds and is worthy of being called a Kshatriya, the greatest of men.

I will now tell you, Yudhishtira, what the eternal dharma of the Vaisya is. A Vaisya should give gifts, study the Vedas, perform sacrifices and acquire wealth by fair means. He should also protect and rear all domestic animals with proper care, like a father nurturing his sons. Anything else that he does will be inappropriate for him. By protecting his domestic animals, he will obtain great happiness, since the Creator, after fashioning these animals, bestowed their care upon the Vaisya. Upon the Brahmana and the Kshatriya he conferred the care of all living things.

I will tell you how the Vaisya is to earn the means of his sustenance. If he looks after six cattle for others, he can take the milk of one cow as his remuneration, and if he keeps a hundred cattle for others, he may take a single pair as his fee. If he trades with others' wealth, he can take a seventh part of the profits as his share. One-seventh also is his share in the profits arising from the trade in horns, but he should take one-sixteenth if the trade is in hooves. If he engages in cultivation with seeds supplied by others, he can receive a seventh part of the yield. This should be his annual remuneration. A Vaisya should always be ready to tend cattle. If he is ready to do so, no one else should be employed for the task.

I will tell you, O Bhaarata, what the duties of a Sudra are. The Creator intended the Sudra to become the servant of the other three varnas, so the service of the three other classes is his duty, one that will obtain great happiness for him. He should wait upon the three other classes according to their order of seniority. A Sudra should never amass wealth, lest he make the members of the three superior classes subservient to him. By doing so, he will incur sin. With the king's permission, however, a Sudra may earn wealth for performing religious acts.

I will now tell you the profession he should follow and the means by which he can earn his livelihood. The shastras say that the three other varnas should certainly maintain the Sudras. Worn-out umbrellas, turbans, beds and seats, shoes and fans should be given to Sudra servants. The Munis should give the Sudra torn clothes no longer fit to wear. These are the latter's lawful acquisitions.

Dharmatman decrees that if the Sudra approaches anyone belonging to the three orders of Munis from the desire of doing menial service, the latter should assign him proper work. To the sonless Sudra, his master should offer the funeral cake. The weak and old among them should be looked after. The Sudra should never abandon his master, whatever the nature or degree of the distress into which the latter may fall. If the master loses his wealth, the Sudra servant should support him zealously. A Sudra cannot have any wealth that is his own, since whatever he possesses belongs lawfully to his master.

The shastras lay down yagna as a duty of the three other varnas— even for the Sudra, O Bhaarata! A Sudra, however, is not competent to utter swaha and swadha, or any other Vedic mantra. For this reason the Sudra, without observing the vows laid down in the Vedas, should worship the gods in minor sacrifices called Paka-yagnas. The dakshina of such sacrifices is the gift called Purnapatra. It is said that in days of old a Sudra named Paijavana gave, in one of his yagnas, dakshina consisting of a hundred thousand Purnapatras, according to the law called Aindragni.

The Vedas prescribe yagnas as much for the Sudra as for the three other varnas. Of all yagnas, devotion is the best, since it is a high deity and cleanses all who perform yagnas. Then again, Brahmanas are the greatest of Devas to their respective Sudra attendants. They worship the gods in sacrifices, for the fruition of various wishes. The members of the three other varnas have all sprung from the Brahmanas. The Brahmanas are the gods of the very Devas. Whatever they say will be for your great good. Therefore, all kinds of yagnas naturally pertain to all the four varnas. The obligation is not optional and must be met. One should always worship as a god the Brahmana who knows the Riks, Yajuses and Samans. The Sudra, who is without Riks, Yajuses and Samans, has Prajapati for his god.

The shastras lay down mental sacrifice for all the varnas, O Bhaarata! It is not true that the gods and other Mahatmans do not wish to share the offerings in such sacrifices of even the Sudra. For this reason, it lays down for all the varnas the sacrifice that consists in devotion.

The Brahmana is the best of the gods. It is not true that they who belong to that varna cannot perform the sacrifices of the other orders. The fire called Vitana, though procured from Vaisyas and inspired with mantras, is still inferior. The Brahmana is the performer of the yagnas of the three other varnas. For this reason all the four orders are holy. All the varnas are related to each other by blood through the intermediate orders, as they have all sprung from Brahmanas. In ascertaining the priority of men in respect of their creation, it will appear that among all the orders, the first created was the Brahmana.

Originally, Saman was one; Yajus was one and Rik was one. In this connection, men who know ancient history sing a verse, O Rajan, in praise of a yagna performed by the Vaikhanasa Munis. Before or after sunrise, a person of subdued senses, with heart filled with devotion, pours libations on the sacrificial fire according to the law. Devotion is a mighty agent. With regard to homas again, the one called Skanna is the initial one, while that which is called Askanna is the last, but the greatest in point of merit.

Yagnas are multifarious, with different rites and fruits. The Brahmana who is devout, who is acquainted with all the shastras and possesses an understanding of them, is competent to perform yagnas. He who wishes to perform a sacrifice is regarded as righteous, even if he happens to be a thief, a sinner or the worst of sinners, and the Rishis applaud such a man. Without doubt they are right.

Thus, in conclusion, all the varnas should always, and by every means in their power, perform yagnas to the best of their abilities, as there is no equal to sacrifice in the three worlds. They should be performed with hearts free from malice, aided by devotion which is sacrosanct.'"

CANTO 61

"Bhishma says, 'O Mahabaho, listen now to me as I name the four varnas and their respective dharmas—Vanaprastha, Bhaikshya, Garhasthya of great merit and Brahmacharya which Brahmanas adopt. Having performed all the dharmas of the stage called Garhasthya—and after undergoing the purificatory pujas necessary to ordain matted locks, following the rites of regeneration and those relating to the sacred fire and study of the Vedas—with soul cleansed and senses restrained, a man should retire, alone or with his wife, to the forest for Vanaprastha.

Having studied the shastras called Aranyakas, drawn up his vital fluid and retired from all worldly affairs, the virtuous Vanaprastha can then attain absorption with the infinite and eternal Atman. This is what the Munis, who have drawn up their vital fluid, suggest that a recluse should practise and perform.

It is well known that the Brahmana who aspires to attain mukti is competent to adopt the Bhaikshya varnasrama after the stage of Brahmacharya. The Brahmana possessed of learning, with no desire to better his situation, wandering without a fixed abode and sleeping wherever he finds himself when evening comes, subsisting on whatever food is obtained in charity, given to contemplation, practising self-restraint with senses under control, free of all craving, without either appetite or aversion, and regarding all beings equally, by adopting this varnasrama attains absorption with the eternal soul that knows no decay.

The man entering the Garhasthya varnasrama, after studying the Vedas, should accomplish all the religious duties laid out for him. He should have children and enjoy pleasures and comforts. He should meticulously perform all the dharma of this varna that sages applaud, which is extremely difficult to observe with purity.

He should be satisfied with his own wedded wife and never approach her except during her season. He should observe the laws of the shastras and not be cunning or deceitful. He should be abstemious in diet, devoted to the gods, grateful, mild-mannered, kind and forgiving. He should be of tranquil heart, tractable and attentive in making offerings to the Devas and the Pitris and always hospitable to Brahmanas. He should be free of pride, not confine his charity to any one sect, and devoutly perform the Vedic rites.

In this connection, the illustrious Maharishis cite an important verse sung by Narayana himself, endowed with mahatapasya. Listen to it: "By truth, simplicity, proper reverence towards guests, acquisition of dharma and artha, and relish of one's own wives, one should enjoy diverse kinds of happiness, both here and in the hereafter." The Maharishis have said that support of sons and wives and study of the Vedas form the dharma of those who lead this great varnasrama.

The Brahmana who, engaged in the performance of yagnas, duly goes through this mode of life and properly discharges its dharma, obtains blessed recompense in Swarga. Upon his death, the rewards he desired become eternal. Indeed, these wait upon him for eternity like menials ever on the alert to execute the commands of their master.

Attending to the Vedas, silently reciting the mantras obtained from his acharya, worshipping all the deities, dutifully serving his guru, with his own body smeared with clay and dirt, the man following the Brahmacharya varna should always observe rigid vows, O Yudhishtira, and, with senses under control, pay heed to the instruction he has received. Reflecting on the Vedas, discharging all the duties of dhyana and karma, he should live dutifully, waiting upon his acharya and always submissive to him. Disengaged from the six kinds of work, such as officiating in the sacrifices of others, never attached to any actions, showing neither favour nor disfavour to any one, doing good even to one's enemies—this is the dharma the shastras lay down for a Brahmacharin!'"

CANTO 62

"Yudhishtira asks, 'Tell us of those duties, in respect of men like ourselves, which are auspicious, produce future happiness, are benevolent, pleasant, agreeable and approved by all.'

Bhishma says, 'The other three orders do not adopt the four varnas that the shastras lay down for the Brahmana, O Bhaarata! I have already mentioned many deeds that lead to Swarga and are appropriate for the Kshatriya. These are not relevant to your present query, for the Vedas lay them down for those Kshatriyas inclined to ruthlessness.

The Brahmana who prefers the practices of Kshatriyas, Vaisyas and Sudras, incurs censure in this world as a man of evil atman, and goes to Naraka in the next world. The names which men give to slaves, dogs, wolves and other beasts, O Pandava, are applied to the Brahmana who engages in pursuits improper for him.

The Brahmana who in all the four varnas is duly engaged in the six-fold deeds, of regulating the breath, contemplation and others, who performs all his duties and is tranquil, who has his passions under control, whose heart is pure and who is ever engaged in tapasya, who has no desire of bettering his prospects and who is charitable, receives inexhaustible regions of bliss in the other world. Everyone derives his own nature from his actions, through their circumstances, place, means and motives.

You should therefore, Rajan, regard the study of the Vedas, of such high merit, to be equal to the exertion of kingly power or the pursuits of agriculture, trade and hunting. The world is set going by Time, and the course of Time settles its operations. Man performs all his karma, good, bad and indifferent, entirely under the influence of Time. Among the good deeds of a man's past life, those that exert the greatest influence on the next are liable to be exhausted. Men, however, are ever engaged in those actions to which their propensities lead. These propensities draw a living entity in diverse directions.'"

CANTO 63

"Bhishma says, 'Improper occupations for a Brahmana are drawing the bow-string, destroying foes, living off agriculture or trade, tending cattle or serving others for money. An intelligent Brahmana, leading a life of the grihasta, should perform the six Vedic deeds. One applauds the retirement of a Brahmana into the vana, after he has duly discharged all the garhapatyas.

A Brahmana should avoid service of the king, wealth obtained through agriculture, sustenance from trade, all kinds of crooked conduct, companionship with any but his wedded wives, and usury. The miserable Brahmana who falls away from his dharma and whose behaviour is impious becomes a Sudra, O Rajan.

The Brahmana who weds a Sudra woman or a dancer or a village servant, who becomes debased in conduct, or otherwise sins, becomes a Sudra. In that case, whether he recites the Vedas or not, he becomes equal to a Sudra, should be assigned a place among Sudras during feasts, and should be excluded from occasions of worshipping the gods. If one distributes food offered to the Devas and the Pitris to any Brahmanas who have transgressed due restraints, who have become impure or addicted to evil pursuits and cruel deeds, or who have fallen away from their legitimate dharma, the giver gets no punya.

For this reason, O Rajan, Brahma has laid down self-restraint, purity and simplicity as the dharma of a Brahmana. Besides these, he has also mentioned the duties of all the four varnas. For Brahma, one is truly a Brahmana who is self-restrained, has drunk the soma in yagnas, is of good conduct, has compassion for all beings and powers of endurance, is frank and simple, mild and forgiving, free from cruelty or any desire to acquire wealth to raise his status.

Men wanting to acquire virtue, O Rajan, seek the assistance of Sudras, Vaisyas and Kshatriyas. Therefore, Vishnu never extends his grace to the members of these three varnas who are not dutiful in helping others to acquire virtue. If one does not please Vishnu, one loses the happiness of all men in Swarga—the merit arising from karma laid down for the four varnas, the declarations of the Vedas, all kinds of yagnas and all other religious deeds and duties in respect of the several varnasramas.

Listen now, O son of Pandu, to those dharmas that you should observe in the four varnasramas. The Kshatriya who wants the members of the three other varnas in his kingdom to adhere strictly to the respective duties of their varnas, should know these.

For a Sudra who wishes to hear shastras that are not forbidden to him, who has accomplished his dharma, who has fathered a son and between whom and the superior varna there is not much difference in purity of conduct, all the varnasramas are for him, except the observance of universal peacefulness and self-restraint, which are not necessary for him.

For a Sudra practising all these, and also for a Vaisya and a Kshatriya, O Rajan, Brahma has laid down the Bhikshu varnasrama. Having discharged the dharma of his varna and having also served his family, a Vaisya of venerable years, with the king's permission, may adopt another varnasrama.

Having studied the Vedas duly and the treatises on the duties of kings, O sinless one, having fathered children and performed other karma of a like nature; having taken the soma and ruled over and protected all his subjects righteously; having performed the Rajasuya, the Aswamedha yagna and other great yagnas; having invited learned Brahmanas for recitation of the shastras, and having made gifts to them according to their desires; having obtained victories, small or great, in battle; having placed on his throne his natural son or some Kshatriya of good birth for the protection of his subjects; having honoured the Pitris with due rites laid down for them; having devoutly worshipped the Devas by performing sacrifices and the Rishis by studying the Vedas; the Kshatriya who in old age desires another varnasrama, can adopt it by leaving the one which immediately precedes it. Thereby he is sure to obtain success in his tapasya.

A Kshatriya, to lead the life of a Rishi, may adopt the Bhikshu varnasrama, but he should never do so for the sake of enjoyment. Having left the Grihastasrama, he can adopt the Bhikshu varna by seeking alms just enough to support his existence. Life as a sannyasi is not obligatory upon the three varnas—Kshatriya, Vaisya and Sudras. However, they can adopt it if they choose and, therefore, this varnasrama is open to the four orders.

Among men, the highest dharma is the one which the Kshatriyas practise. The whole world is subject to the might of their arms. The Vedas have declared that the observance of all the duties, principal and subordinate, of the three other varnas, depends on the duties of the Kshatriya. Know that just as the elephant's footprints encompass those of all other animals, the Kshatriya's duties engulf all the dharma of the other orders, in all circumstances.

Men who know the shastras say that the duties of the other three varnas afford small relief or protection and produce small rewards, while the responsibilities of the Kshatriya afford great relief and produce great rewards. Kingly duties, Rajadharma, are the foremost of all duties, for they protect all the varnas. Every kind of vairagya occurs in Rajadharma, O Rajan, and sannyasa is the eternal and the greatest of all virtues.

If the Dandaneeti, the science of punishment, disappears, the Vedas will disappear. All those shastras that inculcate the dharma of men will also be lost. Indeed, if one abandons the ancient dharma of the Kshatriyas, all the duties in respect of all the varnasramas will be lost.

One sees all kinds of renunciation in Rajadharma. In them occur all kinds of initiation, and connected with them are all kinds of learning and worldly conduct. As with animals, if the commoner slaughters them, it will destroy the virtue and religious actions of the slaughterers. Thus all other duties, deprived of the protection that Rajadharma gives, will fall prey to attack and destruction; anxious men will disregard the practices the Vedas lay down for them.'"

CANTO 64

"Bhishma says, 'The duties in respect of all the four varnasramas, those of Yatis, O Pandava, and the customs relating to the conduct of men in general, are included in Rajadharma, kingly duties, as part of the Kshatriya's dharma. If the functions of royalty are disturbed, evil will overtake all beings.

The duties of men are not obvious, as they have many interpretations. Misrepresented by many false systems, their eternal nature is sometimes violated. Those who pin their trust on the conclusions men have arrived at without really knowing the truths that dharma and the shastras declare, find themselves stranded and confused by creeds whose ultimate ends are unknown.

The dharma imposed upon the Kshatriya is clear, produces great happiness, as is evident from its results, is free from deceit and beneficial to all. The whole world, with all good actions, is subject to Rajadharma, Yudhishtira, since the shastras say that the responsibilities of the three varnas, Brahmanas and of those who have retired from the world, are included within those of the sacred varnasrama called Garhasthya.

I have told you how, in olden days, many brave kings had approached the Lord of all creatures, the divine and mighty Vishnu of great prowess, to resolve their doubts about the Dandaneeti. Mindful of the declarations of the shastras reinforced by examples, those kings waited upon Narayana, after having weighed each of their actions against the duties of each of the varnas. These gods, the Sadhyas, the Vasus, the Aswins, the Rudras, the Viswas, the Maruts and the Siddhas, the first of Devas created in olden days, all observe the Kshatriya's dharma. I will now recite to you a history, rich in inferences, of both dharma and artha.

In olden days, when the Danavas had multiplied and swept away all barriers and distinctions, O Rajan, the powerful Mandhatri became king. He performed a great yagna from a desire to behold almighty Narayana, the God of gods without beginning, middle and end. At this yagna, he humbly worshipped the great Vishnu.

The Supreme Lord, assuming the form of Indra, showed himself to the monarch. Accompanied by many worthy kings, Mandhatri offered worship to the mighty god. An elevated discourse followed between this lion among kings and the illustrious Deva in Indra's form, regarding Vishnu of great effulgence.

Indra asked, "What is your object, O Mahatman, in seeking to behold that Ancient and First of Devas, Narayana of inconceivable tejas and infinite maya? Neither I, nor Brahma himself, can obtain a sight of the God of universal form. I will grant you any other wish of your heart, for you are the greatest of mortals: your soul abides in peace; you are devoted to dharma; you have your senses under control; and you are possessed of heroism. You are unflinching in wanting to do what is agreeable to the Devas. For your intelligence, devotion and high faith as well, I will grant you whatever boon you desire."

Mandhatri replied, "I bow my head to you, O divine Lord. Certainly I desire to see the foremost of Devas! Casting off all earthly longings, I wish to earn punya and to lead the most important varnasrama, the path of the good esteemed by all. By exercising the mahadharma of a Kshatriya, I have spread my fame and earned many realms of inexhaustible merit in the next world. I do not, however, know how to discharge the duties flowing from the first of Devas, which are the best in the world."

Indra said, "They who are not kings, however observant they may be of their duties, cannot easily attain the highest rewards of dharma. Kingly duties first flowed from the original God, while other dharma followed later from his body. Many were other responsibilities of the Vanaprasthasrama, which God later created, but the fruits of all these are exhaustible. Rajadharma, however, is esteemed above them since it subsumes all other duties. For this reason, the shastras consider the Kshatriya dharma to be the highest.

In olden days Vishnu, acting according to the Kshatriya dharma, forcibly suppressed and destroyed his foes and thereby afforded relief to the Devas and the Maharishis. If the divine Vishnu of inconceivable tejas had not slain all his enemies among the Asuras, then the Brahmanas as well as Brahma, the Creator of the world, would have been destroyed. The Kshatriya dharma and the responsibilities that first flowed from the Paramatman would all have been lost.

If the first and foremost of Devas had not by his prowess subjugated the earth's Asuras, they would have destroyed the Brahmanas and, as a consequence, all the dharma of the four varnas, the four varnasramas and the sanatana dharma. They were revived through the exercise of the Kshatriya dharma.

In every yuga, the dharma of Brahmanas in respect of attaining Brahman is prescribed first. However, since kingly duties protect all, we regard them as the most important. Death in battle, compassion for all beings, knowledge of the affairs of the world, protection of men from danger, relieving the distressed and the oppressed, all are part of the Kshatriya dharma that kings practise.

Men who disregard wholesome restraints, whom lust and wrath govern are kept from sin by the fear of kings. As a result, others who are docile men of dharma are able to perform all their responsibilities.

For this reason, we regard Kshatriya duties as righteous. Without doubt, all beings live happily in the world, protected by kings exercising the Kshatriya dharma, like children protected by their parents. The Kshatriya dharma is eternal and the greatest of all duties, and one regards it as the best in the world, as it embraces the protection of every being. Itself eternal, it leads to eternal mukti.'"

CANTO 65

'Indra said, "The Kshatriya dharma, possessing such energy, including in its application all other dharmas and being the greatest of all dharmas, should be observed by men who are like you, O Rajan, noble and always in quest of the good. If these duties are not properly discharged, ruin will overcome all living things. Kings who have compassion for all beings should regard the following to be the most important of their duties: reclaiming the land for cultivation and fertilizing it, performing great purificatory yagnas, protecting their subjects and disdaining beggary.

The best dharma, the Rishis and Munis say, is to give. Of all gifts, that of one's body in battle is the greatest. You have seen yourself how the rulers of the earth, ever observant of the Kshatriya dharma, having duly waited upon their acharyas and acquired great learning, in the end cast off their bodies in battle. The Kshatriya wanting to acquire punya, after having gone through the Brahmacharyasrama, should lead a life of a grihasta, which is always meritorious.

In adjudicating ordinary questions of right and wrong between his subjects, the king should be thoroughly impartial. The shastras declare that, to ensure that the varnas observe their respective duties, for the protection of all, for diverse schemes and stratagems and competence in accomplishing objectives, most important is the Kshatriya dharma, which includes all other duties within its scope.

The other varnas are able to observe their respective dharmas due to Rajadharma. For this reason, the former are said to be dependent upon the latter in respect of the merit they produce. Those who disregard all wholesome restraints and are attached to the pursuit of worldly objects are brutes in nature. The exercise of kingly duties compels them to act righteously. These duties therefore, are of the greatest importance.

Every Brahmana who follows the three Vedas should observe the course of conduct prescribed for him, as well as the varnas that the scriptures lay down for his varna. If a Brahmana acts in any other way, he should be treated like a Sudra.

A Brahmana should follow the dharma of the four varnas and the rituals prescribed in the Vedas, beyond which he has no duties. A Kshatriya should not make any arrangement for the sustenance of a Brahmana who lives in any other way. His religious merit grows as a result of his actions. A Brahmana is like dharma's self and, if he is employed in deeds that are not appropriate for him, he deserves no respect and should not be trusted.

These are the duties that pertain to the several orders, and it is the responsibility of the Kshatriyas to protect them so that their observance can be improved. For these reasons, Rajadharma, I believe, is the most significant duty of heroes, who are foremost in practising it."

Mandhatri then asked, "What are the duties that should be performed by the several castes that have sprung up from Brahmanas, Kshatriyas, Vaisyas and the Sudras, who reside in the dominions of Arya kings—the Yavanas, Kiratas, Gandharvas, Chinas, Savaras, Barbaras, Sakas, Tusharas, Kankas, Pathavas, Andhras, Madrakas, Paundras, Pulindas, Ramathas, Kambojas? What is the dharma of kings like us regarding the tribes who subsist by robbery? I want to hear about this. O illustrious Deva, instruct me since you are the friend of us Kshatriyas."

Indra said, "All the robber tribes should serve their mothers, fathers, their acharyas and other elders, as well as Rishis and Munis living in the vana and their kings. They should also follow the duties and rites prescribed in the Vedas. They should perform yagnas in honour of the

Pitris, dig wells and dedicate them to universal service, give water to thirsty travellers, give away beds and make other appropriate gifts to Brahmanas.

Duties that every person of this class who desires his own prosperity should practise are truth, abstention from injury, suppression of wrath, support to Brahmanas and kinsmen by giving them their due, maintenance of wives and children, purity, peacefulness and presenting gifts to Brahmanas at yagnas of every kind. Such a person should also perform all kinds of Paka-yagnas with costly gifts of food and wealth. These and similar duties the shastras lay down from olden days, for those of this class. The robber class should also perform all these actions which the shastras lay down for all others, O Rajan."

Mandhatri said, "In the world of men, such wicked men may be seen living in disguise among all the four varnas and in all the four varnasramas."

Indra said, "Upon the disappearance of Rajadharma and the Dandaneeti, all creatures are exceedingly afflicted by the tyranny of kings. After the end of this the Krita yuga, confusion will set in regarding the different varnas, and innumerable Bhikshus will appear with sectarian marks of different kinds. Disregarding the Puranas and the high truths of religion, men, driven by lust and anger, will deviate onto erroneous paths.

When Mahatmans restrain sinful men from evil deeds with the aid of Dandaneeti, which is paramount, eternal and the source of all, virtue becomes firmly established. Gifts, libations and offerings to the Pitris of any man who disrespects the ruler become fruitless. The very Devas do not disregard a Dharmarajan, who is truly an eternal god. The divine Lord of all, having created the universe, intended the Kshatriya to rule men's inclinations in respect of duties. I revere and worship one who employs his understanding to watch over the course of duties that men perform. Upon such supervision rests the Kshatriya dharma.'"

Bhishma continues, 'Having uttered these words, the divine and mighty Narayana, in the form of Indra, accompanied by the Maruts, returned to his eternal abode of inexhaustible happiness. When such was the manner in which the virtuous practised duties in the olden days, which learned Mahatman can disregard the Kshatriya?

Like blind men lost on the way, living beings acting or abstaining in an unrighteous manner meet with destruction. O Naravyaghra, adhere to the circle of dharma the ancients first set going. I know you are capable of doing so.'"

CANTO 66

"Yudhishtira asks, 'You have spoken about the four varnasramas of human life. Please expand on them further, as I seek to know more.'

Bhishma replies, 'O Yudhishtira Mahabaho, you know all the duties that Dharmatman practise in this world just as well as I do. Listen, and I will explain to you the merit acquired by a king on account of the duties practised by those leading other varnasramas, O foremost of virtuous men. All the merit that belongs to men practising the obligations of the four varnasramas accrues to Dharmarajans. A king free of lust and hate, who rules with the aid of Dandaneeti and looks equally on all creatures, fulfils the objective of Bhaikshyasrama.

An adept ruler who makes gifts to deserving men on proper occasions, who knows how to favour and to punish, who conducts himself in all things according to the injunctions of the shastras, and who has tranquillity of soul, attains the object of Garhasthyasrama. The king who venerates those who deserve worship by giving them their due, completely fulfils the objective of Bhaikshyasrama.

The monarch who strives to rescue from distress his kinsmen, relatives and friends, O Yudhishtira, fulfils the objective of Vanaprasthasrama. The king who on every occasion honours the noblest among men and the best among Yatis, meets the objective of Vanaprasthasrama, as does the king who daily makes offerings to the Pitris and generous offerings to all living beings. The king who subdues other kingdoms to protect the righteous, O Naravyagahra, also attains the object of the same mode of life.

For shielding all creatures, as well as properly defending his own kingdom, a king earns the merit of as many yagnas as the number of beings protected, and accordingly attains the objective of the Sannyasasrama.

The daily study of the Vedas, propitiation and worship of acharyas and services rendered to one's own guru, lead to attainment of the objective of the Brahmacharyasrama.

The king who silently recites his mantras every day and worships the Devas according to the law, O Naravyaghra, attains the objective of the Garhasthyasrama.

The king who engages in battle resolved to protect his kingdom or meet death, who is liberal to men leading Vanaprasthasrama and to Brahmanas versed in the three Vedas, attains the objective of the Vanaprasthasrama.

The king who is merciful towards all creatures and abstains from cruelty attains the objective of all the varnasramas. The king who shows compassion to the young and the old under every circumstance fulfils the objective of every varna, O Yudhishtira.

The king who affords relief to all oppressed people seeking his protection, who defends all creatures, mobile and immobile, and honours them as they deserve, attains the purpose of Garhasthyasrama.

Bestowing favours and inflicting punishment upon wives and brothers, older and younger, and upon sons and grandsons, are the Garhapatya of a king and constitute his best penances. By honouring those who are righteous and deserving of reverence, and by protecting those who have by their penances acquired knowledge of self, O Purushavyaghra, a king attains the purpose of the Garhasthyasrama.

The Garhapatya of a king, Bhaarata, lies in inviting to his home and feeding men who have taken themselves to Vanaprastha and other modes of life. The king who duly adheres to the duties laid down for him by the Creator obtains the blessed merits of all the varnas. The virtuous king is the greatest of men, and the learned say that such a king in effect accomplishes Vanaprastha and all the other varnasramas.

The king who duly honours the office or rank, the race or family, of veterans deserving of honour, it is said, O Kaunteya, lives in all the varnasramas. The king, by observing the duties of his country and those of his family, acquires the merits of all the modes of life. The king who on proper occasions bestows upon men of dharma wealth or gifts of value, earns the merits of all the modes of life. The king who, while overcome with danger and fear, nevertheless keeps his eye on the duties of all men, earns the merits of all the varnas.

The king obtains a share of the merit earned under his protection by men of dharma in his realm. On the other hand, if kings do not protect the righteous within their dominions, Naravyaghra, they take upon themselves the sins of omission and commission. The men who assist kings in protecting their subjects also become equally entitled to a share of the merit earned by others, by virtue of the protection granted.

The learned say that the Garhasthya, which we have adopted, is superior to all the other varnas. In this respect, the conclusions are clear and hallowed. The man who regards all creatures as himself, who does no harm and has his anger under control, obtains great happiness both here and hereafter. A king can easily cross the ocean of samsara with kingly duties, urged on his fast boat by the breeze of gifts, with the shastras for its tackle and intelligence for the strength of its helmsman, kept afloat by the power of righteousness.

When he withdraws from every earthly object the feeling of desire in his heart, he is regarded as resting on his understanding alone. In this state, he soon attains Brahma. Becoming beatific by meditation, by restraining desire and other passions of the heart, O Naravyaghra, a king engaged in discharging the duty of protection will obtain great merit. Therefore, O Yudhishtira, work carefully to protect pious Brahmanas and those devoted to the study of the Vedas, as well as other men. Merely by exercising the duty of extending shelter, the king earns merit a hundred times greater than Munis can earn in their asramas within the vana.

I have now described the various duties of men, O eldest son of Pandu. You must adhere to Rajadharma that is eternal, which great men have practised since olden days. If you occupy yourself with concentration with the duty of protecting your subjects, Naravyaghra, you will obtain the merits of all the four varnasramas and of all the four varnas!'"

CANTO 67

"Yudhishtira asks, 'You have told me the dharma of the four varnasramas and the four varnas. Tell me now, O Pitamaha, the principal duties of a kingdom.'

Bhishma replies, 'The selection and coronation of a king is the first duty of a kingdom, as anarchy makes it weak and robbers soon come to infest it. In states racked by anarchy, righteousness cannot dwell and inhabitants destroy one another. It is the worst possible state for a kingdom.

The Srutis declare that in the coronation of a king, it is Indra himself who is crowned in the person of the king. A man who desires prosperity should worship the king as he would Indra. No one should dwell in kingdoms where anarchy prevails, because Agni does not convey to the Devas the libations that people there offer. If a powerful king desires to annex kingdoms weakened by anarchy, the people should go forward and receive the invader with respect, for this is consistent with wisdom. There is no evil greater than anarchy, but only if the powerful invader is inclined to equity will everything be set right, otherwise he could annihilate all.

The cow that cannot be easily milked has to endure great pain, whereas the cow lending itself to being easily milked does not suffer at all. The iron that bends easily does not need to be heated. The tree that bends easily does not suffer at the hands of the gardener. Guided by these instances, O Kshatriya, men should bend before the powerful. He who bows to a powerful man actually bends his head to Indra. For these reasons, men who wish for prosperity should elect and crown someone as their king.

Men who live in countries where anarchy prevails cannot enjoy their wealth and wives, because the lawless man derives great pleasure from robbing them. However, when others steal his own ill-gotten wealth, he wishes for a king. It is evident, therefore, that in times of anarchy, even evil men cannot be happy, because two evil men together may snatch away the wealth of a third, and many men banding together may in turn rob those two of their wealth. Such evil men could enslave those who are free, and forcibly abduct women. For these reasons, the Devas created kings to protect the people.

If there were no kings on earth to wield the Dandaneeti, the strong would then prey on the weak, as fish do in water. We have been told that in olden days of anarchy, men destroyed one another like stronger fish devouring weaker ones. We hear that a few among them then joined together to make certain compacts, saying, "We will cast off one who becomes harsh in speech or violent in temper, one who seduces or abducts other men's wives or who robs others of their wealth."

They made such an agreement to inspire confidence in all classes of people. However, after some time, they found the arrangement unsatisfactory and approached Pitamaha Brahma, saying, "Without a king, O divine lord, we are facing doom. Appoint someone as our king so that all of us will revere him and he will protect us."

The Pitamaha requested Manu but he did not assent, saying, "To govern a kingdom is exceedingly difficult, especially among men whose ways are always false and deceitful. I fear all sinful deeds."

The inhabitants of the earth then said to him, "Do not fear. Sins that men commit will affect only those who commit them, without tarnishing you in the least. To increase your treasury, we will give you a fiftieth part of our animals and precious metals, and a tenth part of our grain. When our maidens wish to marry, we will give you the most beautiful ones among them. Those among men who are foremost in the use of weapons, in riding and driving chariots will follow you as the Devas do Indra.

With your strength so enhanced, you will become invincible and powerful. As our king, you will protect us gladly, like Kubera protecting the Yakshas and the Rakshasas. A fourth part of the punya men will earn under your protection will be yours. Strengthened by the punya that you will so easily obtain, protect us, O Rajan, as he of a hundred yagnas protects the gods. Like the sun scorching all with his rays, go and win victories. Crush the pride of your foes and let dharma always triumph in the world."

Thus addressed by the inhabitants of the earth, the tejasvi Manu of high lineage appeared, accompanied by a large force, blazing with power. Beholding the might of Manu, like the Devas perceiving the might of Indra, the inhabitants of the earth became quiet and set their minds to their respective duties. Manu then went through the world like a rain-charged cloud in its mission of beneficence, keeping evil in check and getting all to perform their respective dharma.

The men on earth who desire prosperity, Yudhishtira, should first choose and crown a king for the protection of all. Like disciples prostrating themselves in the presence of the acharya, or the Devas in the presence of Indra, all should humble themselves before the king. A ruler honoured by his own people becomes an object of respect for his enemies, while a king disappointing his people is overthrown, despised by his subjects.

Therefore, parasols, chariots, outward ornaments, meat, drink, mansions, seats, beds and all utensils for use and show, should be assigned to the king. By such means he will succeed in discharging his dharma as protector and become irresistible. He should speak with smiles and, addressed sweetly by others, should in turn address others amiably. Grateful to those who serve him, firmly devoted to those who deserve his respect, and with passions under control, he should give all their due. Looked after by others, he should look upon them mildly, sweetly and generously.'"

CANTO 68

"Yudhishtira asks, 'Why, O Bharatarishabha, have the Brahmanas said that the king, the ruler of men, is a god?'

Bhishma replies, 'There is an old story concerning this about a discussion between the wise Brihaspati and the intelligent king of Kosala, Vasumanas. The king, aware of the value of humility, ever devoted to the welfare of all and desirous of securing the happiness of men, duly observed the proper obsequies, circumambulating the great sage and bowing to him, and questioned the virtuous Brihaspati about the laws of a kingdom.

Vasumanas asked, "By what means do creatures grow, and what destroys them? O you of deep understanding, whom should they worship in order to find eternal happiness?"

Thus questioned by the Kosala king of infinite tejas, the wise Brihaspati conversed with him calmly about the respect that one should pay kings.

Brihaspati said, "The duties of all men, O sagacious one, can be seen to have their root in the king. It is only through fear of the king that men refrain from destroying one another. It is the king who brings peace on earth, through due observance of dharma, and by curtailing lawlessness and all kinds of lust. When he achieves this, he shines in glory.

O Rajan, if the sun and the moon do not rise, all creatures are unable to see one another in utter darkness, just as fish in shallow waters and birds in sanctuaries swim and rove without restraint, attacking and oppressing one another till they meet with extinction. Men, too, like a herd of cattle without a herdsman to look after them, will sink into utter darkness and certain destruction if they have no king to protect them.

If the king did not exercise the duty of protection, the strong would by force appropriate the possessions of the weak and, if the latter refused to surrender them readily, take their very lives. Nobody then would be able to say of anything, 'This is mine.' Wives, sons, food, all kinds of property, would not exist. In the absence of royal protection, ruin would overtake everything: evil men would forcibly appropriate the carriages, robes, ornaments, precious stones and other kinds of property belonging to others, and all kinds of oppression would fall upon those who were righteous, forcing them to take to the path of adharma. Men would disregard or even injure their own aged parents, their very acharyas, guests and elders.

If the king did not offer protection, all those possessing wealth would have to encounter death, confinement and persecution, and the very idea of property would disappear. Everything would be destroyed prematurely, brigands would overrun the country and everybody would fall into hell.

If the king did not offer protection, all restrictions of marriage and intercourse due to consanguinity and other kinds of kinship would dissolve. All affairs relating to agriculture and trade would fall into confusion. Dharma would sink and be lost, and the three Vedas would disappear. Yagnas completed with gifts according to the law would no longer be performed; no marriage would take place, and society itself would cease to exist. If the king did not exercise the responsibility of protection, the very bulls would not cover cows, milk-jars would not be churned and people living by rearing cattle would be ruined. In the absence of royal protection, all creatures, howling and frantic through fear and anxiety, would meet their end in no time at all. No sacrifices extending for a year and completed with gifts according to the shastras would occur.

In the absence of royal protection, Brahmanas would never study the four Vedas or undergo austerities or be cleansed by knowledge and rigid vows, and the slayer of a man guilty of Brahmahatya would not obtain any reward, while the perpetrator would enjoy perfect immunity.

In the absence of royal protection, men would snatch others' wealth, wholesome barriers would be swept away, everybody, terrified, would seek safety in flight and all kinds of injustice would set in. An intermixture of castes would take place and famine would ravage the kingdom.

Were the king to exercise the responsibility of royal protection, men everywhere could sleep at their ease without shutting up their houses and bolting and barring their doors. Nobody would hear evil talk, or fear actual attacks. Women decked with ornaments could confidently wander anywhere without male relatives to escort them. Men would adopt the path of dharma and serve one another because the king exercised his duty of protection. The members of the three varnasramas would be able to perform great yagnas and concentrate on acquiring learning. The Vedas protect the world that depends on farming and trade.

The king duly protects all people by following his principal dharma with the aid of a mighty force and, by taking a heavy load upon himself, enables his subjects to live in happiness. Who will not worship the king whose existence allows people to survive and in whose downfall they are ruined? Those who do what is agreeable and beneficial to the king, and who share the burden of royal duties that overawe every varna, conquer both this and the next world. He who even thinks of doing an injury to the king will certainly come to grief and go to hell hereafter.

No one should disregard the king by taking him for a mere man, for he is in truth a divinity in human form. The king assumes five different forms according to five different occasions. He becomes Agni, Aditya, Mrityu, Vaisravana and Yama. When, confronted by falsehood, he burns the offenders before him with his fierce energy, he assumes the form of Agni. When he scrutinizes through his spies the actions of all men and does what is necessary for the general good, he assumes the form of Aditya. He assumes the form of the Destroyer when in wrath he cuts down hundreds of evil men with their sons, grandsons and relatives. He assumes the form of Yama when he restrains the evil by inflicting severe punishments on them and favours the righteous by bestowing rewards upon them. He assumes the form of Kubera on earth, O Rajan, when he gratifies with profuse gifts those who have rendered him valuable service and confiscates the wealth and jewels of those who have offended him, when he bestows prosperity upon some and takes it from others.

No one who is clever, who is capable of work, who aspires to virtue and is free from malice, should ever spread evil reports about the king. No man by acting against the king can ever be happy, even if he happens to be the king's son, brother, companion or one whom the king regards as his second self. Where Agni, assisted by Vayu, blazing forth among inflammable things, may leave a remnant, the wrath of the king leaves nothing to the man who incurs it.

One should turn away at a distance from whatever belongs to the king, as though from death itself, else one will meet a speedy end like a deer at the touch of poison. The man of intelligence should protect as his own whatever belongs to the king, else he will sink senseless into a deep hell of eternal gloom and infamy.

Who will not worship a king whom such terms adorn as 'delighter of the people', 'giver of happiness', 'possessor of prosperity' and, most important of all, 'healer of injuries', 'lord of earth' and 'protector of men'?

Therefore, one should always attach to the king a minister who is solicitous of his prosperity, who observes all wholesome restraints, who has his soul under control and is master of his passions, who has intelligence and memory, and who is adept in the transaction of business.

The king should duly honour a minister who is grateful, endowed with wisdom, large-hearted, loyal, possessed of mastery over his senses, virtuous and observant of the dictates of policy. He should entertain the man who is loyal, grateful, virtuous, possessed of self-control, brave, magnanimous in his deeds and competent to accomplish tasks without assistance.

Knowledge makes men proud, while the king makes men humble. The man whom the king chastises can never find happiness, while one whom the king favours, rejoices. The king is the heart of his people; he is their great refuge; he is their glory and their greatest happiness. O Rajan, men who are attached to the king succeed in conquering both this and the other world. Having governed the earth with the aid of self-restraint, truth and friendship, and having adored the Devas with great yagnas, the king, earning great glory, obtains an eternal abode in Swarga."

Being thus instructed by Brihaspati, son of Angirasa, the heroic Vasumanas, ruler of Kosala, the best of kings, from then on, began to protect his subjects.'"

CANTO 69

"Yudhishtira asks, 'O Bhaarata, what other special duties remain for the king to discharge? How should he protect his kingdom and subdue his foes? How should he employ his spies? How should he inspire confidence in the four varnas of his subjects, his own servants, wives and sons?'

Bhishma says, 'Listen, O Rajan, with attention to the diverse duties of kings, to the work which the king, or one who is in the position of a king, should first do. The king should first master himself, and only then seek to subdue his foes. How will a king who has not been able to conquer himself be able to conquer his enemies? The conquest of the five senses is regarded as the conquest of self, and the king who successfully subdues his senses is competent to resist his enemies.

He should place foot-soldiers within his own palace, in his forts, frontiers, towns, parks, pleasure gardens and also in all places he personally visits. He should employ as spies men who look like simpletons or appear to be blind and deaf. They should all be adroit men who have been thoroughly tested for their abilities, and who are able to endure hunger and thirst. With proper attention, the king should set his informers upon all his counsellors, friends and sons, as well as in his city, in the provinces and in the dominions of the chieftains under him.

His agents should be so employed that they do not know one another. He should also, O Bharatarishabha, discover the spies of his enemies by setting informers in shops, places of amusement where people congregate, among beggars, in his pleasure gardens and parks, in meetings and conclaves of the learned, in the country, in public places, in places where he holds his own court and in the homes of the citizens. In this way the intelligent king will discover the agents his foes dispatch and will derive great benefit, O Pandava.

When the king, through a survey of his own, finds himself weak, he should, after consulting his counsellors, make peace with an enemy who is stronger. The wise king should quickly make peace with a foe, even when he knows that he is not weak, if any advantage can be derived from it. He should be engaged in protecting his kingdom righteously, and should make peace with those rulers who are accomplished, capable of great exertion, virtuous and honest.

When the king finds himself threatened with danger and on the verge of ruin, he should kill all offenders whom he had overlooked in the past and all those the people identify as being his enemies. A king should ignore men who can neither benefit nor injure him, or those who cannot rescue themselves from distress.

As regards military operations, a king who is confident of his own strength should, after first making arrangements for the protection of his own capital, march at the head of a large force, cheerfully and bravely, without declaring his destination. He should attack those who are without allies and friends, or those already at war with another and therefore careless of danger from another quarter, or those weaker than himself.

A king should not forever live in subjection to another more powerful. Though weak, he should resolve to undermine the stronger, while continuing to rule his own kingdom. He should subvert the stronger by means of weapons, fire, application of poison and fomenting discord among his counsellors and servants.

Brihaspati has said that an intelligent king should always avoid war for acquisition of territory. The wise king should acquire dominions by means of conciliation, gifts and stirring up dissension.

The king should take a sixth of the incomes of his subjects as tribute to meet the expenses of safeguarding them, O Kurusthama. For the protection of his subjects, he should also forcibly take away wealth, much or little as the case may be, from the ten kinds of offenders mentioned in the shastras. A king should certainly look upon his subjects as his own children. However, in determining their disputes, he should not exhibit emotion. To hear complaints and responses of disputants in judicial suits, the king should always appoint wise men possessing knowledge of the affairs of the world, for the state in truth rests upon the proper administration of justice. The king should have honest and trustworthy men supervise his mines, salt, grain, ferries and elephant corps.

The king who always properly conducts the Dandaneeti earns great punya. Regulation of punishment is the lofty duty of kings and deserves acclaim. The king should be conversant with the Vedas and their branches, possess wisdom, engage in tapasya, be charitable and devoted in performing yagnas. All these traits should always be present in a king, for if he fails to administer justice he can attain neither Swarga nor fame.

If a stronger king attacks a weaker the latter, if intelligent, should seek refuge in a fort. Assembling his friends for consultation, he should devise proper means to defend himself. Adopting the policy of conciliation and sowing discord among his enemies, he should devise means to wage war with the assailant. He should set the inhabitants of the woods on the high roads and, if necessary, cause whole villages to be removed, transplanting all the inhabitants to minor towns or the outskirts of great cities. Reassuring his wealthy subjects and the principal officers of his army, he should cause the inhabitants of the open country to take refuge in forts that are well protected.

He should himself withdraw all stores of grain from the open country into his forts. If that becomes impossible, he should destroy them completely by fire. He should set men to destroy the enemy's crops by producing disunion among the enemy's subjects or else, if he fails to do so, he should have those crops destroyed by his own troops. He should demolish all the bridges over the rivers in his kingdom. He should empty the waters from all the tanks in his dominions or alternatively, have them poisoned.

Disregarding the duty of protecting his friends, in view of both present and future circumstances, he should seek the protection of another ruler who is the enemy of his enemy, and who may be strong enough to vanquish his rival on the field of battle. He should destroy all the smaller forts in his kingdom and cut down all the smaller trees and branches of the larger trees, but he should not touch even a leaf of the Chaitya tree.

He should raise outer ramparts round his forts with enclosures in them and fill his trenches with water, pointed stakes at their base and crocodiles and sharks. He should keep small openings in his walls to enable sallies from his fort and make careful arrangements for their defence like that of the greater gates. At all his gates and on the ramparts of his forts he should place weapons and destructive engines such as the Sataghnis.

He should store wood for fuel and dig and repair wells for supply of water to the garrison. He should cause all houses made of grass and straw to be plastered over with mud and, if it is summer, withdraw to a place safe from fire all the stores of grass and straw. He should order all food to be cooked at night so that no fire is lit during the day except for the daily homa. Particular care should be taken of fires in smithies and dormitories, and fires kept within the houses of the inhabitants should be well covered. For the effectual protection of the city, he should proclaim that severe punishment will be meted out to anyone who lights fires during the day.

During such times, O greatest of men, you should drive out of the town all beggars, eunuchs, lunatics and mimes, for if you permit them to remain, evil will follow.

Into places of public resort, tirthas, assemblies and in the houses of the citizens, the king should send competent spies. He should cause wide roads to be constructed and order shops and places for the distribution of water to be opened at proper stations. Depots of diverse necessaries, arsenals, camps and quarters for soldiers, stables for horses and elephants, trenches, streets and bypaths, houses and gardens for retirement and pleasure, should be so ordered that their sites are concealed.

A king threatened by a hostile army should gather and store wealth, oil, fat, honey, clarified butter, medicines of all kinds, charcoal and fuel, grass and leaves, munja grass, arrows, poisoned arrows, weapons of every kind such as darts, swords, lances and others. He should especially keep ready drugs of every kind, roots and fruits, the four kinds of physicians, scribes, draftsmen, actors, dancers, athletes and men capable of assuming diverse disguises. He should decorate his capital and cheer all his subjects.

The king should lose no time in bringing under his control men of whom he has reason to be afraid, be they his servants, counsellors, citizens or neighbouring monarchs. When any assigned task of the king is performed, he should reward those who helped him to accomplish it with wealth, proportionate gifts and words of gratitude. The shastras say that a king pays off his debt when he oversets his enemy or slays him outright.

Listen to me as I recite the seven things a king should take care of. They are his own self, his counsellors, his treasury, his machinery for meteing out punishments, his friends, his provinces and his capital. He should take care to protect these seven limbs of his kingdom. The king who is conversant with the aggregate of six, the triple aggregate and the high aggregate of three, will succeed in winning the sovereignty of the whole earth.

Listen, O Yudhishtira, to what is termed 'the aggregate of six'. These are: ruling in peace after concluding a treaty with the foe, marching to battle, producing disunion among the enemy, concentrating forces for inspiring fear among his enemies, preparing for war with readiness for peace and alliance with others.

Listen now attentively to what is termed 'the triple aggregate'. They are: decreasing what is, maintaining it and increasing it. The 'high aggregate' of three consists of dharma, artha and kama. These should be pursued judiciously. With dharma, a king will succeed in ruling the earth for ever.

On this subject, Angirasa's son Brihaspati himself has sung the following two verses which you should hear: "Having discharged all his duties and protected the earth as well as his cities, a king will attain great happiness in Swarga. What is tapasya to the king who protects his people properly, and what need has he of yagnas? Such a king should be regarded as one who knows every dharma!'"

Yudhishtira says, 'There is the Dandaneeti, the Raja and the Praja. Tell me, O Pitamaha, what advantage they derive each from the other.'

Bhishma says, 'Listen to me, O Bhaarata, as I expound in sacred and solemn words the great blessedness of the Dandaneeti. Dandaneeti forces all men to observe the svadharma of their varnas. Properly administered, it compels people to be virtuous.

Understand that men become truly happy when the four varnas attend to their respective duties, when they maintain all wholesome boundaries, when peace and happiness are brought to flow from Dandaneeti, when the people are freed from all fear, and the three higher varnas endeavour, according to their respective duties, to maintain harmony.

You should entertain no doubt about the question whether it is the king who makes the age, or the age that makes the king. The truth is that the king makes the age. When the king rules with a complete and strict reliance on Dandaneeti, one says that the foremost of ages, called the Krita yuga prevails, where dharma rules and adharma does not exist.

The hearts of men belonging to all the four varnas take no pleasure in adharma. Assuredly, all men succeed in acquiring the objects they desire and preserving those acquired. All the Vedic rites become punya karma, all the seasons become delightful and free from evil, and the voices, enunciation and thinking of all men become clear and cheerful. Diseases disappear and all men become long-lived. Wives do not become widows and no one is a miser. The earth yields crops without being tilled, and herbs and plants grow in luxuriance. Trees, leaves, fruits and roots become vigorous and abundant. No evil is to be seen, and only dharma exists.

These are the characteristics, O Yudhishtira, of the Krita or Satya yuga. When the king relies upon only three parts of Dandaneeti, leaving out the fourth, the yuga called Treta sets in. A fourth part of adharma follows in the train of such observance of the great science by three-fourths. The earth yields crops only if tilled, and herbs and plants grow depending upon tillage.

When the king observes only a half of the great science, leaving out the other half, then the yuga that sets in is called Dwapara. Adharma follows in the train of such observance. The earth requires tillage, and yields crops by half.

When the king, abandoning the great science totally, oppresses his subjects by evil means of diverse kinds, one calls the yuga that sets in Kali. During the Kali yuga, adharma becomes pervasive and nothing of dharma is seen. The hearts of men of all the varnas fall away from their respective dharmas. Sudras live by adopting lives of mendicancy, and Brahmanas live by serving others. Men fail to acquire the objects they desire and preserve those already acquired.

Intermixture of the four varnas takes place. Vedic rites fail to produce fruit. All the seasons cease to be delightful and become laden with evil. The voices, enunciation and minds of men lose vigour. Diseases appear and men die prematurely. Wives become widows and one sees many cruel men. The clouds do not rain in season, and crops fail. When the king does not protect the subjects with proper attention to the great Dandaneeti, drought sets in.

The king is the creator of the Krita yuga, the Treta and the Dwapara. He is the cause of the fourth yuga called Kali. If he causes the Krita yuga, he attains everlasting Swarga. If he causes the Treta yuga, he acquires Swarga for a period that is limited. If he causes the Dwapara, he attains to blessedness in Swarga according to the measure of his merits. By causing the Kali yuga, the king incurs a heavy load of sin. Tarnished by evil, he rots in hell for innumerable years and for the sins of his subjects, he himself incurs great sin and infamy.

Keeping the great science in mind, the learned Kshatriya should satisfy his Purusharthas and protect those he has already acquired. Dandaneeti, which establishes all men in the observance of their respective duties, which is the groundwork of all wholesome distinctions and which, if properly administered, truly upholds the world and sets it going, shields all men like a mother and father protecting their children. Understand, O Bharatarishabha, that the very lives of creatures depend upon it.

The highest merit a king can acquire is to acquaint himself with Dandaneeti and administer it properly. Therefore, O scion of Kuru, protect your subjects righteously with the aid of the great science. By doing so and ruling with dharma, you will surely attain blessedness in Swarga.'"

CANTO 70

"Yudhishtira asks, 'O Pitamaha, since you are familiar with every kind of conduct, tell me if, by adopting the way of Dandaneeti, a king can succeed in easily acquiring happiness in the end, both here and hereafter.'

Bhishma says, 'A king should observe these thirty-six virtues which are connected with thirty-six others. By attending to these qualities a dharmatman can certainly acquire great merit. The king should observe his dharma without anger or malice and adhere to kindness. He should have faith and acquire wealth without persecution and cruelty. He should pursue pleasure without attachment.

He should cheerfully utter agreeable words and be brave without bragging. He should be liberal, but should not make gifts to undeserving men. He should exercise his powers without cruelty, make alliances, avoid those who are evil, not behave with hostility towards friends, never employ as spies and secret agents men not devoted to him, and never try to accomplish his objectives by persecution.

He should never disclose his purposes before evil men and should speak of the merits of others, never of his own. He should take wealth from his subjects but not from those who are good, and should never employ or take the help of base, vile men.

He should not inflict punishment without careful enquiry, never disclose his counsels and give generously, but not to covetous men. He should repose confidence in others, but never in those who have injured him. He should not be malicious. He should protect his wedded wives and not indulge too much in female companionship. He should take only wholesome food, not things that harm him.

He should be pure, and not be swayed by emotion. He should pay reverence humbly to those who deserve it and serve his acharyas and elders sincerely and meekly. He should worship the Devas without pride, seek prosperity, but never do anything that brings infamy.

He should be clever in business but always wait for the proper time. He should comfort men, never send them away with hollow words and, having shown favour to someone, he should not abandon him. He should not strike out in ignorance and, once having slain his foe, he should never indulge in remorse. He should display temper, but not without occasion. He should be mild, but never to those who have committed offences.

While ruling your kingdom, conduct yourself in this manner, if you wish to have prosperity. The king who behaves otherwise incurs great danger, while the king who observes all these virtues that I have mentioned, reaps many blessings on earth and great rewards in Swarga.'

Earnestly attending to these instructions of Santanu's son, the perspicacious king Yudhishtira, protected by Bhima and others, worships his Pitamaha and from that time on begins to rule according to his teachings."

CANTO 71

"Yudhishtira asks, 'Tell me, Pitamaha, in what way should the king protect his subjects without causing grief and violating his dharma?'

Bhishma says, 'I will recite the eternal duties in brief, O Rajan, for if I were to list them in detail, I would never reach the end. You must revere learned Brahmanas who are devoted to their dharma, regular in worshipping the Devas, observe stringent vows and have other accomplishments, and employ them to officiate in your yagnas when they come to your abode.

With your priest accompanying you, you should rise when they approach, touch their feet in reverence and do everything else that is necessary. Performing these acts of piety and discharging other karma that are for your own good, you should, by giving them gifts, make them shower blessings on you for the success of your enterprises.

O Bhaarata, you should be sincere, wise and intelligent and adopt satya while avoiding kama and krodha. The foolish king who pursues artha without driving away kama and krodha fails to acquire dharma, and ultimately sacrifices artha as well. Never employ those who are covetous and foolish, in matters connected with kama and artha. You should always employ in all your work those who are not covetous and possess intelligence. Sullied by kama and krodha and unskilled in the transaction of business, foolish men, if vested with authority in matters of artha, always oppress the people by diverse methods which lead to mischief.

A king should fill his treasury with a sixth part, upon fair calculation, of the yield of the soil as his tribute, with fines and forfeitures imposed upon offenders, with levies according to the shastras upon merchants and traders, in return for the protection he grants them.

Realizing this just tribute and governing the kingdom properly, the king should meticulously work so that that his subjects do not feel the pressure of want. Men become deeply devoted to the king who discharges the duty of protection properly, who is endowed with charity, steady in the observance of dharma, vigilant and free from lust and anger.

Never seek to fill your treasury through adharma or from lobha, greed. The king who does not rule in accordance with the shastras fails to earn wealth and religious merit. The king who is mindful only of acquiring wealth can never acquire religious merit as well. The wealth that he acquires by such means is lavished on unworthy objects.

The avaricious king who, through folly, oppresses his subjects by levying taxes that the shastras do not sanction, wrongs his own self. Just as a man wanting milk cannot obtain any by cutting off the udders of his cow, a kingdom ruled by improper means never yields any profit for the king. As one who treats a milch cow with tenderness always gets milk from it, a king who rules his kingdom wisely reaps the rewards.

By protecting a kingdom properly and ruling it judiciously, a king will always obtain great wealth, O Yudhishtira. The earth well protected by the king yields crops and gold to ruler and ruled alike, like a gratified mother yielding milk to her child. Imitate the example of the gardener who waters his trees and plants and gathers only their produce, O Rajan, not of the charcoal-maker who uproots trees and plants and burns them for making coal. Thus, by discharging the duty of protection, you will be able to enjoy the earth forever.

If in attacking an enemy's kingdom your treasury is exhausted, you may refill it by taking wealth from all except Brahmanas. Do not let your heart be moved, even when you are in great distress, upon seeing wealthy Brahmanas. I need not speak then of what you should do when you are in affluence. You should give them wealth as they deserve and you can afford, and protect and comfort them on all occasions. Thereby you will gain regions after death that are most difficult to attain.

With such dharma you will gain fame that is great, pure and everlasting. Follow your dharma and shield your subjects from injury, O son of Pandu, and you will have no feelings of regret or pain, since virtuous men regard protection and compassion to all creatures as the highest merit of a king.

The sin incurred by a king for failing for a single day to defend his subjects from fear is such that he has to suffer for it in hell for a thousand years, while the merit he earns by protecting them for a single day is reward in Swarga for ten thousand years. A king soon acquires, by this dharma, all the regions that men find who lead the Garhasthya, the Brahmacharya and the Vanaprastha varnasramas.

O son of Kunti, observe painstakingly the duty of protection and you will gain the reward of righteousness. No grief or pain will afflict you and you will obtain great prosperity in Swarga. It is impossible for men who are not kings to acquire punya like this. None other can earn such rewards. Because of your wisdom, you have gained a kingdom. So, safeguard your subjects through dharma, gratify Indra with offerings of soma and fulfill the desires of your friends and well-wishers.'"

CANTO 72

"Bhishma says, 'The king should appoint as his priest one who will protect the good and punish the evil, O Rajan. In this regard, there is told an old story about the discourse between Pururavas, the son of Aila, and Matariswan.

Pururavas asked Matariswan, "From where have the Brahmana and the three other varnas sprung, and why has the Brahmana become the foremost?"

Matariswan answered, "The Brahmana has sprung from the mouth of Brahma, the Kshatriya from his two arms and the Vaisya from his two thighs. In order to wait upon these three varnas a fourth, the Sudra, sprang to life, created from the feet of Brahma.

Thus the Brahmana takes birth on earth as the lord of all creatures, his duty being the custody of the Vedas and the other shastras. Then, to rule the world, wield the Danda and protect all creatures, Brahma created the second varna, the Kshatriya. He created the Vaisya to support the two other varnas and his own by cultivation and trade and, finally, he ordained that the Sudra should serve the three other varnas as a menial."

Pururavas said, "Tell me truly, O god of winds, to whom does this earth rightly belong—to the Brahmana or to the Kshatriya?"

The god of winds said, "Everything that exists in the universe belongs to the Brahmana as a result of his birth and precedence according to the Dharmatmans. What the Brahmana eats is his own, the place he inhabits is his own and what he gives away is his own. He deserves the veneration of all the other varnas, as he is the first-born and the foremost.

Just as a woman, in the absence of her husband, accepts his younger brother in his place, the earth, because of the refusal of the Brahmana, has accepted his next-born, the Kshatriya, for her lord. This is the first rule. In times of distress, however, there is an exception to this rule. If you seek to discharge the duties of the order and wish to obtain the highest place in Swarga, then give the Brahmana all the land you conquer, provided he possesses learning and virtue, knows his duties, observes penances, is satisfied with his svadharma and not greedy for wealth.

Wise and humble, the well-born Brahmana by his own perspicacity guides the king in every matter. By his sound counsels he brings prosperity to the king and instructs him in his dharma. As long as a wise king observes the dharma of his varna and is willing to listen to the advice of the Brahmana without pride, he is honoured and enjoys fame. The king's priest, therefore, has a share in the merit that the king acquires. When the king himself behaves thus, all his subjects, relying upon him, become virtuous in their behaviour, attentive to their duties and free from every fear.

The king obtains a fourth part of those righteous deeds which his subjects, properly defended by him, perform in his kingdom. The Devas, Manushyas, Pitris, Gandharvas, Uragas and Rakshasas, all depend upon the offerings made at yagnas for their support and subsistence. Yagna, therefore, depends upon the king and in a country without a king there can be no yagnas.

In the summer season, men seek comfort from the shade of trees, cool water and cool breezes, while in the winter they derive comfort from fire, warm clothes and the sun. The heart of man may find pleasure in sound, touch, taste, vision and scent, while the man who is afraid finds no pleasure in these things. Therefore, he who dispels the fears of men obtains great merit. There is no gift more valuable in the three worlds than the gift of life. The king is Indra. The king is Yama. The king is dharma. The king in different forms sustains and supports everything."'''

CANTO 73

"Bhishma says, 'With an eye on both punya and artha, whose considerations are often complex, the king should without delay appoint a learned priest who has thorough knowledge of the Vedas and other shastras. Those kings who have mahatmans as priests familiar with policy and who have similar qualities themselves, enjoy prosperity in every way. Both priest and king should have qualities worthy of respect and should observe vratas and tapasya. They will succeed in supporting and pleasing their praja, their Pitris and the Devas.

The shastras lay down that the Brahmana and Kshatriya should possess similar feelings and should be friends, as a result of which their subjects become happy. If they do not respect each other, destruction will overtake the people, for the shastras say that the Brahmana and the Kshatriya are the progenitors of all men.

In this connection, listen, Yudhishtira, to an old story about the discourse between Aila's son and Kasyapa.

Aila asked Kasyapa, "When the Brahmana forsakes the Kshatriya, or the Kshatriya abandons the Brahmana, who among them should be regarded superior, and upon whom should the other varnas rely and maintain themselves?"

Kasyapa answered, "Ruin overtakes the kingdom of the Kshatriya when the Brahmana and Kshatriya fall out, for when confusion prevails, thieves and brigands soon infest the kingdom and all good men regard the ruler as a Mlechcha, devoid of dharma. Neither their oxen nor their children thrive. No one churns their pots of milk and no one performs yagnas. In kingdoms where Brahmanas abandon Kshatriyas, wealth does not increase, children do not study the Vedas or shastras or perform yagnas. The Kshatriyas who abandon Brahmanas become impure in blood and assume the nature of robbers.

The Brahmana and the Kshatriya are connected with each other naturally; each protects the other and each is responsible for the other's growth. When each helps the other, both attain great prosperity. If their friendship, existing from days of old, breaks, chaos sets in. No one who wants to cross the ocean of life succeeds in his task, like a small boat floating on the bosom of the sea.

The four varnas become confused and ruin overtakes all. If one protects the Brahmana who is like a tree, it showers gold and honey. If the Kshatriya does not protect him, the tree sheds tears and sorrow. In the absence of a Kshatriya ruler, if Brahmanas abandon the Vedas and the protection of the shastras, Indra does not bless them with rain, and all kinds of calamities ceaselessly afflict the kingdom.

When, having slain a woman or a Brahmana, a vile sinner does not face disgrace and shame in society and is not afraid of the king, danger threatens the Kshatriya king. As a result of the evils that sinful men perpetrate, Rudra, the god of vengeance, appears in the kingdom to destroy everyone, the honest and the evil alike, without distinction."

Aila then asked, "From where does Rudra spring, and what is his form? One sees creatures killing other creatures. Tell me everything, O Kasyapa!"

Kasyapa answered, "Rudra exists in the hearts of men and he destroys the bodies in which he dwells and also the bodies of others. Rudra is like atmospheric visitations and his form is like that of the god of winds."

Aila said, "Neither does the wind, by blowing, visibly kill men on all occasions, nor does the god of the clouds do so by rain or floods. On the other hand, one sees that men slay each other through lust and malice."

Kasyapa said, "Fire, blazing forth in one house, burns a whole quarter or an entire village. Similarly, this Deva stupefies the senses of a few men and soon that confusion touches all—the honest and the evil alike, without any distinction."

Aila asked, "If as a result of the sins committed by the evil, punishment touches all, the honest and the wicked alike, why should men, do good deeds? Why should they not wantonly sin?"

Kasyapa replied, "By avoiding all connection with the sinful, men become pure and untainted. However, if they are interpolated with the sinful, punishment will overtake them, just as fire consumes even wood that is wet, if it is stored with wood that is dry. The sinless, therefore, should never mingle with the sinful."

Aila said, "The earth contains the honest and the evil, for whom the sun shines, the wind blows and water cleanses, equally."

Kasyapa said, "Such indeed, is the course of this world, O Rajan! However, it is not so in the other world, where there is a great difference between the dharmatman and the sinner. The regions that good men acquire are full of honey, possessed of the splendour of gold or of a fire upon which one pours clarified butter, similar to the navel of ambrosia. The good man enjoys great happiness as death, old age and sorrow do not there exist. The place for the sinful is Naraka—hell, and it is full of sorrow, darkness and ceaseless pain. Sinking in infamy, the man of sin suffers with remorse in hell for many years.

Thus, as a result of disunion between Brahmanas and Kshatriyas, unbearable grief comes to afflict the people. Knowing this, a king should appoint an experienced and sagacious Brahmana priest. He should install the priest before even his own coronation, as laid down by the laws proclaiming the Brahmana as the best of all creatures.

Men who know the Vedas say that Brahma first created the Brahmana and invested in him all things that are good in this world and made him the rightful owner of all the best things that have flowed from the Creator, because of the precedence of his birth. Consequently, he is worthy of the respect and the worship of all creatures.

A king, however powerful, should bestow upon the Brahmana

according to the dictates of the shastras, whatever is best, distinguished and above others. The Brahmana and the Kshatriya contribute to increasing each others' wealth, prestige and power. Therefore kings should, above all, always worship the Brahmanas.'""

CANTO 74

"Bhishma says, 'The preservation and growth of the kingdom rest upon the king, while the protection and development of the king rest upon the king's priest. That kingdom enjoys true happiness where the Brahmana dispels the invisible fears of his subjects and the king dispels all their visible fears by the might of his arms. Listen to this old tale of the discussion between King Muchukunda and Vaisravana.

King Muchukunda, having subjugated the whole earth, went to Vaisravana, the lord of treasures and the lord of Alaka, to test his strength. King Vaisravana created by his ascetic power a large force of Rakshasas, who annihilated the forces of Muchukunda. Seeing the slaughter of his army, Muchukunda began to rebuke his own learned priest, Vasishtha. The Dharmatman Vasishtha sat in severe tapasya and, causing the Rakshasas to be slain, ascertained the true reason behind Muchukunda's action.

While his Rakshasas were being slaughtered, Vaisravana showed himself to Muchukunda and said to him "Many ancient kings, more powerful than you, aided by their priests, have approached me, but never like this. All of them, mighty and skilful warriors, regarded me as the granter of happiness and sorrow and came to me to offer worship. In truth, if you have might of arms, by all means, display it. But why, aided by a Brahmana's might, do you act so proudly?"

Muchukunda boldly replied in apt and just words: "The swayambhuva Brahma created the Brahmana and the Kshatriya and they have a common origin. If they applied their forces separately, they would never be able to defend the world. He bestowed upon Brahmanas the power of tapasyas and mantras, and upon Kshatriyas the power of arms and weapons. Supported by both kinds of might, kings should protect their subjects. This is the reason why I am doing what I do. Why do you, O Lord of Alaka, then rebuke me?"

Vaisravana said to Muchukunda and his priest, "Understand that I neither bestow sovereignty upon anyone without Brahma's command, nor do I ever take it away! You are free to rule the whole world."

Muchukunda replied, "'Rajan, I want to enjoy sovereignty obtained by the might of my own arms, not as a vara from you!" Vaisravana, seeing the king fearless in the observance of Kshatriya duties, was filled with surprise.

King Muchukunda, devoted to Kshatriya dharma, continued to rule all the earth obtained by the might of his own arms. So the Dharmaraja who rules his kingdom, helped by and yielding precedence to the Brahmana, will succeed in subjugating the earth and achieving great fame. The Brahmana should perform his religious rites every day and the Kshatriya should always be armed. Between them they are the rightful owners of everything in the universe.'"

CANTO 75

"Yudhishtira asks, 'Tell me O Pitamaha, about the conduct by which a king can make his people great and thereby earn regions of felicity in the other world.'

Bhishma says, 'The king should be liberal, perform yagnas, O Bhaarata, do tapasya, observe vows and remain devoted to the duty of guarding his subjects by following the path of dharma. He should honour all men of dharma by standing up when they come, and by giving them gifts.

If the king follows dharma, it is respected everywhere. Whatever work and other things the king likes, his subjects too like. To his enemies the king should always be like Death, with the Dandaneeti uplifted in his hands. He should exterminate bandits everywhere in his kingdom and never pardon anyone impulsively.

The king earns a fourth part of the punya that his subjects earn under his protection, O Bhaarata, and by protecting them, he obtains a fourth part of the merit that his subjects acquire through study, by giving gifts, by pouring libations and by worshipping the Devas. The king acquires a fourth part also of the sins that his subjects commit, if there is any distress in the kingdom arising from his neglect in discharging his duty. Some say that the king gains a half, and some say the full measure, of whatever sins he earns by becoming cruel and untruthful in speech.

Attend now to the means by which the king can be cleansed of such sins. If he fails to restore to a subject the wealth that thieves have stolen, he should compensate the victim from his own treasury or, in case he is unable to do so, with wealth obtained from his dependants.

All the varnas should protect the property of a Brahmana, just as they would the Brahmana's son or his life. The man who offends Brahmanas should be exiled from the kingdom, for everything is saved by guarding the Brahmana's wealth. Through the grace of the Brahmana thus obtained, the king is crowned with success. Men seek the protection of an able king like creatures seeking relief from clouds or birds seeking refuge in a large tree. A cruel and covetous king with a lustful soul, always seeking the gratification of his desires, will never be able to protect his subjects.'

Yudhishtira says, 'I do not for a moment wish for the happiness that sovereignty bestows, or sovereignty for its own sake; I desire it for the punya I can acquire from it. It seems to me that the shastras attach no punya to sovereignty, hence I have no need for kingship. I will retire into the sacred vanas, lay aside the danda, subdue my senses and seek to acquire the merit of dharma by becoming a Rishi subsisting upon fruit and roots.'

Bhishma says, 'I know your heart, Yudhishtira, and how inoffensive your nature is. However, by inoffensiveness alone you will not succeed in ruling your kingdom. Your heart is inclined to mildness; you are compassionate, honourable, virtuous and full of mercy. People, therefore, do not regard you much.

Follow the example of your father and your Pitamaha. Kings should never adopt the conduct which you espouse. Do your duty and never be touched by anxiety or adopt such inoffensiveness, for by doing so you will not earn the merit of following your dharma, which arises from protecting your subjects.

The behaviour you wish to adopt, impelled by your own intelligence and wisdom, is not consistent with the blessings which your father Pandu or your mother Kunti prayed for to the Devas. Your father always prayed that you become courageous, mighty and truthful, while your mother Kunti prayed that you become high-minded and liberal.

The Pitris and the Devas always ask for the offerings with Swaha and Swadha in sraddhas and yagnas from children. Whether gifts, study, sacrifices and the protection of subjects are meritorious or sinful, you have been born to practise and perform them. O son of Kunti, the fame of those men who fail to bear the burdens placed on them and to which they are yoked in life, is tarnished.

When a properly trained horse can successfully bear a burden without falling down, why cannot a man like you? Success depends upon work and words, and one incurs no censure as long as one's deeds and words are proper. No one, be he a man virtuously following the Grihastasrama, or a king, or a Brahmacharin, has ever succeeded without failing at some time.

It is better to do some work which is good and in which there is small merit, for total abstention from karma is most sinful. When a high-born dharmatman becomes affluent, his king will obtain prosperity in all his affairs. A Dharmarajan, having obtained a kingdom, should seek to subdue some enemies by gifts, some by force and some by sweet words.

There is no one more virtuous than one upon whom noble and learned men rely, from fear of losing their means of sustenance, and upon whom they depend to live in contentment.'

Yudhishtira asks, 'What actions, O Pitamaha, lead to Swarga? What is the nature of the great happiness that one derives from them? What is the high prosperity that one can then obtain? Tell me all this, if you know.'

Bhishma says, 'Anyone amongst us who is able to give a moment of relief to someone afflicted with fear is worthy of Swarga. This is verily so, Yudhishtira; hence, gladly be the king of the Kurus, protect the good and slay the evil, gain Swarga.

Let your friends and all honest men derive their support from you, like creatures from the deity of the clouds and like birds from a large tree with delicious fruits. Men seek his protection who is dignified, courageous, capable of punishing, compassionate, with senses under control, affectionate towards all, equitable and just.'"

CANTO 76

"Yudhishtira asks, 'O Pitamaha, among Brahmanas some engage in duties proper to their varna, while others engage in other work. Tell me the difference between these two classes!'

Bhishma says, 'Rajan, the Brahmanas who are learned and magnanimous, and who look impartially upon all creatures, are equal to Brahma. They who know the Riks, the Yajuses and the Samans and who devote themselves to the practices of their order are equal to the very Devas. However, those among them who are not well-born, not devoted to the duties of their varna and take to evil practices, are like Sudras.

A virtuous king should realize tribute from, and press into public service without remuneration, Brahmanas who do not possess Vedic knowledge or their own fires for worship. Those who are employed in courts of justice for summoning people, who perform worship for others for a fee, who perform the yagnas of Vaisyas and Sudras, who officiate in yagnas on behalf of a whole village and who make voyages on the ocean—these five are regarded as Chandalas among Brahmanas.

Among the Brahmanas, those who become Ritwikas, Purohitas, counsellors, envoys and messengers, become equal to Kshatriyas. Those among them who ride horses, elephants, chariots or become foot-soldiers, become equal to Vaisyas.

If the king's treasury is not full, he can realize tribute from these, but should exclude the Brahmanas who, because of their conduct, are equal to the Devas or Brahma. The Vedas say that the king is the lord of the wealth belonging to all the varnas, except Brahmanas. He can take the wealth of those Brahmanas who stray from their svadharma. But the king should never be indifferent towards those Brahmanas who do not observe their duties. For the sake of making his people virtuous, he should punish and separate them from their superiors.

The learned regard the king in whose territories a Brahmana becomes a thief, as responsible for the sin, O Rajan. Men who know the Vedas declare that if a Brahmana well versed in the Vedas, who observes vows but, through want of sustenance, becomes a thief, it is the duty of the king to provide for his support. If even after he has obtained provision for his support, the Brahmana does not abstain from theft, O Parantapa, he should be banished from the kingdom with all his kinsmen.'"

"Yudhishtira asks, 'Tell me, O Bharatarishabha, of whose wealth is the king regarded to be the lord, and what conduct should he adopt?'

Bhishma says, 'The Vedas declare that the king is lord of the wealth that belongs to all men, except Brahmanas, and also of those Brahmanas who do not follow their dharma. The king should not spare such Brahmanas, and the sages say that this is the ancient custom of kings.

One regards the king in whose dominion a Brahmana becomes a thief, to be responsible for that misdeed, O Rajan, and to have become sinful and worthy of reproach on that account. Therefore, all kings who follow dharma provide Brahmanas with the means of sustenance.

There is an old story of what a king said to a Rakshasa when the latter was about to abduct him. Once a Rakshasa forcibly seized the king of the Kaikeyas who observed strict vratas and had mastered the Vedas while living in the forest.

The king said, "There is no thief in my territories, nor any evil person, nor any one who drinks alcohol. There is no one in my dominions who has not his sacred fire or who does not perform yagnas. How then have you been able to possess my heart?

There is no Brahmana in my realm who is not learned or who does not observe vows or who has not drunk soma. How then have you been able to possess my mind?

In my dominions, no one performs a sacrifice without completing it with dakshina, or studies the Vedas and does not observe vows. How then have you been able to possess my soul?

The Brahmanas in my kingdom teach, study, sacrifice, officiate at others' sacrifices, give and receive gifts. All of them observe these six sacred karmas and all are devoted to the performance of their swadharma. Venerated and provided for, they are mild and truthful in speech. How then have you been able to possess my atma?

The Kshatriyas in my kingdom are all devoted to their swadharma. They never beg but give, and are truthful and virtuous. They never teach but study, and perform sacrifices but never officiate at the yagnas of others. They protect the Brahmanas and never flee from battle. How then have you been able to possess my atma?

All the Vaisyas in my dominion follow their svadharma. With simplicity and without deceit, they derive their sustenance from farming, cattle-rearing and trade. They are all careful, observe all religious rites, keep admirable vratas and are truthful in speech. They give to atithis their due and are self-restrained, pure and close to their relatives and kinsmen. How then have you been able to possess my heart?

The Sudras in my kingdom observe their svadharma, humbly and duly serve and wait upon the other three varnas without entertaining any malice towards them. How then have you been able to possess my heart?

I support the helpless and the old, the weak, the ill and women without guardians, by supplying them with all the necessities of life. I have never destroyed any customs of families or of countries existing from ancient days. How then have you been able to possess my heart?

I protect and worship the Mahatapasvins in my kingdom and honour and entertain them with food. I never eat without feeding others from my table. I never go to other men's wives and never sport or recreate alone. How then have you been able to possess my heart?

No one in my kingdom who is not a Brahmacharin begs his food, and no one who leads the Bhikshu varnasrama wishes to be a Brahmacharin. No one who is not a Ritwij pours offerings of clarified butter upon the sacrificial fire. How then have you been able to possess my soul?

I never disregard the learned, the old or those who are engaged in tapasya. When the whole world sleeps, I keep awake and vigilant. How then have you been able to possess my heart?

My priest possesses knowledge of the Self. He is given to tapasya and is a man of dharma. Highly intelligent, he has absolute power over my kingdom. By gifts I aspire to acquire knowledge, and by truth and the protection of Brahmanas I aspire to attain regions of blessedness in Swarga. By service, I attach myself to my acharyas. I have no fear of Rakshasas.

In my kingdom there are no widows, no evil Brahmanas, no Brahmana who has deviated from his dharma, no deceitful men, no thief, no Brahmana who officiates in the yagnas of people for whom he should never officiate and no perpetrator of sinful deeds. I have no fear of Rakshasas. There is no space in my body, of even two fingers' breadth, that does not bear the scar of a weapon-wound. I always fight for the cause of dharma. How have you been able to possess my heart?

The people of my kingdom ever invoke blessings upon me, that I may be always able to protect cattle and Brahmanas and perform sacrifices. How then have you been able to possess me?"

The Rakshasa answered, "Since you observe your dharma under all circumstances, O king of the Kaikeyas, go back to your home. I set you free. Blessed are they who protect cattle, Brahmanas and all their subjects, for they have nothing to fear from Rakshasas and even less from sinful men. Those kings who support the Brahmanas, whose might depends upon that of the Brahmanas and whose subjects discharge the duties of hospitality, will always succeed in acquiring Swarga."

You should, therefore protect the Brahmanas. They will protect you in return. Their blessings will surely descend upon kings of dharma.

For the sake of dharma, Brahmanas who do not observe their swadharma should be punished and segregated into a distinct class from their superiors. A king who conducts himself in this way towards the people of his kingdom obtains prosperity here and lives in Swarga with Indra.'"

CANTO 78

"Yudhishtira asks, 'The shastras say that, in times of adversity, a Brahmana can support himself by doing the work of a Kshatriya. Can he, however, at any time support himself by doing the work of Vaisyas?'

Bhishma replies, 'When a Brahmana loses his means of support and falls into distress, he can certainly do the work of a Vaisya and derive his support from farming and keeping cattle, but only if he is not competent to perform Kshatriya dharma.'

Yudhishtira then inquires, 'If a Brahmana does the work of a Vaisya, O Bharatarishabha, what trade can he engage in without losing his prospect of Swarga?'

Bhishma responds, 'A Brahmana in all circumstances should avoid trading in wine, salt, sesamum seeds, animals with manes, bulls, honey, meat and cooked food, Yudhishtira, for by selling these he will go to Naraka.

A Brahmana, by selling a goat, incurs the sin of selling Agni Deva; by selling sheep, the sin of selling Indra, the god of rain; by selling a horse, the sin of selling Surya Deva; by selling cooked food, the sin of selling land; and by selling a cow, the sin of selling sacrifice and the soma rasa. Therefore a Brahmana should not sell these things. Good men do not approve the purchase of uncooked food by giving cooked food in exchange. Uncooked food, however, can be exchanged for cooked food,

O Bhaarata. "We will eat your cooked food if in exchange you cook these raw things that we give you," is an acceptable arrangement bearing no sin.

Listen, Yudhishtira, I will tell you the age-old practice of men following approved customs. "I will give you this, and you will give me this in return." Such barter is permissible. To take things by force, however, is sinful. This is the convention the Rishis and others followed and, without doubt, this is righteous.'

Yudhishtira says, 'When all the varnas disregard their svadharma and take up arms against the king, of course the power of the king will decrease. How then can he become the protector and refuge of the people? Clear my doubt, Pitamaha, by explaining this to me in detail.'

Bhishma says, 'All the varnas that the Brahmanas head should, on such occasions, seek their own good by gifts, tapasya, yagnas, peacefulness and self-restraint. Those who have Vedic strength should rise up on every side and like the Devas strengthening Indra, contribute by Vedic rites to enhance the strength of the king.

One says that the Brahmanas are the refuge of the king when his power wanes. A wise king seeks the enhancement of his power through that of the Brahmanas. When the king, crowned with victory, seeks the re-establishment of peace, all the varnas then take themselves to their swadharma. When bandits and thieves, breaking all restraints, spread devastation, all the varnas should take up arms. They incur no sin by doing so, O Yudhishtira!'

Yudhishtira says, 'If all the Kshatriyas become hostile towards the Brahmanas, who then will protect the Brahmanas and their Vedas? What then should be the duty of the Brahmanas, and who will be their refuge?'

Bhishma says, 'By penances, Brahmacharya, weapons and physical might, applied with or without the aid of deceit, they should subjugate the Kshatriyas. If the Kshatriya himself commits sins especially towards Brahmanas, the Vedas themselves will subdue them.

The Kshatriyas have sprung from the Brahmanas, fire from water, and iron from stone. The energy of fire, the Kshatriya and iron, are irrcsistible. But when these come into contact with the sources of their origin, their force becomes neutralized. When iron strikes stone, or fire battles with water, or the Kshatriya becomes hostile to the Brahmana, the strength of each of these three is destroyed. Thus, Yudhishtira, the strength and might of Kshatriyas, however great and irresistible, become quelled as soon as they are directed against the Brahmanas.

When the energy of the Brahmanas turns mild, when Kshatriya energy turns feeble, when men misbehave towards the Brahmanas, those who engage in battle then without fear of death, in order to protect the Brahmanas, dharma and their own selves—these men, moved by righteous indignation and possessed of great strength of mind, will win high regions of bliss hereafter.

Everybody should take up arms for the sake of Brahmanas, because those brave men who fight for them attain a felicitous region in Swarga reserved for men who have always studied the Vedas attentively, who have performed the severest tapasya and who have, after fasting, cast their bodies into blazing fires.

The Brahmana, by taking up arms for the three varnas, does not incur sin, for people say there is no higher duty than casting away life under such circumstances. I bow to them, and blessed be they who so lay down their lives in seeking to destroy the enemies of Brahmanas. Let us attain the realm intended for them. Manu himself has said that these heroes go to Brahmaloka. Just as men become cleansed of all their sins by undergoing the final bath in an Aswamedha yagna, men who die at the edge of weapons while fighting evil are cleansed of their sins.

Dharma becomes adharma, and adharma becomes dharma, according to circumstances. Such is the power of place and time in determining the character of human actions. Friends of humanity, even if they have been cruel, have attained Swarga. Kshatriyas of dharma have attained blessed ends, even by sinning. By taking up arms on three occasions—to protect himself, to compel the other varnas to do their dharma and to punish brigands—the Brahmana does not incur sin.'

Yudhishtira asks, 'When robbers raise their heads and Kshatriyas become incompetent, and an inter-mixture of varnas begins as a result of chaos, what happens if some powerful man other than a Kshatriya tries to subdue these outlaws for the sake of protecting the people? Indeed, if this powerful man happens to be a Brahmana, a Vaisya or a Sudra, O best of kings, and if he is successful in protecting the people through dharma by applying the Dandaneeti, is he justified, or do the laws restrain him? It seems that others should take up weapons, when the Kshatriyas prove unworthy.'

Bhishma says, 'Be he a Sudra or a member of any other varna, he who becomes a raft on a raftless current, or a means of crossing where there are none, certainly deserves respect in every way. He by whose aid helpless men whom brigands have oppressed and made wretched come to live happily, O Rajan, deserves to be lovingly revered by all as if he were a near kinsman.

O Kurusthama, he who dispels the fears of others always deserves respect. Of what use are bulls that do not bear burdens, cows that do not yield milk or a wife who is barren? Similarly, what need is there of a king who is not able to provide protection? Are not a Brahmana void of Vedic lore and a Kshatriya incapable of granting protection like an elephant made of wood, a deer made of leather, a man without wealth, a eunuch or a sterile field? Both of them are like a cloud that does not yield rain.

He who always protects the good and restrains the evil deserves to become a king and to rule the world.'"

CANTO 79

"**Y**udhishtira asks, 'Tell me O Pitamaha, what should be the work and behaviour of men employed as priests in our yagnas, and what sort of men should they be?'

Bhishma says, 'The shastras decree that those Brahmanas who are eligible to act as priests should know the Chhandas, including the Samans, and all the rites prescribed in the Srutis, and be able to perform all religious karma and kriya that lead to the prosperity of the king.

They should be devoted and loyal, and should shower eulogies on their kings. They should also be friendly towards one another and treat everybody equally. They should be devoid of cruelty and truthful in speech. They should never be money-lenders and always be simple and sincere.

One who has a peaceful temperament, is without vanity, modest, charitable, self-restrained, contented, intelligent, knowledgeable, truthful, observant of vows, harmless to all creatures, without lust and malice, endowed with the three excellent qualities and devoid of envy, deserves the seat of Brahma himself. Men with such qualities make the best priests and deserve all respect.'

Yudhishtira says, 'There are Vedic texts about giving Dakshina at sacrifices, but there is no law which lays down how much should be given on such occasions. This law about Dakshina has not proceeded from motives connected with the distribution of wealth. The command of the law, because of the provision in cases of incapacity, is terrible and is blind to the ability of the sacrificer. The prescription of the Vedas is that one should perform a sacrifice with devotion. But what can devotion do when the sacrificer is deceitful?'

Bhishma says, 'No one acquires punya by disregarding the Vedas, by deceit or falsehood. Do not ever think so. Dakshina is one of the limbs of sacrifice and contributes to the nourishment of the Vedas. A yagna without Dakshina can never lead to moksha. However, the worth of a single Purnapatra—two hundred and fifty-six handfuls of rice, is equal to that of any Dakshina, however lavish. Therefore, everyone belonging to the three varnas should perform yagnas.

The Vedas say that, to the Brahmanas, soma is like the king himself. One can sell it for performing sacrifices, but never for gaining a livelihood. Maharishis who agree on the dictates of dharma have declared that a yagna performed with the proceeds of the sale of soma serves to extend sacrifices. However, these three—man, sacrifice and soma—must be of good character. A man of bad character is neither for this nor for the other world. We have heard that the sacrifice great Brahmanas perform by wealth earned by excessive physical labour does not produce great punya.

The Vedas declare that tapasyas are higher than yagnas. Pay attention to me, O learned prince, while I tell you about tapasyas. The wise regard as penances not the emaciation of the body, but refraining from causing injury, truthfulness in speech, benevolence and compassion. Disregard of the Vedas, disobedience of the dictates of the shastras and violation of all wholesome restraints lead to self-destruction.

Listen, O son of Pritha, to what those who pour ten libations upon the fire ten times a day have laid down. For those who perform the sacrifice of tapasya, the Yoga they endeavour to effect with Brahma is their ladle; the heart is their clarified butter; and great knowledge constitutes their Pavitra. For them all kinds of crookedness mean death, and all kinds of sincerity are Brahma. This is the subject of knowledge which the rhapsodies of system-builders cannot affect.'"

CANTO 80

"Yudhishtira says, 'No man can accomplish even the most trifling work, O Pitamaha, without help. How then can a king manage, who has to rule a kingdom? What should be the conduct and the work of the king's minister? In whom should the king repose confidence, and in whom should he not?'

Bhishma says, 'Kings, O Rajan, have four kinds of friends: those who have the same objective, those who are devoted, those related by birth and those won over by gifts and kindness.

A Dharmatman who will serve only dharma is the fifth kind. With such a man, the king should never disclose his full intention, since it might not enlist his sympathy.

Kings who want success are obliged to adopt both kinds of paths—of dharma and of adharma. Of the four kinds of friends, the second and the third are best, but he should always regard the first and the fourth with suspicion. However, he should not trust any of the four with work that he is required to do himself.

The king should never be careless in the matter of watching his friends, as he could be overthrown. An evil man assumes the garb of honesty, and he who is good becomes dishonest. An enemy will become a friend and a friend an enemy, for a man cannot always be of the same mind. Who can trust him completely? A king should ensure that his chief works are carried out in his own presence. A complete reliance on his ministers will destroy both dharma and artha.

However, a want of trust in respect of everyone is worse than death. Trustfulness is premature death and dangerous. If one trusts another completely, it is said, one lives at the mercy of the trusted person. For this reason, everyone should be trusted and at the same time viewed with suspicion. This eternal rule of policy should always be kept in view.

One should always mistrust the man who is covetous of wealth, for the wise declare such a man to be one's enemy. A person whose joy knows no bounds upon seeing the elevation of the king, and who is made miserable by the king's downfall, is one of the best friends. You should trust completely one whose fall is linked to your own, as you would trust your own father. You should promote him to the best of your power when you are successful.

He who seeks to rescue you from harm in your religious rites will try to rescue you from harm in every other business. You should regard such a man as your best friend. They who wish you harm, on the other hand, are your enemies. One says that a friend filled with dread when calamity overtakes you and with joy when prosperity shines on you is like your own self. A handsome man, fair-complexioned, of excellent voice, liberal, benevolent and of good birth, cannot be such a friend.

An intelligent man with a good memory, who is clever in the transaction of business, who is by nature not cruel, never angry and never dissatisfied, whether given recognition or not, be he your priest, acharya or honoured friend, should always receive your regard, if he accepts the office of your counsellor and lives in your home. Such a man can be trusted with your most secret counsels and the true state of all your affairs, religious or pertaining to matters of business. You may confide in him as you would in your own father.

One task should be given to one man and not to two or three, because they may not tolerate each other and will generally disagree among themselves. Your leading minister should be one who achieves celebrity, observes all restraints, is never jealous of others, is able and competent, does no evil, never abandons dharma from lust, fear, greed or wrath, is clever in the transaction of business and possesses the gift of wise and weighty speech.

You should appoint as ministers to supervise all your affairs men of good birth and good conduct, liberal, not boastful, brave and respectable, learned and resourceful. They will work for your good and be of great help to you if you honour them and reward them with wealth. Appointed to offices connected with revenue and other important matters, they will always bring great prosperity. Motivated by healthy rivalry, they will discharge all duties connected with profit, consulting with one another when necessary.

You should fear your kinsmen as you would death itself. A kinsman can never bear another relative's prosperity, just as a feudal chieftain cannot bear to see the prosperity of his overlord. None but a kinsman can feel joy at the destruction of a relative blessed with sincerity, mildness, liberality, modesty and truthfulness of speech.

No one, on the other hand, can be more pitiable than those who have no kin, for they are unhappy and easily overcome by enemies. Kinsmen are the refuge of one assailed by other men, for relatives will not tolerate seeing outsiders destroy a kinsman. When even his friends trouble a kinsman, any relative of the persecuted person would regard it as a personal injury.

In having kinfolk, therefore, there are both merits and faults. A man without relatives neither bestows favours nor humbles himself to anyone. One should, for this reason, always honour and respect one's kinsmen in words and deeds and give them agreeable offices, never injuring them in any way. Remaining sceptical at heart, one should behave towards them as if one completely trusted them. If one reflects upon their nature, it would seem that they have neither faults nor merits. One who mindfully conducts himself in this way will find even his enemies disarmed of hostility and converted into friends. One who always behaves thus to kinsmen and relatives and treats his friends and enemies accordingly, will win everlasting fame.'"

CANTO 81

"Yudhishtira says, 'If one does not gain influence over one's kinsmen and relatives by this method, they become enemies. How then should one conduct oneself so that the hearts of both friends and foes can be won?'

Bhishma says, 'Listen to an old discourse between Krishna and the Devarishi Narada.

Once, Krishna told Narada, "Neither an illiterate and foolish friend, nor a learned friend of fickle soul, deserves to know one's secret counsels. Because of your friendship with me, let me tell you something, O Muni who can visit Swarga at will!

One should speak to another only if one is convinced of his intelligence. I never flatter my kinsmen by complimenting them on their prosperity. I give them half of what I have and forgive their evil words. As a man who wants to light a fire grinds a fire-stick, my kinsmen grind my heart with their cruel words. Indeed, O Maharishi, these burn my heart every day.

Might resides in Sankarshana, mildness in Gada and, as for Pradyumna, he surpasses even me in personal beauty. Although I have all these on my side, yet I am helpless, O Narada! Many others among the Andhakas and the Vrishnis possess great prosperity, power, enduring courage and perseverance. He who does not side with them meets with death, while he whom they support achieves everything.

Dissuaded in turns by both Ahuka and Akrura, I do not support either of them. What can be more painful for one than to have both Ahuka and Akrura on his side or against him? I am like the mother of two brothers gambling against each other, invoking victory for both. Both afflict me, O Narada. Only you can tell me what is good for both my kinsmen and me."

Narada replied, "Calamities are of two kinds, O Krishna, external and internal. They arise, O Vrishni, from one's own actions or from the deeds of others. The calamity that has now overtaken you is an internal one and is born of your own actions. Baladeva and others of the Bhoja race are supporters of Akrura and have taken his side, either for the sake of wealth, or out of mere impulse, or moved by words, or by hate. As for you, you have given away to another the wealth that you have obtained. Though you have men who should be your friends, you have by your own actions brought calamity on your head. You cannot take back that wealth, just as one cannot swallow again the food one has vomited.

O Krishna, you cannot take back from Babhru and Ugrasena the kingdom you gave them, for fear of creating internal strife. Even if you succeed, it will be after much trouble and with great difficulty. A great slaughter and loss of wealth will ensue, perhaps even total annihilation. Use, then, a weapon that is not made of steel, that is very mild and yet capable of piercing all hearts. Sharpening and re-sharpening this weapon, correct the evil tongues of your kinsmen."

Krishna said, "What is this weapon, O Muni, which is not made of steel, which is mild, which still pierces all hearts and which I should use to correct the tongues of my kinsmen?"

Narada said, "Distributing food to the best of your power, forgiveness, sincerity, mildness and honour to whom honour is due—these constitute a weapon that is not made of steel. With soft words alone turn away the anger of kinsmen who say cruel things, and mollify their hearts, minds and slanderous tongues.

None other than a great man, accomplished, with a pure soul, who has friends, can bear such a heavy burden. Take up this great weight of governing the Vrishnis and bear it on your shoulders. All oxen can carry heavy loads on a level road, but only the strongest can sustain such burdens on a difficult road. From disunity will spring destruction and overtake all the Bhojas and the Vrishnis.

You, O Kesava, are the greatest among them. Work in such a manner that the Bhojas and the Vrishnis will not be destroyed. Naught but intelligence and forgiveness, restraint of the senses and liberality operate in a wise man. Advancing one's own race is always praiseworthy, glorious and conducive to a long life. Therefore, Krishna, act in such a way that your clan will not be destroyed.

There is nothing, Lord, that you do not know of policy and the art of war. The Yadavas, the Kukuras, the Bhojas, the Andhakas and the Vrishnis all depend on you, Mahabaho, as do the worlds and all the regents of the worlds. The Rishis always pray for your success, O Madhava. You are the lord of all creatures. You know the past, the present and the future. You are the greatest among all the Yadavas, and they rely on you to live in happiness.""""

CANTO 82

"Bhishma says, 'I have told you what constitutes the first method. Listen now, Yudhishtira, to the second one. The king should always defend those who seek to advance his interests.

If someone who is paid or unpaid comes to tell you of the damage being done to your treasury by a minister who is embezzling its resources, you should grant him an audience in private and protect him from the accused minister, since officials guilty of misappropriation will seek to kill such informants. They who plunder the royal treasury combine together to oppose the man who seeks to protect it, and if you leave him defenceless he is sure to be finished.

Listen to an old story of what the sage Kalakavrikshiya once narrated to the king of Kosala. Once upon a time, the Rishi Kalakavrikshiya came to Kshemadarsin who had ascended the throne of the kingdom of Kosala. Wanting to examine the conduct of all the officers of Kshemadarsin, the Rishi, with a crow in a cage in his hand, repeatedly travelled through every part of the king's dominions, telling all men, "Study the corvine science. The crows tell me the present, the past and the future."

Proclaiming this in the kingdom, the sage, accompanied by a large number of men, began to observe the misdeeds of all the officers of the king. Having examined all the affairs of the kingdom and having learnt that all the officers of the king were guilty of wrongdoing, the Rishi of stern vows, with his crow, came to the king and said to him, "I know everything about your kingdom."

In the presence of the king, he said to his appointed minister that his crow had informed him that the minister had committed a crime in a particular place and that such and such men knew that he had plundered the royal treasury.

"My crow tells me this. Admit or prove the falsehood of the accusation quickly," he told the minister. The sage then proclaimed the names of other officers who had similarly been guilty of embezzlement, adding, "My crow never says anything that is false."

Thus accused and arraigned by the Muni, all the officers of the king, O Kurusthama, united and killed the crow while the sage slept at night. Seeing his crow pierced with a shaft within the cage, the Maharishi went to Kshemadarsin in the morning and said to him, "O king, I seek your protection. You are all-powerful and the master of the lives and wealth of all. With your permission, I will tell you what is good for you.

Grieved on your account, I have come to you, whom I regard as a friend, impelled by devotion and ready to serve you with my whole heart. You are being plundered of your wealth and I have come to you to disclose the truth without showing any consideration for the robbers. Like a rider who urges a good steed, I have come here to awaken you, whom I regard as a friend. A friend who is alive to his own interests and wants his own prosperity and growth, should forgive another who intrudes, urged by devotion and anger, for what is beneficial."

The king replied, "Why should I not listen to what you say, since I am not blind to what is for my good? I grant you permission, O Maharishi! Tell me what you please and I will certainly obey your instructions."

The Rishi said, "I have come to you compelled by my devotion, to tell you everything about your servants after ascertaining their merits and faults, and also the dangers you incur at their hands. Our ancient Rishis have described the plight of those who serve others. The condition of men who serve the king is painful and wretched, akin to associating with virulently poisonous snakes. Kings have many friends and also many enemies; so they who serve kings have to fear all of them, including the king himself, O Rajan.

A man serving the king cannot with impunity be guilty of negligence in doing the king's work, especially one who wants to win prosperity. His inattention can move the king to wrath and may bring down doom upon him.

One should learn to behave in the presence of the king as one would in the presence of a blazing fire. Prepared to lay down life itself at any moment, one should serve the king attentively, for he is all-powerful and master of the lives and the wealth of all, therefore like a venomous snake. One should always be afraid to speak evil before the king, to sit gloomily or in irreverent postures, to wait in attitudes of disrespect, to walk disdainfully or display insolent gestures and motions of the limbs. If the king becomes gratified, he can shower prosperity like God. If he becomes enraged, he can consume a man to the very roots, like a blazing fire.

Yama said this, O Rajan. Its truth is seen in the affairs of the world. By these precepts, I will now do that which will enhance your prosperity. Friends like us can give you the aid of their intelligence in times of peril. They have killed my crow for serving you. I cannot, however, blame you for this. Those who killed this bird do not love you.

Ascertain who your friends are and who your enemies. Do everything yourself without surrendering your intelligence to others. I have incurred the hostility of your servants, who are all embezzlers and do not desire the good of your subjects. Conspiring with those among them who have constant access to you, they covet your kingdom by planning your downfall. However, on account of unforeseen circumstances, their designs have not succeeded.

Through fear of these men, O Rajan, I will leave this kingdom for some other refuge. I have no worldly desire, yet these deceitful men have shot this shaft at my crow, despatching the bird to Yama's abode. I have seen this, O king, with eyes whose vision tapasya has rendered keen.

With the help of this single crow I have crossed your kingdom that is like a river abounding with alligators, sharks, crocodiles and whales. Indeed, with the help of the bird, I have passed through your dominions as if to a Himalayan valley, impenetrable and inaccessible because of fallen tree trunks, scattered rocks, thorny shrubs, lions, tigers and other beasts of prey.

The learned say that a region inaccessible on account of darkness can be passed through with the aid of a torch and a wide river can be crossed by a boat. No means, however, exist for penetrating or passing through the maze of kingly affairs.

Your kingdom is like an inaccessible forest enveloped in darkness. When you who are the lord cannot trust it, how then can I? Here you view good and evil in the same light, so staying here cannot be safe. Here a Dharmatman meets with death, while a sinner incurs no danger.

Justice requires that you slay a man of adharma but never a Dharmatman. It is not proper for me to stay long in this kingdom, and a sensible man should leave it quickly. There is a river called Sita, O Rajan, where boats sink. Your kingdom is like that, for a net of ruin seems to have been cast over it.

You are like the fall from the tree that awaits collectors of honey, or like delectable food containing poison. Your nature now resembles that of dishonest men, not the good. You are like a pit abounding with snakes of virulent venom, or a river full of sweet water but exceedingly difficult to access, because of its steep banks overgrown with kariras and thorny canes.

You are like a swan surrounded by dogs, vultures and jackals. Grassy parasites, deriving their sustenance from a mighty tree, swell into luxuriant growth and finally overspread it completely. A forest conflagration breaks out and, catching these grassy plants first, consumes the lordly tree along with them. Your ministers, O Rajan, resemble those parasites of which I speak. Check and correct them.

You have nourished them, but conspiring against you, they are destroying your prosperity. Concealing from you the faults of your servants, I live in your palace in constant dread, like a man inhabiting a room with a snake, or like the lover of a hero's wife.

My object is to ascertain the conduct of the king who is my fellow-lodger. I want to know whether he has his passions under control, whether his servants are obedient to him, whether they love their king and whether he loves his subjects. It is to ascertain all this that I have come to you.

As food to a hungry person, you have become dear to me. However, I dislike your ministers as one whose thirst, once slaked, feels averse to drink. They find fault with me because I seek your good—there is no other cause for their hostility towards me. I do not have any hostile intentions towards them. I am engaged only in pointing out their faults. As one fears a wounded snake, one should fear an evil-hearted enemy."

The king said, "Dwell in my palace, O Brahmana! I will always treat you with respect and honour and venerate you. They who dislike you will not live with me. You may do whatever is necessary to those of whom you have spoken. Ensure that the Dandaneeti is wielded appropriately and that everything is orderly in my kingdom. Please reflect upon all this and guide me so that I obtain prosperity."

The sage said, "Shut your eyes to their first offence—the slaughter of my crow, and gradually weaken them one by one. Prove their faults and then strike them, one after another. When many men are guilty of the same offence, they can, by acting together, soften the very sharpness of thorns.

In the case of those of your ministers whom you suspect work against you and disclose your secret counsels, I advise you to proceed with caution. As for us, we are Brahmanas, naturally compassionate and unwilling to cause pain to anyone. We desire your good and also the good of others, just as we wish our own.

I speak of myself, O Rajan! I am your friend. I am known as the Rishi Kalakavrikshiya and I always adhere to truth. Your father regarded me affectionately as his friend. When this kingdom was in distress during your father's reign, I performed many tapasyas to drive it away, abandoning every other karma. I tell you this from my affection for you, so that you may not repeat the fault of reposing confidence in undeserving men. You have gained a kingdom without trouble, so reflect upon everything connected with its welfare. You have ministers in your kingdom but why, O Rajan, should you be guilty of negligence?"

After this, the king of Kosala chose a minister from the Kshatriya varna and appointed him as his minister and the sage Kalakavrikshiya, bull among Brahmanas, as his Purohita. Following these changes, Kshemadarsin, the king of Kosala, subjugated the whole earth and acquired great fame. The Rishi Kalakavrikshiya worshipped the Devas with many grand yagnas performed for the king. Having benefited from the Rishi's counsels and conquered the earth, the king of Kosala ruled his kingdom exactly as the Rishi directed.'"

CANTO 83

"Yudhishtira asks, 'What should be the characteristics, O Pitamaha, of the legislators, the ministers of war, the courtiers, the warlords and the counsellors of a king?'

Bhishma says, 'You should have as your legislators men of modesty, self-restraint, truthfulness and sincerity, who have the courage to say what is proper. O son of Kunti, for ministers of war at times of distress, look for those who like you and will be always by your side, who are courageous, by nature Munis, and are learned and persevering.

You should have as courtiers those who are of noble birth and who, treated with honour, always put forth their utmost powers for you, O Bhaarata, and who will never abandon you in good or bad times, sickness or death. You should employ as officers of your army, noble men born in your kingdom, who are wise, handsome, learned, dignified and loyal to you. Men of low descent and covetous dispositions, who are cruel and shameless, will court you only as long as they stand to gain from you.

The king should appoint as ministers in all his affairs those who are of good birth and conduct, who are shrewd and pragmatic, not cruel, and who always seek the good of their master. Those whom you have won over with gifts of wealth, honours, public regard, and whom you can regard as men from whom you will benefit in all your affairs, should always be given a share of your happiness.

Those who are steadfast, learned, well-behaved, large-hearted and truthful in speech, and those who observe solemn pledges, will always be attentive to your affairs and will never abandon you. On the other hand, you should always restrain those who are disreputable, profligate, immoral and inclined to evil.

When you have to choose between two parties, you should not side with one man and abandon the majority. However, when one man's accomplishments transcend all the others', you should abandon the many for him. Ability, self-discipline and devotion to work that brings fame should be regarded as marks of superiority.

You should employ as your counsellors those who honour all able men, who are never jealous of persons of merit, who do not abandon dharma from the urges of kama, bhaya, krodha or lobha, who are humble, truthful in speech and forgiving in temper, who have their soul under control, who have dignity and whom you have tried in every situation.

High descent, purity of blood, forgiveness, sagacity and purity of soul, bravery, gratefulness and truth, O son of Pritha, are marks of superiority and goodness. A wise man who conducts himself thus will disarm his enemies and convert them into friends.

A king who has his atman under restraint, who is wise and who wants prosperity, should carefully examine the merits and flaws of his ministers. A king who wants prosperity and to shine among his contemporaries, should have for ministers men connected with his trusted friends who are noble, born in his own kingdom, incorruptible, untarnished by adultery and similar vices, well-tested, who belong to good families, are descendants of former ministers and are learned and humble.

The king should employ five men to look after his affairs who are intelligent, not proud, who have a pleasant disposition, who are energetic, patient, forgiving, pure, loyal, firm, courageous, mature, responsible, free from deceit, capable of hard work, and whose merits and faults have been well tried. The king should employ in all affairs of the kingdom men who are wise in speech, heroic, resourceful, of noble origin, truthful, intelligent, free from cruelty, pragmatic and who desire the good of their sovereign.

One who is lethargic and abandoned by friends can never work with perseverance. Such a man, if employed, fails in almost every business. A minister who possesses little learning, even if noble and attentive to dharma, artha and kama, becomes incompetent to choose a proper course of action. Similarly, a man of low descent, even if learned, will always err in all actions requiring dexterity and foresight, like a blind man without a guide. A man who is indecisive, even if intelligent and learned, and even if he has the means, cannot be successful for long. An evil-hearted man who is not learned will set his hand to work but will fail to foresee the results of his work.

A king, should never repose trust in a minister who is not devoted to him and should, therefore, never disclose his counsels to such. An evil minister, combining with the other ministers of the king, can ruin his master, like a fire helped by the wind consuming a tree by entering its entrails through holes in its trunk. Giving way to rage, a master can one day pull down a servant from his office or reprove him in harsh words, and restore him to power again. None but a servant devoted to the master will endure and forgive such treatment.

Ministers can sometimes become highly offended with their royal masters. The king should consult in all his affairs only one who can control his resentment from a desire of doing good to his master and sharing with the king his good and ill fortune.

The king should never consult one who is crooked, even if he is devoted to his master, is clever and possesses numerous virtues. He who is allied with foes, and who does not regard the interests of the king's subjects, should be considered an enemy. The king should not consult him, or anyone who is not learned, who is not pure, who is arrogant, who courts the king's enemies, or is boastful, hostile, wrathful and covetous.

The king should not consult one who is a stranger, even if he is devoted to him and greatly learned in his affairs, although he may honour him and employ him. Nor should he ever consult a man whose father had been unjustly banished by royal edict, even if the king may have subsequently bestowed honours upon him and employed him. The king should not consult a well-wisher whose property he had once confiscated for a slight transgression, even if he has every accomplishment.

He who is a wise man, intelligent and learned, who is born within the kingdom, who is pure and righteous in all his actions, deserves to be consulted by the king. One who is knowledgeable and judicious, who understands the dispositions of his friends and enemies, who is like a second self to the king, deserves to be consulted. One who is truthful in speech, modest and mild, who is contented and honoured, truthful and dignified, who hates evil and bad men, who knows policy and is pragmatic and courageous, and who is a hereditary servant of the king, deserves to be consulted.

The king who wants to rule according to the dictates of Dandaneeti, O Rajan, should consult those who are competent to win over all men by conciliation, in whom the inhabitants of both the capital and the provinces repose confidence for their dharma, who are competent to fight and who know the rules of policy.

Thus, the king should honour and appoint as his ministers men who have such qualities, who discern the dispositions of all and want to achieve great deeds. Their number also should not be less than three. The king should employ ministers to observe the lapses of their masters, of themselves, of subjects and of the foes of their lord.

The kingdom has its root in the counsels of policy that flow from ministers, and its growth proceeds from the same source. Ministers should work in such a way that the enemies of their monarch will not detect his lapses. On the other hand, when their shortcomings become visible, they should be prosecuted. Like the tortoise protecting its limbs by withdrawing them into its shell, ministers should keep their own counsels and conceal their lapses. Those ministers of a kingdom who can conceal their counsels are wise.

Counsels constitute the armour of a king and the limbs of his subjects and officers. A kingdom has its roots in spies and secret agents and its strength in counsels of policy. If master and ministers depend on one another for support, subduing pride, anger, vanity and envy, they will all become happy.

A king should also consult ministers who are free from the five kinds of deceit. He should ascertain first the different opinions of the three among them whom he has consulted, and for all subsequent deliberations consult his priest, informing him of their opinions and his own. His guru should be a Brahmana well versed in all matters of dharma, artha and kama, and the king should, with collected mind, ask his opinion. When he arrives at a decision after deliberation with his priest, the king should then carry it out impartially.

They who know the conclusions of the science of consultation say that kings should always hold consultation in this manner. Having settled counsels in this way, they should then be reduced to practice, for then they will be able to win over all the subjects.

There should be no dwarfs, hump-backed men, no one of an emaciated constitution, no lame or blind men, no idiots, no women or eunuchs in the place where the king holds his consultations. Nothing should move there: before or behind, above or below, or in transverse directions. Getting up on a boat, or going to an open and bare space without grass or undergrowth, from where he can clearly see the surrounding land, the king should hold his consultations at the proper time, avoiding faults of speech and gesture.'"

CANTO 84

"Bhishma says, 'An ancient tale has been told, O Yudhishtira, about a conversation between Brihaspati and Indra.

Indra asked Brihaspati, "O Maharishi, what single act should a man accomplish to become famous and an object of regard for everyone?"

Brihaspati replied, "Only by agreeable and pleasant speech, O Indra, can a man become an object of regard for all, acquire great celebrity and give happiness to all. With this sole skill, one can always obtain everybody's love. Everyone dislikes the man who does not speak a word, whose face is always furrowed with frowns and who cannot make agreeable conversation. He who, upon meeting others, addresses them first and does so with a smile, will please everyone.

Even gifts, if not made with pleasant words, are like rice without curry and do not delight the recipients, O Sakra, whereas if someone even takes away the possessions of men with sweet words, they become reconciled to the robbery. A king, therefore, even when he wants to punish, should use kind words. Sweetness of speech never fails in its purpose and never pains any heart. A man of good deeds and agreeable and pleasing words has no equal."

Thereafter, Indra began to follow the advice of his guru. O son of Kunti, you too should practise this virtue.'"

CANTO 85

"Yudhishtira asks, 'O greatest of kings, by what method can a ruler obtain great blessings and eternal fame?'

Bhishma says, 'A king of cleansed soul, who attends to the duty of protecting his subjects, by conducting himself as a man of dharma will earn merit and fame, both here and hereafter.'

Yudhishtira says, 'O wise one, tell me how a king should behave and with whom, for I believe that the desirable virtues which you have already described in a man, cannot be found to exist in any single individual.'

Bhishma says, 'You are very intelligent, O Yudhishtira; it is just as you say. A man who has all these good qualities is very rare. To be brief, such good conduct in one possessing all the virtues mentioned, is most difficult to find even after diligent searching. I will however, tell you what kind of ministers you should appoint.

Four Brahmanas, learned in the Vedas, dignified, belonging to the Snataka order, of untainted behaviour; eight physically strong Kshatriyas, capable of wielding weapons; twenty-one wealthy Vaisyas and three humble Sudras of pure conduct, devoted to their daily duties, and one of the Suta caste, with knowledge of the Puranas and the eight cardinal virtues, should be your ministers.

Each one of them should be fifty years of age, possess a sense of dignity, be free from envy, familiar with the Srutis and the Smritis, humble, impartial, competent to make ready decisions in the midst of disputes, suggesting different courses of action, free from covetousness and from the seven dreadful vices called Vyasanas. The king should consult with those eight ministers and lead them. He should then publish, for the information of the subjects in his kingdom, the results of such deliberation.

You should always watch over your subjects and never confiscate what they deposit with you, or appropriate disputed things. Such conduct will tarnish the administration of justice, and you and your state will incur sin, instilling fear in your subjects akin to what little birds feel at the sight of a hawk. Your kingdom will then sink like a boat wrecked at sea. If a king governs his subjects without dharma, fear will take possession of his heart and the door of Swarga will be closed to him.

A kingdom, O Bharatarishabha, has its root in dharma. The minister or the king's son occupying the seat of justice who works without dharma, and those officers who, having accepted charge, act unjustly, moved by self-interest, all go to hell, along with the king himself. Those helpless men whom the powerful oppress and who lament piteously and copiously, look to the king for protection. In cases of dispute between two parties, the decision should be based upon the evidence of witnesses. If one of the disputants has no witnesses and is helpless, the king should give the case his best consideration.

The king should punish offenders according to the measure of their offences. The wealthy should be punished with fines and confiscations; the poor, with loss of liberty. He should mete out corporal punishments to those who are evil. He should cherish all good men with praise and gifts of wealth.

He who plans the death of the king should be punished with death, to be effected by varied methods. The same should be the punishment of one who becomes guilty of arson, or theft, or co-habitation with women which may lead to a confusion of varnas. A king who inflicts punishments appropriately according to the dictates of Dandaneeti, incurs no sin by the deed, but earns eternal merit. The foolish king who inflicts punishments capriciously earns infamy in this world and sinks into hell hereafter.

A king should not punish a man for the fault of another. A man should be convicted or acquitted, purely based upon the criminal law. A king should never slay an envoy under any circumstances, else he will go to hell with all his ministers. The king who espouses the Kshatriya code, if he kills an envoy who is only faithfully delivering the message entrusted to him, stains the reputation of his ancestors with a sin equal to the sin of killing a foetus.

An envoy should possess these seven accomplishments: he should be of a noble family, eloquent and of sweet speech, faithful in delivering the message with which he is charged, clever and possessing a good memory. The king's bodyguard and the governor of his capital or citadel should have similar qualities.

The king's minister should know the conclusions of the shastras and be competent in directing wars and making treaties. He should also be intelligent, possess courage, be modest and capable of keeping secrets. He should also be of high birth, with a strong mind and pure in conduct. If he possesses these qualities, he should be regarded as worthy.

The commander of the king's forces, his Senapati, should possesses similar accomplishments. He should also be an expert in different kinds of battle array and in the uses of war engines and weapons. He should be able to bear exposure to rain, cold, heat and wind and remain watchful of the movements of his enemies.

The king, O Rajan, should be able to lull his foes into a false sense of security. He should not however, himself trust anyone, including his own son. I have now, O sinless one, explained to you what the conclusions of the shastras are. The refusal to trust anyone is said to be one of the highest mysteries of the ways of a king.'"

CANTO 86

"Yudhishtira asks, 'Tell me, O Pitamaha, in what kind of city should the king himself dwell? Should he select an already made one or should he get one constructed?'

Bhishma replies, 'It is proper, O Bhaarata, to enquire about the conduct one should follow and the defences that one should adopt for the city in which a king lives. I will talk to you about it, referring especially to the defences of forts, so that you will know and do what is necessary.

Keeping his eye on the six different kinds of citadels, the king should build his cities abounding in every kind of necessity and comfort. The six kinds are: water-citadels, surrounded on all sides by a river, earth-citadels, built on plains fortified with high walls and encircled with trenches; hill-citadels, human-citadels, unfortified cities properly protected by guards and a loyal population, mud-citadels and forest-citadels.

Along with ministers and an army completely loyal to him, the king should have a citadel with impenetrable walls and a trench. It should be well provisioned with an abundant stock of rice and weapons, teem with elephants, horses and chariots and be inhabited by skilled men also versed in the mechanical arts.

The city should have a population that is virtuous and clever in business and consists of strong and energetic men and animals. Blazing with beauty and resounding with music and song, it should contain many open squares and rows of well-stocked shops.

The houses where many brave and wealthy men live are all spacious and echo with the chant of Vedic hymns; there are frequent festivities and celebrations and the inhabitants always worship the gods. Here all men follow dharma, peace prevails and no danger exists. Dwelling here, the king should employ himself in filling his treasury, increasing his forces, enhancing the number of his friends and establishing courts of justice.

He should check all abuses and evils in his cities and his provinces and employ himself in filling his arsenals with care, in collecting provisions of every kind and increasing his store of rice and other grain, and in strengthening his councils with wise men. He should further enhance his supplies of fuel, iron, chaff, charcoal, timber, horns, bones, bamboo, marrow, oils and ghee, fat, honey, medicines, flax, resinous exudations, weapons, shafts, leather catgut for bow-strings, canes, strings and cords made of munja grass and other plants and creepers.

He should also increase the number of tanks and wells with large quantities of water, and protect all shady fruit trees. He should entertain with honour and attention acharyas of different sciences, Ritwijas, other priests, mighty bowmen, architects, astronomers, astrologers, physicians, all wise and intelligent men who are self-restrained, clever, courageous, learned, noble, energetic of mind and capable of close application to all kinds of work. He should honour men of dharma and punish the unrighteous.

Working with determination, the king should set the several varnas to their respective duties. Ascertaining diligently through spies the outward behaviour and the state of mind of the inhabitants of his city and provinces, he should take necessary action based on what he learns.

The king should himself supervise his spies and advisors, his treasury and the agencies for inflicting punishments, for everything depends upon these. With spies acting as his eyes, the king should watch all that his enemies do and intend, as well as his friends and neutrals. He should then carefully plan his own course of action, honouring those who are loyal to him and punishing those who are hostile.

The king should worship the Devas in yagnas and distribute gifts without hurting anybody. He should protect his subjects, never doing anything to obstruct or thwart dharma, always supporting and protecting the helpless, the masterless, the old and widows.

The king should honour Rishis and give them gifts of clothes, vessels and food at appropriate times. The king should take care to inform the Munis who live within his dominions of his own condition, of all his actions and of the state of the kingdom, and should always behave with humility in their presence. When he sees noble Rishis or Munis of high birth and great learning who have abandoned all earthly goods, he should honour them with gifts of food, beds and seats.

Whatever the nature of the distress into which he may fall, he should confide in a Rishi, for even robbers trust such men of character. The king should place his wealth in charge of a Muni and should glean wisdom from him. He should not, however, always show favour to such men or pay homage to them on all occasions, as it might expose them to robbers.

From among those living in his own kingdom, he should select one sage as a friend. Similarly, he should choose another Muni who lives in the kingdom of his foe, as a friend. He should pick a third from among those dwelling in the vana and a fourth from the kingdoms paying tribute to him. He should show hospitality, bestow honours and give them the means for their sustenance.

He should behave towards the Rishis dwelling in the kingdoms of his enemies and in the forests, in the same way as towards those who live in his own kingdom. Engaged in tapasya and rigid vows, they will, if calamity befalls the king and he solicits their protection, grant him his wish.

I have now summarized for you the features of the city in which the king should dwell.'"

CANTO 87

"Yudhishtira asks 'I want to know how a kingdom can be consolidated and protected. Tell me all about this, O Bharatarishabha!'

Bhishma says, 'Listen to me with concentrated attention while I tell you how this can be done. A headman should be selected for each village, and over ten headmen there should be one supervisor, and over two such supervisors there should be one officer who controls twenty villages. Above him should be appointed men to oversee a hundred villages, and above them officers who control a thousand villages.

The headman should ascertain the characteristics of everyone in the village and also all the faults that need correction. He should report everything to the supervisor above him in charge of ten villages, who again, should report the same to the officer above him, in charge of twenty villages. This officer, in his turn, should report the conduct of all men within his dominion to the one above him who is in charge of hundred villages.

The village headman should have control over all the produce and property of the village. Every headman should contribute his share for the use of the lord of ten villages, and the latter should do the same to support the lord of twenty villages. The lord of a hundred villages should receive every honour from the king and should have for his support a populous, wealthy and large village. Such a village, so assigned to a lord of hundred villages, should be within the control of the lord of a thousand villages.

The lord of thousand villages should have a minor town for himself and he should enjoy the grain, gold and other produce from it. He should perform all the duties that pertain to it, such as conduct of wars and other internal affairs.

A virtuous minister should exercise strict supervision over the administration and mutual relations of officers. Again, in every town, there should be an officer to attend to all matters in his jurisdiction. Like some fearsome planet moving above all the stars below, this officer should be placed with comprehensive powers over all the officers subordinate to him. He should ascertain the conduct of those under him through his spies and protect the people from all deceitful men, those of murderous disposition or evil deeds, robbers and those possessed by demons.

Taking note of sales and purchases, the state of the roads, stocks of food and clothing and the profits of traders, the king should levy taxes on them. He should first ascertain the extent of production, the receipts and expenses of those engaged in trade, and the condition of the arts, and only then levy taxes upon the various artisans.

The king can levy high taxes, O Yudhishtira, but never such that will emasculate his people. He should levy no tax on a product without ascertaining the output and the amount of labour that has gone into it, for nobody will produce anything without a sufficient margin of profit. The king should thoughtfully levy taxes so that both he and the man who produces the article taxed share the profit.

The king should not, on account of greed, destroy his own foundations along with those of others. He should always avoid deeds which will make his people detest him, and try instead to win their approval. Subjects hate a ruler who is rapacious in the matter of taxes and levies. How can a king who becomes an object of hatred have prosperity? Such a ruler can never acquire any wealth.

An intelligent king should treat his kingdom like a calf. If you permit the calf to suckle, it grows strong and can carry heavy loads. If, on the other hand, O Yudhishtira, you milk the cow too much, the calf grows up weak and incapable of doing much work for the owner. Similarly, if you drain the kingdom, the subjects fail to prosper. The king who protects his kingdom himself, is considerate to his subjects in the matter of taxes and duties, and collects only what he can easily obtain, will achieve great success.

This should not lead to the king obtaining so much wealth that the entire kingdom becomes his treasury and his treasury becomes his bedchamber. If the inhabitants of the cities and the provinces are poor, the king should show them compassion to the best of his powers, whether they are dependent upon him or not.

The king should punish all bandits who infest the outskirts of his villages, protect his people and make them happy. The subjects then become partners in the king's welfare and feel exceedingly obliged to him.

To accumulate wealth in the first instance, the king should visit the prosperous areas of his kingdom, one after the other, and endeavour to alarm the people. He should tell them, "Calamity threatens us and there is a great danger from our enemies. However, there is every reason to hope that the danger will pass, for the enemy, like a bamboo that has flowered, will very soon meet his end. Many enemies of mine have combined with a large number of brigands to destroy our kingdom. In view of this imminent danger, I need your wealth to devise your protection. When the danger passes, I will return what I now take.

Remember, our enemies will not give back what they will forcibly take from you if unopposed, but will kill all your relatives, even your wives. You desire wealth only for the sake of your children and wives. I am glad at your prosperity and I entreat you as I would my own children, allow me to take from you what is within your power to give. I do not wish to trouble any one, but in times of calamity and danger, wealth should not be so dear to you and you should, like strong bulls, bear such burdens."

A king who understands the circumstances that change with time, should send his agents to collect taxes from his people with agreeable, sweet and complimentary words. He should point out to the Vaisyas of his realm the need for him to repair his fortifications and to meet the expenses of his establishment and other heads, alarm them with an impending foreign invasion and impress them with the need for protection which will allow them to live in peace. If he disregards them, they will abandon his dominions, take to the forests and become lost to him. He should therefore behave with leniency towards the Vaisyas, conciliate and protect them, give them a sense of security and always do what is agreeable to them, to ensure that they enjoy their possessions.

The king, O Bhaarata, should always work in such a way towards the Vaisyas that their productive powers can grow. Since the Vaisyas increase the strength of a kingdom, improve its agriculture and develop its trade, a wise king should always gratify them. Acting with thoughtfulness and leniency, he should levy mild taxes upon them. It is always easy to behave with kindness towards the Vaisyas, as there is nothing more profitable for a kingdom.'"

CANTO 88

"Yudhishtira asks, 'Tell me, O Pitamaha, what the king should do if, despite his great wealth, he desires more.'

Bhishma replies, 'A king who wants to earn religious merit should devote himself, to the best of his abilities, to the good of his subjects and protect them, taking existing circumstances into account. He should adopt all such measures in his dominions that he estimates will secure their mutual good.

A king should exploit his kingdom like a bee gathering honey from plants, without injuring the source. He should be like a dairy farmer, who milks his cow without injuring her udders, or starving her calf. In the matter of taxes, the king should work like the leech drawing blood mildly. He should conduct himself towards his subjects like a tigress carrying her cubs, touching them with her teeth but never piercing them. He should be like a mouse, which, despite having sharp and pointed teeth, nibbles the feet of sleeping animals in such a manner that they remain unaware of it.

A flourishing subject should be shorn little by little, the demand increased gradually until what is taken assumes a fair proportion. The king should enhance the burden of his subjects by degrees, like a man gradually increasing the load on a young bullock. If in the end he gently and carefully puts the harness on them, they will accept it without complaint.

Indeed, adequate measures should be employed for making the people obedient, for mere entreaties will not reduce them to subjection. Since it is impossible to behave equally towards all men, the common people should be compelled to be obedient by appeasing their leaders. After using the leaders to bring about disunity among the people who bear the burden, the king should himself come forward to conciliate them. He will then be able to enjoy without trouble what he can extract from them.

The king should never enforce taxes unreasonably and on men unable to bear them. He should impose them progressively, at the proper time, formally and with conciliation. The methods that I tell you are legitimate means of Rajadharma, and are not considered deceitful.

He who wants to control horses by violent methods only makes them furious. Drinking shops, public women, pimps, actors, gamblers and keepers of gambling houses and others of this kind, who are sources of disorder to the state, should all be checked. Dwelling within the realm, they cause trouble and harm the better class of subjects.

Manu himself in the olden days has laid down the injunction that nothing should be asked of anyone when there is no distress. If all men were to abstain from work and take to demanding and begging, the world would certainly come to a stop.

The king alone is competent to control and regulate. Since the Srutis declare that the king who does not restrain his subjects earns a fourth part of the sins that they commit, due to the absence of royal protection, he should check his subjects who are sinful. The king who neglects to restrain them becomes sinful and earns a fourth part of their sins, just as he would otherwise have earned a fourth part of their merits. The evil that a man governed by passion will do will impoverish everyone. Such men, capable of anything, indulge in stimulants and meat, appropriate the wives and the wealth of other men, and set a bad example for others.

Those who do not live on alms may beg in times of distress. The king should observe true dharma and give gifts to them from compassion, but not from fear. Let there be neither beggars nor robbers in your kingdom.

It is robbers, not virtuous men, who give alms to beggars, for such givers are not real benefactors of men.

Let the men who live in your dominions be such as advance the interests of others and bring them benefit, not such as exterminate them. The officers who take from subjects more than what is due, Rajan, should be punished and replaced by others who will collect only what is due.

Agriculture, rearing of cattle, trade and other work of similar nature should be popularized, based on the principle of the division of labour. If a man engaged in agriculture, cattle-rearing or trade feels a sense of insecurity on account of thieves and tyrannical officers, the king will be disgraced. He should always honour his subjects who are rich and say to them, "Advance the interest of the people with me."

In every kingdom, the wealthy are assets to the realm and without doubt constitute its foremost estate. He who is wise or courageous, wealthy or influential, righteous, engaged in penances, truthful in speech or gifted with intelligence, assists in protecting his fellow men.

For these reasons, O Rajan, love everyone and display the qualities of truth, sincerity, absence of anger and abstention from doing injury. You should wield the Dandaneeti and swell your treasury, support your forces and friends and thus consolidate your kingdom!'"

CANTO 89

"Bhishma says, 'Do not cut down the fruit trees in your dominions, Yudhishtira. Fruits and roots are the property of the Brahmanas. The sages have declared this to be a law of dharma. The surplus, after supporting the Brahmanas, should go to meet the needs of other people. Nobody should take anything by doing an injury to Brahmanas.

If a Brahmana wants to leave the kingdom because he has been unable to find any livelihood in it, the king should, with affection and respect, provide him the means of sustenance. If he still wants to leave, the king should call an assembly of Brahmanas and say, "If such a Brahmana leaves the kingdom, the people lose in him a friend, teacher and guru. In whom will my people then find an authority to guide them?" If even after this, he does not give up his intention to leave, the king should ask his forgiveness and say to him, "Forget the past."

This, O son of Kunti, is the eternal way of Rajadharma. The king should further tell him, "Indeed, O Brahmana, people say that only as much should be assigned to a Brahmana as will be just sufficient to maintain him. I do not accept this opinion, but think rather that a Brahmana should be given the means to procure even items of luxury, if he so wishes," and he should be requested to stay.

Agriculture, cattle-rearing and trade provide all men with the means of livelihood. Knowledge of the Vedas however, provides them with the means to reach heaven. Therefore, one regards those who obstruct the study of the Vedas and Vedic practices as enemies of society. It is for their extermination that Brahma created Kshatriyas. Subdue your foes, protect your subjects, worship the Devas in sacrifices and fight battles with courage, O Kurupravira!

A king should shield those who deserve protection, and he who does this is the best of rulers. The kings who do not exercise this duty live in vain.

For the benefit of his subjects, the king should always try to discover the behaviour and thoughts of all, through informers and secret agents. Look after your people, O Yudhishtira: protect others from your own, your own from others, others from others and your own from your own.

Wise men say that everything has its root in the self. The king should first protect himself and then the earth. The king should always reflect upon what his shortcomings are, what bad habits he is addicted to, and what the sources of his weakness and faults are. He should employ trusted agents to wander through the kingdom and ascertain whether his conduct of the previous day has met with the approbation of the people of the provinces, and whether or not he has earned a good name in his kingdom.

Among those who are wise and virtuous, Yudhishtira, you should not disregard those who never retreat from battle, those who do not live in your kingdom, those who are dependent on you, those who are independent of anyone, those who are your ministers and those who praise or blame you. No man can earn the good opinion of everybody in the world, since everyone has friends, foes and those who are neutrals.'

Yudhishtira asks, 'Among men equal in might of arms and accomplishments, how does one gain superiority over all the others and succeed in ruling over them?'

Bhishma replies, 'Creatures that are mobile devour things that are immobile; animals that have teeth devour those that have no teeth; poisonous snakes devour smaller ones of their own species. Similarly, among human beings too, the king who is strong preys upon weaker ones. He should always pay attention to his subjects and his enemies, or else they will fall upon him like vultures.

Take care, Yudhishtira, that the imposition of heavy taxes does not crush the traders in your kingdom. They buy diverse goods at varying prices, high and low, to sell, and in the course of their journeys have to seek repose in forests and inaccessible areas and undergo many privations.

Let not your farmers desert your kingdom due to oppression, for they, too, bear the burdens of the king and support the other inhabitants of your land. The gifts you make in this world support the Devas, Pitris, Manushyas, Nagas, Rakshasas, birds and animals. These are the methods of governing a kingdom and protecting its rulers. I will talk to you again on the subject, O son of Pandu!'"

CANTO 90

"Bhishma says, 'I will tell you now, O Yudhishtira, everything that Utathya of Angirasa's race, the leading authority on the Vedas, once told Yuvanaswa's son, King Mandhatri.

Utathya said, "One becomes a king in the interests of dharma and not to indulge in caprice. Understand this, O Rajan: the king is indeed the protector of the world. If he acts righteously, he attains the position of a Deva and goes to heaven, and if he does not, he sinks into hell. All creatures rely upon dharma, which in its turn, depends upon the monarch. The ruler, therefore, who upholds dharma is truly a king.

The king who is a Dharmatman and has every kind of grace is said to be an embodiment of virtue. If a king fails to punish adharma, the Devas desert his palace and he comes to be defamed among men. The efforts of men who observe their swadharma will always be crowned with success. For this reason, all men seek to obey the dictates of dharma, which is the root of prosperity. When one continues to sin, adharma increases greatly and righteousness comes to an end.

The scriptures lay down that when one does not restrain adharma, no one can claim the rights of property and say, 'This is mine and this is not mine.' Men cannot enjoy ownership of their wives, animals, fields and houses; the Devas receive no worship, the Pitris no offerings, the Atithis no hospitality; the Dvijas do not study the Vedas or observe great vratas, or perform yagnas. When one does not restrain adharma, the human mind becomes weak and confused, O Rajan, like the minds of wounded men.

The Rishis, with their eyes on both worlds, made the king the superior being, intending him to be the embodiment of dharma on earth. They called him Rajan—one in whom righteousness shines. The king in whom there is no dharma they call a Vrishala. Divine dharma or righteousness has another name, Vrisha, and he who weakens Vrisha is Vrishala. All creatures grow in the development of righteousness and decay with its decline. A king should, therefore, advance the cause of dharma, and should never permit it to deteriorate.

We call righteousness dharma because it fosters the acquisition and preservation of wealth—dhana. The Rishis have declared, O Rajan, that dharma restrains and limits all evil actions of men. The Swayambhuva Brahma created dharma for the advancement and growth of men. So a king must work according to the dictates of dharma—the greatest of all things, for the benefit of his subjects.

The best of men who rules his subjects righteously is called a king. Disregard kama and krodha, and observe the dictates of dharma. It is the greatest above all things, O Naravyaghra, that contribute to the prosperity of kings. Dharma, again, has sprung from the Brahmana. For this reason, one should always revere the Brahmana. You should humbly satisfy the wishes of Brahmanas, O Mandhatri. By neglecting to fulfill their wishes, the king draws danger to himself, because he fails to gain any more friends, while his enemies increase in number.

Once upon a time, Lakshmi, the goddess of prosperity, became enraged and left the Asura Bali—the son of Virochana, with whom she dwelt—because of his malice towards the Brahmanas, and went to Indra, the chief of the Devas. Seeing the goddess living with Indra, Bali was filled with vain regret. This is what comes of malice and pride. Wake up, O Mandhatri, so that the Devi of prosperity does not desert you in wrath!

The Srutis declare that Adharma fathered on Lakshmi Devi a son named Ahamkara, Pride. This Ahamkara led many amongst the Devas and the Asuras to ruin. Many Rajarishis also suffered destruction due to him. Wake up O Rajan! He who can conquer Ahamkara becomes a king, while he whom Ahamkara conquers becomes a slave. If you wish for a life of eternal happiness, live as a king who does not indulge in these two—Ahamkara and Adharma.

Abstain from becoming friends with one who is proud, dishonest, mocks faith, or is cold-blooded, and on no account keep company with anyone who has all of these faults. Keep yourself aloof from ministers whom you have once punished, from women too, and stay away from mountains, uneven lands, inaccessible fastnesses, elephants, horses and poisonous snakes.

You should also give up wandering in the night, and avoid being stingy, vain, boastful or angry. Never have intercourse with those who are lewd or of ambiguous sex, unknown women, the wives of other men or virgins. When the king does not restrain vice, a confusion of castes follows and sinful Rakshasas, hermaphrodites, crippled children, or thick-tongued imbeciles and idiots begin to take birth even in respectable families.

Therefore the king should take particular care to act with dharma for the benefit of his subjects. If he acts thoughtlessly, great evil follows and adharma increases, causing a confusion of castes. Cold sets in during the summer months and disappears when its proper season comes. Drought, flood and pestilence afflict the people. Ominous stars arise, terrifying comets appear and other portents are seen, indicating destruction of the kingdom.

If the king does not take measures for his own safety and protect his subjects, the latter meet with destruction, followed by the king himself. Two men get together to snatch the wealth of a single individual, many join hands to rob them in turn, and men rape maidens. One says that such a state of affairs arises from the king's fault in abandoning dharma and being thoughtless, and consequently, all rights of property and dhana come to an end among men.'"

'Utathya said, "If Indra, the Deva of the clouds, ensures rain at the right season, and if the king works with dharma, the prosperity that follows will bring happiness to his subjects. The washerman who does not know how to wash out the dirt from cloth without fading it is not skilled in his profession. The king becomes a Sudra, as among the Brahmanas, Kshatriyas or Vaisyas, one who has disregarded the proper duties of his varna can be compared to a washerman.

Menial service is for the Sudra; agriculture for the Vaisya; the Dandaneeti for the Kshatriya; and Brahmacharya, penances, mantras and truth for the Brahmana. The Kshatriya who knows how to correct the faults in the behaviour of the other varnas and to wash them clean like a washerman, is really their father and deserves to be their king.

The four yugas called Krita, Treta, Dwapara and Kali are all dependent on the conduct of the king, O Bharatarishabha, for it is he who constitutes the yuga. The four varnas, the Vedas and the dharma of the four varnasramas, all become confused and weakened when the king behaves carelessly. The three kinds of Agni, the three Vedas and yagnas with dakshina, all are lost when the king becomes heedless.

The king is the creator of all creatures and he is their destroyer. One regards the king who is a Dharmatman as the creator, and a sinful king as the destroyer. The king's wives, sons, kinsmen and friends all become unhappy and grieve when the king becomes neglectful. Elephants, horses, cattle, camels, mules, asses and all other animals lose their vigour when the king becomes unrighteous.

Brahma created Shakti, which the king represents, O Mandhatri, in order to protect weakness. He who defends the weak wins heaven, while he who persecutes weakness goes to hell. Weakness is indeed a great being, for everything depends upon it.

All men worship the king and are the children of the king. If, therefore, the king takes the path of adharma, all men come to grief. One should regard as terrible the reproachful eye of the weak, the curse of a Muni and the bite of a deadly poisonous snake. Do not, therefore, make an enemy of the weak, or forget that the weak are always subject to humiliation. Make sure that the curse of the helpless does not turn you and your kinsmen to ashes. No children are born in a lineage which has been cursed by the weak, for they destroy the family to its very roots. Hence, do not earn the ill-will of the weak, for weakness is more powerful than even the greatest power and can even totally exterminate it.

If one who has been humiliated or beaten cries out in vain for help and fails to obtain a protector, divine punishment will overwhelm the king and destroy him. While you enjoy power, do not take wealth from the weak. Take care that the curses of the weak do not burn you like a blazing fire. The tears shed by men wronged through falsehood slay the children and livestock of those who have lied.

A sin does not produce immediate consequences. It is like a cow, and the sinner has to wait for milk till it calves. If the effects are not evident in the sinner himself, one notices it later in his progeny or descendants. When a weak person fails to find a protector, divine punishment falls on the king. When distress reduces all subjects of a king to penury and obliges them to live by begging like Brahmanas, it will bring destruction upon the king.

When all the officers of the king posted in the provinces unite and act unjustly, it is the king who becomes responsible for the great evil that will visit his kingdom. When his officers, by unfair means, or from kama or lobha, extort wealth from men who piteously solicit mercy, then a great destruction is sure to befall the king.

O Mandhatri, when a mighty tree first sprouts into life and grows large, numerous creatures come and seek its shelter. When, however, it is cut down or consumed in a fire, all those who took shelter become homeless.

When the subjects of a kingdom perform righteous deeds, carry out religious rites and applaud the good qualities of the king, the latter reaps the rewards. On the other hand, if they take to adharma, due to ignorance, the king will suffer. When you allow sinful men, known for their misdeeds, to move among the righteous without being punished, Kali then overpowers the rulers of those realms; while the king who punishes all evil men thrives in prosperity.

The king who pays proper honours to his ministers, employs them in matters of policy and in battles, enjoys the wide earth forever and his kingdom certainly thrives. The ruler who duly rewards all good work and words, earns great merit. Enjoyment of good things after sharing them with others, paying proper respect to the ministers and subjugating vain and powerful men, constitute the responsibility of a king.

Protecting all men by words and physically by deeds and pardoning no one who has committed an offence, be it even his own son, constitute the great obligation of the king. To share his possessions with those who are weak and thereby to increase their strength, to support them and protect the kingdom, to exterminate thieves and to conquer on the battlefield, embody the duty of the king.

Never to forgive anyone, however dear, if he has offended by deed or word, constitutes the mahadharma of the king. His duty is to protect those who seek shelter, as he would his own children, never to deprive anyone of the honours to which he is entitled, to worship the Devas with devotion in yagnas completed by gifts and to subdue lust and envy.

His duty is also to wipe the tears of the distressed, the helpless and the old and to make them rejoice, to praise friends, to weaken foes and to honour the good, and to observe with alacrity the obligations of truth.

To make gifts of land, to entertain guests and to support dependants are also duties of the king.

The king who shows favours to the deserving and disciplines those who deserve punishment, earns great merit both here and hereafter. He is Yama himself, O Mandhatri, the Deva incarnate to all, because they expect everything from him. By controlling his senses he will acquire great wealth and by not subduing them, he incurs sin.

The duty of the king is to pay proper honours to Ritwijas, priests and gurus and to do good work for them. Yama governs all creatures with an even hand, without prejudice. The king should do the same in dealing with all his subjects. It is said that the king resembles the thousand-eyed Indra in every respect, and that one should regard as righteous those whom Indra regards as such, O Bharatarishabha.

You should carefully cultivate forgiveness, intelligence, patience and love towards all creatures. You should also ascertain the strengths and weakness of men and learn to distinguish between right and wrong. Conduct yourself with propriety towards all, give gifts and say agreeable and sweet words. You should maintain the people of your city and the provinces in happiness.

A king who is not clever will never be able to protect his subjects. Sovereignty is a very happy burden to bear, but only a wise and courageous king who knows Dandaneeti can protect a kingdom. One who is without energy and intelligence, and who is not well versed in this great science, is incompetent to bear the burden of sovereignty.

Aided by handsome, learned and devoted ministers of noble birth, who are clever in business, you should examine the hearts and actions of all men, including the Rishis in the vana. If you conduct yourself in this manner, you will be able to learn the duties of all varnasramas. This will help you to observe your svadharma when you are in your country, or when you go to other lands.

Among dharma, artha and kama, dharma—virtue—is the greatest, and a dharmatman obtains great happiness both here and hereafter. If you treat men with respect, they will even, for the sake of the honour you give them, abandon their own wives and sons.

A king can win great prosperity by attracting good men to himself by such favours as gifts, sweet words, thoughtfulness and purity of behaviour. Do not, therefore, O Mandhatri, take these qualities and actions lightly.

The king should never be unconcerned about his own shortcomings or those of his enemies. He should act in such a way that his foes are not able to detect his lapses and he should attack them when theirs become evident. This is the way in which Indra, Yama, Varuna and all the Rajarishis have fought. Do you likewise, O Rajan, quickly adopt this behaviour and take the heavenly road which the Rajarishis followed. The Devas, the Rishis, the Pitris and the Gandharvas, of great tejas, sing the praises, both here and hereafter, of the king whose conduct accords with dharma."'

Bhishma continues, 'Mandhatri unhesitatingly did as Utathya directed and became the sole lord of the wide earth. Therefore, O Rajan, take the path of dharma like Mandhatri. After ruling the earth, you will find a home in Swarga.'"

CANTO 92

"Yudhishtira asks, 'Tell me, O Pitamaha, how should a righteous king behave who wants to adhere to the path of dharma?'

Bhishma replies, 'An old story has been told of what the wise, all-knowing, mahatapasvin Rishi Vamadeva related long ago to the knowledgeable, courageous and chaste king, Vasumanas, who entreated him, "Guide me, O holy one, in morality, on how I should conduct myself, so that I do not fall away from the dharma prescribed for me."

The mahatapasvin Vamadeva said to the handsome golden-complexioned Vasumanas of great tejas, seated at his ease like Yayati, son of Nahusha, "Act with dharma, as there is nothing superior to righteousness. The kings who are righteous are able to conquer the whole world. The king who regards dharma to be the most effective means to accomplish his objectives, and who conducts himself according to the counsels of men of dharma, blazes forth with righteousness. The king who disregards dharma and works with brute force soon falls away from righteousness and loses both dharma and artha.

His subjects should slay that king with his entire family who acts on the advice of a vicious and sinful minister and thus destroys dharma. The ruler who is not competent to discharge his duties of Rajaneeti, whom caprice governs in all actions and who brags, very soon meets with destruction, even if he happens to be the ruler of all the earth.

On the other hand, the king who wants prosperity, who is free from malice, who has his senses under control and who is gifted with intelligence, thrives and is prosperous, like the ocean swelling with the waters discharged into it by a hundred rivers. He should never regard himself as possessing enough virtue, pleasures, wealth, intelligence and friends.

Upon these depends the conduct of the world. By listening to these counsels, a king gains fame, achievements, prosperity and subjects. Devoted to dharma, the king who seeks wealth only by such means and who begins all his enterprises after reflecting on their objectives will obtain great prosperity. The king who is illiberal, without affection, who inflicts undue punishments on his subjects and is rash in his actions, soon meets with destruction. The king who is not intelligent fails to see his own faults. Covered with dishonour in this world, he sinks into hell hereafter.

If the king pays due honour to those who deserve it, gives gifts and, recognizing the value of sweet words, always uses them, his subjects will take on any calamities that might overcome him, as if these had fallen upon themselves.

The king who has no acharya to instruct him on the ways of dharma, who never asks others for advice and who seeks to acquire wealth as his fancy suggests, will not long enjoy happiness, while one who listens to the instructions of his gurus in matters of dharma, who supervises the affairs of his kingdom himself, and whom dharma guides in all his acquisitions, will possess happiness for a long time.'''

CANTO 93

'Vamadeva continued, "When a powerful king behaves with adharma towards the weak, others, including his descendents, emulate his conduct. The universal imitation of such a king soon brings destruction upon the kingdom.

While men in general will accept as a role model in conduct a king who observes his proper duties, his very kinsfolk will not tolerate a king who strays from dharma. The rash king who disregards the injunctions of the shastras and rules his kingdom high-handedly very soon meets with ruin.

The shastras say that the Kshatriya who does not follow the conduct observed traditionally by other Kshatriyas, victor or vanquished, fails in his dharma. Having captured in battle a royal foe who had done some favour to the conqueror in the past, if he, out of malice, does not pay him honour, he has failed in his Kshatriya dharma.

The king should display his power, live happily and do what is necessary in times of danger. Such a ruler becomes beloved of all and prosperity never abandons him. If you do a disservice to anyone, you should, when the opportunity arises, make amends and do him some favour.

He whom no one loves becomes an object of love if he does what is pleasant. Avoid empty words. You should do good to others without being asked, and never abandon dharma from kama or krodha. Do not reply harshly when someone questions you, or speak in an undignified manner. Never be in a hurry to do anything, or indulge in malice. This is how you can win over an enemy.

You should neither be overcome with joy when anything agreeable occurs, nor overwhelmed with sorrow when anything unpleasant happens. Never be grieved when you face financial distress, and always remember the dharma of doing good to your subjects. The kind king who does what is beneficial will succeed in all his endeavours and remain prosperous.

The king should always cherish the devoted servant who works for his benefit and refrains from doing anything to injure his master. He should appoint to all great affairs of his kingdom devoted men who have control over their senses, who are loyal, virtuous and competent. In addition, they should please the king and should never be thoughtless in looking after his interests. The king loses his prosperity if he appoints to important offices foolish men who are slaves to their senses, covetous, disreputable, deceitful, hypocritical, malicious, evil, ignorant, low-minded, or drunkards, gamblers, womanizers or addicted to shikar.

The king who first protects himself and then others who deserve protection, will have the satisfaction of finding his subjects growing in prosperity and will attain greatness. He should watch over the conduct and deeds of other kings, so that he can gain superiority over them through devoted secret agents. Having injured a powerful king, he should not develop a false sense of security by the great distance between them. Such an affronted king could very well fall upon him like a hawk swooping down upon its prey. A ruler who has consolidated his power and is confident of his own strength should attack a neighbour who is weaker than himself, never one who is stronger.

A king devoted to dharma, having acquired the sovereignty of the earth by his prowess, should protect his subjects righteously and destroy his enemies in battle. In this world, everything is destined for destruction, as nothing here is durable. But one who pays heed to five imperatives is the best of kings and will succeed in safeguarding and enlarging his kingdom. These five are defence of forts, administration of justice, conduct of war, consultations on questions of policy and keeping subjects happy.

It is impossible however, for one man alone to oversee all these matters. Handing over such supervision to his ministers, a king can rule the earth forever. The people want a liberal man as their king who shares all objects of enjoyment with others, who has a mild disposition, who is virtuous and who will never abandon his subjects.

People in the world obey one who accepts wise advice, abandoning his own opinions. The ruler who does not tolerate and attend to the advice of a well-wisher because it is contrary to his own views, and who does not follow the conduct of mighty and noble men, victor or vanquished, strays from the path of the Kshatriya dharma.

The king should always be careful to protect himself, from ministers whom he has earlier punished, from the arts of women, and while he is climbing mountains or entering inaccessible regions such as forests and wooded valleys. He should not ride untamed elephants or horses and should guard himself against poisonous reptiles.

The king who, abandoning his chief ministers, favours base men, soon falls into difficulties and never fulfills his plans. The weak-souled ruler who yields to the influence of anger and malice and does not love and honour his kinsmen who have noble qualities, lives on the very verge of destruction; while the king who attaches to himself accomplished men by showing them favour, even though he might not like them at heart, enjoys lasting fame.

Never impose taxes unseasonably. You should neither grieve if anything disagreeable occurs, nor rejoice exceedingly if anything agreeable happens. Try and accomplish good deeds. Ascertain who among the dependent kings is truly devoted to you, who is loyal to you from fear, and who among them has faults.

Even a powerful king should not trust a weak one, for in moments of inattentiveness the weak may assail the powerful like a flock of vultures seizing their prey. A sinful man seeks to injure his master even if the latter is sweet-tempered and possesses every virtue. Do not, therefore, place your confidence in such men. In declaring the mysteries of Rajaneeti, Nahusha's son Yayati said that a ruler should slay enemies who are contemptible.'"

CANTO 94

'Vamadeva said, "The king should win victories without battles. The wise do not speak highly of victories that wars achieve, O Rajan. Till a king's sovereignty is established, it is not proper for him to make any new conquests.

The authority of a king is established when his dominions are wide and abound with wealth, when he has a large number of officers and his subjects are loyal and contented. Even with a small force, a king can subjugate the very earth, if his soldiers are happy with pay and plunder and are competent to deceive foes. The power of the king is established when his subjects, whether of the cities or the provinces, have compassion for all creatures, are wealthy and possess grain.

When the king thinks that his power is greater than that of an enemy, he should intelligently set out to acquire the latter's territories and wealth. A king whose resources are increasing, who is compassionate to all creatures, who never loses time by procrastination and who is careful in protecting himself, makes progress indeed. The king who betrays his own innocent people injures himself like a man cutting down a forest with an axe. If he does not always attend to the task of slaying his foes, they will not diminish. The king who knows how to control his own temper will have no enemies. If he is wise, he will never do anything that good men disapprove. He will, on the other hand, always engage himself in work that will benefit him and others.

The king who, having accomplished all his duties, is happy in the approval of his own conscience, has never to incur the reproach of others nor feel any regrets. The monarch who observes such conduct towards men will subjugate both the worlds and enjoy the fruits of victory."'

Bhishma continues, 'King Vasumanas did as Vamadeva directed him. Without doubt, you, too, by following such advice will conquer both worlds.'"

CANTO 95

"Yudhishtira asks, 'Tell me, Pitamaha, how should a Kshatriya who has conquered another Kshatriya in battle behave after the victory?'

Bhishma replies, 'The sovereign, with or without an army at his back, should enter the dominions of the king he has subjugated and say to all the people, "I am your king and I will always protect you. Give me just tribute or encounter me in battle."

If the people accept him as their king, there is no need to fight, for kings should only fight other kings. If men who are not Kshatriyas by birth show signs of hostility, he should restrain them by every means, as the shastras do not prescribe the practice of warfare for them. People of the other varnas sometimes do take up arms to resist the invader if they find that their Kshatriyas are unarmed, unprepared and afraid to protect them.'

Yudhishtira says 'Tell me, O Pitamaha, how a Kshatriya king should conduct himself in war against another Kshatriya king.'

Bhishma replies, 'A Kshatriya must not put on armour to fight another Kshatriya who is not clad in mail. He should engage him in single combat and stop when the opponent is disabled. If the enemy comes clad in mail, he should also put on mail. If the enemy advances with an army, he should, taking his own army, challenge him to battle.

If the enemy fights with deceit, he should be similarly met. If, on the other hand, he fights fairly, you should engage him by fair means. You should not ride on horseback against a war chariot, for only a Maharatha should battle another Maharatha. You should not attack an unhorsed enemy, a vanquished opponent, one who has lost his chariot or weapons, or one who is frightened.

Neither poisoned nor barbed arrows should be used, as these are the weapons of the evil. You should fight righteously, without yielding to anger or wanting to kill. You should not slay a weak or wounded man; one who does not have an heir; one whose weapon has broken; one who is wounded; one whose bow-string has been cut; or one who has lost his ratha. You should send a wounded opponent to his own home or, if you bring him to your own, you should get skilful surgeons to attend to his wounds.

When, in a battle between kings who follow dharma, a righteous warrior is wounded and falls, you should have his wounds attended to and, when healed, you should set him free. This is the eternal duty and Manu, the son of the Swayambhuva Brahma, has said that battles should be fought fairly. The upright should always be righteous towards those who follow dharma, adhering to it without destroying it.

If a Kshatriya, whose duty is to fight nobly, wins a victory by adharma, he becomes sinful. A man of deceitful conduct in effect kills himself, for he practises evil. Even those who are iniquitous should be subdued only by fair means.

It is better to lay down your life in the observance of dharma, than to win victory by sin. O Rajan, sin when committed does not produce its effects immediately but overwhelms the sinner after eating away his roots and branches. A sinful man acquiring wealth by sinful means rejoices greatly, but in the process becomes wedded to sin. Thinking that dharma has no value, he jeers at men of upright conduct. Disbelieving in dharma, he meets in the end with destruction. Though enmeshed in Varuna's noose, he still regards himself immortal.

Like a large leather bag puffed up with wind, the sinner dissociates himself entirely from dharma. Soon, however, he disappears like a tree on the riverside washed away from its very roots. Then people compare him to an earthen pot broken on a stony surface and say that he deserved it. The king should, therefore, seek both victory and enrichment by just means.'"

CANTO 96

"Bhishma says, 'A king should never try to subjugate the earth through adharma, even if it makes him the supreme sovereign. Which king will rejoice after having won victory by unfair means? A victory achieved through adharma is uncertain and never leads to Swarga because, O Bharatarishabha, it weakens both the king and the country.

A warrior whose armour has fallen off, or who begs for quarter saying, "I am yours," or by joining his hands has surrendered, should simply be captured, never killed. If the troops of the invader vanquish a hostile king, the invader should not himself fight his vanquished enemy. On the other hand, he should bring him to his palace and for a whole year, try and persuade him to admit, "I am your slave!" Whether he says this or not, the vanquished enemy, by living for a year in the house of his victor, gains a new lease of life.

If a king brings by force a maiden from his vanquished foe's house, he should keep her for a year and ask her whether she will marry him or anyone else in his kingdom. If she does not agree, she should then be sent back. You should behave similarly in respect of all other kinds of wealth, such as slaves, that you acquire by force.

The king should never appropriate wealth confiscated from thieves or men awaiting execution. Cattle forcibly taken from the enemy should be given to Brahmanas so that they can drink their milk. Bulls taken from the enemy should be sent for agricultural work or returned to the enemy.

The shastras lay down that a king should fight only another king, and that one who is not a king should never strike a king. If a Brahmana desirous of peace fearlessly goes between two contending armies, both should immediately stop the battle. If any Kshatriya commits Brahmahatya or wounds a Brahmana, he breaks an eternal law and earns the contempt of his varna.

The Kshatriya who destroys dharma and transgresses all reasonable restrictions does not deserve to be considered a Kshatriya, and should be banished. A king who wants victory should never follow such conduct.

What gain can be greater than victory won fairly? It is good policy for the triumphant king to conciliate the frightened people of a kingdom recently conquered, be it with soothing words or with gifts. If he rules these conquered people roughly, they will leave the kingdom to side with his enemies and wait for a chance to strike back. Then in times of danger other discontented men, watching for such an opportunity, O Rajan, will promptly side with the king's foes.

An adversary should not be deceived through unfair means and in no case should he be wounded mortally in a fight. If a lesser king is happy, he too, will also regard life as great. That king, it is said, has his roots firm whose dominions are extensive and wealthy, whose subjects are loyal and whose servants and officers are all contented.

That king, it is said, knows the ways of the world, whose Ritwijas, priests, acharyas and others about him are well-versed in all shastras and in whose kingdom the deserving are honoured and duly respected. Indra thus won the sovereignty of the worlds, and earthly kings will gain the status of Indra if they conduct themselves in this way.

Similarly, King Pratardana, subjugating his foes in a great battle, took all their wealth, including their very grain and medicinal herbs, but left their land untouched. King Divodasa, however, after subjugating his enemies, brought away the very remnants of their sacrificial fires, their clarified butter intended for libations and their food. For taking what he should not have seized, he lost all the merit of his conquests.

King Nabhaga, after his conquests, gave away entire kingdoms, except the wealth of learned Brahmanas and Munis, along with their rulers, as sacrificial gifts to the Brahmanas. The conduct of all ancient kings was irreproachable, O Yudhishtira, and I completely approve of it. The king who desires his own prosperity should seek to conquer through every kind of excellence but never by deceit or with pride.'"

CANTO 97

"Yudhishtira asks, 'There is no dharma more sinful than that of the Kshatriyas, for the king kills multitudes in wars. Tell me, O Bharatarishabha, by what deeds, then, can the king win realms of felicity?'

Bhishma says, 'Kings become purified by punishing the evil, by attracting and cherishing the good, through yagnas and charity. It is true that kings who desire victory cause suffering to many creatures, but after that they change and improve the conditions of all.

By the power of dana, yagnas and tapasya, they destroy their sins and their punya swells so as to enable them to do good to all. The farmer who weeds his paddy field takes up the blades of the paddy, as well as the weeds. His action, however, does not destroy the blades or paddy, but makes them grow more vigorously.

Those who wield weapons destroy many who deserve destruction, but that does not retard the growth and advancement of those who remain. One who protects the people from plunder, slaughter and affliction by brigands is regarded as the giver of wealth, life and food, and similar to one who performs a yagna yielding punya.

By thus worshipping the Devas, by unifying all yagnas whose dakshina is the dispelling of fear, the king enjoys every kind of happiness here and lives in Swarga hereafter.

One regards the king who lays down his life in battle for the sake of

Brahmanas as the embodiment of a yagna with limitless gifts. If a king with his quivers full of arrows shoots them fearlessly at his enemies, the very gods will not find anyone on earth superior to him. He will enjoy eternal realms of felicity, in which his wishes will be granted, equal in number to the shafts with which he pierced the bodies of his enemies.

The blood that flows from his body cleanses him of all his sins, along with the pain that he feels. Authorities on the shastras say that the pain a Kshatriya suffers in battle operates as penance to enhance his punya. Timid men of dharma stay in the rear and beg the Kshatriyas who have rushed into battle for their lives, as men solicit rain from clouds. Great becomes their merit if they protect these fearful men and go forward themselves to face the danger.

These timorous men can free themselves from fear only if they do what is proper and just, which is to appreciate such valorous deeds and always respect their defenders. There is a great difference between men apparently equal. Some rush into battle, amid its terrible din, against armed ranks of enemies. Indeed, the Kshatriya who charges hosts of enemies takes the road to Swarga.

He who feels dread seeks safety in flight and deserts his comrades in danger. Let not such wretches be born as Kshatriyas. The very Devas, with Indra at their head, send calamities to those who desert their comrades in battle and return without a wound. One should beat with sticks or pelt with stones, or roll in a mat of dry grass and burn to death, one who deserts his comrades to save his own life. One should kill like animals any among Kshatriyas who are guilty of such conduct.

It is sinful for a Kshatriya to die in bed, spitting phlegm and passing urine, uttering piteous cries. Men who know the shastras do not applaud the death of an uninjured Kshatriya. The death of a Kshatriya at home is not praiseworthy. They are heroes, and any action that is not heroic is sinful and inglorious. In disease, he may be heard to lament, "What misery! What agony! I must be a great sinner." With a face emaciated and a stench issuing from his body and clothes, the sick man plunges his relatives into grief. Coveting the condition of those who are healthy, such a man amidst his tortures repeatedly wishes for death. He who is a hero, dignified and proud, does not deserve such a dishonorable end.

A Kshatriya should die by the sword, surrounded by kinsmen and slaughtering his enemies in battle. Frenzied with battle lust, he fights furiously and does not feel the wounds his enemies inflict on him. If he encounters death in battle, he earns that high punya filled with the fame and respect of the world due to him, and ultimately gains a place in Swarga.

The Kshatriya who does not show his back but fights with all his might at the forefront of the battle, utterly reckless of his very life, obtains the companionship of Indra. All Kshatriyas who die in the midst of their enemies without displaying shameful fear or despair earn admittance to the realms of eternal bliss.'"

CANTO 98

"Yudhishtira asks, 'Tell me, O Pitamaha, to what realms do Kshatriyas go who encounter death in battle?'

Bhishma, replies, 'There is an old story, O Yudhishtira, of a conversation which took place long ago, between Ambarisha and Indra. Ambarisha, the son of Nabhaga, went to Swarga and in those heavenly regions, so difficult to reach, he saw his own powerful general Sudeva in the company of Indra, in a celestial form blazing with every kind of energy and travelling in a very beautiful vimana. Seeing the prosperity of his Senapati and observing how he was journeying further up towards still loftier regions, the noble Ambarisha, filled with surprise, questioned Indra.

Ambarisha said, "Having ruled the whole earth bounded by the seas and wanting to earn punya, I practised all the dharma that the shastras declare are common to the four varnas. I practised with strict austerity the dharma of Brahmacharya. I waited with dutiful obedience upon my acharyas and other reverend elders and studied with due observances the Vedas and the shastras on Rajadharma. I gratified the Devas with many mahayagnas, Atithis with food and drink, the Pitris with offerings in Sraddhas and the Rishis with attentive study of the scriptures, after proper initiation into religious mysteries.

I duly observed the Kshatriya dharma according to the injunctions of the scriptures. I fearlessly faced hostile armies and won many victories in

330 || THE COMPLETE MAHABHARATA: SANTI PARVA

battle. This Sudeva, O Indra, was once the general leading my forces. It is true that he was a warrior of tranquil soul, but how has he exceeded me? He never worshipped the Devas in mahayagnas or gratified the Brahmanas with frequent and costly gifts according to the laws. Why then has he succeeded in surpassing me?"

Indra replied, "Sudeva has often performed the great yagna of battle, like anyone who engages in battle. Every warrior wearing armour who advances against his foes in battle array becomes installed in the yagna. Indeed, such a man is indisputably regarded as the yajamana of the yagna of battle."

Ambarisha said, "What constitutes the libations in this yagna? What constitutes its liquid offerings? What is its dakshina? Who, again, are its Ritwijas? Tell me all this, O performer of a hundred yagnas."

Indra said, "Elephants constitute the Ritwijas of this sacrifice and horses are its Audharyus. The flesh of enemies constitutes its libations and blood is its liquid offering. Jackals, vultures, ravens and also arrows, constitute its Sadasyas as they drink the remnants left of the liquid offering in this yagna and eat the remnants of its offerings. Heaps of lances, spears, swords, darts and axes, blazing, sharp and well-tempered, constitute the ladles of the sacrificer. Straight and well-tempered arrows with keen points that can pierce the bodies of enemies, loosed from well-stretched bows, constitute its large double-mouthed ladles.

Swords kept in sheaths of tiger skin, with handles made of ivory and capable of cutting off the elephant's trunk, form the Sphises of this sacrifice. Strokes inflicted with blazing and keen lances, arrows, swords and axes, all made of hard iron, constitute its great wealth collected from illustrious people by agreement regarding the amount and period.

The blood that runs over the battlefield from the fury of an attack constitutes the final libation, full of great punya and capable of granting every wish, in the homa of this yagna. Cries that one hears in the front ranks such as 'Cut!' and 'Pierce!' constitute the Samans that its Vedic chanters sing in the abode of Yama. The front ranks of the enemy's battle array form the vessel to store its libations.

The herd of elephants, horses and men equipped with shields one regards as the Syenachita fire of the sacrifice. The headless trunks that rise up after thousands have been slaughtered constitute the octagonal stake, made of Khadira wood, for the Kshatriya who performs the sacrifice. The screams of elephants goaded with hooks constitute its Ida mantras. The drums struck by palms forming the Vashats, O Rajan, are its Trisaman Udgatri.

When someone takes away the property of a Brahmana, the man who sacrifices his own body, so dear to him, in order to protect that property, thereby acquires the guna of a sacrifice with infinite gifts. The Kshatriya who, for the sake of his master, displays prowess at the van of the army and does not show his back through fear, earns those regions of felicity that are mine.

He who strews the altar of the battle yagna with swords cased in blue scabbards and severed arms resembling heavy bludgeons, will win regions of happiness like mine. The warrior who, intent upon victory, penetrates into the midst of the enemy's ranks without waiting for any help, succeeds in winning regions of bliss like mine.

The warrior who in battle creates a river of blood, terrible and difficult to cross, with kettle-drums for its frogs and tortoises, bones of heroes for its sands, blood and flesh for its marsh, swords and shields for its rafts, the hair of slain warriors for its floating weeds and moss, herds of horses, elephants and chariots for its bridges, standards and banners for its rushes, the bodies of slain elephants for its boats and huge alligators, swords and scimitars for its larger vessels, vultures, kankas and ravens for the rafts that float upon it, obtains regions of felicity like mine.

The warrior who creates such a river, difficult of passage even for those who possess courage and power, filling all timid men with dread, is said to complete the sacrifice by performing its final ablutions. The Kshatriya whose altar in such a yagna is strewn with the severed heads of enemies, horses and of elephants, obtains regions of happiness like mine.

The Rishis say that the warrior who regards the vanguard of the hostile army as his antapura, the front of his own army as the vessel for the sacrificial offering, the warriors standing to his south as his Sadasyas and those to his north as his Agnidhras, and who looks upon the hostile forces as his wedded wife, will attain all realms of happiness.

The open space between the two hosts drawn up for the battle constitutes the altar of such a sacrificer and the three Vedas are his three sacrificial fires. Upon this altar, aided by the chanting of the Vedas, he performs his yagna.

There is no doubt that the cowardly warrior who runs away from the fight in fear and is slain by the enemy sinks into hell, while the combatant whose blood drenches the sacrificial altar already strewn with hair, flesh and bones is sure to attain Swarga.

The powerful warrior who, having slain the commander of the hostile army, mounts the ratha of his fallen antagonist, is regarded as possessing the power of Vishnu himself and the intelligence of Brihaspati, the guru of the Devas. He who can capture alive the commander of the hostile army, or his son, or some other honoured leader, will win regions of happiness like mine.

One should never grieve for a hero slain in battle. A slain hero, if nobody grieves for him, goes to Swarga and earns the respect of its habitants. Neither do men desire to dedicate food and drink for the hero's salvation, nor do they bathe after receiving the news of his death, nor go into mourning for him.

Listen to me as I enumerate the joys that are in store for such a man. The best of Apsaras, numbering thousands, rush out to receive the spirit of the slain hero, coveting him for their lord. The Kshatriya who does his duty in battle acquires the punya of tapasya and of dharma, since his conduct conforms to the sanatana dharma. Such a man gains the punya of all the four varnasramas.

You should not kill the aged, children or women; those who flee, one who holds a straw in his lips to indicate unconditional surrender, or one who says, 'I am yours.' After killing in battle Jambha, Vritra, Vala, Paka, Satamaya, Virochana, the irresistible Namuchi, Sambara of innumerable illusions, Viprachitti—all these sons of Diti and Danu and also Prahlada, I myself have become the Lord of the Devas."

King Ambarisha came to understand by these words of Indra how, by means of fighting battles, Kshatriyas can win the blissful regions of Swarga.'"

CANTO 99

"Bhishma says, 'Let me tell you the old story of the battle between King Pratardana and Janaka, the Dharmarajan of Mithila. Janaka, who knew the truth of everything, showed both Swarga and Naraka to his own warriors and gladdened them on the eve of the battle.

He told them, "Look, these are the regions of great splendour for those who fight fearlessly. Full of Gandharva girls, these realms are eternal and grant every wish. There, on the other side, are the regions of hell, intended for those who flee from battle. They will have to rot there for eternity in everlasting disgrace. Resolve, then, to cast away your very lives and conquer your enemies. Do not fall into inglorious hell. The laying down of life in battle is the happy door to heaven for Kshatriyas."

Thus addressed by their king, O subjugator of hostile towns, the warriors of Mithila vanquished their enemies in battle and gladdened him. Those who are resolute should take their stand in the forefront of battle. The maharathas should be placed in the midst of elephants, with the horsemen behind them. At their back should be the foot-soldiers, all clad in mail. The king who forms his battle vyuha in this manner will vanquish his enemy. O Yudhishtira, you should always adopt this vyuha formation.

Filled with rage, heroes want to earn punya in Swarga by fighting fairly. Like makaras agitating the ocean, they charge the ranks of the enemy, exhorting one another, so that they hearten even those among them who are slackening.

The victor should protect the newly conquered land from aggression. Rajan, you should not allow your troops to hound the vanquished foe too far, since the enemy who rallies after being routed is desperate for safety, and will assail pursuers ferociously. Another reason why you should not pursue the defeated enemy is that brave warriors do not strike at those who run away.

Creatures who are mobile devour things that are immobile; those that have teeth devour those that are toothless; the thirsty drink water; heroes devour cowards. Cowards ensure defeat though they have the same limbs, backs and stomachs as the victors. Those who are afraid join their hands and bend their heads before the courageous.

This world rests on the arms of Kshatriyas, like a son on those of his father. Hence, he who is a Kshatriya deserves respect under every circumstance. There is nothing higher in the three worlds than heroism. The heroic Kshatriya protects and cherishes all, and all things depend upon him.'"

CANTO 100

"Yudhishtira asks, 'Tell me, O Pitamaha, how kings who want victory, should lead their troops in battle, Bharatarishabha, even if they have to offend dharma slightly!'

Bhishma replies, 'Some say that one makes dharma secure by truth; some by upapatti or reasoning; some by good conduct, and some by the application of authority. I will now tell you what the method and strategy of authority are which produce immediate results.

Robbers who break all laws very often become destroyers of property and punya. Listen to me and I will tell you about the successful methods the shastras prescribe for resisting and restraining them. The king should be acquainted with both kinds of wisdom—straight and crooked—but never apply dishonest means to injure others, only to defend himself against the dangers that may overtake him. Enemies frequently undermine a king by sowing seeds of disunity among his ministers, troops, allies or subjects. The king, aware of such deception, may use deception to counter these foes.

You should manufacture and store in abundance armour made of leather for protecting the bodies of elephants and bulls, bones, thorns and keen-pointed weapons made of iron, coats of mail, yak-tails, sharp and well-tempered weapons, all kinds of yellow and red armour, banners and standards of diverse hues, sharp swords, lances, scimitars, battle-axes, as well as spears and shields. The weapons should all be properly whetted and the warriors filled with courage and resolution.

It is proper to start your campaign and move your troops in the month of Chaitra or Agrahayana, when crops ripen and water is not scarce. This time of year, O Bhaarata, is neither very cold nor very hot. If, however, the enemy is in trouble, troops should immediately be set in motion without waiting for a favourable season. These two are the best times to start a campaign to subjugate your enemies.

While moving your troops, you should take that road which has an abundance of water and grass, which is level and easy to march on. You should ascertain the route in advance, through skilful spies who have intimate knowledge of the adjoining terrain and forests. Kings who want victory should march their armies along good roads and not through forests like animals. In the van should be an akshauhini, a division of brave and strong men of noble birth.

Regarding forts, only those which have walls, a moat and a single entrance are favourable, because resistance can be offered from within them against invading armies.

Experienced warriors consider an area lying near a wood much better for pitching a camp than one under the open sky, so that the foot-soldiers are in a position which they can defend. Danger and distress can be warded off if they engage with the enemy as soon as it comes.

If the warriors fight keeping the Saptarishis behind them and take up their stand, immoveable as the hills, they will vanquish even irresistible foes. You should have the army in such a position that the wind will blow, and the sun and the planet Saturn shine, from behind them. As a force for ensuing victory, O Yudhishtira, the wind is superior to the sun, and the sun is superior to Sukra.

Warriors prefer for the operations of cavalry a region that is not miry, soggy, uneven or full of bricks and stone, while a field free from mire and holes is suitable for rathas. A region overgrown with bushes and large trees and one under water is appropriate for elephant-warriors, while an area that has many inaccessible spots, that is overgrown with large trees and groves of cane or is a mountainous or woody tract is well-suited for the operations of infantry.

One regards an army with a large infantry force as very strong, O Bhaarata, and one in which chariots and horsemen predominate as very effective on a clear and sunny day. An army in which foot-soldiers and elephants predominate is effective in the rainy season.

Having attended to these points about the character of various forces and the manner of marching, quartering and leading them, the king should turn his attention to the characteristics of place and time. He should set out on his expedition on an auspicious day, determined by the phases of the moon and the positions of stars and planets. This will ensure that if he leads his troops adroitly, he will gain victory.

No one should kill one who is asleep, thirsty, fatigued, disarmed or one who has his heart set on nirvana, one fleeing, one walking unsuspecting along a road, one drinking or eating, one deranged, one mortally wounded or severely weakened by his wounds, one who is unaware of the fight, one who is conducting a yagna, one who is an expert in some special art like mining, one who is in mourning, one who is out of the camp foraging, men who set up camps or are camp-followers, dwarapalakas of the king or his ministers, or those who do menial services for the chieftains of the army, or the overseers of such servants.

You should honour and double the pay of those warriors who break the ranks of enemies, or rally your retreating troops with food, drink and seats equal to your own. You should promote those among them who are chiefs of ten warriors to chiefs of a hundred, and the Kshatriya who is the chief of a hundred warriors, to chief of a thousand.

Gathering together your principal warriors, you should address them saying: "Let us swear to conquer, and never to desert one another. Let those who are afraid remain here, who will cause their chiefs to be slain by being cowardly in the cauldron of battle. Let such men come who will never break in battle or cause their own comrades to be slain, for they can protect themselves as well as their comrades and will certainly kill the enemy in a fight. The consequences of fleeing from battle are reproach and infamy, loss of wealth and death. He who flees from battle, who is shameless, who casts away his weapons or is captured by the enemy, will have to hear sharp words. Let such evil always befall the warriors of our enemies."

Those who flee from battle are the most despicable of men. They are a shame on earth and devoid of true manhood, here or hereafter. Bards sing the praises of victorious warriors who readily pursue their fleeing enemies with taunts. In battle, when an enemy tarnishes the fame of a man, the misery he feels is more painful than death itself.

Understand that victory is the root of punya and of every kind of happiness. Kshatriyas bear cheerfully that which cowards regard as the highest pain. One should be resolved to fight on, regardless of life itself, determined to conquer or die and attain a blessed end in heaven."

Having sworn such an oath and prepared themselves to throw away life itself, Kshatriyas should valiantly charge the enemy's ranks. In the van you should place an akshauhini of men armed with swords and shields, and in the rear the ratha akshauhini. In between you should position other kinds of warriors. This should be the array for attack.

Battle-hardened veterans should fight in the van so that they can protect their comrades behind them. Those who are afraid should be solicitously cheered and encouraged. You should position the strongest and most courageous men in the van. You should keep the weaker men on the field without withdrawing them, at least to make the army appear larger to the enemy.

If your troops are few, you should draw them close together for the fight or, if their leader wants, the close vyuha can be extended. When a small number of troops fight with a greater army, you should form the Suchimukha vyuha, in which you draw up the warriors into a wedge-like formation.

When you engage a small force with a large one, the leader of the former should shake his men's hands and utter loud cries saying, "The enemy has broken! The enemy has broken!" Those who are strong should stand firm against the enemy and shout loudly to their comrades, "Fresh comrades have arrived! Fearlessly strike our foes!"

Those who are in advance of the rest should utter loud shouts and make all kinds of noises and blow and beat krakachas, cow-horns, drums, cymbals and kettle-drums.'"

CANTO 101

"Yudhishtira says, 'Of what temperament, behaviour and physique should warriors be, and how clad and armed so that they are fit for battle?'

Bhishma replies, 'Brave soldiers, when they engage in battle, use those weapons and chariots with which they are familiar.

The Gandharvas, the Sindhus and the Sauviras are brave and very strong and fight best with their swords and lances. Their armies are capable of vanquishing all forces. The Usinaras possess great strength and are skilled in all kinds of weapons. The Easterners are accomplished in fighting from elephant-back and also know how to fight unfairly. The Yavanas, the Kambojas and those who dwell around Mathura are skilled in fighting with bare hands, and the Southerners with swords.

It is well known that strong and courageous men are born in almost every country. Listen, and I will describe their distinguishing features. Those who have voices, eyes and bearings like those of the lion or the tiger, and those who have eyes like those of the pigeon or the snake, are all Kshatriya parantapas, while those who sound like the deer and have eyes like those of the leopard or the bull, are highly energetic. Those who have voices that resemble the sound of bells are excitable, malevolent and wrathful, while those who have voices deep as that of the clouds, visages angry or like those of camels' hooked noses and tongues, possess great speed and can shoot or hurl their weapons great distances.

Those who have bodies curved like a cat, thin hair and skin, possess great speed and are eager, near-invincible in battle, while some of those who have eyes closed like those of the iguana, a mild disposition and the speed and voice of a horse, can face all foes.

Those who are handsome, well-built with symmetrical frames, broad chests, who become angry upon hearing the enemy's drum or trumpet, who delight in affrays of every kind, who have grave eyes, eyes that bulge, or green eyes, or eyes like those of the mongoose, who have faces darkened with frowns, are all brave and will gladly give their lives in battle.

Those who have crooked eyes, broad foreheads and cheekbones not covered with flesh, arms strong as thunder-bolts and fingers bearing circular marks with arteries and nerves that are visible, will rush in with great speed when the clash of battle takes place. They then resemble infuriated elephants and become irresistible.

Those who have greenish hair ending in curls, flanks, cheeks and faces plump and fleshy, elevated shoulders, thick necks, fat calves, who have fearful visages and are fiery like Vasudeva's horse Sugriva, or like the offspring of Vinata's son Garuda, or have round heads, large mouths, faces like those of cats, shrill voices and quick tempers, who rush wildly into battle guided by its din, who are evil and full of haughtiness, who have fearsome faces and who live in the outlands, are all reckless of their lives and never retreat from battle.

You should keep such troops in the vanguard. They always slay their foes or die without turning back. Of wild conduct and outlandish manners, they regard soft speech as a sign of weakness. If treated mildly, they show contempt towards their king.'"

CANTO 102

"Yudhishtira says 'I would like to know the well-known signs, O Bharatarishabha, that portend the success of an army.'

Bhishma replies, 'I will tell you all the well-known indications that predict the success of an army. A learned astrologer and a wise priest see the future with the eye of celestial knowledge and can perform various auspicious karmas and expiatory rites, including homa and the silent recitation of mantras, to ward off calamities that unpropitious fate and the wrath of the Devas may have in store.

The army where the troops and animals are all happy and cheerful, Yudhishtira, is sure to win a decisive victory. The wind blows favourably behind such troops, rainbows appear in the sky, the clouds cast their shadows upon them and at times the sun shines upon them. Jackals, ravens and vultures become auspicious to them. When these show such regard to the army, great victories are sure to be won.

Their yagna fires blaze up with a pure splendour, the light going upwards and the smokeless flames slightly bending towards the south. The libations poured on it emit an agreeable fragrance; the conches and drums, blown and beaten, send forth sonorous peals, and the warriors are inspired with eagerness. These are indications of success.

If we see deer and other quadrupeds behind or to the left of those who have already set out for battle, or of those who are about to set out, we regard them as auspicious. If they appear to the right of the warriors when they are about to engage in battle, we regard it as an indication of success. If, however, they make their appearance in front, it indicates disaster and defeat. If certain birds, swans, cranes, satapatras and chashas utter auspicious cries and all able-bodied warriors become lively, these are omens of success.

The vyuha, which blazes with splendour and becomes terrible to look at because of the reflection from its weapons, war-machines, armour, standards and the radiant faces of the warriors who stand within the formation, will always succeed in vanquishing its enemies. If they are of pure conduct, modest deportment and attend to one another with loving kindness, it as an indication of success to come.

If because of the agreeable commands and connections the warriors become grateful and patient, we can know this as the root of success. A crow on the left of a warrior engaged in battle and on the right of him who is about to engage in it, we regard as favourable; again, if it appears at his back, it indicates failure, while its appearance in front forebodes danger.

Even after enlisting a large army consisting of the four kinds of forces, you should strive to make peace, O Yudhishtira. Only if your efforts for peace fail should you engage in battle. The victory won by battle is inferior because it is dependent on luck or destiny.

When a large army breaks and the troops begin to flee, it is exceedingly difficult to check its flight. The spontaneity of the flight resembles that of a powerful current of water or of a frightened herd of deer. If a single division takes flight the rest will follow, because fear is contagious. Some armies have broken without adequate cause, while others break even when they are brave and skilled in battle.

A great army consisting of even brave soldiers is like a large herd of Ruru deer. Sometimes even fifty men, resolute and relying upon one another, confident and prepared to lay down their lives, succeed in routing enemies numerically far superior. Sometimes even five, six or seven great Maharathas, unyielding and standing close together, can vanquish large armies.

Armed conflict is never desirable if it can be avoided. You should first try the policy of conciliation, or causing internal dissension and giving gifts as bribes; battle should be the last resort. At the very sight of a hostile force, fear paralyses the timid, like the sight of a blazing bolt from heaven. They ask, "Oh, upon what will it fall?"

Once a battle is raging, sweat drenches the limbs of those who go to join it, and of those who are winning. The entire country where a war rages, with all its resident and floating population, O Rajan, is agitated and affected. The very marrow of living men scorched by the heat of action suffers intense pain.

So a king should on all occasions adopt conciliatory methods, mixing them with severity. Men always show a disposition to make peace when an enemy oppresses them. Send secret agents to create dissension among the allies of the enemy. Discord having been kindled, the enemy will want peace with the king who is more powerful than himself, whom he once sought to crush.

If the invader does not proceed in this manner, he can never completely conquer his foe. In dealing with the enemy, take care to hem him in from all sides. Forgiveness always comes to those who are good and never to those who are evil. Listen now, O Partha, to the uses of forgiveness and sternness. The fame of a king who displays clemency after a conquest spreads widely. The very enemies of a man who is of a forgiving disposition trust him, even when he commits a grave transgression.

Sambara has said that an enemy should be subjugated first and compassion shown afterwards, for a wooden pole, if made straight without the application of heat in the first instance, very soon assumes its former crookedness. However, men skilled in the shastras do not advocate this or regard it as an indication of good kingship. Rather, they say, an enemy should be subdued and disciplined as a father does a son, without anger and without destroying him.

If a king is cruel, O Yudhishtira, he becomes a universal object of hatred. If, on the other hand, he becomes mild, everybody disregards him. Do, therefore, practise both severity and mildness. Before striking, O Bhaarata, and while striking, utter sweet words; and having struck, show your enemies compassion and let them understand that you grieve for them.

After he has vanquished an army, the king should address the survivors and say, "I am not glad that my troops have slain so many of you. Alas, they did not listen to me, though I repeatedly dissuaded them. I wish that all your dead were all alive. They did not deserve such deaths. They were all good men and true, who did not retreat from battle. Such men are rare. I surely do not approve of those who have slain such kshatriyas in battle."

Having spoken thus to the survivors of the vanquished enemy, the king should, in secret, honour those among his own troops who bravely slew the foe. To soothe the wounded slayers from their sufferings at the hand of the enemy, and to win them over, the king should even weep, seizing their hands affectionately. Thus, in all circumstances, the king should behave with conciliation.

A Dharmarajan who is fearless becomes trusted and beloved of all. Winning the people's faith, he succeeds in ruling over the earth as he pleases. If he wants to rule the earth, the king should abandon deceit, attempt to gain the trust of all and try to protect his subjects from fear.'"

CANTO 103

"Yudhishtira says, 'Tell me, O Pitamaha, how should one behave towards an enemy who is mild, one who is fierce and towards one who has many allies and a large force?'

Bhishma replies, 'There is an old tale, Yudhishtira, of a conversation between Brihaspati and Indra which took place long ago. Once upon a time, Indra, the lord of the Devas, approached Brihaspati and, saluting him with folded palms, said, "How, O Maharishi, should I behave towards my enemies? How can I subdue them other than by killing them? In a war between two armies, either side can win. What should I do so that I do not lose this blazing wealth that I have won from my enemies, that scorches them?"

The wisest Brihaspati, skilled in dharma, artha, kama and rajadharma, replied, "One should never seek to subdue one's foes by force. Only boys, cruel and volatile by nature, pick an open fight. One who wants to destroy an enemy should not put him on his guard and should never exhibit anger, fear or joy, but should conceal these within oneself. Without actually trusting one's enemy, one should behave towards him as if one trusts him completely.

One should always speak sweetly to one's enemy and never do anything displeasing to him. One should abstain from pointless hostility and from insolent speech. Just as a fowler, carefully imitating the cries of the birds he wants to catch or kill, lures and captures them, a king should first lull his enemies and then strike them down, if he so chooses.

Having overcome one's enemies, one should not sleep at ease. A foe who is evil raises his head again, like a carelessly put out fire flaring up later. When either side can win, you should avoid a battle. Lull an enemy into a false sense of security and then overpower him and gain your objective.

Consult your ministers and intelligent men who understand statecraft. If you disregard and forget an enemy who has actually not been subdued at heart, he will lie in wait and strike at you at an opportune moment, especially when you take a false step. Such an enemy can employ his own trusted agents and by sowing dissension, neutralize your forces.

Feelings of hostility towards his enemies should be nourished in secret by a king, and at the same time he should collect definite information about his enemy and learn everything he can about him. He should undermine his adversary's forces by bribery, poisoning and fomenting discord.

A king should never be too friendly with his foes, but wait patiently for the right opportunity, so that he can strike at a time when he is least expected to, and then make his kill. He should never slay too large a number of the enemy's troops, although he must certainly ensure a decisive victory. He should neither do an injury to his enemy that would rankle in the latter's heart, nor cause needless hurt by insults or rudeness.

If the opportunity to strike comes, he should not let it slip. This is what a king who wants to annihilate his enemies should do, O Indra, because if such a chance is missed, it will never come again.

A king should consult his advisors and only break the strength of his enemy. However, he should neither try to accomplish this when the opportunity is unfavourable, nor persecute his enemy even when the opportunity is at hand. The king should work carefully, giving up kama, krodha and ahamkara and all the while continually watch for any lapses by his enemy.

Extreme mildness, harshness of punishments, idleness, and recklessness: these four faults, and the deceit of his enemy, will ruin a foolish ruler,

O king of the Devas. The king who can eradicate these and counteract the cunning of his enemies will certainly succeed in vanquishing all.

When one minister can accomplish the king's secret project without any help, the king should consult him and no other. If many ministers are consulted, they will endeavour to pass the responsibility to one another and even give publicity to a project which should have been kept secret. Only if there is a need to consult another should the king do so.

When the enemy is invisible, you should invoke the Brahmadanda divine punishment, upon them; when visible, the army consisting of four kinds of forces should be deployed on the field. The king should first try and create dissension, as well as use conciliation, depending upon the need of the moment.

At times the king should even abase himself before a powerful enemy. He should work carefully and seek to ensure the victor's destruction when the latter becomes careless. One should humble oneself before a more powerful king by prostrating oneself, with gifts of tribute and by uttering sweet words when the occasion demands, never doing anything to arouse the suspicions of a powerful enemy. The weaker ruler, under such circumstances, should carefully avoid every action that can awaken doubts.

A victorious king, again, should not trust his defeated enemy, for they who are vanquished always remain alert. Men of a restless nature find it hard to acquire wealth, Devaraja, so their very existence is dangerous. Kings should carefully ascertain who their friends are and who their enemies.

If a king is mild, people disregard him, but if he is fierce, he instills fear in them. Therefore, instead of being either fierce or mild, be both. As a rapid current ceaselessly eats away a high river-bank and causes large land-slips, carelessness and mistakes ruin a kingdom. Never attack many enemies at the same time. By adopting a policy of conciliation, giving gifts or creating dissension, O Purandara, you should subdue them one by one.

As for the rest, when they are few in number the victor should behave peacefully towards them. An intelligent king, even if he is able to do so, should not try to crush all his enemies at once. He should openly strike without hesitation only when he thinks he is superior to his enemy in many respects, when he has a large army packed with the six-fold forces, consisting of foot-soldiers, horses, elephants, rathas, war engines, treasure and traders following the camp, all loyal to him.

If the enemy is strong, adopting a strategy of conciliation towards him would be a mistake. On the other hand, you should plan to harass such enemies by secret means and not try to be mild in your conduct to him. Repeated expeditions would also be a blunder, for you would be risking the loss of your crops, the poisoning of your wells and tanks, and suspicion in respect of the seven branches of administration.

On such occasions, you should apply diverse kinds of deception, various methods for setting your enemies against one another and different forms of misinformation. You should also ascertain, through trusted agents, what is happening in the cities and provinces of your enemies, Kings, after pursuing their enemies and entering their forts, O slayer of Bala and Vritra, should sack, pillage, plunder and simultaneously devise proper plans to safeguard their own cities and dominions.

Making gifts of wealth to them in private and confiscating their possessions publicly, proclaiming them as offenders punished for their misdeeds without injuring them physically, kings should send their agents to the cities and provinces of their enemies. At the same time, in their own cities, they should arrange for killing rites to be performed for the enemy, by means of powerful mantras through men who are accomplished, learned, authorities in the shastras and acquainted with the regulations of the sacred books."

Indra said, "O best of Munis, what are the signs of an evil person? Tell me how I am to identify a wicked man."

Brihaspati said, "An evil man is one who proclaims the faults of others behind their backs, who is consumed with envy at the accomplishments of others and who remains silent, reluctant to join in when someone proclaims the merits of others in his presence. Mere silence on such occasions is no indication of wickedness; however, an evil person at such times breathes heavily, bites his lips and shakes his head.

Such a man always mixes in society, speaks irrelevantly, never does what he promises when the eye of the man to whom he has made the pledge is not upon him, or even allude to the subject in his presence. He eats by himself and not with others at the same table and finds fault with the food set before him, saying, 'All is not right today, as on other days.' His disposition shows itself when he sits, lies down or rides.

Mourning on occasions of sorrow and rejoicing on occasions of joy are the signs of a friend, while the opposite behaviour indicates an enemy. Keep in mind, O ruler of the Devas, that the nature of evil men can never be concealed. I have now told you, O greatest of deities, what the signs of an evil man are. Now that you have heard the truths that the shastras lay down, follow them duly."

Purandara, when the opportunity came, conducted himself strictly according to the advice of Brihaspati and, determined to be victorious, the Parantapa successfully reduced all his enemies to subjection.'"

CANTO 104

"Yudhishtira says, 'What should a Dharmaraja do to acquire happiness whose own officers oppose him, whose treasury and army are no longer under his control and who has no wealth?'

Bhishma replies, 'Listen, Yudhishtira, to the oft-told story of Kshemadarsin, the Kosala Rajan. Long ago, Kshemadarsin lost his power and fell into great distress.

He went to the Rishi Kalakavrikshiya and, saluting him humbly, asked, "What should a man like me do who deserves wealth but who has failed to recover his kingdom despite repeated efforts; what should I do other than commit suicide or theft, take sanctuary with others or resort to other such degrading actions? O Brahmana, tell me, for one like you, who knows dharma and is full of kindness, is the refuge of a man suffering from mental or physical illness.

I have heard that a man like me should give up his desires, abandon joy and sorrow, and he will find happiness after he has earned the plenitude of knowledge. I grieve for those who believe that worldly happiness is dependent on wealth, which after all vanishes like a dream. Those who can abandon vast riches achieve a difficult feat, because we are unable to give up even wealth which has been lost. I have lost all my prosperity and fallen into a miserable and joyless existence. Tell me, O Brahmana, what happiness I should still strive for."

The sage said, "You have already understood, it seems. You are wise and should do as your intellect tells you. You are right in your belief that all that you see, as well as yourself and everything that you have, are evanescent, as am I and all that I have. Know, O Rajan, that those things which you regard as substantial, are in reality non-existent. The wise man knows this and is never troubled when confronted by sorrow.

Once you know what everyone should know, which is that whatever has happened and whatever will take place, all are unreal, you will be freed from adharma and its misery.

Whatever those who came before earned and acquired, and whatever those who succeeded them got, all have perished. Reflecting on this, who will yield to misery? Things that were are no more. Things that are will again not exist. Sorrow has no power to restore them. One should not, therefore, indulge in grief.

Where, is your father today, O Rajan, and where is your grandfather? You do not see them now, nor do they see you. If you think of your own instability, for whom then do you mourn? Reflect carefully and you will understand that it is certain that you will cease to exist. I, you, your friends, your enemies and indeed everything, will without any doubt cease to be. Those men who are now twenty or thirty years of age will all definitely die within the next hundred years.

If a man does not have the heart to give up his possessions, he should then endeavour to regard them as being not his own, and with that seek to do good. One should regard future acquisitions as well as those that have disappeared as being not one's own, of destiny as being all-powerful. Those who reason thus are wise, and the habit of seeing things like this an attribute of the good.

Many men who are equal or superior to you in intelligence and application, though deprived of wealth, are not only alive but are not kings. But unlike you, they are not unhappy. So, stop distressing yourself in this way. Are you not superior to these men, or at least equal to them in intelligence and hard work?"

The king said, "I won my kingdom and everything else with no great effort. However, all-powerful Time has swept it away as a river does sand, O Maharishi, and I am obliged to subsist on charity."

The Muni Kalakavrikshiya said, "Your frame of mind, based on the knowledge of reality, should be such that you never mourn for anything in life, O prince of Kosala, either in the past or the future. Your desire should be to obtain only that which is attainable, and so to enjoy your present possessions, not to suffer for what is not there.

Be delighted, O Kosala Rajan, with whatever you easily win. Even if you become poor, do not grieve, but seek to preserve a pure character. Only a foolish man, when he loses his wealth, instead of being contented with his remaining possessions censures the Supreme Ordainer. Such a man regards others, however undeserving, as blessed. For this reason, they suffer more who are malicious, vain and filled with self-importance.

However, such vices do not tarnish you, O king, so endure the wealth of others although you are poor. The wise succeed in enjoying the riches of others, while prosperity deserts the man who envies others.

Men of dharma and wisdom who know the duties of Yoga renounce of their own accord material possessions, as well as sons and grandsons. Others who know earthly wealth to be unstable and unattainable, dependent as it is upon ceaseless action and effort, also renounce it. You appear to be wise; why then do you grieve and yearn for things undesirable and dependent on others?

You wish to know that frame of mind which would enable you to enjoy happiness despite the loss of your possessions. My advice is that you renounce all these objects of desire.

Objects that should be avoided appear attractive, while objects that should be pursued appear undesirable. Some lose their wealth in the pursuit of riches, while others regard wealth as the root of infinite happiness and pursue it avidly. Again, some delighted with wealth think nothing superior to it and a man, in his eagerness to acquire material goods, loses all the other purusharthas.

If a man loses his hard-earned and legitimate riches, he despairs, falls inert and gives up all hope of material possessions. Some noble men of dharma pursue virtue and renounce every kind of worldly pleasure, from a desire to win felicity in the other world.

Some men lay down life itself to amass riches, for they think life without affluence is useless. Look at their pitiable condition, their foolishness. When life is so short and uncertain, these men, moved by ignorance, set their eyes on wealth. Who would set his heart upon hoarding possessions when destruction is their end, upon life when death is its end, and upon union when separation is its end?

Sometimes a man renounces wealth, and sometimes wealth abandons a man. What wise man would mourn the loss of wealth? There are many others in the world who lose their worldly possessions and friends. Use your intelligence, O Rajan, and you will understand that the calamities which overtake men are all due to their own conduct.

The remedy is to restrain your senses, mind and speech, for if those become weak and inclined to evil, there is no man who can keep himself free from the temptation of external objects which always surround him. As no one can form an adequate idea of the past or foresee the future because of the mutability of time and place, a wise man like you who has such an ability should never grieve for union and separation, for good or evil.

A man of mild disposition such as you, mature and with a disciplined soul, observant of brahmacharya, never gives in to woe or becomes restless from a desire to acquire or a fear of losing anything of little value.

It is not proper for a man like you to adopt a deceitful life of begging, a life that is sinful, evil, cruel, which only a wretch deserves. Take refuge in the great vana and lead a life of happiness there, alone, subsisting upon fruit and roots, restraining your speech and soul and filled with compassion for all creatures. He is wise who cheerfully leads such a life in the forest, with great-tusked elephants for companions, with no human being by his side, contented with the produce of the wilderness.

A large lake, when it becomes turbid, also becomes clear by itself. Similarly, a wise man, when disturbed in such matters, will become tranquil on his own. I know that someone who has fallen into a plight such as yours can still live happily. When it is near-impossible for you to recover your wealth, and when you have no ministers and counsellors, such a path opens to you.

Do you hope to reap the benefits that destiny has in store for you?'"

CANTO 105

'The Rishi Kalakavrikshiya said, "On the other hand, O Kshatriya, if you think that you still have any ability, and if you want me to, listen attentively while I disclose to you in detail the strategy you can adopt to have vast riches and, indeed, to recover your kingdom, kingly power and great prosperity."

King Kshemadarsin replied, "Tell me, O holy one, what you want me to know. I am eager to listen and do whatever you say. Let my meeting with you today prove fruitful to my enterprise."

The sage said, "Renounce ahamkara, moha, krodha, sukha and bhaya; humble yourself and wait upon your very enemies with folded hands. Serve Janaka, the king of Mithila, by always doing pure and goodly deeds. Firmly devoted to truth, you will then gain the trust of everyone and become as that king's right hand, and the Rajarishi of Videha will certainly give you great wealth.

As a result, you will gain many valiant and resolute allies, pure as fire in their deeds and free from the seven principal faults. A man of disciplined soul, with his senses under control, who adheres to his karma, will raise himself and gladden others. Honoured by the intelligent and prosperous Janaka, you will certainly become the right hand of the king and enjoy the confidence of all.

Then muster a large force, consult able ministers, bring about dissension among your enemies, set them against one another and break them all, like one who breaks a hard bilwa fruit with another. Or, make peace with the enemies of your opponent and destroy the latter's power. Arrange for your enemy to become addicted to such things as are not easily attainable—beautiful women, inordinately expensive clothes, beds, seats, carriages, mansions, birds and animals of diverse species, juices, perfumes and fruits, so that he ruins himself through indulgence.

You could either deal with your enemy thus, or show him indifference. One who wants to pursue a successful strategy should never alert the enemy to his intentions.

Follow the conduct that the wise approve of, enjoy every kind of pleasure in the dominions of your enemy, imitate the ways of the dog, the deer and the crow and behave with apparent friendship towards your enemies. Induce them to undertake tasks that are grand and difficult to accomplish. See, also, that they engage in hostilities with other powerful enemies.

Draw their attention to pleasant gardens and costly beds and seats; offer them objects of enjoyment and thereby drain your enemy's treasury. Advise him to perform sacrifices, make gifts and gratify Brahmanas to excess. Since they received the gifts through you, they will do good to you in return and perform tapasyas, Vedic yagnas to devour your foes like wolves. Without doubt, a dharmatman of virtuous deeds will earn realms of the highest felicity in Swarga.

If you cause the treasury of your enemies to be exhausted, every one of them can be subdued. The exchequer is the root of felicity in Swarga and victory on earth, and it is because of their treasuries that enemies enjoy such happiness. You should, by any means, drain their coffers.

Do not praise Parishrama or exertion in the presence of your enemies but speak highly of Vidhi or destiny. Without doubt, the man who relies too much on the worship of the Devas soon meets his destruction. Get your enemy to perform the great Viswajit yagna and by that strip him of all his possessions. Thus, your objective will be fulfilled.

You should then inform your enemy that the best men in his kingdom are being oppressed with levies to refill the exhausted coffers, and suggest some eminent Rishi who knows the duties of Yoga, who will then wean him away from his earthly possessions. Your enemy will then want to adopt renunciation and retire to the vana to seek mukti. You should then, with the help of drugs prepared by boiling potent poisonous herbs and plants with artificial salts, kill the elephants, horses and men of your enemy's dominions.

These and many other well-devised schemes are available, all connected with fraudulence. An intelligent man can destroy the entire population of a hostile kingdom with poison."

CANTO 106

'King Kshemadarsin said, "I do not desire to live by deceit or fraud, O Brahmana, for I do not want wealth, however great, earned other than through dharma. When we began our discussion I explained that I will live in this world only by means that would benefit me but not lead to censure, and I will only do things that have no harmful consequences. I am incapable of following the strategy that you recommend. Indeed, your advice does not become you."

Rishi Kalakavrikshiya replied, "Your words prove, O Kshatriya, that you are truly a man of dharma in temperament and understanding. I will strive for the benefit of both you and Janaka, the ruler of Videhas. I will arrange a bond, eternal and unbreakable, between you and him.

Who is there that would not be glad to have a minister like you, born of a noble race, learned, who follows dharma, abstains from cruelty, is versed in the art of governance and knows how to pacify everyone? I say this because, though dispossessed of your kingdom and plunged into great misery, you still want to follow dharma. Janaka, who firmly adheres to truth, will come soon to my asrama. I have no doubt that he will do what I ask of him."

The sage then summoned Janaka and said to him, "Kshemadarsin is of royal birth. I know his very heart and soul are as pure as the surface of a mirror or the disc of the autumn moon. I have tested him in every way and I do not see any fault in him. You should be friends. Repose in him the same confidence that you have in me.

A king who is without a competent minister cannot rule his kingdom for even three days. The minister should be courageous and highly intelligent. With these two attributes you can conquer both the worlds. Understand, Janaka, that these two qualities are essential to rule a kingdom and Dharmarajans have no greater support than a minister who possesses them.

Kshemadarsin is of royal birth and walks the path of dharma. He who always has dharma in his mind is a valuable acquisition. If you treat him with honour, he will reduce all your foes to subjection. If he fights you, he will do what a Kshatriya should. Indeed, like his father and grandfathers, if he fights, it will be to conquer you, and it will then be your duty to fight him, observing the Kshatriya dharma.

However, listen to my advice and you will benefit if you employ him and refrain from fighting him in battle. Keep your eyes always on dharma and renounce greed, for it is inappropriate for you to abandon the duties of your varna from lust for battle.

Neither Jaya nor Parajaya, victory or defeat, are predictable. Remember, peace should be made with an enemy by giving him food and wealth. One can see victory and defeat in Kshemadarsin's own case. Those who seek to destroy an enemy are sometimes themselves destroyed."

King Janaka saluted and gave due honour to the Maharishi and replied, "You are immensely learned and wise and I have no hesitation in saying that your sincere advice is sure to be advantageous for us both."

King Janaka then addressed the prince of Kosala, "I have conquered the world through the Kshatriya dharma and with the help of Neeti. However, Rajan, you have conquered me with your qualities. If you remain by my side, I will honour you and you will live with me as a victor—a Praptajaya. I honour your intelligence and your prowess, and I will not slight you by saying that I have conquered you. Live with me in my home with honour, and as a victor."

Both kings then performed obsequies to Rishi Kalakavrikshiya and, with mutual trust, went to the capital of Mithila. King Janaka invited

Kshemadarsin into his home and duly honoured him with water to wash his feet, honey, curds and the other customary offerings. King Janaka also gave him the hand of his own daughter, as well as all kinds of gems and jewels. The establishment of peace is the greatest dharma of kings, since victory and defeat are both uncertain."'

"Yudhishtira says, 'You have, O Pitamaha, described the path of dharma, the general conduct, the means of livelihood of Brahmanas, Kshatriyas, Vaisyas and Sudras, and its consequences. You have also spoken about the duties of kings, of their treasuries and the means to fill them, and about conquest and victory.

You have explained the character of ministers, the measures that lead to the betterment of one's subjects, the characteristics of the six-fold limbs of a kingdom, the qualities of armies, how to identify evil, the marks of those who are good, the attributes of those who are equal, inferior or superior to oneself, how a king who desires progress should conduct himself towards his people, and the manner in which the weak should be protected and cherished.

You have discussed all these subjects and laid down instructions that are lucid and as prescribed in the sacred texts. You have also discussed what kings should do if they wish to conquer their enemies.

Tell me now, Pitamaha, how I should behave towards the multitude of noble Kshatriyas that gather round a king's court. I want to know how their number can be increased, how they can be made loyal to the king, and how they can subjugate their enemies and acquire friends. It seems to me that disunity alone can bring about their destruction.

I also think that it is difficult to keep a secret that concerns many men. I would like to hear about all this in detail, Parantapa. Tell me also how to prevent the nobles from becoming inimical towards the king.'

Bhishma replies, 'Lobha and krodha, greed and anger, O Rajan, cause enmity between noblemen and kings. If the king yields to greed, the nobles become angry, and if each works with intent to weaken and harm the other, both are destroyed. The two sides war with each other; they employ spies, use ploys, physical force, adopt the strategy of conciliation, offer bribes, cause disssension, try to weaken each other, pillage and spread fear.

The noblemen of a kingdom, a close-knit body, will dissociate themselves from the king if he tries to take too much from them. Once distanced from the king, all of them become dissatisfied and, from fear, will side with the enemies of their ruler. If the Kshatriyas are not united amongst themselves, they will fall easy prey to ouside enemies and will be destroyed. The nobles should always work in concert; by their strength and prowess they can acquire wealth, and many outsiders will seek their alliance.

Men of knowledge laud those noblemen who are united with bonds of love. If they stand together, they will all prosper and, by their example, establish dharma in the kingdom. They become prosperous if they restrain their sons and brothers, if they teach them their dharma, and behave kindly towards all men who have disciplined their ahamkara through gyana.

The nobles become prosperous if they ensure that their spies are active, Mahabaho, if they formulate policy, fill their treasuries, show proper reverence to the wise, the courageous and the persevering, and display steady proficiency in work.

By being wealthy and resourceful, through their knowledge of the shastras, the arts and sciences, the aristocracy rescues the ignorant masses from suffering and danger. A show of anger by the king, disagreement, terror, punishment, persecution, oppression and executions, O chief of the Bhaaratas, speedily cause the nobility to break from him and side with his enemies.

The king should honour the leaders among the nobility, for Rajaneeti depends to a great extent on them. You should hold consultations with only those who are the leaders, Parantapa, and have secret agents to watch them. The king should not consult every member of the nobility, O Bhaarata, but work together with the leaders and do whatever is for the good of the entire Kshatriya varna.

When the nobility fall out or become disunited and leaderless, you should adopt other methods, for if they quarrel and act independently without unity, their prosperity dwindles and they fall prey to all kinds of evil. Those among them who are learned and wise should quell a dispute as soon as it arises, because if the elders of a royal house look on with indifference, such quarrels will soon destroy them and disunite the entire varna of Kshatriyas.

Fears that arise from outside are of little consequence, Rajan, but protect yourself from all fears that arise from within, for this can cut your very roots in a single day. When men equal to one another in family and blood, provoked by the wrath and greed inherent in their nature, cease to speak with one another, it is an omen of imminent defeat and destruction.

It is not by employing courage, intelligence, beauty, or wealth that enemies destroy the nobility. It is only through conflict and bribery that they can be subjugated. For this reason, one says that unity is the greatest protection of the nobility.'"

CANTO 108

"Yudhishtira says, 'The path of dharma is long, O Bhaarata, and has many branches. Which are the most important duties that I must practise to earn the highest punya, both here and hereafter?'

Bhishma replies, 'I think that the worship of Mata, Pita and guru is most important. The man who attends to this duty here will acquire great fame and many regions of felicity hereafter. Yudhishtira, you should revere them and obey unhesitatingly whatever they command, be it consistent with dharma or not! One should never do what they forbid.

They are the three worlds, the three varnas, the three Vedas and the three sacred fires. The Pita, one's father, one says is the Garhapatya fire; the Mata, mother, the Dakshina fire, and the guru is that fire upon which you pour libations. These are pre-eminent and, if you attend attentively to these three fires, you will conquer the three worlds.

If one serves one's father steadfastly, one can cross this sea of samsara. If one serves one's mother in the same way, one can attain regions of felicity in the next. If one serves one's acharya with devotion, one can obtain the realm of Brahma. Behave properly towards these three, O Bhaarata, and you will gain great fame in the three worlds and be forever blessed.

Great will be your punya and reward. Never disobey them in any matter. Never eat before they eat, or eat anything that is better than what they eat. Never blame them for anything, and always serve them humbly. You can earn fame, merit, honour and regions of felicity hereafter, if you perform these deeds of great punya.

All the worlds honour those who revere these three. On the other hand, those who disregard these three will fail to find any punya, fame or merit from his karma, either in this world or in the next.

All that I have given away in honour of these three has returned a hundredfold or a thousandfold to me. It is because of this punya, O Yudhishtira, that even now the three worlds are clearly before my eyes. One acharya is superior to ten Brahmanas learned in the Vedas, and one Upadhyaya superior to ten acharyas. The father, again, is superior to ten Upadhyayas, and the mother greater in importance than ten fathers or perhaps the whole world. It is said that no one deserves as much reverence as the mother.

In my opinion, however, the guru is worthy of greater reverence than the father or even the mother. The father and the mother are authors of one's being, O Bhaarata, but they only create the body. The life of the spirit, on the other hand, one receives from one's Acharya, and that is divine. It is subject to no decay and is immortal.

You should never injure your father and mother, however much they offend you, and one does not incur sin if one refrains from punishing a parent, even if punishment is deserved. Indeed, a parent who enjoys impunity does not tarnish the image of a king, and the Devas and the Rishis do not withhold their favours from men who strive to cherish reverently even sinful fathers.

One should regard as both father and mother those who favour us and impart to us true and immortal knowledge of the Vedas. The disciple in gratitude should never do anything that would injure the acharya.

Those who do not respect the acharyas who instruct them, and do not obey them dutifully in thought and deed, incur the sin of killing an unborn, and there is no greater sinner in this world. Gurus always show great affection for their shishyas, so the latter should show their acharyas equal reverence. He who wishes to earn this great punya, which has existed from ancient days, should revere and love his acharyas and cheerfully share with them every object of enjoyment.

He who makes his father happy pleases Prajapati himself, and he who pleases his mother gratifies the earth herself, but he who pleases his guru gratifies Brahma by his karma. For this reason, the acharya is worthy of greater reverence than either the father or the mother.

If you worship your acharyas, the very Rishis and the Devas, together with the Pitris, all are pleased. The guru is worthy of the highest reverence and the shishya should never disregard him in any manner. Neither the mother nor the father deserves as much respect as the acharya. One should never insult the father, the mother or the guru, or find fault with anything they do.

The Devas and the great Rishis are pleased with one who behaves with reverence towards his gurus. Those who hurt in thought or deed their acharya, father or mother, incur the sin of killing a foetus in the womb, and there is no sinner in the world equal to them. The son of the father's loins and the mother's womb, raised by them, who does not support them in his turn when he comes of age, incurs the sin of killing an unborn child, and there is no greater sinner in the world than him. We have heard that these four, he who injures a friend, he who is ungrateful, he who kills a woman and he who kills his guru, will never be able to purify themselves.

I have now told you generally all that a man should do in this world. Besides these duties that I have indicated, there is nothing that will bring greater happiness. I have told you the essence of all dharma.'"

CANTO 109

"Yudhishtira says, 'You are wise, O Bhaarata, so tell me how one who wants to adhere to dharma should work. Truth and falsehood exist in all the worlds. Which of these two should a man of dharma accept? What is truth, what is falsehood and what is sanatana dharma? When can a man tell the truth and when an untruth?'

Bhishma replies, 'To speak the truth is consistent with dharma, because there is nothing higher than truth. I will now tell you that which men do not generally know. You should not speak the truth where falsehood can appear to be the truth. Then again, you should even lie where truth will appear to be false.

The ignorant man incurs sin when he tells a truth which is not connected to dharma. He who can distinguish truth from falsehood knows dharma. Even a disreputable, cruel man with an evil, impure soul, can earn great punya, like the hunter Valaka, who killed the blind beast that threatened to destroy all creatures.

It is extraordinary that even a Rishi, though foolish, who wanted to acquire punya by tapasya, could incur the sin of murder by telling the truth to a company of robbers and pointing out the place where certain innocent men were hid.

Again, an owl who did an evil deed and with his beak broke a thousand eggs on the banks of the Ganges, obtained great punya and went to Swarga, because the eggs were of a deadly poisonous she-serpent.

The question you have asked me is a complex one, and no one who discusses the subject can define dharma accurately. Brahma declared that whatever leads to the advancement and growth of all creatures is dharma. He declared that whatever restrains creatures from injuring one another is dharma.

Dharma is so called because it supports all creatures. Some say that dharma is in the Srutis, while others do not agree. I would not fault those who disagree, since the Srutis do not lay down every duty.

Sometimes brigands seek information to help them identify a victim to rob. It is one's duty never to answer such queries. If by one's silence, a victim can escape, one should remain silent. If, on the other hand, one's silence at a time when one must speak rouses suspicion, it would be better to tell a lie.

It is accepted that there is no sin if one can escape from evil men even by swearing a false oath. One should not give wealth to sinful men, for that affects even the giver. If a creditor desires to enslave a debtor unable to pay off his debt, the witnesses should all lie if the creditor summons them to establish the truth of the contract. When life is at risk, or on a matter of marriage, one can lie.

One who seeks dharma does not commit a sin by telling a lie if he says it to save the property of others, or for sake of dharma. One is liable to fulfill all promises to pay one's debts and, upon failure, the defaulter may be forcibly enslaved. If a man does not fulfill his responsibilities, he should certainly be punished with the Dandaneeti.

A deceitful man who fails in all the duties of his own varna will begin to adopt practices of Asuras and live dishonestly. You should never tolerate such men but kill them by any means, for they think there is nothing in this world higher than wealth. No one should eat with them, and you should regard them as inhuman evildoers—pisachas shut out from the grace of the gods. Since they do not perform yagnas or tapasya, stay away from their companionship for, if they lose their wealth, they will even perform that most wretched act, suicide. Among these evil men, there is no one to whom you can say, "This is your duty. Let your heart turn to it." Their strong belief is that there is nothing in this world equal to wealth. He who slays such a creature would incur no sin, for his own karma has killed him, and he is already dead.

He who swears to slay these mindless men should keep his vow. Such evil men are like the crow and the vulture, dependent on deceit for their living, and after the dissolution of their human bodies they are reborn as crows and vultures. You should behave towards others in the same manner as they behave towards you. You should deal with one who practises deceit with deceit, and treat an honest man honestly.'"

CANTO 110

"Yudhishtira says, 'We see men suffer almost continually on various counts. Tell me, O Pitamaha, in what way can one overcome all these travails?'

Bhishma replies, 'The Rishis who duly practise the dharma decreed by the scriptures for the several varnasramas surmount all their difficulties. Those who never practise deceit, who are disciplined and who are in control of their worldly desires, master all their troubles.

Those who do not respond even when provoked, who do not injure others though they are themselves hurt, who give but do not take, overcome all hardships. Those who are always hospitable to guests, who are not malicious, who regularly study the Vedas, overcome all their difficulties. Those who know their duties, behave appropriately towards their parents, who do not sleep during the day, master all their troubles. Those who do not commit any kind of sin in thought, word or deed, who practise ahimsa, overcome all tribulations.

Kings who are not influenced by moha and lobha, who do not levy oppressive taxes and protect their own dominions, overcome all problems. Those who go to their own wedded wives in season and do not seek the companionship of other women, who are honest and attentive to their Agnihotras, surmount all difficulties.

Those who are courageous and engage in battle by fair means, unmindful of death, overcome all troubles. Those who always adhere to truth in this world, even when life is at stake, and who are models for all men to imitate, overcome all obstacles. Those who never deceive by their actions, whose words are always agreeable and whose wealth is always well spent, overcome all ills.

Those Brahmanas who study the Vedas only at hours intended for study and who practise tapasya with devotion, overcome all obstacles. Brahmanas who take to a life of celibacy and brahmacharya, who perform tapasya and whom learning, Vedic knowledge and proper vows have cleansed, overcome all travails.

Those who have controlled the gunas of rajas and tamas, are Dharmatmans who practise the quality of sattva, and they can overcome all pain and sorrow.

Those whom no creature fears, who do not themselves fear any, and look upon all creatures as their own selves, overcome all difficulties. Those bulls among men who are good, who are not envious of other people's prosperity and who are noble in their conduct, overcome all difficulties.

Those who bow to all the Devas and listen to the doctrines of all dharmas, have faith and tranquil souls, and overcome all troubles. Those who do not desire honour for themselves, who reward others, who bow down to those deserving of their worship, overcome all difficulties.

Those who perform sraddhas on the proper lunar days with pure minds for the sake of progeny are blessed with fine children. Those who restrain their own anger and pacify the wrath of others, who never lose their temper, overcome all difficulties. Those who abstain all their lives from honey, meat and intoxicants, overcome all grief.

Those who eat only in order to support life, who seek the companionship of women only for the sake of begetting children, and who open their lips only to speak the truth, overcome all difficulties. Those who worship with devotion Narayana, the Supreme Lord of all creatures and the origin and destruction of the universe, overcome all trials.

This Krishna here, of eyes red as the lotus, clad in yellow robes, this Mahabaho who is our well-wisher, brother, friend and relative, is

Narayana of unfading glory. He covers all the worlds like a leather case, at his own pleasure. He is the powerful Lord of unimaginable Soul. He is Govinda, the greatest of all beings. This Krishna who always does what pleases and is beneficial to Vishnu and also to you, Yudhishtira, is the first and best of all beings, the irresistible one, the abode of eternal felicity.

Those who devoutly seek the refuge of Narayana, also called Hari, will overcome every obstacle. Those who read these verses about how to surmount difficulties, who recite them to others and speak of them, will surely overcome.

I have now, O sinless one, told you all those acts by which men can transcend all their woes and sorrows, both here and hereafter.'"

CANTO 111

"Yudhishtira says, 'Many men here who are not serene souls outwardly appear calm, while others who are really peaceful souls appear otherwise. How, O Pitamaha, can we distinguish between them?'

Bhishma replies, 'Let me relate, O Yudhishtira, a conversation between a tiger and a jackal.

Long ago, in a prosperous city called Purika, there was a king named Paurika. He was the worst of men, exceedingly cruel, who delighted in causing injury to others. On the expiry of his lifespan he died miserably and, as a result of the evil deeds of his human life, was reborn a jackal.

He, however, remembered his former prosperity and in grief, gave up meat even when others of his kind brought it to him. He became compassionate to all creatures, truthful in speech, firm in the observance of strict vratas, and ate only wind-fallen fruits from the trees. The jackal continued to live in the vast crematorium where he was born and never wished to change it for a better locality.

Unable to suffer the purity of his conduct, the other members of his species tried to make him change his resolve and told him with humility, "Though you dwell in this terrible smasana, you still want a lofty life. Isn't this a perversity, since you are by nature a carrion-eater? Be like us. All of us will give you food. Eat what is your natural diet, and abandon this virtuous conduct."

The jackal listened attentively and replied reasonably in these words of ahimsa, "I am of low birth, but it is conduct that determines varna, not varna that decides conduct. I wish to live in such a way that my fame will spread.

Although I dwell in this smasana, I observe my vratas according to dharma. One is the cause of one's karma and the varnasrama one takes is not for religious deeds. If one who follows any varnasrama kills a Brahmana, will he not incur the sin of Brahmahatya? If, on the other hand, one gives away a cow, though one does not observe any particular varnasrama, will that pious gift yield no punya?

Motivated by selfish needs, you only want to fill your stomachs. You are confused and foolishly do not see the three sins that will be the final result. I do not want to adopt the life you lead, which is evil both here and hereafter and will surely lead to discontentment, temptation and loss of virtue."

A renowned tiger happened to overhear this conversation and, finding the jackal to be a learned one of pure conduct, greeted him respectfully and said, "Righteous one, I know what you are. Come and share the duties of kingship with me as my minister. Enjoy whatever you wish and leave behind what you do not want. But let me tell you that tigers are known to be fierce. If you behave with mildness, you will reap the benefits."

The jackal, flattered by these words of the mahatman among animals, hung his head a little and said humbly, "O king of beasts, I thank you for your kind words. Your wish to seek ministers of pure conduct, familiar with dharma and worldly affairs, does you credit. You cannot remain a great leader without a pious minister, or with an evil one who is on the lookout to destroy you.

You should regard the ministers who are devoted to you, who understand policy, who are independent, who want to crown you with victory, who are not greedy, who are free from deceit, wise, ever engaged in your welfare and have mental vitality, just as you look upon your acharyas or your parents.

But as I am perfectly happy with my present position, I do not want to change it for anything else. I do not covet luxury or the happiness associated with it.

My conduct will not agree with that of your old servants. If they are evil, they will produce discord between us. It is not desirable or praiseworthy to depend upon another. I am a Dharmatman and highly blessed. I cannot show severity even to sinners. I have foresight and a capacity for great exertion and do not look at insignificant things. I possess great strength, follow dharma and never work fruitlessly. I have every object of enjoyment and am never satisfied with a little.

I have never served another and am unskilled in the matter. I live according to my pleasure in the vana. All those who dwell with kings have to endure great apprehension because of evil talk against them. Vanavasis pass their days fearlessly, without anxiety and contentedly in the observance of vratas, living on fruits and roots, with no fear that arises in the heart of one whom the king summons.

Reflect, and you will see that simple food and drink obtained without effort, and sumptuous food procured with fear, differ widely from each other. I am of the opinion that happiness prevails where there is no anxiety. Only a few among those who serve kings are justly punished for their offences. A large number of them are falsely accused and suffer death.

If you still appoint me as your minister, O king of beasts, I want to make a compact with you regarding your conduct towards me. You should always heed my advice, which will ever be for your good. You will not interfere later with the arrangements that you will make for me.

I will never consult your other ministers because, if I do, they will find various faults in me to put me down. I will meet you alone, in secrecy, and advise you. In all matters regarding your kinsmen, you will not seek my advice. After you have consulted me, you will not punish your other ministers later in rage, nor will you punish my followers and dependants."

To this the king of beasts answered, "Tathaastu, let it be so!" and showed him every respect. The jackal then became the minister of the tiger.

When they saw the jackal treated with respect and honour, the previous servants of the king conspired together and began to show their hatred towards him. These evil servants at first tried to gratify and win him over with friendly overtures so that he would permit the misappropriation and abuse of the property of others, which they had so long enjoyed.

When they were unable to do as they pleased, they began to lure him with sweet talk and large bribes, but the wise jackal showed no signs of yielding to these temptations. Then some of them colluded to destroy him, stole the well-dressed meat intended for the tiger and placed it secretly in the jackal's house. The jackal knew who had stolen the meat and who the conspirators were, but he did nothing because of his covenant with the king. When he was made a minister, he had said, "You want my friendship, O Rajan, but you will not mistrust me without cause."

When the king of beasts, feeling hungry, came to eat, he did not see any meat for his dinner and roared, "Find the thief!"

His deceitful ministers reported to him that his learned minister, the jackal, who was so proud of his own wisdom, had stolen the meat. Hearing this, the tiger became filled with rage and ordered his jackal to be seized. Seeing their opportunity, the former ministers told the king, "The jackal is always ready to steal our food."

They spoke of the jackal robbing the king of his food and said, "Such then is he! What is there that he would not venture to do? He is not as you had heard. He is righteous in speech but he is sinful and has disguised himself by putting on the garb of dharma. For selfish reasons he has practised austerities in diet and vows. If you do not believe us, we will show you proof."

They then caused the meat to be discovered in the jackal's home and reported it to the king. Based on this evidence and the complaints of his old servants, the king ordered the jackal to be executed.

The venerable mother of the tiger heard of this and came to awaken his good sense with wise advice. "Son, you should not accept this deceitful accusation. Evil men, out of envy and rivalry, impute faults to an honest man, as they cannot endure his exploits and success.

They ascribe faults even to a Dharmatman engaged in tapasya. Even for a Muni in vanavasa, harmlessly practising his svadharma, friends, neutrals and foes spring up. They who are greedy hate those who are pure; the idle hate the active; the uneducated hate the learned; the poor hate the rich; the evil man hates the man of dharma; and the ugly hate the beautiful. Many among the learned, the ignorant, the rapacious and the deceitful, would falsely accuse an innocent one, even if the latter possessed the virtues and intelligence of Brihaspati.

If the meat has really been stolen from your house, remember, while you search for the thief, that the jackal never takes any meat that anyone gives him. We notice that evil men sometimes appear good, and the good sometimes appear evil. A thorough examination is absolutely necessary.

The sky appears to be the solid base of a vessel and the firefly a spark of actual fire. In reality however, the sky has no base and there is no fire in the firefly. Ensure that there is close scrutiny, even of what appears to the eye, so that you don't regret it later.

It is not at all difficult, O son, for a master to put his servant to death. Forgiveness in the powerful, however, is always laudable and celebrated. You appointed the jackal as your prime minister and earned great fame among all our neighbouring jungle kings. A good minister cannot be found easily and, since the jackal is your well-wisher, you should support him.

The king who condemns an innocent one falsely accused by his enemies soon meets destruction at the hands of evil counsellors who influenced that decision."

After the tiger's mother had spoken, a good servant of the jackal, stepping out of the ranks of his foes, described how his enemies had fabricated the false accusation. The jackal's innocence was proved and the tiger acquitted and feted him, affectionately embracing him again and again.

The jackal, who knew Rajaneeti, however, burned with grief. He saluted the king of beasts and sought his permission to give up his life by observing the praya vrata. The tiger looked at the virtuous jackal, his eyes brimming with affection, and respectfully sought to dissuade him.

The jackal, seeing his master emotional, bowed to him and in a voice choked with tears, said, "You first honoured and later insulted me. Your conduct towards me is calculated to make me your enemy. It is not proper that I should stay with you any longer.

Servants who are discontented, who have been stripped of their office or deprived of their honour, who have been impoverished or whose enemies have ruined them through their master's anger, who have been weakened, who are rapacious, enraged, alarmed, deceived by their employers, whose property has been confiscated, who are proud and want to achieve great feats but do not have the means to earn wealth, and who burn with grief or rage due to some injury done to them, always hope for calamities to overcome their masters. Deceived, they leave their masters and become effective instruments in the hands of enemies.

You have insulted me and pulled me down from my place. How will you trust me again? How will I on my part continue to stay with you?

You thought me competent and gave me high office. However, you violated our compact and humiliated me. If you refer to someone as a Dharmatman, you should not then term him evil, if you want to maintain your steadfastness.

You no longer have any confidence in me, and this fills me with alarm and anxiety. Your suspicion and my fear will give our enemies opportunities to injure us, leaving your subjects uneasy and anxious.

Such a state of affairs has many faults, and the wise do not regard a situation as happy in which there is honour first and dishonour later. It is difficult to reunite two that you have separated, just as it is difficult to separate two who are united. If men reunite after separation, their conduct will not be affectionate.

There is no servant who does anything only to benefit his master.

Service proceeds from the motive of doing good to the master, and also to oneself. One lives from selfish motives, because unselfish deeds or motives are rare, almost unknown. Kings whose hearts are restless and unquiet cannot acquire a true knowledge of men. Only one in a hundred can be found to be able or fearless. The prosperity of men and their fall, adversity and greatness, all proceed from weakness of understanding."

These conciliatory words of advice about dharma, kama and artha made the king happy. The intelligent jackal then left for the forest. Disregarding the entreaties of the king of beasts, he sat in praya, cast off his body and went to Swarga as the reward for his good karma on earth.'"

CANTO 112

"Yudhishtira says, 'Tell me in detail, O Dharmatman, what efforts a king must make to be happy.'

Bhishma replies, 'I will tell you the established truth about what a king should do in this world, and his dharma, so that he can be happy. Yudhishtira, a king should not behave like the camel in the story that I am about to relate to you!

There was, in the Krita yuga, a huge camel who could recollect all the events of his former life. He sat in tapasya and observed the most rigid vratas in the vana. This pleased the great Brahma so much that he granted him a boon.

The camel said, "Let my neck become long by your grace, O Holy One, so that I may be able to reach food that lies even at the end of a hundred yojanas."

The Mahatman, giver of boons said, "Tathaasthu!" and granted the wish.

Having obtained the boon, the camel returned to his own vana. The foolish animal, from the day of gaining the boon, became idle and did not go out to graze. One day, while the animal had extended his neck of a hundred yojanas and was grazing without any effort, a great storm arose. The camel, placing his head and a portion of the neck within the cave of a mountain, resolved to wait till the storm passed.

Meanwhile, it began to pour in torrents, inundating the whole terrain.

A jackal, with his wife, drenched by the rain and shivering with cold, dragged himself with difficulty towards the very same cave and ran into it for shelter. Living as he did upon meat, and famished and tired as he was, O Bharatarishabha, the jackal, seeing the camel's neck, began to eat as much of it as he could. The camel strove desperately to shorten it, but the jackal and his wife did not lose their hold. Within a short time the foolish camel was dead. Having eaten the camel's head and throat, the jackals came out of the cave after the storm had abated. Thus the stupid camel met its death, which followed in the train of idleness.

As for yourself, control your senses, avoiding idleness, and do everything in the world conscientiously. Manu himself has said that victory depends upon intelligence. All karma accomplished with your intelligence is regarded as the best; karma achieved with the help of arms is average; that attained by the use of feet is inferior, while work done by carrying loads is the lowest. If the king is clever in the transaction of business and restrains his senses, his kingdom will thrive.

Manu has also maintained that with intelligence an ambitious man can achieve victory. Sinless one, in this world those who listen to advice that is not generally known, who have allies and who act only after careful consideration, achieve all their goals and rule the earth.

Yudhishtira, you who are powerful as Indra himself, the wise men of ancient times who know the shastras have held this view and I, too, say the same to you: In this world, Rajan, think before you act!'"

CANTO 113

"Yudhishtira says, 'Tell me, O Bharatarishabha, how a ruler who has won possession of a precious kingdom behaves towards a powerful enemy.'

Bhishma replies, 'Let me relate to you the old story of the conversation between the Ocean and the rivers.

Long ago, the eternal Ocean, the lord of rivers, the refuge of the foes of the Devas, asked all the rivers to clear a doubt that had arisen in his mind. "I see that all you rivers bring away along with your rapid currents large tree trunks, torn off with their roots and branches. However, you do not ever bring me the cane that grows on your banks, which is thin and not strong. Tell me, do you refuse to uproot it out of contempt, or because it is of no use to you? Indeed, why do you not wash away the stalks of cane uprooted from the banks where they grow?"

The Ganga river replied to the Ocean, the lord of all rivers, wisely and sensibly: "Trees stay in one place and do not yield the spot where they stand. As a result, they resist our currents and we are obliged to uproot them. The cane, seeing the swelling currents, behaves differently. It bends and after the flood has subsided, resumes its former posture. The cane knows the virtues of time and opportunity, kaala and avasara. It is docile and obedient, yields without being obstinate and inflexible, and so remains where it grows, without us carrying it away. The plants, trees and creepers that bend and rise before the force of wind and water have never to suffer the fate of being uprooted."

He who does not yield to the power of an enemy greater in might, and in a position to imprison or kill him, soon meets with destruction. The wise man who acts only after he has fully ascertained the relative strengths and weaknesses, the stamina and energy, of himself and his enemy, has never to suffer embarrassment. An intelligent man, when he finds his enemy to be more powerful than himself, should be like the cane. This is true wisdom.'"

CANTO 114

"Yudhishtira says, 'How should a learned and modest man behave, O Bhaarata, when an ignorant and conceited braggart assails him with harsh words in a gathering?'

Bhishma replies, 'Listen, O lord of the earth, to what the shastras prescribe as the conduct of a mahatman when he is confronted in this world by abuse from unintelligent men. If he does not yield to anger, he is sure to take away the punya of all the good karma of the abuser. The sufferer in such a case transfers the paapa of all his own bad karma to the angry abuser. An intelligent man should disregard insulting language, which, after all, is merely like the screeching of a tittibha bird.

He who yields to hate, lives in vain. A fool can often be heard to say, "I addressed that respectable man in these words before an assembly of men," and to even boast of that vicious deed. He will add, "Abused by me, the man remained silent as if dead with shame."

A shameless man brags about something of which no one should boast. You must disregard such a wretch. The wise man should endure anything that fools say, for what can a vulgar fellow achieve by his praise or blame? He is like a crow that caws pointlessly in the vana.

If those who accuse others verbally could establish the charges by some means, then perhaps their words would be of some value. But empty words are as effective as those spoken by fools invoking death upon those they abuse.

Such a man only proclaims his own bastardy by his vile conduct; he is like a peacock that dances displaying its intimate body parts, which should properly be concealed. A man of pure conduct should never even speak with such sinful men, who have no scruples and say or do anything without shame.

He who speaks of someone's merits when his eyes are upon him, and speaks ill of him behind his back, is truly like a dog. Such a man loses prospect of bliss in Swarga as well as the fruits of any knowledge and dharma that he has earned. He who speaks ill of others behind their backs soon loses the punya earned from all his yagnas, libations and gifts made even to a hundred men.

A wise man should unhesitatingly avoid one who is sinful at heart and shunned by all honest men, just as he would avoid eating the flesh of a dog. The evil one who proclaims the faults of a Mahatman, actually demonstrates his own vile nature, just as a snake displays his hood when others excite it. The sensible man who seeks to rebut such a back-biter at his favourite work, is like a donkey sunk in a heap of ashes.

A man who always speaks ill of others should be avoided like a ferocious wolf, an infuriated elephant which trumpets in madness, or a rabid dog. Shame on the sinful, mean men who take to such a senseless path and abandoning all wholesome restraints and modesty, who always do what is injurious to others without care for their own welfare.

If an honest man wants to bandy words with such despicable men when they set out to humiliate him, you should advise him: "Do not allow yourself to be upset." Men of calm temperament never approve of an argument between a high and a low man. We know that an angry, slanderous, enraged man can slap another, pelt him with dirt, frighten him with snarls or grind his teeth at him. He who endures the complaints and abuse of evil men made in public, or who frequently reads these injunctions, never suffers any distress through verbal abuse.'"

CANTO 115

"Yudhishtira says, 'Wise Pitamaha, as you care for the future of our family, you must clear some other doubts that perplex me, apart from how to deal with evil men who speak maliciously about us. I want to ask you further about what would be beneficial to a kingdom and will produce happiness, benefits and advancement in the present and the future to the royal line, about beneficial food and drink, and about a healthy body.

How should a ruling king, surrounded by friends, ministers and servants, make his people happy? The king who becomes a victim of his baser passions falls into evil company, looks for debased companions, finds that all his noble, wellborn and moral servants have abandoned him, and so loses their good advice. Such a king never succeeds in gaining the objectives whose accomplishment depend upon having good men around him.

You are equal to Brihaspati himself in intelligence and must explain to me the Rajadharma, which is difficult to understand. You, Naravyaghra, are constantly striving to achieve the good of our vamsa and advise us about the dharma of Rajaneeti.

The learned Kshatri Vidura, too, gives us valuable instructions. I could pass my days in happiness like a man who has quaffed amrita, listening to your teachings that are so beneficial to us Kshatriyas and the kingdom.

Which class of servants can one regard as inferior and which competent? What type of retainers, of what birth, can help us discharge our Rajadharma? If the king chooses to work alone and without assistance, he will never succeed in protecting his people. All noble men of high birth covet the power of sovereignty.'

Bhishma replies, 'The king, O Bhaarata, cannot rule his kingdom alone. Without retainers to help him, he cannot accomplish any goal. Even if he succeeds in gaining his objective, he cannot retain it alone. The king whose servitors are all knowledgeable and wise, devoted to the good of their master, of noble birth and of tranquil disposition, succeeds in enjoying the happiness of sovereignty.

That king enjoys the satisfaction of sovereignty whose ministers are of high birth, who cannot be lured away from him by bribes and other influences, who live with him and give him advice, who are wise, good, and have a knowledge of how matters are interrelated, who can provide for future events and contingencies, who have knowledge of the virtues of Time and never grieve for what is past. The king whose officials share with him his joys and sorrows, who are all faithful, strive to please him and direct their attention to the accomplishment of their master's objectives, enjoys the happiness that comes with sovereignty.

That king enjoys the true happiness of power whose subjects are always cheerful, distinguished and tread the path of dharma. He is the best of kings if contented and trustworthy men, experts in matters of finance, manage and supervise all the sources of his income. The king acquires wealth and great punya when incorruptible, trustworthy, devoted and generous servants supervise the replenishment of his granaries and stores.

The king who in his city administers justice lawfully and delivers criminal law in the manner of Sankha and Likhita, earns the punya of kingship. The king who binds his subjects to himself through kindness, who knows the Rajadharma, earns the punya of sovereignty.'"

CANTO 116

"Bhishma says, 'An ancient tale relevant to our subject has been told which good and wise men regard as an important precedent. I heard many Maharishis recount it in the asrama of Rama, the son of Jamadagni.

In a certain large vana, uninhabited by humans, there dwelt a Rishi who, with his senses under control, lived upon fruit and roots and observed rigid vratas. He was a most perspicacious man, of tranquil and pure soul, who always recited the Vedic mantras, observed strict laws and self-restraint and, with a heart cleansed by fasts, lived a life of kindness towards all creatures.

When he sat in tapasya, all the creatures that lived in the forest who knew of his goodness and wisdom would approach him with affection. Fierce lions and tigers, huge choleric elephants, leopards, rhinoceroses, bears and other fierce carnivores, blood-drinkers, came and conversed with the Rishi, who knew all their tongues. They would greet him courteously and depart. Indeed, they always did what pleased him and behaved towards him like disciples.

One domestic animal, a dog, lived there permanently. He had a heart like that of a human being, was devoted and exceedingly attached to the Rishi and never left him at any time. Weak and emaciated with fasts, he subsisted upon fruit, roots and water. He was tranquil and inoffensive in nature and always lay at the feet of the great sage because of the love he received.

One day, a vicious leopard of cruel intent, always on the lookout for prey, a veritable second Yama, arrived hungry and thirsty, with slavering jaws, his tail flicking from side to side, and eyed the dog for his prey.

When he saw the fierce beast coming, O Rajan, the dog, in fear of his life, said to the Rishi, "O Maharishi, this leopard is an enemy of all dogs and it wants to kill me. Save me from this beast, wise Mahabaho!"

The Rishi could read the thoughts of every animal and understood that the dog had ample cause for fear. Possessed of the six attributes and fluent in the voices of all creatures, the Rishi said, "You will have no fear of death from leopards any longer. Let your natural form disappear and become a leopard, my son!"

Instantly, the dog was transformed into a leopard with skin bright as gold, spots on his body and large fangs, and thereupon began to live in the vana fearlessly. Meanwhile, the predatory leopard, seeing before him an animal of his own species, lost all feelings of animosity towards it.

Some time later a fierce and hungry tiger visited the asrama and padded with open mouth towards the dog that the Rishi had transformed into a leopard. Seeing the hungry tiger, the transfigured leopard sought the Rishi's protection. The Rishi, who had great affection for the leopard because it lived with him, now changed him into a powerful tiger. The other tiger, when he saw a beast of his own species, Rajan, did him no injury.

In course of time, the dog, now turned into a powerful carnivore, gave up his former diet of fruit and roots. Indeed, from that time, Rajan, the transformed tiger lived upon the flesh of other animals of the forest, like a true king of beasts.'"

CANTO 117

"Bhishma says, 'The transfigured tiger, replete with the flesh of slain animals, slept easy. One day, as he lay in the yard, an infuriated elephant who looked like a great cloud, with rent cheeks, a lofty forehead, freckled with the dust of lotus filaments on his body, with long curved tusks and a trumpet deep as thunder, came to the asrama.

The tiger saw the enraged elephant approach him and, frantic with fear, sought the protection of the Rishi. The Rishi transformed the tiger into an elephant. The real elephant, when he saw one of his own kind, big as a mass of clouds, was scared away. The Rishi's elephant from then on frolicked in lakes overgrown with lotuses and wandered on their banks riddled with rabbit holes.

A considerable time elapsed in this way. One day, as he cheerfully strode along near the asrama, he was confronted by a maned mountain lion accustomed to killing elephants. When he saw the lion coming, the Rishi's elephant trembled with fear and sought the sage's protection. The Rishi transformed that prince of elephants into a lion. As the wild lion was of the same species, the Rishi's lion no longer feared him. On the other hand, the wild lion, seeing a stronger beast of his own kind before him, was intimidated.

The Rishi's lion began to live in the asrama within the forest, which the other animals no longer ventured to approach as they all feared for their lives. One day, a fierce Sarabha with eight legs and eyes on its forehead, who preyed on all other animals and petrified them with fear, came to that asrama hunting the Rishi's lion. The Rishi transformed his lion into a fiercer and more powerful Sarabha, who quickly put the other to flight.

Thereafter it lived happily with the Rishi in the asrama and all the animals that dwelt in the forest were afraid of it. Their dread and desire to save their lives led them to flee the vana. The Sarabha blithely continued every day to kill animals for his food and became a carnivorous beast, as it no longer cared for the fruit and roots upon which it had once subsisted.

One day, that ungrateful creature who had first been a dog but who was now a Sarabha, thirsting for blood, wanted to kill the Rishi. The wise Rishi, through his ascetic power, understood the intentions of the beast and cursed him, "O dog, I first converted you into a leopard and then into a tiger. From a tiger I changed you into a bull elephant in musth, and then into a lion. From a mighty lion I transformed you into a Sarabha. I changed you into these diverse shapes out of affection for you. You never belonged by birth to any of these species. Since you now want to kill me, one who has done you no injury, O sinful one, become a dog again!"

Immediately, the low, foolish and wicked animal resumed his own natural form of a lowly dog.'"

CANTO 118

"Bhishma says, 'The dog, after he assumed his natural form, was very cast down. The Rishi reprimanded him and drove the sinful creature away from his asrama.

Guided by this precedent, an intelligent king should appoint servants fit for the office assigned to each and exercise proper supervision over them. He should first ascertain their truthfulness, purity, sincerity and general disposition, knowledge of the shastras, conduct, birth, self-restraint, compassion, strength, energy, dignity and forgiveness. A king should never appoint a minister without first evaluating him.

If a king gathers round him men of low birth, he will never be happy. A man of noble birth, even if unfairly persecuted by his royal master, will never try to injure him, while one of mean and low birth who becomes rich and powerful through his royal connection, will become his master's enemy even if only verbally rebuked.

A minister should be of high birth and strength; he should be forgiving, self-restrained, with his senses under control; he should not be greedy but contented with his just acquisitions, delight in the prosperity of his master and friends and know the requirements of time and place— kaala and avasara.

He should always recruit useful men who keep their lord's dharma in mind, remain attentive and faithful in the discharge of their svadharma, are masters in the strategy of war and peace, and are loved both by the citizens and the inhabitants of the provinces.

The minister should be a master of all kinds of vyuhas that can cleave and shatter his enemies' ranks, a general skilled in leading the army on the march, able to inspire his master's army with courage and to read signs and gestures, adept in the art of training elephants, confident of his own powers, free from pride and clever in the transaction of business.

He should always do what is right, follow svadharma, select noble friends, be sweet of speech, good-looking, with marked qualities of leadership, well-versed in policy, accomplished, energetic in action, active, ingenious, of a sweet temper, modest in appearance, patient, brave, rich, and adaptable to the requirements of time and place. The king who finds such a minister will never be humiliated or overpowered by anyone. Indeed, his kingdom will gradually spread over the earth like the light of the moon.

A king who knows the shastras, who recognizes the supremacy of dharma, who always protects his subjects and who has the following virtues, obtains the love of all. He should be patient, forgiving, pure in conduct, severe when required, believe in hard work, be respectful towards all his elders, know the shastras, remain ready to listen to those who are competent to instruct, to give advice and be able to judge correctly between conflicting courses of action suggested to him.

He should be intelligent, have a retentive memory, be just in action, self-restrained, sweet-spoken, forgiving even to enemies, practise personal charity and have perfect faith in God. He should be of pleasing aspect, ready to extend a helping hand to men in distress, be free from egoism, never without a wife, refrain from acting in haste, and appoint ministers who always seek his good.

He should always reward his ministers when they achieve anything singular. He should avoid idleness, attract men to himself by doing them good and cherish those devoted to him. He should always be cheerful and attentive to the wants of his servants, and never give way to anger. He should be magnanimous and wield the Dandaneeti justly. He should make all men around him follow dharma.

He should use spies for his eyes, to supervise his subjects' concerns and all matters connected with their dharma and artha. A king who has these hundred qualifications earns the love of all, so every ruler should strive to emulate him.

The king who wants his own advancement should never disregard his army and should enlist able warriors to help him protect his kingdom. If his commanders are brave in battle, grateful, well versed in the shastras, if the foot-soldiers are familiar with the treatises on religion and dharma, if the elephant-warriors are fearless, if the Maharathas are skilled archers and can wield other weapons, he will conquer the whole world.

The king who strives to win over all men, who is ever eager for hard work, who has many friends and allies, becomes the greatest of rulers. A king who can bond all men to himself, will conquer the whole world, O Bhaarata, with just a thousand brave horsemen.'"

CANTO 119

"Bhishma says, 'The king who is guided by the moral of this dog's story and appoints his courtiers to offices for which they are fit, enjoys the happiness that comes with sovereignty. You should not praise and elevate a dog in a position above his competence because he will become intoxicated with pride. Ministers should be appointed to offices for which they are fit and should be suitably qualified for their occupations. The wise do not approve appointments of unworthy men.

The king who confers on his servitors offices for which each is competent will enjoy the happiness that comes with sovereignty. A Sarabha should occupy the position of a Sarabha; a lion should bristle with the might of a lion; a tiger should be a tiger, and a leopard should remain a leopard.

Ministers and servitors should be appointed to offices for which each is suitable according to the law. If you want to achieve success, never appoint them to situations higher than their deserving. The foolish king who, ignoring precedent, appoints servants to offices for which they are unfit, will not please his subjects.

A king who wants accomplished retainers should never appoint unintelligent, petty-minded men who cannot control their senses and who are of low birth. Men who are honest, of noble birth, brave, learned, devoid of malice and envy, lofty-minded, pure in conduct and clever in business matters, deserve to be appointed as ministers.

Humble men, prompt in discharging their duties, tranquil in disposition, pure in mind, with diverse natural abilities and who are above reproach should be advisors to the king.

A lion should always have only a lion as a companion, otherwise the companion will earn all the advantages of the lion, and the lion, none. The lion that has only a pack of dogs for his associates will never benefit from such a friendship in accomplishing his dharma.

A king can succeed in subduing the whole world if he has for his ministers men of courage, wisdom, learning and high birth. Yudhishtira, kings should never keep counsellors who are not learned, sincere, wise and wealthy. Men who devote themselves to the service of their master are never hindered by any impediments, so kings should always speak to them in peaceful terms.

The king should look after his treasury with great care and always try to augment it, since therein lie his roots. Let your granary be filled with corn and increase your wealth; but let their supervision be entrusted to honest retainers.

Let your officers be always attentive to their work, acquire skill in battle and in managing horses. Yudhishtira, look after the interests of your kinsmen and friends, always be in their midst and seek the good of your city.

With this story of the dog, I have instructed you about your dharma towards your subjects. What else do you want to hear?'"

CANTO 120

"Yudhishtira says, 'You have, O Bhaarata, discoursed upon the many duties of Rajaneeti that wise men who knew the Rajadharma of old observed and passed down. You spoke in detail of those duties that they approved. Will you now give me a summary of all this, O Bharatarishabha, so that I can commit it firmly to memory?'

Bhishma says, 'Listen, Rajan, to how the protection of all creatures, the greatest duty of the Kshatriya, is to be exercised. A king who knows his duties should assume many forms, like the peacock that puts forth plumes of diverse hues. Keenness, crookedness, truth and sincerity, are the qualities that should be present in him.

With thorough impartiality, he should practise the qualities of goodness, if he is to earn happiness. He must assume that particular hue or form which is suitable for the particular object he seeks to accomplish. A king who can adopt diverse forms will be able to carry out even the most subtle objectives. Dumb like the peacock in autumn, he should conceal his counsel. He should speak little and the little he speaks should be sweet. He should be attractive and well versed in the shastras.

He should always carefully guard those gates through which danger can overcome him, like men taking care of breaks in embankments through which the waters of large tanks can rush out and flood their fields and houses. He should seek the refuge of Mahatman Brahmanas, like men who seek the refuge of great rivers engendered by rainwater collected in mountain lakes.

The king who wishes to amass wealth should behave like religious hypocrites who wear a coronal lock. He should retain the danda of chastisement uplifted in his hands and levy taxes only after he has carefully examined the incomes and expenses of his subjects, as one selects a full-grown palmyra tree for drawing its juice.

He should behave equitably towards his own subjects, get his cavalry to trample the crops of his enemies, march against foes when his own wings have become strong and, most of all, understand his own weakness. He should proclaim the faults of his enemies, crush their supporters and collect wealth from outside like a man who plucks flowers from the vana. He should destroy the mightier kings who stand with uplifted heads like mountains, by placating the governors of their citadels and the garrisons, and by ambuscades and sudden attacks.

He should enter his nightly quarters alone and unseen, like the peacock in the rainy season, and enjoy within his inner apartments the companionship of his wives. He should protect himself, not take off his armour, and avoid the nets that spies and secret agents of his enemies spread for him. He should also win over the spies of his enemies, but kill them when an opportunity occurs.

Like the peacock, the king should kill his powerful and angry foes of crooked policy, destroy their forces and drive them away from their homes. Similarly, he should do what is good for himself and gather wisdom from everywhere, as the peacock collects insects from the forest.

A wise king should thus rule his kingdom and adopt a policy that is beneficial to him. He should exercise his own acumen, decide what to do, and then consult others to either abandon or confirm such decisions. The shastras are useful because they sharpen the intellect and help one to choose a proper course of action.

By the art of conciliation, a king should inspire confidence in the hearts of his enemies. He should display his own strength, form his own conclusions, and judge different courses of action in his own mind, using his intelligence. The king should be wise and well-versed in the arts of diplomacy; he must do what is necessary and avoid what is not.

A wise and intelligent man does not require advice or instruction. If, for instance, a man like Brihaspati is disgraced, he soon regains his natural disposition, like heated iron dipped in water. A king should accomplish all objectives, his own or those of others, in accordance with the shastras. A king who knows to acquire wealth should always employ men who are of mild disposition, courageous, wise and powerful. When he sees his servitors employed in activities for which each is fit, he should work in harmony with all of them, like the several strings of a musical instrument tuned to their intended tones.

He should do good to all and never transgress the dictates of dharma. The king of whom everybody thinks, "He is mine," stands unshaken like a hill. When he adjudicates between litigants, he should not differentiate between whom he likes and dislikes, but uphold justice.

He should appoint to all his offices men who know the characters of particular families, of the masses of the people and of different countries; who are mild in speech; of middle age; who have no faults; who are devoted to good work; who are never careless; who are free from greed; who are learned and self-restrained; who are firm in virtue and always prepared to uphold the interests of both dharma and artha. Thus, when he has decided on his courses of action and their final objectives, he should proceed to achieve them carefully and, advised by his spies in all matters, he can live happily.

The king who never gives way to wrath and joy without sufficient cause, who supervises all his actions himself and personally controls his income and expenditure, will find great wealth in this world. It is said that the king who rewards his officers and subjects publicly for any good they do, who chastises those who deserve punishment, who protects himself and his kingdom from every evil, knows the dharma of Rajaneeti. Like the sun, who casts his rays upon everything below, the king should always look after his kingdom himself and, using his intelligence, supervise all his agents and officers.

The king should take wealth from his subjects at the proper time and never publicize what he does. Like an able man who milks his cow, he should milk his kingdom every day. As the bee collects honey from flowers, the king should draw wealth little by little from his kingdom and store it. After he has kept apart a sufficient portion, the remainder should be spent on the acquisition of punya and the gratification of kama. A sensible king who knows his dharma would never waste what he has stored, or disregard any wealth for its meagreness; he should never ignore enemies for their being powerless; he should exercise his own intelligence, be self-aware and never repose confidence in stupid men.

Steadiness, cleverness, self-restraint, intelligence, health, patience, bravery and attention to the demands of time and place: these eight qualities lead to the increase of wealth, be it small or great. A little fire, fed with clarified butter, may blaze forth into a conflagration. A single seed may produce a thousand trees. A king, therefore, even when he hears that his income and expenditure are great, should not disregard what appear to be small things. Just as an enemy, whether he happens to be a child, a young man, or an aged one, can kill a careless man, an insignificant enemy, when he becomes powerful, can exterminate a king. A king who is conscious of the requirements of time is the best of all rulers.

A strong or weak enemy can very soon out of malice destroy the reputation of a king, obstruct his acquisition of religious punya, and even deprive him of his vitality. Therefore, a king with a disciplined mind should never be heedless of his foes.

If a disciplined king desires riches and victory, he should, after he has evaluated his expenditure, income, savings and administration, make either peace or war. For this reason, the king should seek the help of a clever minister, because shrewdness weakens even a mighty protagonist; power that is increasing will be protected by astuteness; a growing enemy is weakened through cunning. Every action that is undertaken intelligently is praiseworthy.

A patient and impeccable king can satisfy all his wishes even with the support of a small force. However, the king who is vain and covetous, who surrounds himself with self-seeking flatterers, will never prosper in the least. For these reasons, the king should act with consideration when he taxes the wealth of his people, for if he continually oppresses them, he will be destroyed like a flash of lightning that blazes forth for only a moment.

Knowledge, tapasya, riches, indeed everything, can be earned through hard work. Parisrama, as it occurs in living creatures, is governed by intelligence, and one should regard it as the greatest of all things. In the human body live many intelligent entities of great energy, like Sakra, Vishnu and Saraswati. An intelligent man, therefore, should never disregard the body.

A greedy man can be dominated by constant gifts, as he is never satisfied with seizing the wealth of others. However, everyone becomes jealous in the matter of enjoying happiness. If a man becomes poor, he loses both dharma and kama, which are objects that artha can attain.

An envious man will try to take the wealth, the enjoyments, the sons and daughters and the affluence of others. We can see every kind of fault in covetous men, so the king should never take such a man for his minister or officer.

A wise king lacking proper agents should despatch even a low functionary to ascertain the disposition and actions of his enemies, in order to frustrate their efforts and designs. The trustful and noble king who seeks the advice of learned and virtuous Brahmanas, and who is protected by his ministers, will be able to keep all his vassals and chieftains under control.

Rajan, I have briefly spoken to you of all the duties laid down in the shastras. Attend to them intelligently, for the king who does so, in obedience to his acharya, will surely rule the whole world. The king who disregards the satisfaction that comes from following a plan, and depends upon what chance will bring, neither enjoys the happiness of kingship nor wins the regions of bliss hereafter.

A king who is vigilant and attentive to the requirements of war and peace will be able to destroy even enemies who are famed for their wealth, who are esteemed for their intelligence and good conduct, who are brave in battle, accomplished and hard-working.

A king should discover the consequences of different kinds of activities and procedures, and never depend upon destiny. One who sees defects in faultless men cannot become prosperous and famous. When two friends try to complete the same work, a wise man always commends the one who takes upon himself the heavier share. Practise this Rajadharma that I have told you, be determined to do your duty to protect all your subjects, and you will easily obtain the rewards of dharma.

All the regions of felicity in the hereafter depend upon dharma and punya!'"

CANTO 121

"Yudhishtira says, 'Pitamaha, you have finished your discourse on Rajadharma. From what you have said it is clear that Neeti has a crucial position and is the key, for everything depends upon chastisement. It seems that Neeti possesses great energy, is omnipresent and is the greatest among the Devas, Rishis, high-souled Pitris, Yakshas, Rakshasas, Pisachas and Sadhyas, or any of the living beings in this world, including beasts and birds.

You have said that the entire universe, mobile and immobile, including Devas, Asuras and Manushyas, depends upon danda. I now want to know from you, O Bharatarishabha, who Neeti is truly, of what kind, of what form and disposition. Of what is he made, what is his origin, what are his features and his grandeur? How does he manage to remain eternally wakeful among living creatures, protecting this universe? Who is he, this supreme personage called Neeti? Upon what does Neeti depend, and what is his path?'

Bhishma replies, 'Listen, Kurusthama, to who Neeti is and why he is also called Vyavahara, and why danda is that upon whom Vyavahara depends. Law, sometimes called Vyavahara, is that which upholds the dharma of a vigilant and alert king.

In olden days, Manu first declared this truth: "He who protects all creatures, the loved and the hateful equally, impartially wielding the Dandaneeti, is the embodiment of dharma."

Since Manu began with these words, they are known as the first words and represent the transcendent word of Brahma. Since it is with the Dandaneeti that we stop the misappropriation of people's possessions, we call it Vyavahara. The traiguna always rests on well-administered chastisement.

Danda is a great Deva. In form, he looks like a blazing fire. His complexion is dark like that of the petals of the blue lotus. He has four teeth, four arms, eight legs and many eyes. His ears are pointed like shafts and his hair stands upright. He has matted locks and two tongues. His face is the hue of copper and he is clad in a lion's skin. This irresistible deity assumes a fierce shape.

Danda moves in the world assuming the form of the sword, the bow, the mace, the dart, the trident, the mallet, the arrow, the bludgeon, the battle-axe, the discus, the noose, the heavy club, the rapier, the lance and in fact of every kind of weapon that exists on earth. Indeed, punishment moves on earth, piercing, cutting, smiting, lopping, dividing, striking, slaying and attacking his victims.

These, Yudhishtira, are some of the names which Danda bears: Sword, Sabre, Dharma, Fury, the Irresistible, the Parent of Prosperity, Victory, Punisher, Checker, the Eternal, the shastras, Brahmana, Mantra, Avenger, the Greatest of First Legislators, Judge, the everlasting God, the One whose course is irresistible, the Unceasing, the First-born, the individual without affections, the Soul of Rudra, the eldest Manu and the great Benefactor.

Dandaneeti is the holy Vishnu, the powerful Narayana, and because he always assumes a terrible form, he is called Mahapurusha. His wife Dharma is also known by the names of Brahmana's daughter, Lakshmi, Vriti, Saraswati, and Mother of the universe. Dandaneeti thus has many forms.

Blessing and curse, pleasure and pain, dharma and adharma, strength and weakness, fortune and misfortune, merit and demerit, virtue and vice, desire and aversion, season and month, night, day and hour, care and carelessness, joy and anger, peace and self-restraint, destiny and exertion, salvation and condemnation, fear and fearlessness, injury and ahimsa, tapasya, yagna and nirvritti, poison and healthy food, the beginning, the middle and the end, the result of all murderous deeds, insolence, insanity, arrogance, pride, patience, policy, disorder, powerlessness and power, respect, disrespect, decay and stability, humility, charity, timeliness and untimeliness, falsehood, wisdom, truth, belief, disbelief, impotence, trade, profit, loss, success, defeat, ferocity, mildness, death, acquisition and loss, agreement and disagreement, that which should be done and that which should not, strength and weakness, malice and good-will, disgrace and honour, modesty, prosperity and adversity, energy, action, learning, eloquence, keenness of understanding: all these, Yudhishtira, are the multiple forms of the Dandaneeti in this world.

If the Law had not existed, all living creatures would have harassed or killed one another, for it is fear of punishment that restrains them. When the Dandaneeti protects subjects it enhances the might of their ruler, for Danda is the best refuge of all.

It quickly sets the world on the path of dharma, which depends upon satya and dwells in Brahmanas. Empowered by dharma, the greatest of Brahmanas become attached to the Vedas. From the Vedas the sacrifices flow which please the Devas. The gratified Devas then recommend the inhabitants of the earth to Indra, who gives them food in the form of rain, without which crops and vegetation would fail. The life of all creatures depends upon food which provides them with nourishment for growth.

For this purpose, Danda assumes among them the form of a Kshatriya ruler, who remains alert, protecting them, always vigilant and never failing.

Law has these other eight names—God, Man, Life, Power, Heart, the Lord of all creatures, the Atman of all things, and the Living Entity. God gave both wealth and the rod of chastisement to the strong king in the form of military forces which are a combination of five constituents: Dharma, Vyavahara, Dandaneeti, Ishwara and Prani.

Yudhishtira, the king should seek noble blood, wealthy ministers, knowledge, power in the form of strength of body and energy of mind, with the eight instruments—elephants, horses, chariots, foot-soldiers, boats, slaves as camp followers for doing other work, increase of population and cattle—and the other force which depends upon a well-filled treasury.

The army accoutered in mail and livery, with Maharathas, elephant-warriors, cavalry, infantry, officers and surgeons constitute the limbs. Beggars, principal judges, astrologers, priests who perform propitiatory and Atharvan rites, the treasury, allies, grain and all other requisites, composed of seven attributes and eight limbs, constitute the body of a kingdom. Law is another powerful limb of a kingdom and in the form of an army is the very creator of a kingdom. God himself has with great care sent Danda for the use of the Kshatriya, and this eternal universe is impartial Neeti's self.

There is nothing more worthy of respect by kings than Danda, by which the ways of dharma are defined. Brahma, for the protection of the world and for establishing the dharma of different individuals, created chastisement. The common law or Vyavahara, arising out of the dispute of litigants, has also sprung from Brahma.

When a suit, civil or criminal, is instituted, the king or those who work in the king's name must call for evidence and decide in favour of one or the other party. There follows danda or punishment. Principally characterized by a belief in either of the two parties, this Vyavahara is seen to bring about good. There is another kind of Vyavahara which has the Vedas for its soul and its cause. There is a third kind of Vyavahara, O tiger among kings—Kulachara, which deals with family customs consistent with the shastras.

Vyavahara, based on the belief that either of two litigant parties is right, is inherent in the king, and should be also known as Evidence. Although judgement and punishment are regulated by Evidence, yet one says it has its soul in Vyavahara, which is based upon Vedic precepts.

That Vyavahara which has the Vedas for its soul, is dharma or duty, and benefits all men who believe in it. Mahatmans have spoken of the

Vyavahara as they have done of ordinary law.

The third kind of Vyavahara is also an acharya of men and also has its roots in the Veda, O Yudhishtira. It upholds the three worlds. It has Truth for its soul and produces prosperity. That which is Danda we have seen to be the eternal Vyavahara and is actually the Veda, dharma and duty.

That which is morality and duty is the path of dharma from the beginning, and is Pitamaha Brahma, the Lord of all creatures. Brahma is the Creator of the entire universe with the Devas, Asuras, Rakshasas, Manushyas, Nagas, and of every other entity. Hence the Vyavahara which is based on the belief that either of two litigant parties is right, also flows from Him.

For this reason Manu has laid down the following in respect of Vyavahara: Neither mother, nor father, nor brother, nor wife, nor priest, are above punishment by the king who rules strictly according to his dharma.'"

CANTO 122

"Bhishma says, 'An old story is told about great Vasuhoma, king of the Angas. He and his queen were always engaged in pious work and practised the most rigid tapasya.

He went to Munjaprishtha, held in high esteem by the Pitris and the Devarishis, where on the summit of Himavat, near the golden mountains of Meru, the great Brahmana Rama had sat under the shade of a renowned banyan tree, his hair matted in jata. Rishis of rigid vratas call Munjaprishtha the favourite haunt of Rudra.

King Vasuhoma lived there, acquired many spiritual powers, gained the esteem of the Brahmanas and came to be regarded as a Devarishi. One day, the great Parantapa King Mandhatri, the mighty friend of Indra, came to the mountain retreat and stood before Vasuhoma of austere tapasya in an attitude of humility.

Vasuhoma offered arghya to his guest and water to wash his feet, and enquired about the well-being of all seven limbs of his kingdom. He then asked his royal guest, who faithfully followed the practices of the ancient men of dharma, "What can I do for you, O Rajan?"

Mandhatri, the best of kings, highly gratified, answered the wise Vasuhoma seated at his ease, "You have studied all the doctrines of Brihaspati, Rajan, and those laid down by Usanas. I want to know what the origin of Neeti is. What was awake before Chastisement? What is said to be its end? How did Danda come to depend upon the Kshatriya?

Tell me all this, O you of great wisdom! I come to you as a shishya, acknowledge you as my guru and am ready to give you gurudakshina."

Vasuhoma said, "Listen, Mandhatri, to how Neeti, the upholder of the world, arose. The soul of dharma is eternal, ananta, and was created to uphold the appropriate governance of all creatures. We hear that, once upon a time, the Pitamaha of all the worlds, the divine Brahma, wanted to perform a sacrifice, but failed to find a priest whose competence equalled his own.

He then conceived such a priest in his head and held the embryo there for long years. After a thousand years had passed, the great God sneezed, and the embryo fell out of his head. The divine being that thus took birth from Brahma came to be called Kshupa, a great lord of creatures, who possessed enormous powers and became the priest at the yagna of the Mahatman Pitamaha.

When the yagna began, Brahma assumed the mild and peaceful aspect of a sacrificer and Chastisement, which had dwelt in his furious form, disappeared, causing great confusion among all creatures. There was no longer any distinction between what should be done and what should not, between clean and unclean food, and between what drink was permissible and what was not.

All creatures began to do violence to one another, and there were no restraints in the matter of the union of the sexes. All ideas of property ceased, all creatures began to rob and lawlessly take meat from one another. The strong began to kill the weak, and nobody had the slightest consideration for his neighbour.

The Pitamaha then worshipped the divine and eternal Vishnu, the great boon-giver and said, "Kesava, show mercy and remove this pervasive chaos."

Thus addressed, the best of gods, Vishnu, reflected long and created his own self in the form of Danda. From that form, which had Dharma for its legs, Goddess Saraswati created the Dandaneeti, the science of Punishment, which soon became celebrated the world over. Mahavishnu again reflected awhile and appointed some among the Devas as the lords or rulers of their respective varnas.

It was then that he made the divine Indra, the thousand-eyed, the king of the Devas; Yama, the son of Vivaswat, the lord of the Pitris; Kubera, the lord of treasures and of all the Rakshasas; Meru, the king of mountains; and Sagara, the lord of rivers. He installed the powerful Varuna with the sovereignty of the waters and the Asuras, made Yama the lord of life and all living things and Agni the lord of all things possessed of energy.

He made the powerful Isana, Mahatman and eternal Mahadeva of three eyes, the lord of the Rudras; Vasishtha, the lord of the Brahmanas, and Jatavedas the chief of the Vasus; Surya, the lord of all luminous bodies, Chandramas, the king of stars and constellations, Ansumat, the lord of all herbs; and the mightiest of deities, Kumara or Skanda, of twelve arms, the chief of all the spirits and ghostly beings, the ganas that wait upon Mahadeva.

He made Kaala, Time, who possesses the seeds of both destruction and growth, the sovereign of all creatures and also of the four portions of Death—weapons, diseases, Yama and deeds and, lastly, of grief and joy. The Srutis declare, Rajan, that the supreme God Mahadeva, the Lord of Lords armed with his Sula, is the lord of the Rudras. The danda of punishment was given to Brahma's son Kshupa, the lord of all creatures and the best of all Dharmatmans.

On the completion of the yagna according to the prescribed rites, Mahadeva Brahma, with due reverence, gave Neeti, the protector of dharma, to Vishnu. Vishnu gave it to Angiras Maharishi, who in turn passed it down to Indra and Marichi. Marichi gave it to Bhrigu, who gave the Dandaneeti, meant for the protection of dharma, to all the Rishis. The Rishis gave it to the regents of the world and the Lokapalas gave it again to Kshupa. Kshupa then gave it to Manu, the son of Surya and Manu, the Deva of Sraddhas, gave it to his sons for the sake of true dharma and artha.

Chastisement, which is intended to restrain evil, should be applied with discrimination, always guided by dharma and not by caprice. Fines and forfeitures are meant to strike fear, and not to fill the king's treasury. Sentences of maiming a person's body or inflicting death or physical pain by various means, hurling from mountain-tops and banishment, should never be imposed for trivial causes. Surya's son Manu gave the Dandaneeti to his sons for the protection of the world. Danda in the hands of its successive bearers remains awake to protect all creatures.

Above, the divine Indra is awake with the Dandaneeti; below him, Agni of blazing flames; followed by Varuna, then Prajapati, then Vairagya, whose essence is restraint and discipline, after whom come Dharma, the son of Brahma, the eternal Neeti, and then Tejas, always awake and employed in the work of protection.

After Tejas, come the herbs offered in yagnas to support the Devas and used as food and medicines; after the herbs, the mountains; after the mountains, all kinds of juices and their essences; after these, the Devi Niriti; after Niriti, the planets and the luminous bodies in heaven; after these, the Vedas; after the Vedas, the powerful Vishnu as Hayagriva; after him, the almighty and eternal Pitamaha Brahma. After Pitamaha, the divine and blessed Mahadeva; after Mahadeva, the Viswadevas; after them, the Maharishis; after the Rishis the divine soma; after soma, the Nitya Devas; after them, know that the Brahmanas are awake.

After the Brahmanas, the Kshatriyas righteously protect all creatures. The Kshatriyas keep awake the eternal universe, which consist of mobile and immobile creatures, and Chastisement is awake among them. With magnificence akin to that of Pitamaha himself, Neeti keeps together and upholds everything. Kaala, O Bhaarata, is always awake, in the beginning, the middle and the end. The master of all the worlds, the lord of all creatures, the powerful and blessed Mahadeva, the Devadeva, is always awake. He is called by these names also—Kapardin, Sankara, Rudra, Bhava, Sthanu and Umapati, the lord of Uma. Thus, Danda also keeps awake in the beginning, the middle and the end. A king of dharma should rule justly, guided by the Dandaneeti."

He who listens to this teaching of Vasuhoma and conducts himself according to its spirit is sure to have all his wishes fulfilled. O Bharatarishabha, I have now, told you everything about Danda—the restrainer of the universe, which is governed by dharma.'"

CANTO 123

"Yudhishtira says, 'I want to hear, O Pitamaha, the generally accepted conclusions on the subject of dharma, artha, kama, their respective roots and outcomes. On which of these does the course of life depend? We sometimes observe them to mingle with one another and sometimes to exist separately, independent of one another.'

Bhishma replies, 'When men in this world endeavour with good intentions to earn artha with the help of dharma, then the three, dharma, artha and kama, will co-exist in a state of union in respect of time, cause and action.

Artha has its root in dharma and kama is the fruit of artha. All three again have their root in will. Will is concerned with objects. All objects, again, in their entirety, exist for gratifying kama. Upon these does the traiguna depend. Complete withdrawal from all objects is mukti.

Dharma is needed for the protection of the body, artha for the acquisition of dharma, and kama for the gratification of the senses. All three have the quality of rajas or passion.

If one seeks dharma, artha and kama for the sake of Swarga or other such rewards, they are remote because the rewards themselves are distant. When one seeks them for the sake of the Knowledge of the Self, the rewards are immediate. One should seek dharma only for achieving purity of soul; artha to devote to work undertaken without desire of any reward, and kama only to support the body.

One should not cast off dharma, artha and kama even mentally, until one has freed oneself through tapasya. The aim of the first three purusharthas is the fourth one, mukti, if only man can obtain it!

Actions, undertaken and completed even with intelligence, may or may not yield the expected results. Dharma is not always the root of artha, for things other than virtue lead to wealth, such as service and agriculture. There is also a contrary opinion, for some say that one acquires wealth through chance, or birth, or other like causes. In some instances, the attainment of artha produces evil, while others hold the view that artha spent on sacrifices has led to the acquisition of dharma.

Therefore a dullard, whose understanding ignorance has debased, can never acquire the highest aim of dharma and artha, which is mukti. Dharma is worthless if sought for reward; artha is impure if wealth is hoarded; but when purged of these impurities, they produce great results.

A discussion is said to have taken place long ago between Rishi Kamandaka and King Angaristha. One day, Angaristha saluted Kamandaka as he was comfortably seated and, taking advantage of a long-sought opportunity, asked him, "If a king impelled by lust and folly commits sins for which he later repents, through what actions, O Rishi, can he wash away those sins? If an ignorant man commits a sin in the belief that he is acting righteously, how will the king stop this sin from gaining currency among men?"

Kamandaka said, "The man who abandons dharma and artha and pursues only kama reaps the destruction of his intelligence. Heedlessness then follows, destroys both virtue and wealth, and leads to godlessness and inveterate wickedness of conduct.

If the king does not restrain such evil men of sinful conduct, all good subjects will live in fear of him, like the inmates of a room where a snake has hidden itself. The subjects, including Brahmanas and all pious men, will not follow such a king. As a result, he incurs great danger and ultimately the risk of death itself. Disgraced and insulted, he has to drag on a miserable existence equal to death.

Men learned in the shastras have indicated the following method for checking sin. The king should always dedicate himself to the study of the three Vedas, be devoted to dharma and make alliances of marriage with noble families. He should respect the Brahmanas, give them good offices and wait upon high-minded ones who possess the virtue of mercy. He should perform ablutions, chant sacred mantras and thus pass his time righteously and happily.

Banishing all evil subjects from himself and his kingdom, he should seek the companionship of Dharmatmans. He should please all with his speech or good karma. He should tell everyone 'I am yours,' and proclaim the virtues of even his enemies. Thus, he will soon cleanse himself of his sins and win the high regard of all.

You should complete all the important duties your elders and gurus tell you to perform, and you will be certain to gain great benefits as a result of their blessings."'"

CANTO 124

"Yudhishtira says, 'Everyone on earth, O greatest of men, lauds conduct that conforms to dharma. However, I have grave doubts about this praise. If we are to understand this, I want to hear everything about the way in which virtuous behaviour can be acquired and what its characteristics are.'

Bhishma replies, 'Once, Duryodhana asked his father Dhritarashtra the same question, when he was afire with jealousy at the sight of you and your brothers' opulence in Indraprastha, and for the jeers he received when made to look a fool in your magnificent court, the Mayasabha. Listen to what happened then, O Bhaarata. When he had seen your grand sabha and your great prosperity, Duryodhana spoke of it to his father.

Dhritarashtra then asked his son and Karna, "Tell me, why do you grieve, Duryodhana? If there is adequate reason for your sorrow, I will try to advise you. O subjugator of hostile towns, you too have obtained great riches; all your brothers, friends and relatives are obedient to you and you also wear the best clothes, eat the richest food and ride the finest horses. Why, then, have you become pale and emaciated?"

Duryodhana said, "Tens of thousands of ascetic Snataka Brahmanas daily eat at Yudhishtira's palace from golden plates. When I see the great prosperity of my enemies, the sons of Pandu, Yudhishtira's splendid palace adorned with beautiful flowers and fruit, his horses of the Tittiri and the Kalmasha breeds, his diverse raiment and his wealth that equals that of Vaisravana himself, I burn with grief, father!"

Dhritarashtra said, "If you wish to become prosperous like Yudhishtira, or even richer, endeavour to be virtuous, my son, for then without doubt you can conquer the three worlds by conduct alone. There is nothing impossible that dharma cannot attain. Mandhatri conquered the whole world in course of one night, Janamejaya, in three and Nabhaga, in seven. All these kings possessed compassion and were men of dharma, and so won the earth with their virtue."

Duryodhana said, "I want to hear, O Bhaarata, of that dharma by which the kings you named won the earth so swiftly."

Dhritarashtra said, "Let me relate the story that Narada once recounted on the subject of dharma. Long ago, the Daitya Prahlada, by the punya of his karma, snatched from noble Indra his sovereignty and reduced the three worlds to subjection. Then Indra, Lord of the Devas, approached the wise Brihaspati with folded hands and said to the great Devaguru, 'I want you to tell me what the source of happiness is.'

Brihaspati replied that the knowledge which leads to mukti is the source of the highest happiness. Indra then asked him again whether there was anything still higher.

Brihaspati said, 'There is something still higher. The Mahatman Bhargava-Usanas will instruct you better. Go and ask him, O king of the Devas!'

Indra then went to the great Rishi Sukra Bhargava and obtained from him the knowledge of what would be of great good for him. After he had the permission of the Maharishi Bhargava, Indra again asked the Rishi whether there was any higher happiness to acquire than what the Muni had already taught him.

The omniscient Bhargava said, 'The Mahatman Prahlada has better knowledge of this.'

Indra, the percipient vanquisher of Paka, was delighted and, assuming the form of a Brahmana, went to Prahlada and entreated him, 'I want to know what causes happiness.'

Prahlada answered, 'O Mahamuni, I have no time to instruct you for I am occupied in the task of ruling the three worlds.'

The Brahmana said, 'Rajan, when you have leisure, I wish to receive instruction from you on what course of conduct produces happiness.'

At this King Prahlada was pleased and said, 'Tathaasthu!'

He then found a favourable opportunity to impart to Indra the deep truths of knowledge. Indra duly showed to Prahlada the reverence expected from a sishya towards his guru and began with his whole heart to do what Prahlada wanted. Many a time he enquired, 'Parantapa, how have you been able to win the sovereignty of the three worlds? Tell me, Dharmarajan, what those means are.'

Prahlada said, 'I neither feel any pride in being a king, nor do I cherish any hostility towards Brahmanas. On the other hand, I accept and follow the guidance they give me on matters of policy, based upon the teachings of Sukra. With complete confidence they tell me whatever they wish and restrain me from sinful deeds or straying from dharma.

I am always obedient to the teachings of Sukra. I wait upon and serve the Brahmanas and my elders. I bear no malice to any creature; I am a Dharmatman. I have conquered wrath, and all my senses are under my control. These Munis who are my masters pour beneficial teachings on me like bees dropping honey into the cells of their comb. I taste the nectar these learned men let fall and, like the moon among the constellations, I live among those of my varna.

To listen to the teachings of Sukra from the lips of Brahmanas and to follow their advice, is like nectar on earth, like the clearest eye. In these consist the good of a man.' So said Prahlada to the Brahmana by whom he was dutifully served.

'Maharishi, I am gratified by your reverential behaviour towards me. You are blessed. Ask me for a boon and I will grant you whatever you wish for.'

Indra the Brahmana said, 'If you are gratified with me, and if you wish to give me what I desire, I want then to acquire your dharma. This is the boon that I beg.'

At this, though he was pleased, Prahlada became filled with a great fear. Indeed, when Indra asked for his boon, the Daitya king guessed that the Brahmana could not be an ordinary man. Wondering, Prahlada at last said, 'Tathaasthu. Let it be so!'

The Brahmana went away, but deep anxiety filled Prahlada, and he did not know what to do. While he sat brooding over the matter, a flame of light emerged from his body. It had a shadowy form of great splendour and huge proportions.

Prahlada asked the form, 'Who are you?'

The form answered, 'I am Neeti, the embodiment of your conduct. Cast off by you, I am leaving. I will henceforth, Rajan, dwell in that faultless and best of Brahmanas who has become your devoted disciple.' The form disappeared and soon entered the body of Sakra.

After the disappearance of that form, another of similar shape issued from Prahlada's body. The Daitya king addressed it, 'Who are you?'

The form answered, 'Know me, Prahlada, for the embodiment of Dharma. I will go where the greatest of Brahmanas is, for I reside where Neeti dwells.'

Upon the disappearance of Dharma, a third form, ablaze with splendour, came out of the body of the ascetic. Asked by Prahlada who he was, the magnificent form answered 'Know, O Lord of the Daityas, that I am Satya. I will leave you, and follow the way of Dharma.'

After Truth had left Prahlada, in the wake of Dharma, another great one issued out of his body. Asked who he was by the Daitya king, the mighty being answered, 'I am the embodiment of good deeds. Know, O Prahlada, that I live where Satya lives.'

After this one had left Prahlada, another being emerged, roaring loudly. Questioned by Prahlada, he answered, 'Know that I am Might, and dwell where good deeds are.' Then Might went away to where good deeds had gone.

After this, a Devi of great brilliance issued out of Prahlada's body. The Daitya king asked her who she was, and she told him that she was Sree, the embodiment of prosperity, adding, 'I dwelt in you, O hero, incapable of being obstructed! Cast off by you, I will follow Might.'

The noble Prahlada, stricken with fear, once more asked the goddess, 'Where do you go, Devi, you who live amid lotuses? You are always devoted to truth and are the greatest of deities. Who is that best of Brahmanas who was my disciple? I want to know the truth.'

The goddess of prosperity said, 'That Brahmana whom you instructed, O mighty one, was Indra, assuming the vow of Brahmacharya. He robbed you of the sovereignty that you had over the three worlds. Maharishi, it was by your conduct that you had reduced the three worlds to subjection. Knowing this, the king of the Devas robbed you of your Neeti. Righteousness, Truth, Good deeds, Might and Prosperity, O wise man, all have their root truly in Neeti, conduct.'"

Bhishma continues, 'With these words, the goddess of prosperity went away like all the rest, Yudhishtira!

Duryodhana once more addressed his father, "Kurupravira, I want to know the truth about Neeti. Tell me how it can be acquired."

Dhritarashtra told him, "The noble Prahlada revealed these to Indra. However I will tell you in brief how you can acquire Dharmaneeti. Abstention from injury by act, thought and word, towards all creatures, compassion and charity, constitute conduct that is worthy of praise.

You should never do anything which does not benefit others, or which makes you ashamed. On the other hand, you should do what will win praise in society. Kurusthama, I have now told you in brief what Dharmaneeti is. If men of evil conduct ever win prosperity, O King, they do not enjoy it for long and are exterminated by the root.

Now that you know all this, be of good conduct if you want to have prosperity greater than that of Yudhishtira."

This even was what King Dhritarashtra said to his son. Act according to these instructions, son of Kunti, and you will surely find their reward.'"

CANTO 125

"Yudhishtira says, 'You have said, O Pitamaha, that Neeti is the primary requirement for any man. But tell me, what is hope, and from where does it arise? Only you can clear this grave doubt, which has risen in my mind. I had great hope that Suyodhana would do what was proper, even when the battle was about to begin.

Every man cherishes hope and when that hope is dashed, he feels grief almost equal to death. Fool that I am, Dhritarashtra's evil son destroyed the hope that I had nurtured. Look at the idiocy of my mind! I think that hope is larger than a mountain with all its trees, or perhaps it is vaster than the firmament itself, truly immeasurable. Hope is veritably difficult to fathom, and equally difficult to subdue. What else, Pitamaha, is as unconquerable as hope?'

Bhishma replies, 'Listen, Yudhishtira, while I narrate to you the discussion between Sumitra and Rishabha that took place long ago.

A Rajarishi of the Haihaya vamsa, called Sumitra, went out to hunt. He pursued a deer, which he had struck with an arrow but could not kill. That strong deer ran ahead with the arrow sticking out of him, with the virile king in hot pursuit. The fleet animal quickly cleared a low ground and then a level plain, with the king, young, active, strong, armed with bow and sword and clad in mail, still in chase. Alone in the hunt, Sumitra followed the deer through the vana, crossing many rivers, streams, lakes and copses. The swift animal, struck by many shafts of the king, ran on through one forest after another, showing itself now and then tantalizingly to the king as if in sport, and lessening the distance between itself and its pursuer.

At last, that Parantapa drew his sharpest and most terrible arrow, capable of piercing the very vitals of any creature, and fitted it to his bowstring. The great and mighty deer, as if mocking his pursuer's efforts, suddenly raced away and flew four yojanas out of range, and the magnificent shaft fell harmlessly to the ground. The deer entered a large vana, but the king still continued the chase.'"

"Bhishma says, 'The king entered that great vana and came upon an asrama of Rishis. Exhausted by the chase, he sat down to rest. The Rishis, when they saw him armed with bow, worn out and hungry, approached him and duly honoured him. The king accepted the honours the Rishis offered and enquired about the progress of their tapasya. Having answered the king's questions, the Rishis endowed with the wealth of tapasya asked him what had led him to their asrama.

They said, "Blessed Rajan, what delightful pursuit brings you to this asrama on foot, armed with sword, bow and arrows? Tell us your vamsa and your name."

The king gave all the Brahmanas an account of himself, O Bhaarata, and said, "I am born into the race of the Haihayas, my name is Sumitra and I am the son of Mitra. I chase herds of deer and hunt them in thousands with my arrows.

Accompanied by a large force, my ministers and the women of my household, I came out on a hunt. I shot a deer with an arrow, but the animal, with the shaft stuck in his body, sped away. While chasing it, I have accidentally arrived in this vana and find myself in your presence, in this pitiable condition—shorn of all splendour, weary and disappointed. I am not at all sorry, august Rishis, at my present plight, being without the signs of royalty or far from my capital. However, I feel a poignant grief at my hope being dashed. Just as Himavat, prince of mountains, and Sagara, vast receptacle of waters, cannot measure the extent of the sky, O Maharishis, I cannot measure the limits of hope.

You are endowed with the punya of tapasya and are infinitely wise; there is nothing unknown to you. You are also highly blessed. I beg you to resolve my quandary. Which of these two appears vaster to you—hope cherished by man, or the wide firmament? I want to know why hope is so unconquerable.

If the subject is not improper for you to discuss, then tell me without delay. I do not want to hear from you anything, Maharishis, that is a mystery that cannot be revealed, or is harmful to your tapasya, or not a worthy matter to speak of. Otherwise, I would like to hear of this, and in detail. Devoted to tapasya as you are, I beg you to instruct me."'

CANTO 127

"Bhishma says, 'The Maharishi Rishabha, who sat in the midst of all the other Rishis, smiled a little and said, "Once, Sumitra, while I was on a tirtha yatra, I went to the delightful Badrikasrama, the beautiful hermitage of the sages Nara and Narayana, near the lake where the sacred Ganga rises and where the sage Aswasiras always reads the eternal Vedas. I performed my ablutions in that lake, offered, with due rites, oblations of water to the Pitris and the Devas and entered the asrama where the spirits of those two immortal Rishis, Nara and Narayana, always pass their time in true bliss.

I then went to another asrama not far away to make my home. While seated there I saw a very tall and emaciated Rishi named Tanu, clad in rags and skins, approaching me. Blessed with a wealth of tapasya, he was eight times taller than other men, Mahabaho, and I can say that I have never seen anyone like him. His body was as thin as one's little finger, his neck, arms, legs and hair extraordinary, with his head, ears and eyes, proportionate to his body. His speech and his movements were exceedingly feeble.

When I saw this emaciated Brahmana, Bharatarishabha, I was frightened and full of dread. I touched his feet, stood before him with joined hands, informed him of my name and family, my father's name, and then slowly sat down on a seat that he indicated. Then Dharmatman Tanu, in the midst of the Rishis living in that asrama, began to discuss the issues of dharma and artha, O Rajan.

While the discourse was going on, a king with eyes like lotus petals came to the asrama in a chariot drawn by fleet horses, accompanied by his forces and his women. He was the handsome and famed Viradyumna, who was unhappily looking for his missing son Bhuridyumna and had come there in the course of his search in the vana. He had urged himself on through that forest for days thinking, 'Surely I will find my son here! I will surely find my son here!'

Addressing the macilent Rishi Tanu he said, 'My noble son, my only child, is lost. I had great hopes of finding him, but with my hope being constantly dashed, I am on the point of death.'

When he heard this, the great Rishi Tanu remained for a short while with his head hanging down and sunk in dhyana. Seeing him thus engrossed, the king became exceedingly disturbed. In great grief, he asked slowly and softly, 'Devarishi, what is unconquerable and what is greater than hope? Tell me this, if there is no impropriety in my hearing it.'

The Rishi said, 'Your son has insulted a holy Maharishi through his ill-luck and foolishness. The Rishi asked your son for a golden jar and herbal bark, which he contemptuously refused to give. His conduct infuriated the Maharishi.'

Thus addressed, the king paid homage to that Rishi whom the whole world revered. Viradyumna sat there, spent with fatigue, as you are now. The Maharishi Tanu, in return, according to the rites vanavasis observed, offered the king water to wash his feet and the usual ingredients that make up the arghya. Then all the Rishis sat around him like the Saptarishis around Dhruva, and questioned the unvanquished king about the reason for his arrival at the asrama.'"

CANTO 128

"The king said again, 'I am a king called Viradyumna and my fame has spread in all directions. My son Bhuridyumna is lost and I have come to this forest in search of him, O noble Brahmanas. He is my only son, sinless ones, and of tender years. Since I cannot find him here, I wander everywhere in search of him.'

Rishi Tanu hung down his head again, remained perfectly silent and did not utter a single word. In the past, the king had not honoured Tanu and, in chagrin, the ascetic had practised austere tapasya for a long time, resolving that he would never accept any gift from either kings or members of any other varna, saying to himself, 'Hope agitates every man of foolish understanding. I will drive hope from my mind.' Such was his determination.

King Viradyumna once more questioned the Maharishi: 'What is the measure of the thinness of hope? What in this world is exceedingly difficult of acquisition? Tell me this, holy one, for you know dharma and artha well.'

The sage Tanu of the straw-lean body remembered all the past incidents about the King's neglect of him, and now brought them to the recollection of the king. He said, 'There is nothing, Rajan, that equals hope in flimsiness. I solicited many kings and found that nothing is as difficult to attain as an image that Hope sets before the mind.'

The king said, 'From your words, Brahmana, I understand what is thin and what is not. I understand also, how difficult it is to acquire the images set by hope before the mind. I regard your words as Sruti, but I have one doubt in my mind. If it pleases you, and it is a subject that you can discuss without impropriety, explain it in detail to me. What is more slender than your body?'

The emaciated sage said, 'A contented supplicant is exceedingly difficult to meet. Perhaps there is no such person in the world. Rarer still is one who never disregards a supplicant. The hope that rests upon such men who, after swearing promises, do not render service to others to the best of their abilities and according to the supplicant's merit, is even leaner than my body.

The hope that rests upon an ungrateful man, or on one who is cruel, or an idle man, or one who injures others, is even slenderer than my body. The hope a father who has but one son cherishes of seeing him once more after he has been lost, is slenderer than even my body. The hope that old women entertain of giving birth to sons, Rajan, and that which rich men cherish, is even thinner than my body. The hope of marriage that springs up in the hearts of old maids when they hear anybody talk of it, is leaner than my body.'

Hearing these words, Rajan, King Viradyumna and the women of his household prostrated themselves before the great Brahmana and touched his feet with their bent heads.

The king said, 'By your grace, O holy one, I want to find my child. What you have said is true. There is no doubt of the verity of your words.'"

Rishabha continued, "The holy Tanu, foremost of Dharmatmans, smiled, and with his gyana and his tapasya caused the king's son to be brought to the place. The sage rebuked the king and then revealed himself to be Dharma Deva, the god of righteousness himself. After displaying his own wonderful and celestial form, he entered an adjacent vana, with heart freed from wrath and the desire of revenge.

I saw all this, Rajan, and heard the words I have said. Drive out your hope that is even slenderer than any mentioned by the sage.'"

Bhishma continues, 'Thus addressed by the Dharmatman Rishabha, King Sumitra cast off the hope that was in his heart and which was slimmer than any of the kinds of hope the skeletal Rishi had indicated. You, too, O son of Kunti, pay heed to what I have said and be calm as Himavat. Overcome with distress, you have questioned me and heard my reply. Now that you have heard it, Rajan, you should dismiss your regrets!'"

CANTO 129

"Yudhishtira says, 'Like one who drinks amrita, I am never satiated listening to you speak. Just as a person who has knowledge of the Atman is never content with meditation, I am never satisfied after I drink the nectar of your discourse on dharma. Therefore, Pitamaha, speak again on dharma.'

Bhishma replies, 'Then let me tell you the old story of the discourse between Maharishi Gotama and the illustrious Yama. Gotama owned an extensive asrama on the Paripatra hills, where for sixty thousand years the sage sat in tapasya. One day, O Naravyaghra, the regent of the world, Yama, arrived there and saw him engaged in the most stern tapasya.

The Muni, understanding that it was Yama who had come, quickly saluted him and sat attentively with folded hands, awaiting his command. Lord Dharma in return saluted that bull among Brahmanas and enquired what he could do for him.

Gotama asked, "What does one do to liberate oneself from the debt one owes to one's mother and father? And how does one win regions of pure bliss that are so difficult to attain?"

Yama replied, "One should devote oneself to the dharma of satya, practise purity and tapasya ceaselessly, and worship one's mother and father. One should also perform Aswamedha yagnas, with gifts in plenty for Brahmanas. Through such deeds one wins many wonderful regions of felicity."'"

CANTO 130

"Yudhishtira says, 'O Bhaarata, what course of conduct should a king adopt who is without friends and troops, who has many enemies and an exhausted treasury? What should be his conduct when evil ministers surround him, when all his counsels are divulged, when he does not see his way clearly before him while he is attacking or subduing a hostile kingdom, or when, though weak, he is at war with a stronger ruler?

What should be the conduct of a king in whose kingdom affairs are ill-regulated, who disregards the requirements of place and time, who is unable to bring about peace and cause dissension among his enemies because he is oppressed? Should he seek to acquire wealth by evil means, or should he lay down his life and not seek artha?'

Bhishma replies, 'Though you know your dharma, O Bharatarishabha, you asked me a question that relates to a mystery about duty. This dharma is not something I would have spoken about had you not asked me. Dharma is very subtle, and one can understand it with the shastras.

Some men may become Dharmatmans when they practise the good deeds they remember having heard about. By clever and ingenious methods, the king can acquire wealth, or he may fail. Now, using your own intelligence, can you think of an answer to your question?

Listen, Bhaarata, to methods which have great punya, and which kings can use during times of distress, although I would not say that they conform to true dharma. If the king fills the treasury by oppression, this will bring him to the verge of destruction. This is also the conclusion of all wise men who have deliberated upon the subject.

The kind of shastras one studies only gives one knowledge which it is capable of bestowing and is to his liking. Ignorance stunts the development of methods, while knowledge promotes ingenuity and becomes the source of great happiness.

Without any scruples or malice and with a pure heart, listen to these teachings. Through the decrease of the treasury, the king's forces diminish, so he should fill his coffers by any means possible, just as he would locate water in an arid wilderness. However, in conformity with the code of ethics that the ancients practised, the king should show compassion to his people, when this times arrives. This is the eternal dharma.

Under ordinary circumstances, for men who are able and competent, dharma is of one kind, while in times of misfortune one's duties are different. A king without wealth may acquire religious punya by tapasya and the like. Since life is much more important than punya, and one cannot support it without wealth, no punya should be sought which stands in the way of gaining wealth.

A weak king can never obtain just and proper means of sustenance or power through religious merit. Since he cannot, even by his best exertions, acquire power with the aid of punya, practices during times of misery can be condoned, even though the learned opine that they lead to sin.

When the time of trial is over, the Kshatriya should conduct himself in such a way that he does not destroy his punya. He should also work so that he will not have to succumb to his enemies. Even these are declared to be his dharma. He should not sink into despondency or seek to rescue from the peril of destruction his own punya or that of others. On the other hand, he must preserve himself. This is the well-established judgement on dharma.

There is this Sruti, which decides that Brahmanas who know dharma should have the expertise to perform. Similarly, the Kshatriya should be proficient in exertion, since might of arms is his greatest possession.

When a Kshatriya has no means of support, what should he take, other than what belongs to Munis and Brahmanas? Even a Brahmana in times of distress can officiate at the yagna of one for whom he should never officiate during ordinary times, and he may even eat forbidden food; so, also, there is no doubt that a Kshatriya in distress can take wealth from everyone, except Rishis and Brahmanas.

For one troubled by an enemy and trying to escape, what can be a forbidden recourse? For a man imprisoned within a dungeon who wants to escape, what outlet can be an improper one? For someone in difficulty, even a normally forbidden way out is permissible.

For a Kshatriya who is in distress because of an empty treasury and a weak army, neither a life of mendicancy nor the profession of a Vaisya or a Sudra has been prescribed. The profession ordained for a Kshatriya is the acquisition of wealth by battle and victory. He should never beg from a member of his own varna.

One who supports himself in ordinary times by following the practices primarily prescribed for him, can in times of distress follow alternative practices which the shastras have laid down. In times of travail, when a Kshatriya cannot follow his ordinary dharma, he may live by even unjust and improper means.

Brahmanas are seen do the same when their means of livelihood are destroyed. When they can conduct themselves in this manner, what doubt need there be in respect of Kshatriyas? One, indeed, accepts this. Without sinking into despondency and ruin, a Kshatriya may forcibly take what he can from rich men with a view to protecting the people in the longer term, for he is their defender and destroyer as well.

No one in this world, Rajan, can support life without injuring other creatures. Even the Muni who leads a solitary vanavasa is no exception. A Kshatriya should not rely upon destiny, especially he who wants to rule. The king and the kingdom should always mutually protect each other. This is an eternal duty. As the king protects the kingdom when it sinks into danger, by making use of all his possessions, the kingdom should also protect the king when he is in trouble.

Even as a last resort, the king should never give up his treasury, his weapons to punish evildoers, his army, the chieftains of his kingdom, his friends and allies, and other necessary institutions.

Men who have knowledge of dharma say that one must save one's seeds by deducting them from one's very food. This is a truth cited from the treatise of the Asura Sambara, well-known for his great powers of illusion: "Shame on that king whose kingdom languishes! Shame on the life of that man who, from want of means, goes to a foreign country for a living! The king's roots are his treasury and army. His army has its roots in his treasury, and his religious punya is the root of all."

One can never fill the treasury without oppressing others. How, then, can the army be kept without oppression? The king in times of distress incurs no fault when he persecutes his subjects to fill the treasury. To perform yagnas, many adharmic deeds are done, and a king whose object is to fill his treasury in times of misfortune incurs no fault by any of these, since otherwise evil is certain to befall both him and his kingdom.

Institutions which cause death and misery exist to collect wealth. An astute king must decide what his policy should be in times of distress. He should remember that animals and other things are necessary for yagnas, which one requires as sacrifices to purify the heart, and that yagnapasus, yagnas and purity of the heart are all essential for final mukti. Similarly, policy and danda exist for the treasury, which in turn exists for the army, while policy, treasury and army, all three exist to vanquish enemies and protect or enlarge the kingdom.

I will give you an example which illustrates the true ways of dharma. When a great tree is cut down for making a sacrificial stake, other trees that stand in its way have also to be felled. These, when they fall, in turn knock down others in their path. Similarly, one should eliminate those who stand in the way of a treasury being filled. I do not see how else success can be had.

Through wealth both worlds, this and the next, can be gained, as well as truth and punya. A man without wealth is more dead than alive. One should acquire wealth by any means for the performance of yagnas. The sin that attaches to an action done during times of hardship is not equal to that which attaches to the same deed done at other times.

You cannot possibly see both the acquisition of wealth and its abandonment in the same person, Rajan! I have never seen a rich man in the forest. All the wealth one sees in this world is attended by struggle. All contend with others, saying, "This must be mine! This will be mine!"

There is nothing more meritorious for a king than the possession of a kingdom. While in ordinary times it is sinful for a king to oppress his subjects with heavy taxes, in times of trouble it is quite different. Some acquire wealth through gifts and yagnas, some who prefer tapasya acquire it by penance, and some through their intelligence and ingenuity. A man without wealth is considered weak, while he who has wealth is regarded as powerful, for he can buy everything.

A king who has a well-filled treasury can accomplish anything and thus earn punya, gratify his kama, and gain this world and the next. One should, however, always fill the treasury with the help of dharma, not by practices that can pass for dharma in times of need and distress.'"

PART II

Apaddharmanusasana Parva

CANTO 131

"**Y**udhishtira says, 'What, besides this, should a weak and procrastinating king do, who shrinks from battle through anxiety for his friends' lives, who is timorous and lacking in discretion? What should that king do whose cities and kingdom his enemies have annexed and partitioned among themselves, who has lost his wealth, who from poverty cannot honour and win friends to his side, whose ministers are disunited or bought over by his adversaries, who is obliged to face his foes, whose army has declined, and whose heart is being agitated by a strong enemy?'

Bhishma replies, 'If the invader is principled and conversant with both dharma and artha, a king of the kind you have described should immediately sue for peace and negotiate for him to restore those parts of the kingdom that have been seized. If the invader is powerful and seeks victory through unprincipled means, the king should make peace with him abandoning a portion of his territories. If the invader is bent upon hostilities, the king should abandon his capital and all his possessions and make his escape. If he saves his life, he can hope for equivalent gains in the future. Which man, knowing his dharma, would sacrifice himself, his most precious possession, to encounter danger from which he can escape by abandoning his treasury and army? A king should protect the women of his household, but if they fall into the hands of the enemy, he should not be moved to risking his own capture to save them. As long as he can, he should never surrender his own person to the enemy.'

Yudhishtira says, 'When his own people are dissatisfied with him, when invaders oppress him, when his treasury is empty, and when his secrets are divulged, what then should a king do?'

Bhishma says, 'Under such circumstances, a king, should make peace, if his enemy is righteous. If he is not, the king should then show courage and try to drive the enemy out of his kingdom; or, fighting bravely, he should lay down his life and ascend to Swarga. A king can conquer the whole earth with the help of even a small force if it is loyal, spirited, and devoted to him. If he kills his enemies, he is sure to enjoy the earth, while, if he is killed in battle, he is sure to ascend to heaven. By laying down one's life in battle, one obtains the companionship of Indra himself.'"

CANTO 132

"Yudhishtira says, 'When dharmic rule and practices for the good of the world disappear, when all the means and resources for supporting life fall into the hands of brigands, at such a calamitous time, how should a Brahmana survive, O Pitamaha, who from affection is unable to abandon his sons and grandsons?'

Bhishma replies, 'When such a time comes, the Brahmana should live by his knowledge. Everything in this world is for those who are good, and nothing for the evil. He who makes himself an instrument of acquisition, taking wealth from the evil and giving it to the good, is said to know the dharma of adversity. The king who wants to maintain his rule without driving his subjects to indignation and rebellion, can seize what the owner does not give voluntarily, saying, "This is mine!" This conduct of the wise man, blameworthy in ordinary times, does not deserve to be censured in times of necessity when cleansed by knowledge and power. They who always support themselves by force, prefer no other method of living. Those who are powerful, Yudhishtira, always live by their strength.

A king should practise what the ordinary shastras prescribe for times of distress without any exceptions. An intelligent king, however, should also do something more, such as levy more taxes upon the evil and punishable among his own subjects and upon the subjects of other kingdoms. At such times, the king should not oppress Ritwijas, Purohitas,

Acharyas and Brahmanas, who are honoured and esteemed. Even during bad times, he will incur censure and sin if he afflicts them. This is the eternal eye, the authority by which one should be guided in the world. By this, one judges whether a king is to be called good or evil.

One sees that many men in villages and towns bring accusations against one another from jealousy and anger. The king should never honour or punish anybody based on such reports. Slander should be neither spoken nor heard. When slanderous conversation takes place, one should close one's ears or walk right out, for such talk is characteristic of evil men, an indication of depravity. Conversely, those who speak of the virtues of others in assemblies of the good, are honest men.

Just as a pair of sweet-tempered bulls, governable and well-broken, bend their necks to the yoke and draw the cart willingly, the king should bear his burden in troubled times. Others say that a king at such times should conduct himself so as to gain a large number of allies. Some regard ancient usage as the highest indication of dharma. Others, such as those who favour the conduct of Sankha when his brother Likhita stole a few fruits from him, are of a different opinion, but not from malice or covetousness. One sees examples of Maharishis who are of the opinion that even acharyas, if given to evil practices, should be punished, although no authority has approved of such a proposition. The Devas can be left to punish men who are vile and guilty of evil practices.

The king who fills his treasury by fraudulent means certainly falls away from dharma. The code of morality should be followed which good men honour in every respect in affluent circumstances, and which every honest heart approves. He is said to be conversant with dharma who knows that it stands on four foundations, as elusive as the legs of the snake. Just like a hunter who tracks a shaft-struck deer by observing spots of blood on the ground, one should seek to discover the basis of dharma. A man should tread humbly along the ancient path trodden by the virtuous, as this was the dharma of the great Rajarishis of old, O Yudhishtira!'"

CANTO 133

"Bhishma says, 'The king should fill his coffers by drawing wealth from his own kingdom and from those of his enemies. From his treasury springs his punya, O son of Kunti, and from it extend the roots of his kingdom. For these reasons a king must fill his treasury, augment it and carefully husband it by reducing needless expenditure. This is the eternal practice. The treasury can neither be filled by pure and dharmic actions, nor by heartless cruelty. One should fill it by adopting a middle course. How can a weak king acquire a treasury? How can a king who has no treasury have strength? How can a weak man have a kingdom? From where can one without a kingdom obtain prosperity?

For a man of high rank, adversity is like death. For this reason the king should always increase his resources, army, allies and friends. Men do not heed a king with an empty treasury, and his servants will not show any zeal in his business if he pays them little. It is on account of his wealth that a king succeeds in obtaining great honour, as it covers up his sins like clothes that conceal parts of a female body that should not be exposed to view.

Those with whom the king has formerly quarrelled become jealous at the sight of his new affluence, and like dogs they once more take service under him. Though they only wait for an opportunity to destroy him, he takes to them as if nothing has happened. How, O Bhaarata, can such a king obtain happiness?

The king should strive to acquire greatness, and never bend down meekly. Exertion is manliness, He should rather break in adverse conditions, take to vanavasa and live there with the wild animals, than bend before anyone or dwell among ministers and officers who behave like robbers, without restraints. Even the brigands of the forest can furnish a large number of fighters for the accomplishment of the fiercest of deeds. O Bhaarata!

If the king transgresses wholesome restraints, everyone becomes alarmed. The very robbers, strangers to compassion, dread such a king. For this reason, the king should always establish rules and restraints for the well-being of his people. The people welcome rules in respect of even trivial matters.

There are men who think that this world is nothing, and the future a mirage. One should never trust atheists of this type, even if secret doubts agitate his heart. If the brigands of the forest, while observing other dharma, commit depredations only to property, one can regard them as harmless, since they do not threaten the lives of thousands of people. Even brigands regard as evil actions like killing an enemy who is fleeing from battle, ingratitude, plundering the property of a Brahmana, depriving a man of the whole of his property, violating maidens, ravishing wives, having adulterous congress with other people's wives and occupying villages and towns as their lawful lords.

Certain kings strive to make peace in order to inspire confidence in the hearts of the bandits, only to destroy them after their ways have been studied. A king should never behave cruelly towards them, thinking that he is more powerful. Rather than exterminate the robbers outright, the king should bring their families, habitations and property under his control. Kings who do not seek to annihilate them need not fear for their own existence, while those who do have always to live with that apprehension.'"

CANTO 134

"Bhishma says, 'Men learned in the shastras declare that an intelligent Kshatriya knows his obvious dharma, the earning of punya and the acquisition of wealth. Subtle discussions on duty and on unseen consequences in respect of a future world should not stop him from performing those two duties. As it is useless to argue, upon seeing certain foot-prints on the ground, whether or not they are those of a wolf, so too is discussion on the nature of dharma and adharma.

Nobody in this world ever sees the fruits of dharma and adharma. A Kshatriya, therefore, should seek to acquire power. He who is powerful is master of everything. Wealth leads to the possession of an army. He who is powerful obtains intelligent advisers, while he who is without means is truly fallen. One regards too little of anything in the world as the unclean remnants of a feast. Even if a strong man performs many bad deeds, everybody is afraid to says or do anything to censure or check him.

Associating power with dharma and truth can rescue men from great peril. If one compares the two, power will appear to be superior, since dharma springs from and rests upon power, as all immobile things do upon the earth, as smoke depends for its motion upon the wind.

Dharma is dependent on the more powerful, as pleasure is contingent upon those who desire enjoyment. There is nothing that powerful men cannot do, and everything they do becomes pure. A powerless man committing evil actions can never escape, because men are alarmed by his conduct as at the appearance of a wolf. One fallen on hard times leads a life of disgrace and sorrow, which is akin to death. The learned have said that when a man is abandoned by friends and companions as result of his sinful conduct, their taunts will pierce him and bring him to burn with grief.

Acharyas versed in the shastras have suggested that to expiate sin, one should study the three Vedas, wait upon and worship the Brahmanas, gratify all men by looks, words and acts, cast off meanness, marry into high families, proclaim the praises of others while confessing one's own worthlessness, recite mantras, perform the usual water-rites, be mild of demeanour and frugal of speech, perform austere yagnas, and seek the refuge of Brahmanas and Kshatriyas. One who has committed evil deeds should do all this without resenting the reproaches of others. By following this course and by sharing his wealth with others, he will redeem himself in the regard of the world and come to enjoy different kinds of happiness here, and great rewards and punya in the next.'"

CANTO 135

"Bhishma says, 'An old story is told of a brigand who practised restraints in this world and so did not meet with destruction in the next. Once there lived a robber called Kayavya, born of a Kshatriya father and a Nishada mother, who practised Kshatriya dharma. Strong, intelligent, courageous, an expert in the shastras, he was devoid of cruelty. He was devoted to the Brahmanas, worshipped his elders and gurus with reverence and protected the Rishis in the observance of their practices. Though a brigand, he earned felicity in Swarga.

Morning and evening he used to chase deer and drive them to frenzy. He knew well all the practices of the Nishadas and the ways of all animals living in the forest. Well versed in the requirements of time and place, he roved over the mountains. His arrows never missed their aim, his weapons were powerful and he could vanquish hundreds of troops single-handedly. He worshipped his old, blind and deaf parents daily in the forest. He was hospitable to everyone who deserved the honour, entertained them with honey, meat, fruits, roots and other kinds of excellent food and did them many favours. He showed great respect for those Brahmanas who retired from the world for vanavasa, and often took meat for them when he killed deer. In the case of those unwilling, from fear of censure, to accept gifts from him because of his profession, he went to their homes before dawn and left meat at their doorstep.

One day the entire band of robbers, pitiless and unbridled as they were, moved to elect him as their leader. The robbers said, "You are familiar with the requirements of place and time, wise and courageous, and committed to everything you undertake. Be our supreme leader, respected by us all, and we will do as you direct. Protect us as a father or mother would."

Kayavya replied, "Never kill a woman, a child, an ascetic or one who from fear abstains from a fight. Never seize women or bring them away with force. None of you should ever, amongst all creatures, kill a female.

Brahmanas should be always blessed, and you must fight for their good. Never sacrifice Truth. Never obstruct wedding ceremonies or destroy houses in which the Devas, the Pitris and Athitis are honoured.

Of all creatures, Brahmanas should be exempt from your plundering raids. You should worship them by giving away even all you have. He who incurs the wrath of the Brahmanas will fail to find a rescuer in the three worlds, if they wish to humiliate him. He who speaks ill of the Brahmanas and wishes for their destruction, himself meets with destruction like darkness at sunrise.

Living here, you will obtain the fruits of your valour, and troops will be sent against those who refuse to give us our dues. The danda of punishment is intended for evil, not for self-glorification. Those who oppress the good deserve death, and those who seek to increase their fortunes by attacking kingdoms in unscrupulous ways, very soon come to be regarded like vermin in a dead body. Those brigands whose conduct conform to the restraints prescribed by the shastras soon win salvation, though they lead a life spent in plunder."

By obeying all the commands of Kayavya and desisting from sin, the robbers obtained great prosperity, while, by doing good to the honest and restraining the robbers from evil deeds, Kayavya won great happiness in the next world. He who bears in mind this story of Kayavya will not fear the denizens of the forest, or any earthly creature, not even wicked men O Bhaarata! If such a man takes to vanavasa, he will be able to live there as secure as a king.'"

CANTO 136

"Bhishma says, 'Regarding how a king should fill his treasury, men who know the shastras cite the following verses that Brahma himself sang. One should never take the wealth of those who perform yagnas, or wealth dedicated to the gods. A Kshatriya should seize the wealth of those who never perform religious rites and yagnas and are regarded as equal to brigands. All the creatures who inhabit the earth, all the pleasures of sovereignty, and all the earth's wealth, belong to the Kshatriya alone, O Bhaarata. The Kshatriya should use this wealth for the upkeep of his army and for the performance of yagnas.

Men weed out creepers and plants that are not of any use and burn them as fuel to cook their food. Similarly the king should, by punishing the wicked, cherish the good. Men who know dharma say that one's wealth is useless if it is not used to feed with libations of ghrita the Devas, the Pitris, and men. A virtuous ruler, O Rajan, should confiscate such wealth so that a large number of good people can be gratified, but he should not hoard that wealth in his treasury. He who makes himself an instrument of acquisition by taking away wealth from the evil and giving it to the good is said to know the whole science of dharma.

A king should extend his conquests in the next world according to his ability, as gradually as vegetables are seen to grow. Like white ants who appear and multiply from no apparent cause, yagnas spring for no particular external reason. As one drives off flies, gnats and ants from the bodies of domestic cattle at the time of milking, one should drive away from the kingdom those who are averse to performing yagnas. This is consistent with dharma. Just as soil becomes finer and finer with pounding between two stones, questions of morality, become finer and finer the more they are reflected on and discussed.'"

CANTO 137

"**B**hishma says, 'One who provides for the future, and one who has presence of mind, both enjoy happiness, while the man of procrastination is lost. Listen attentively to an excellent story concerning these types.

In a lake that was not very deep and which abounded with fish, there lived three Sakula fishes, friends and constant companions. Amongst the three, one always planned ahead and liked to provide for the future, another had great presence of mind, while the third always put things off. One day some fishermen who came to the lake began to drain away its water to a lower ground through different outlets. Seeing the water of the lake gradually decreasing, the fish with foresight perceived the danger and addressed his two companions.

He said, "A great peril is about to overtake all the creatures who live in this lake. Let us speedily escape to some other place before our path is blocked. One who avoids a future evil through good planning will never incur serious danger. Listen to my advice and let us all depart." The lazy one among the three answered, "Well said, but it is my considered opinion there is no need for such haste." The fish with presence of mind said to his procrastinating companion, "When the actual time comes for action, I always come up with a plan."

Hearing the answers of his two companions, the prudent and intelligent fish immediately set out by a flowing current and reached another deep lake. The fishermen, when they saw that the lake had been drained, shut in the remaining fish and, beating the residual water, began to catch numbers of fish, including the procrastinating Sakula, and to tie them as they were caught to a long string. The Sakula noted for his presence of mind thrust himself into the company of those that had been so tied and remained quietly among them, biting the string to give the appearance of having been caught. The fishermen, believing that all the fish attached to the string had been caught, removed them to deeper waters to wash them, at which point the quick Sakula left the string and darted away to safety. However the fish who had been procrastinating, foolish and bemused as he was, was unable to escape, and met with death.

Thus, like the procrastinating fish, anyone who, from want of intelligence, cannot divine the approach of danger, will meet with destruction. He who considers himself clever does not seek his own good at the appropriate time and thereby incurs great danger, like the Sakula fish with presence of mind. Only one who plans in advance, and one with presence of mind, can succeed. One who postpones his decisions meets with destruction.

The divisions of time are many, such as Kashtha, Kala, Muhurta, day, night, Lava, month, fortnight, the six seasons, Kalpa, and year. We call the divisions of the earth place, while Time we cannot see. The success of any object or purpose is achieved or not, according to the manner in which the mind is set to think of it. The man of forethought and the one with the presence of mind, the Rishis declare, in all treatises on dharma and artha and in those that deal with mukti, is foremost among men. He who acts after reflection and scrutiny, and who uses proper means to accomplish his objectives, will always achieve a great deal. However, those who work with due regard to time and place, win results better than the mere man of presence of mind.'"

CANTO 138–1

"Yudhishtira says, 'You say, O Bharatarishabha, that intelligence which provides for future contingencies and meets present emergencies is always superior, while procrastination brings about destruction. I ask you, Pitamaha, about that superior intelligence which will protect a king who knows the shastras, dharma and artha, and guard him from confusion even when he is surrounded by many enemies. I want you to tell me, O Kurupravira, everything that the shastras lay down about the manner in which a king should conduct himself when enemies assail him.

When a king is in trouble, a large number of his enemies, provoked by his past actions, will range themselves against him and try to vanquish him. How can a king, weak and alone, succeed in holding up his head when he is challenged from all sides by many powerful kings in league together? At such times, how does a king make friends and enemies, O Bharatarishabha, and how should he then behave towards both? When those he thought of as his friends become his enemies, what should a king do, if he wants happiness? With whom should he go to war, and with whom should he make peace? Even if he is strong, how should he behave in the midst of enemies? O Parantapa, this to me is the greatest of all questions regarding the discharge of Rajadharma. Few can hear the answer to this question, and none can answer it save Santanu's son. Firmly wedded to truth, with all your senses under control, O blessed one, reflect on this and speak to me!'

Bhishma replies, 'Yudhishtira, this question is certainly worthy of you. I am immensely happy to tell you all the duties generally known that one should practice in times of distress, O Bhaarata. An enemy becomes a friend and a friend also becomes an enemy, for the course of human actions through the play of circumstances is very uncertain. Therefore, what should be done and what should not, whether one should either trust one's enemies or make war depend upon the requirements of time and place. One should exert oneself to make friends with intelligent and knowledgeable men who have one's welfare at heart. You should make peace with even your enemies, O Bhaarata, when your life cannot otherwise be saved. The foolish man who never makes peace with enemies will never gain or acquire any of those fruits for which others strive. He who makes peace with enemies and breaks even with friends, after a full consideration of the circumstances, obtains great benefits.

An old story is told of an exchange between a cat and a mouse under a banyan tree. In the midst of a great forest there was a huge banyan. Covered with many kinds of creepers, it was the resort of diverse birds. It had a large trunk from which numerous branches extended in all directions. Delightful to view, it afforded refreshing shade and was home to animals of many species. A wise mouse named Palita lived happily at the foot of the tree in a hole with a hundred outlets. On the branches of the tree lived a cat called Lomasa, contentedly devouring a large number of birds every day.

After some time, a Chandala came to the vana and built a hut there for himself. Every evening after sunset he spread his traps of leathern strings and, going back to his hut, slept happily till he re-visited his traps at dawn. Diverse animals fell into his nets every night, and it so happened that one day the cat, in a careless moment, got caught in the snare.

O you of great wisdom, the mouse Palita, seeing his enemy the cat thus caught in the net, came out of his hole and began to rove about fearlessly. While confidently wandering through the forest in search of food, the mouse caught sight of the meat spread there as lure. Getting up on the trap, the little animal began to eat the flesh. Laughing to himself, he even climbed over his old foe entangled helplessly in the net. Intent on eating the meat, oblivious to his own danger, he suddenly noticed the presence of a terrible enemy, none other than a coppery-eyed, restless mongoose named Harita. Living in underground holes, it resembled in form the flower of a reed. Attracted by the scent of the mouse, the animal hastened towards his prey, standing on his haunches with head upraised, licking the corners of his mouth with his tongue.

The mouse at the same moment beheld, sitting on the branch of the banyan tree, another arboreal enemy, the sharp-beaked nocturnal bird called Chandraka. When he realized that both the mongoose and the owl had seen him, Palita, surrounded by danger and filled with alarm for his safety, began to think, and made a great resolution: "At times of such peril, when death itself is staring me in the face and fear is all around, what should one do who wants his own good? I must try and save my life, warding off by every conceivable means even multiple dangers.

If I descend from this trap to the ground without measures for my safety, the mongoose will surely devour me. If I remain on this trap, the owl will certainly seize me. If, again, that cat manages to disentangle himself from the net, he too is certain to eat me up. But someone of my acumen should not lose his wits. I must use my intelligence and do my best to save my life. A person of wisdom and intelligence who knows the science of strategy never despairs, however great and terrible the danger that threatens him.

At present, I do not see any refuge other than this cat. He is an enemy, but himself in distress, so the service that I can do him is great. With three enemies trying to make me their prey, what should I do to save my life? I should now seek the protection of one of them, the cat. My plan should be to advise the cat for his good, so that I can escape from all three. Let me try to make this foolish creature understand his own interests in order to get him to make peace with me. When one's life is threatened, say those who profess knowledge of Neeti, one should even conciliate an enemy. It is better to have a learned person for an enemy than a fool for a friend. My life now rests entirely in the hands of my enemy the cat, and so I will now talk to him about his own liberation. Perhaps, at this moment, it would not be wrong to take him for an intelligent and learned foe."

The mouse, surrounded by enemies, pursued his reflections in this strain and, familiar with the science of artha and well acquainted with occasions when one should declare war or make peace, gently addressed the cat, saying, "I speak as a friend, O cat! Are you alive? I wish you to live! I wish for the good of us both. O amiable one, have no fear. You will live in happiness, and I will rescue you, if you do not kill me. There is an excellent plan I have thought of, by which you can escape, and which will benefit me as well. The mongoose and the owl are both waiting with evil intent, and my life is safe only as long as they do not attack me. There, that wretched owl with restless glances and horrid cries is eyeing me from the branch of that tree, terrifying me.

Two good men can become friends in no time by just taking seven steps in a walk together. As you are wise, you are my friend and you need have no fear now. Without my help, O cat, you will not succeed in tearing the net. I will serve you by cutting the net, if you abstain from killing me. You have lived on this tree and I have lived at its foot for many long years together, as you know. The wise do not approve one whom nobody trusts, or one who never trusts another; both are unhappy. For this reason, let our love for each other increase, and let there be union among us both. Wise men do not approve of trying to do something when the moment for it has passed. This is the proper time for such an understanding between us. I wish that you survive, and you also want me to live. A man crosses a deep and large river on a piece of wood, each taking the other across. Similarly, our compact also will bring happiness to both of us, and we will rescue each other."

The mouse Palita waited expectantly for an answer, knowing that his suggestion was reasonable and beneficial to both.

CANTO 138–2

'Hearing the suggestion of the mouse, framed in well-chosen words to make it acceptable, the cat, possessed of foresight and judgment of his own, answered him politely. Regarding the mouse kindly through eyes like lapis lazuli gemstones, the sharp-toothed Lomasa replied, "I am delighted with you, O amiable one! Bless you for wishing me to live! Do not hesitate to do what you think is helpful, as I am certainly in great danger, and you in possibly greater difficulties. Let us have an agreement between us, and I will do what is appropriate and necessary for the success of our efforts. If you rescue me, your service will not be forgotten. I will place myself in your hands, serve you devotedly like a disciple and always obey you."

The mouse Palita, seeing that the cat was now completely under his influence, answered him with grave and judicious words. "You have spoken magnanimously, beyond my expectations. Listen to this plan I have hit upon to our mutual advantage. I will crouch beneath your body, as I am terrified of the mongoose. Save me, do not kill me, for I can rescue you. Protect me also from the owl, for that wretch, too, wishes to seize me for his prey. I swear by Truth that I will cut the net that entangles you, O friend!"

Lomasa gazed at Palita with delight and, now converted to cordiality, lauded him with exclamations of welcome. Losing no time, he said, "Come, quick! You are indeed blessed, a friend dear to me as breath, since through your grace I have almost got back my life. Tell me now whatever is in my power to do for you and I will do it. Let there be peace between us, O friend! Once free from this danger, I and all my friends and relatives will do all that is agreeable and beneficial to you, and will always try to please and honour you for your services. One can one never become equal to the person who did the favour first, even with abundant service in return. One does it in return for help received, while the other acts without any such motive."

Bhishma continues, 'The mouse, once he convinced the cat of his own interests, crept under its breast as trustfully as if it had been the lap of his father or mother. Both Harita and Chandraka were shocked and amazed at this, and gave up all hope of catching the prey so close to them. They had strength, intelligence and enough cleverness to seize their prey, but realized they could not break the compact between the mouse and the cat, and went away to their respective homes.

Then the mouse Palita, who knew what to do when, began to gnaw through the strings of the net slowly, as he lay under the body of the cat, waiting for the opportune moment to finish his work. Distressed by the strings that entangled him, the cat grew impatient at the slow progress the mouse was making and, wishing to hurry him up, said, "O amiable one, how is it that you do not proceed faster with your work? Now that you have succeeded in your purpose, do you disregard me? O Parantapa, do cut these strings quickly, as the hunter will soon be here!"

The clever mouse, with his own interest in mind, replied in politic terms to the impatient cat, who was less acute, "Wait in silence, O amiable one, and drive away your fears. Speed is not essential. We know the requirements of time. It will not be wasted. A venture begun at an improper time cannot succeed, while one started at the right time will always produce splendid results. If I free you at an improper time, I will have to remain in great fear of you. So wait for the right one. Do not be impatient, friend, for I will cut the strings when I see the hunter approach, armed with his weapons, at the moment when both of us are terrified. Set free at that instant, you will scramble up the tree thinking of nothing save your safety and, as you flee in dread, I will enter my hole."

When he heard this, the cat, who was clever and persuasive, and indeed had expeditiously fulfilled his own part of the covenant, said to the recalcitrant mouse, "I rescued you promptly from a great danger, Alas, this is not the way for honest people to do business with their friends! They are happy to do their part, but it turns out otherwise. You should work for my benefit more speedily. O you of great wisdom, do go a bit faster. If you are only waiting for time to slip away, because of our former hostility, know, evil one, that the consequence of your act will be to lessen your own life! If I have in the past unconsciously done you any wrong, I ask your forgiveness."

The wise mouse, who knew the scriptures, replied: "O cat, I have heard what you have to say in your own interest. Now listen to me as I tell you mine. A friendship based and maintained on fear should be sustained with great caution, like the hand of the snake-charmer from the fangs of the snake. He who does not protect himself after contracting an agreement with someone stronger, will find that it causes harm instead of good. Nobody is anybody's friend or well-wisher, for men become friends or enemies only from motives of self-interest. Interest attracts interest, just as tame elephants catch wild individuals of their species. After an act has been accomplished, the doer is barely remembered; therefore all acts should be so done that something remains to be completed. When I set you free, you will flee for your life without a thought to catch me, out of fear of the hunter. See, I have cut all the strings of this net. Only one remains; I will cut that also quickly. Be comforted, Lomasa!"

CANTO 138–3

'While the mouse and the cat were talking to each other, both in serious danger, the night gradually wore away, and a great dread pierced the heart of the cat. When at last morning came, the grim-visaged Chandala, Parigha, appeared on the scene, armed with weapons and accompanied by a pack of dogs. His aspect was fierce and frightful, exceedingly filthy, with black and tawny hair, large hips, long ears, and a large mouth extending from ear to ear. Seeing Parigha, who appeared veritably as an agent of Yama, the cat asked Palita, "What will you do now?" Palita rapidly cut the last string and freed the cat, who sped up the tall banyan tree, while the mouse darted into his own hole. The Chandala saw everything and, with his hopes frustrated, gathered up his nets and returned home.

Liberated from that great peril, and with his precious life intact, the cat, from the branches of the tree, addressed the mouse Palita in his hole: "You ran away so suddenly, without speaking to me. I hope you do not suspect me of any evil intentions. I am certainly grateful for the great service you have done me. Since you inspired me with trust and gave me my life, why don't you approach me now, so that we can enjoy the sweetness of friendship?

He who forgets his friends is a wicked person and will never find comrades in times of danger and need. You have honoured and served me to the best of your power, and it is now proper for you to enjoy the company of my poor self who has become your friend. Like disciples who revere their guru, all my friends and kinsmen will honour and worship you, your friends and your kinsmen, for which grateful individual will not idolize his saviour?

Be the lord of both my body and home, be the disposer of all my wealth and possessions, be my honoured counsellor and rule me like a father. I swear by my life that you have no fear from us. In intelligence you are Usanas himself. By the power of your strategy you have given us our life and by the strength of your understanding you have conquered us."

Soothed by the comforting words of the cat, the mouse, who knew what was good for him, replied in sweet and sensible words: "I have heard you, Lomasa, so now listen to me. Friends should be well scrutinized, and enemies closely studied. In this world, even the learned regard a task like this as difficult, one depending upon acute intelligence. Friends assume the guise of enemies, and foes assume the guise of friends. When pacts of friendship are formed, it is difficult for the parties to understand whether the other parties are really moved by kama and krodha.

There is no such thing as a foe. There is no such thing as a friend. It is force of circumstances that creates friends and foes. He who thinks his own interests to be safe if another person lives, and endangered if he dies, regards him as a friend as long as their interests do not clash. There is no condition that deserves the permanent name either of friendship or hostility. Both friends and enemies arise from considerations of interest and gain.

Friendship changes to enmity in the course of time, and a foe also becomes a friend; self-interest is supreme. He who reposes blind trust in friends, and is always suspicious of enemies, without any guiding principle, will find his life unsafe. He who sets his heart upon affiliating with either friend or foe, without consideration of strategy, is regarded as unhinged. One should neither place trust in someone undeserving, nor too much faith in someone deserving. The danger that arises from blind confidence is that it cuts the very roots of him who reposes such assurance. Interest and advantage guide even a father, a mother, a son, a maternal uncle, a sister's son, or other relatives and kinsmen. One can even see a father and mother discard a dear son faced with disgrace. People take care of themselves; such is the efficacy of self-interest.

O wise one, someone who seeks his enemy's happiness immediately after being freed from danger will find escape very difficult. You came down from the tree-top to this very spot and, due to your limitations of perception, did not notice the net spread here. How can one who fails to protect himself protect others? He is sure to ruin all his work. You tell me in sweet words that I am very dear to you. Listen, friend, to my analysis.

One becomes dear for a reason, and an enemy, too, for some adequate cause. The desire for gain, in some form or other, moves this whole world of creatures. Friendship between two brothers, love between husband and wife, depends upon selfishness. I do not know any kind of affection between men that does not rest upon some motive of self-interest. Sometimes we see blood brothers or husband and wife quarrel and reunite from natural affection; we also see this in men unrelated to each other. You cherish one for his liberality, another for his sweet words and a third for his religious deeds; all are dear to us for the purpose they serve.

The amity between us arose for a sufficient cause. That cause no longer exists. What reason is there for which I am so dear to you, other than your desire to make me your prey? You should know that I will not forget that Time erode these reasons. You seek your own interests, just as other wise men and I value our own welfare. The world rests upon the example of the wise, and I feel that this affection that you show me now is ill-timed. My self-interest makes me constant in both peace and war, themselves very unstable. The circumstances under which one makes peace or declares war change as quickly as clouds change their form.

This very day you were first my enemy, then my friend, and now once more you are an enemy. There was friendship between us as long as there was basis for its existence. Once it passed away, so did friendship.

You are by nature my enemy, but circumstances made you my friend. That state of things has now passed and the old natural state of enmity has returned. As I understand this principle, why should I, for your sake, enter the net that is spread for me? Through your power, I was freed from a great danger. Through my power, you have been freed from a similar danger. Each of us has served the other through our individual abilities and freed the other from peril, and there is no need for us to come together again in friendly conversation.

We have both accomplished our objectives. I am weak and you are strong; I am your food and you are my eater. There cannot be a friendly union between us when we are situated so unequally. I understand your cunning, which is to praise me so that you can all the more easily eat me. You got entangled in the net while searching for food. You are freed, and once again you feel the pangs of hunger. You can now have no further use for me except as a meal. I know you are hungry, and this is your dinner time; your gaze is upon me as you seek your prey. Acute from studying the shastras, you scheme in truth to eat me up today. You have sons and wives. Still you seek a friendly union with me, offer to treat me with affection and do me services. Friend, I cannot accept this proposal. If your dear spouse and loving children see me with you, they would cheerfully eat me up!

I will not, therefore, join you in friendship, for there is no longer any reason for such a union. If, indeed, you wish not to forget my help, think of what will be beneficial for me, and be satisfied. Which wise man would place himself in the power of an enemy who is not a distinguished dharmatma, who is in the pangs of hunger and on the look-out for a prey? Be happy, then. I will presently leave you. I am filled with alarm to see you even from a distance. I will not mix with you, so stop your attempts, Lomasa! If you think I have done you a service, follow then the rules of friendship when I happen to rove confidently or carelessly. Even that would be gratitude enough, coming from you.

Living near a strong and powerful person is never a good thing, even if the immediate danger has receded. I will always stand in fear of one more powerful than myself. If you do not seek your own interests, tell me what I can do for you, and I shall certainly give you everything— except my life. For protecting oneself one should even give up one's own children, kingdom, jewels and wealth. If one lives, one can recover all the affluence that one has lost. Men who protect and commit themselves only after proper consideration and assessment are never in danger. The weak always know him for an enemy who has greater strength. Their understanding, firm in the truths of the shastras, never loses its focus.'"

CANTO 138–4

'Thus rebuked soundly by the mouse Palita, the cat blushed with shame, and said, "Truly, I swear to you that I consider injuring a friend to be detestable. I know you are wise and want to do me good. Guided by Artha, you say that there is cause for a breach between you and me. It does not become you, good friend, to take me for what I am not. I regard you as a great friend, for I owe you my life. I, too, am familiar with duties, and appreciate other people's merits. I am very grateful for services received, and I am committed to the service of friends, especially to you. For these reasons we should fraternize. At your command, I and all my kinsmen and relatives will lay down our very lives. Those who are learned and wise see abundant reason to place their trust in those of such mental disposition as us. So you, who know the truths of dharma, should not suspect me."

The mouse reflected a little, and said gravely, "You are exceedingly good, and I am glad to hear all that you have said. For all that, I cannot trust you. It is impossible for you, by such eulogies or by gifts of great wealth, to induce me to associate with you again. The wise never place themselves in the power of an enemy without sufficient reason. A weak person who has a pact with a stronger one, when both are threatened by enemies, should conduct himself carefully, and with considerations of expediency, when that common danger passes. After he has gained his objective, the weaker of the two parties should not again place confidence in the stronger. One should never trust someone who does not deserve to be trusted, nor should one believe blindly another who merits trust. One should try to inspire others with confidence in oneself, but not repose confidence in enemies. Thus one should, under all circumstances, protect oneself.

One's possessions, children and all, are valuable so long as one is alive. In brief, the highest truth of all treatises on policy is mistrust. For this reason, mistrust of all produces the greatest good. If weak people mistrust their enemies, the latter, even if strong, will never get them under their power. O cat, someone like myself should always guard his life from someone like you. You too should protect your own life from the Chandala whose rage you have excited." The cat, frightened at the mention of the hunter, instantly left the branch of the tree and sped away. The wise mouse Palita, who who knew the truths of the shastras, having displayed his power of understanding, also left and entered another hole.'

Bhishma continues, 'Thus the mouse Palita, though weak and alone, through his intelligence baffled many powerful enemies. A wise man should make peace with a powerful enemy. The mouse and the cat owed their escape to their reliance upon each other's services. I have thus pointed out to you the course of Kshatriya duties at great length. Listen while I summarise it for you.

When two men who were once engaged in hostilities make peace with each other, it is certain that each of them desires to outwit the other. In such a case he who is wise by the power of his understanding, will get the better of the other. On the other hand, he who lacks wisdom will suffer, if he is careless, and will be over-come by the intelligent. It is necessary that one should appear to be fearless even when afraid, and appear to be trustful even while really mistrusting others. One who acts thus never stumbles or, if he stumbles, is not ruined. When the right time comes, one should make peace with an enemy, or wage war with even a friend. This is how one should conduct oneself, O Rajan, as the authorities on matters of peace and war have said.

Knowing this, O Rajan, one should bear in mind the truth of the shastras, and with all his wits about him, behave like one in fear before the cause of fear actually presents itself, and make peace with enemies. Such fear and alertness sharpen the intellect. If one behaves like a nervous man before the cause of fear is at hand, one is not panic-stricken when the cause is actually present. From the fear of someone who always behaves fearlessly, one sees very great fear arising. You should not advise anyone, "Never be afraid." He who is afraid, spurred by the knowledge of his own weakness, seeks the counsel of wise and experienced men. For these reasons, one should appear to be fearless even when afraid, and seem to be trustful when one mistrusts others. But on the most important matters, one should not behave towards others with falsehood.

You have listened, O Yudhishtira, to the old story of the mouse and the cat that I have told. Act as required amidst your friends and kinsmen. Derive insight from this story. Learn the difference between a friend and an enemy, and the proper time for war and peace, and you will discover a means of escape when in danger. Make peace at a time of common danger with a powerful one, and think carefully about uniting with the enemy after the danger has passed. Indeed, having achieved your purpose, you should not trust the enemy again. This path of policy is consistent with the aggregate of three, O Rajan!

Guided by this Sruti, win prosperity by protecting your subjects once more, O son of Pandu. Seek the companionship of Brahmanas in all your work, as they constitute the great source of benefit both in this world and the next. They are teachers of dharma and are always grateful and, if worshipped, are sure to do you good. Therefore, O Rajan, you should venerate them and then you will duly obtain kingdom, great benefits, fame, achievement and progeny, in the proper order. This story of peace and war between the mouse and the cat, this history so persuasive and instructive, should remain always before his eyes when a king conducts himself in the midst of his enemies.'"

CANTO 139–1

"Yudhishtira says, 'You have stated, O Mahabaho, that one should not trust foes. But how can the king maintain himself if he does not trust anybody? You say that kings who trust others face greater danger. How can a king conquer his enemies without depending on others? Clear my doubts, for my mind has become confused by what you say about mistrust.'

Bhishma replies, 'Listen, O Rajan, to the story of King Brahmadatta and a bird named Pujani who lived for a long time within the inner apartments of the king's palace at Kampilya. Like the bird Jivajivaka, Pujani could mimic the cries of all animals. Although a bird by birth, she had great knowledge and knew every truth.

While living there, she had a child of great splendor, at the very same time as the king and his queen also had a son. Pujani, who was grateful for the shelter of the king's roof, used to go every day to the shores of the ocean and bring back a couple of fruits for the nourishment of both her own nestling and the infant prince. One of the fruits she gave to her chick, the other to the prince. Every day she brought them, and every day she distributed them the same way. The fruits she brought were sweet as nectar and most nutritious. The infant prince derived great strength from Pujani's fruit.

One day the prince, while with his nurse, saw Pujani's chick. Getting down from the nurse's arms, he ran towards the little bird, the same age as himself, and, moved by childish impulse, began to play with it happily. At last, picking up the bird in his hands, the prince stifled the chick's life. He went back to his nurse. When Pujani, who had been out in search of the usual fruits, returned to the palace and saw her young one lying dead on the ground, killed by the prince, she wept bitterly. With tears gushing down her cheeks, her heart burning with grief, she said, "Alas, nobody should live with a Kshatriya, or make friends with him, or associate with him. When they have a purpose to serve, they are courteous, and when that object has been served they discard you. The Kshatriyas do evil to all. They should never be trusted. Even after they inflict a wound, they try to pacify the injured, at no cost to themselves. I will exact my retribution from the cruel and ungrateful betrayer of my trust. He is guilty of a triple sin, because he took the life of one who was born on the same day as him, who was reared with him and ate with him, and who was dependent on him for protection."

With these words to herself, Pujani pierced the eyes of the prince with her talons, and, deriving some comfort from her act of reprisal, said again, "A sinful deed, perpetrated deliberately, harms the doer immediately, while those who avenge an injury do not lose their punya." O Rajan, if the consequences of a sinful deed are not visited upon the perpetrator himself, they will certainly be on his descendants.

When Brahmadatta saw his son blinded by Pujani, he understood what had happened, and said to Pujani. "We did you an injury, and you have avenged it. The account has been squared. Do not leave your home, O Pujani; continue to dwell here."

Pujani replied, "If anyone who causes an injury to another continues living with that other, his conduct will not be approved by the learned. In the circumstances, it is always better for him to leave his former place. One should never trust gentle assurances received from an injured party. The fool who trusts such assurances soon meets with death.

Animosity is not quickly cooled. The very sons and grandsons of men who have injured each other can encounter destruction, as enmity is handed down like an inheritance. As a result of their offspring being destroyed, they lose the next world also.

Among men who have injured one another, mistrust can be advantageous. One who has betrayed a confidence should never be trusted; one who does not deserve trust should not be trusted; nor should too much trust be placed in anyone, though he may be deserving of trust. The danger that arises from blind confidence brings wholesale destruction. While one should seek to inspire others with confidence in oneself, one should not repose confidence in others.

One's father and the mother are only the foremost of friends. The wife is merely a vessel for procreation. The son is only one's seed. The brother is an enemy. A friend or companion requires to have his palms oiled, if he is to remain one. You alone enjoy or suffer your own happiness or misery.

It is not advisable to have real peace among men who have injured one another. The reasons for which I lived here no longer exist. The mind of one who has once injured another becomes naturally filled with mistrust, if he sees the injured one pay homage to him with gifts and honours. Such conduct, especially when displayed by those who are strong, always fills the weak with alarm.

An intelligent person should leave the place where he was first given respect, so as not to meet with dishonour and injury again, despite any subsequent honour that he might obtain from his enemy. I have dwelt in your home for a long time, esteemed by you. However, a cause for enmity has now arisen, and I should leave this place without any hesitation."

CANTO 139–2

'Brahmadatta replied, "One who does an injury in return for an injury received, is not considered unjust. Indeed, the avenger only settles his account. Therefore, Pujani, continue to dwell here and do not leave this place."

Pujani said, "No friendship can be restored between one who has injured another and one who has inflicted an injury in return. The hearts of neither can forget what has happened."

Brahmadatta replied, "It is necessary for an injurer and the avenger of injury to get together. One has seen that upon such a union, mutual animosity cools and no fresh injury follows."

Pujani said, "That animosity can never die. The person injured should never trust his enemies and think, 'O, I have been soothed with assurances of goodwill.' In this world, men frequently meet with destruction because of misplaced confidence. We should no longer meet each other. Those who cannot be subjugated even by force and sharp weapons can be conquered by conciliation, as she-elephants are used to capture elephants."

Brahmadatta said, "Even if one inflicts deadly injury upon the other, affection and mutual trust arises naturally between them if they live together, as in the case of the Chandala and the dog. Among men who have injured one another, living together blunts the keenness of animosity. Indeed, it disappears quickly like water poured upon the leaf of a lotus."

Pujani said, "The learned know that enmity springs from five causes: woman, land, harsh words, natural incompatibility and injury. If the person with whom hostility occurs is a liberal man, he should not be killed, particularly by a Kshatriya, openly or by covert means. In such a case, the man's fault should be properly weighed. When there is hostility even with a friend, no further confidence should be reposed in him. Enmity lies hidden like fire in wood and cannot be put out without consuming one of the parties outright. Like the Aurvya fire within the waters of the ocean, the fire of antipathy can never be extinguished with gifts of wealth, by display of prowess, by conciliation or by scriptural knowledge.

If one has injured a person, he should never be trusted again as a friend, even though one might later have lavished wealth and honours on him. The fact of the injury inflicted fills the injurer with fear. I never injured you, nor did you ever harm me, so I lived in your house. All that has changed, and I cannot trust you any more."

Brahmadatta said, "Time is responsible for all action. Karma is of diverse kinds, all of them proceeding from Time. Who, therefore, injures whom? Birth and death happen in the same way: creatures take birth and live as a result of Time, and it is also because of Time that they cease to live. We see some die all at once some die one at a time, and some live long lives. Like fire consuming fuel, Time consumes all creatures.

O Bird, I am not the cause of your sorrow, nor are you the cause of mine. It is Time that decides the happiness or misery of living creatures. So continue to live here at your pleasure, with affection for me and without fear of any injury from me. I have forgiven you for what you have done and you must forgive me too, Pujani!"

Pujani replied, "If Time to you is the cause of all actions, then of course nobody should cherish feelings of enmity towards anybody on earth. Why then do friends and kinsmen seek to avenge the slain? Why too did the Devas and the Asuras in ancient days attack one another in battle? If it is Time that causes happiness and misery, birth and death, why do physicians administer medicines to the sick? If it is Time that moulds everything, what is the need for medicines? Why do grief-stricken people, deprived of their senses, indulge in such delirious lamentations? If Time, according to you, is the cause of karma, how can men acquire punya by performing religious deeds?

Your son killed my child and, impelled by grief, I blinded him for it. I have by that action, Rajan, become liable to be killed by you. Men desire birds either to kill them for food, or keep in cages for their pleasure, and for no other reason. Birds, again, from fear of being either killed or caged by men, seek safety in flight. Men who know the Vedas have said that death and imprisonment are both painful. Life is dear to all. Grief and pain make all creatures miserable. All creatures wish for happiness. Misery arises from various sources, Brahmadatta. Decrepitude is misery. Loss of wealth is misery. The proximity of anything disagreeable or evil is misery. Separation from friends and agreeable objects is misery. Misery arises from imprisonment and death. Misery arises from causes connected with women, and from other natural causes. The misery that arises from the death of children alters and afflicts all creatures tremendously.

Fools say there is no unhappiness in others' misery. Only he who has not felt any pain or sorrow himself can say so in the midst of men, not anyone who has felt distress or anguish himself. One who has experienced pangs of any kind of misery feels the misery of others as his own. What I have done to you, Rajan, and what you have done to me cannot be washed away by even a hundred years; there can be no reconciliation. As often as you happen to think of your son, your resentment towards me will become fresh.

If a man, after he avenges himself for an injury, wants to make peace with the injured, the two can never be properly reunited, even like the fragments of an earthen vessel. Men who know the shastras say that trust never produces happiness. Usanas himself sang two verses to Prahlada in ancient times: 'He who trusts the words of a foe, true or false, meets with death like a honey-gatherer falling into a pit covered with dry grass.'

We see antagonisms survive the very death of enemies, for men speak of the past enmities of their deceased fathers before their surviving children. Kings settle mutual animosities by conciliation but, when the opportunity comes, they shatter their enemies like earthen water-jars dashed upon stone. If the king wrongs someone, he should never trust him again, else he will have to suffer great misery."'

CANTO 139–3

'Brahmadatta said, "No man achieves anything by distrust of others. Nurturing fear obliges one to live like a corpse."

Pujani replied, "He whose feet are sore will certainly fall, however cautiously he tries to walk. Similarly, a man whose eyes have become sore by opening them against the wind will find wind very painful to them. He who sets foot on an evil path and persists in walking along it, without knowing his own strength, will soon lose his life. He who is lazy and tills his land disregarding the season of rain will never reap a harvest. He who eats every day food that is nutritious, be it bitter, sharp, palatable or sweet, will enjoy a long life, while he who ignores wholesome food and takes what is injurious, oblivious of its consequences, will soon meet with death.

Destiny and effort depend upon each other. Mahatmans achieve good and great feats, while eunuchs only pay court to Destiny. Be it harsh or mild, one's karma should be good. The unfortunate man of inaction is always overwhelmed by all sorts of calamity. One should use one's energy to do what is beneficial to oneself and abandon everything else. Knowledge, courage, cleverness, strength and patience are said to be one's natural friends, and wise men live in this world with the aid of these five. Houses, precious metals, land, wife and friends—these are secondary sources of good, the learned say, and can be obtained everywhere.

A wise man can be happy and will stand out everywhere. He never fills anybody with fear, or yields to fear even if frightened. The wealth that he possesses at any time, however little, is certain to increase. Such a man acts with acumen and self-restraint and will win great fame.

Foolish men have to put up at home with quarrelsome wives who devour their flesh like the progeny of a crab eating up their mothers. There are men who, through deficiency of understanding, become disconsolate at the prospect of leaving home. They say to themselves, 'These are our friends! This is our country! Alas, how shall we leave these?' One should certainly leave the country of one's birth if it is afflicted by plague or famine. One should live in one's own country respected by all, or go to a foreign country and live there. For this reason I will go to some other region, as I no longer dare to live in this place, for I have done a great wrong to your child.

Rajan, one should abandon a bad wife, a bad son, a bad king, a bad friend, a bad alliance, and a bad country. One should not place any trust in a bad son, and what joy can one have in a bad wife? There can be no happiness in a bad kingdom, and in a bad country one cannot hope to obtain a livelihood. There can be no lasting companionship with a bad friend, for his attachment is very unreliable, and in a bad alliance, when there is no compulsion for it, there is disgrace. She is a wife indeed whose utterances are agreeable. He is a son who makes the father happy. He is a friend in whom one can trust. That certainly is one's country where one earns one's livelihood. He is a just ruler who does not oppress, who loves the poor and in whose territories there is no fear.

Wife, country, friends, son, kinsmen, and relatives—all these one can acquire if the king is accomplished and is virtuous. If the king is sinful, his subjects will meet with ruin as a result of his oppressions. The king is the root of one's triple aggregate—Dharma, Dana and Kama. He should carefully protect his subjects and take from them only a sixth share of their wealth, or else he is in truth a thief. The king who gives assurances of protection and does not fulfill them due to greed, takes upon himself the sins of all his subjects and ultimately sinks to hell, whereas he who protects all his subjects, is a universal benefactor.

Manu, the lord of all the creatures, has said that the king has seven attributes: he is Father, Mother, Guru, Protector, Fire, Vaisravana and Yama. One calls the king who shows compassion towards his people their father, and the subject who behaves falsely towards him will take birth in his next life as an animal or a bird. By nurturing them and caring for the poor, he becomes a mother to his people. When he destroys evil, he comes to be regarded as Fire; when he restrains the sinful, one calls him Yama; when he gives gifts of wealth to those who are dear to him one regards him as Kuvera, the granter of wishes; when he gives instruction in morality and dharma, he becomes the Guru; and when he exercises the duty of defending his subjects he becomes the Protector.

The king who gladdens the people of his cities and provinces by his achievements in observing dharma is never deprived of his kingdom. The king who knows how to honour his subjects never suffers misery, here or hereafter. The king whose subjects are always anxious or overburdened with taxes and evils of all kinds will be defeated at the hands of his enemies, while he whose subjects grow like a large lotus in a lake will obtain every reward here, and will ultimately be honoured in Swarga. Hostility with one more powerful is never applauded, O Rajan. The king who incurs the hostility of one more powerful than himself loses both kingdom and happiness."

Having said these words to Brahmadatta, the bird left for the place she had chosen. I have narrated to you O foremost of kings, the discourse between Brahmadatta and Pujani. What else do you want to hear?'"

CANTO 140

"Yudhishtira asks, 'When both dharma and men decay due to the gradual decline of the Yuga, and when robbers overrun the world, how then, O Pitamaha, should a king behave?'

Bhishma replies, 'I will tell you, O Bhaarata, the policy the king should adopt at such times of distress, and how he should conduct himself, casting off compassion. There is often told an old story of a conversation between Bharadwaja and Satrunjaya. King Satrunjaya, the Maharathi ruler of the Sauviras, went to Bharadwaja and asked the Rishi about the truths of the science of Artha: "How can one acquire an object? How again, when acquired, can it be increased? How, when increased, can it be protected? And how, when protected, should it be used?"

The Maharishi set out a reasoned explanation of the science of Artha. He said, "The king should always have the rod of Dandaneeti raised in his hand. He should strike everyone with awe and thus rule all creatures. He should display his prowess and make no mistakes himself, but use his eyes to mark the lapses of his foes. Learned men with knowledge of truth applaud Punishment, or Danda. Hence, one says that of the four requisites of governance, Conciliation, Gift, Disunion and Punishment, Danda is the greatest.

All who seek refuge perish when one destroys the foundation that ensures protection. If one cuts away the roots of a tree, how can the branches live? A wise king should cut away the very roots of his enemies, and then win them over and bring their allies and partisans under his control. When calamities occur, the king should lose no time, counsel wisely, display his prowess suitably, fight with ability and even retreat wisely. The king should exhibit humility in words, while at heart remaining sharp as a razor. He should give up kama and krodha and speak sweetly and mildly. When the occasion for a parley with an enemy comes, a king with foresight should make peace, but without blind trust. When the undertaking is over, he should quickly turn away from the new ally.

One should conciliate an enemy with sweet assurances as if he were a friend, but remain wary as though living in a room where there lurks a snake. He whose mind your intellect can dominate should be comforted by assurances given in the past, an evil one by promises of future benefit, and a wise man by present assistance. He who wants to achieve prosperity should join his hands together, make pledges, use sweet words, show reverence by bowing down his head, and shed tears. One should carry one's foe on one's shoulders so long as the time is unfavourable. Then, when the opportunity comes, one should shatter him like an earthen jar on a stone.

It is better, O Rajan, for a king to blaze up in a moment like a charcoal of ebony-wood rather than to smoulder and smoke like chaff for many years. One who has many purposes to serve should have no scruples dealing with even an ungrateful man. If one succeeds, one can enjoy happiness but, if unsuccessful, one loses esteem; therefore, while dealing with such men, one should always leave something unfinished.

A king should for his own good, imitate a cuckoo, a boar, the mountains of Meru, an empty chamber, an actor, and a devoted friend, He should diligently visit the homes of his enemies and, if calamities befall them, enquire about their well-being. Those who are idle will never be wealthy; nor will those who lack manliness and energy; nor those who are vain or fear unpopularity; nor those given to procrastination. The king should work in such a way that his enemy is unable to detect his shortcomings, while he can observe his enemy's weakness. He should imitate the tortoise who conceals its limbs and covers its own weakness. He should think of all matters connected with finance like a crane sitting patiently by the water's edge for hours together waiting for fish. He should demonstrate his skill like a lion. He should lie in wait like a wolf, and fall upon and strike his foes directly like an arrow.

He should be judicious in enjoying drink, dice, women, hunting and music, as addiction to these will produce evil. He should make bows with bamboos and such; he should sleep cautiously like the deer, and seem blind or deaf when necessary. A wise king should show his prowess according to time and place, for if these are not favourable, all his skills will be futile. He should get down to work marking the timeliness of his action, reflect upon his own strength and weakness and improve his own strength in comparison to that of the enemy. The king who does not crush a foe defeated by military force provides for his own death like the crab when she conceives. A tree with beautiful blossoms may not be strong; one bearing fruits may be difficult to climb; and sometimes a tree with unripe fruits may appear like one with ripe fruits. These facts should not depress a king, for if he conducts himself as explained above, he will succeed against all foes.

The king should first strengthen the hopes of those who approach him as supplicants and then put obstacles in the way of their fulfillment. He should represent these obstacles as rare and the circumstances as the results of grave causes. As long as the occasion for fear does not actually occur, the king should make all his arrangements like one who is nervous. When the occasion for fear actually comes, he should strike fearlessly. No man can reap benefits without incurring danger. If he succeeds in preserving his life amidst peril, he is sure to earn great rewards.

A king should ascertain all future dangers when they are present and overcome them before they grow further; he should, even after vanquishing them, consider them unconquered. The abandonment of present happiness and the pursuit of future happiness is never the policy of an intelligent man. The king who, having made peace with an enemy, sleeps happily in tranquility, is like a man sleeping on the top of a tree who awakes only after a fall. When one lapses into difficulties, one should raise oneself by every means in one's power, mild or strong, and practise dharma only after one has recovered.

The king should always honour the foes of his enemies. He should employ as his own spies agents employed by his foes and ensure that his enemies do not discover them. He should use atheists and ascetics as spies and send them into his enemy's territories. Sinful thieves who offend the laws of dharma and who are thorns in the side of everyone enter gardens, places of amusement, places set up for giving drinking water to thirsty travelers, public inns, drinking spots, houses of ill fame, holy places and public assemblies. You should recognise them, arrest them and put them down. The king should not trust one who does not deserve to be trusted, nor should he trust too much one who deserves trust, for danger springs from trust. No one should be trusted without prior scrutiny.

Having by persuasive methods created confidence in the enemy, the king should smite him when he makes a false step. The king should fear him who is without fear, and also those who should be feared. Fear that comes from a quarter one did not suspect can lead to total extermination. By attention, by taciturnity, by wearing the reddish garb, matted locks and skins of ascetics, one should lull one's enemy into confidence and then, when the opportunity comes, spring upon him like a wolf. A king who wants prosperity should not scruple to slay son, brother, father or friend, if any of them tries to thwart his plans. One's very guru deserves to be punished, if he happens to be arrogant, ignorant of what should be done and what should not, and one who treads the path of adharma.

Just as certain insects with their sharp mandibles can cut off all flowers and fruits of the trees on which they sit, the king should deceive his enemy with welcome, honours and gifts and then attack him and take everything from him. One cannot acquire great prosperity without stabbing the very vitals of others, without accomplishing many grim deeds and without slaughtering living creatures like a fisherman. There are no separate species of creatures called enemies or friends; they become that from force of circumstance.

The king should never be moved to allow his foe to escape, even if they plead piteously, as it is his dharma to destroy any who have done him an injury. A king who wants prosperity should take care to win over to himself as many men as he can, doing good to them. He should remain free from malice while dealing with his subjects, but judiciously control and punish the evil and disobedient. After seizing wealth he should say placating words. After striking off someone's head, he should grieve and shed tears. A king who wants to prosper should draw others to himself and bind them to his service by means of sweet words, honours and gifts. He should never engage in fruitless disputes or cross a river with the aid of his own two arms. To eat cow-horns is futile and not invigorating, for their taste is not pleasing and they break one's teeth.

The triple aggregate of dharma, artha and kama has three disadvantages, with three inseparable adjuncts. Pursuit of dharma stands as an impediment in the way of artha; artha stands in the way of dharma; and kama stands in the way of both. Carefully consider these adjuncts, and avoid the disadvantages. The unpaid balance of a debt, the un-extinguished remnant of a fire, and un-slain enemies: these grow and increase, and should therefore be completely put out and exterminated. Debt that grows, defeated foes and neglected ailments are certain to remain, unless totally eradicated, and will lead to a rout. All work should be done thoroughly and carefully, for even a minute thing like a thorn, if extracted clumsily, can lead to incurable gangrene.

A king should destroy a hostile kingdom by slaughtering its population, by tearing up roads and otherwise damaging them, and by burning and pulling down its houses. He should be far-sighted like a vulture, motionless like a crane, vigilant like a dog, valiant like a lion, wary like a crow, and like a snake sneak into the territories of his foes with ease and unconcern. A king should win over a hero by joining his palms, a coward by filling him with fear, and a covetous man by gifts of wealth, while, with an equal he should wage war. He should be alert to any opportunity to produce disunion among leaders of different sects and to conciliate those among them who are dear to him. He should protect his ministers from disunion and destruction.

If the king becomes mild, the people ignore him, but if he becomes stern, the people feel it as hardship. The rule is that he should be stern or mild as the occasion requires. He should treat the mild with mildness, and that may even destroy the fierce, for there is nothing that mildness cannot achieve. For this reason, one says that mildness is more effective than fierceness. The king, who is mild when the occasion requires mildness and stern when sternness is required, will accomplish all his objectives and defeat his foes.

Having incurred the animosity of a knowledgeable and wise man, one should not draw comfort from the conviction that one is at a distance from him. The arms of an intelligent injured man who seeks revenge, reach far. One should not try to cross what cannot really be traversed or snatch from an enemy something he will be able to recover, or dig for something that one will not succeed in unearthing. One should never strike someone whose head one cannot cut off. In times of trouble a king should follow this course of conduct that I have laid down. I have said all this for your own good and to instruct you on how you should bear yourself when enemies attack."

The king of the Sauviras listened to these words of the Brahmana who had spoken out of a desire to do him good, obeyed them cheerfully and as a result he, his kinsmen and friends obtained great prosperity.'"

CANTO 141

"Yudhishtira asks, 'When Mahadharma decays and all disobey it, when dharma assumes a reverse form and becomes adharma; when all good restraints disappear, and all truths in respect of dharma are challenged and disputed; when kings and robbers oppress people; when men of all the four varnashramas become confused about their duties and all actions lose their merit; when, as a result of kama, lobha and ahankara, men have cause for fear from every direction; when all cease to trust one another, when they kill one another treacherously and deceive one another in their mutual dealings; when houses are burned down throughout the land; when the Brahmanas suffer; when the clouds do not bring a drop of rain; when everyone's hand is turned against his neighbor; when all the necessities of life fall under the control of robbers; when such a time of terrible distress sets in, by what means should a Brahmana maintain himself who is unwilling to give up compassion and his children? Tell me this, O Pitamaha. When sinfulness sweeps over the world, O Parantapa, how should the king live so that he will not stray from both dharma and artha?'

Bhishma replies, 'O Mahabaho, the peace and prosperity of subjects, sufficient and seasonal rain, disease, death and other fears, all depend on the king. I have no doubt, O Bharatarishabha, that the setting in of Krita, Treta, Dwapara and Kali yugas depend on the king's conduct. When such a season of misery as you describe sets in, the righteous should support life by their own judgment.

In this connection, a story has been told of the conversation between Viswamitra and a Chandala in a hamlet inhabited by Chandalas. Towards the end of Treta and the beginning of Dwapara yugas, a frightful drought extending over twelve years occurred, as intended by the Devas. At the end of Treta yuga and the commencement of Dwapara yuga, when the time came for many creatures to die of old age, Indra, the thousand-eyed deity of Swarga, sent no rain. The planet Brihaspati began to move in a retrograde course and Soma, abandoning his own orbit, receded towards the south. Not even a dew-drop could be seen, let alone clouds gathering together. The rivers all shrank into narrow rivulets, and as the Devas ordained, lakes, wells and springs everywhere lost their beauty and disappeared.

Water having become scarce, the places set up by charity for thirsty travellers became desolate. The Brahmanas abstained from sacrifices and recitation of the Vedas. They no longer uttered Vashats or performed propitiatory rites. Agriculture and cattle rearing were given up, markets and shops were abandoned and stakes for tethering sacrificial animals disappeared. People no longer collected articles for sacrifices, and all festivals and amusements perished. Heaps of bones lay scattered around and the air was filled with the shrill cries and yells of ferocious creatures. Cities and towns became empty of inhabitants. Villages and hamlets were burnt down. Some people were assailed by robbers, some by weapons, some by evil kings, and all began to flee in fear of one another. Temples and places of worship became desolate. The aged were forcibly turned out of their houses, and cattle—goats, sheep and buffaloes—fought for food and perished in large numbers. Brahmanas began to die on all sides, protection came to an end, and herbs and plants dried up. The earth, shorn of all her beauty, became ghastly and dreadful, like trees in a crematorium.

In that period of terror, when dharma was nowhere, O Yudhishtira, starving men lost their senses and began to eat one another. The very Rishis gave up their vows, abandoned their fires and deities, forsook vanavasa and began to wander about in search of food. The holy and wise Maharishi Viswamitra, leaving his wife and son in a place of shelter and abandoning his homa fire, wandered homeless and hungry, unmindful of clean and unclean food.

One day he came upon a hamlet in the midst of a vana, inhabited by savage hunters engaged in the slaughter of living creatures. The village abounded with broken earthen jars and pots, and dog-skins lay scattered around. Bones and skulls of boars and asses were heaped up, clothes stripped from the dead lay strewn around, and huts were decorated with withered garlands and filled with sloughed-off snakeskins. The loud crowing of cocks and the dissonant bray of asses filled the air, while the inhabitants of the village disputed with one another harshly in discordant voices. Temples of Devas bearing images of owls and other birds resounded with the clang of iron bells, and packs of dogs lolled about.

Maharishi Viswamitra, moved by the pangs of hunger, entered the Chandalas' village in search of food and tried his best to find something to eat. Though he begged and begged, he failed to obtain meat, rice, fruit, root or any other kind of food. At last he exclaimed, "Alas, what misery has overtaken me!" and collapsed from weakness.

The sage began to reflect and asked himself, "What is best for me to do now?" The one thought that seized him was how to avoid immediate death. He found spread on the floor of a Chandala's hut a large piece of flesh, of a recently-killed dog. The sage reflected and decided to steal that meat, saying to himself, "When there is no other means to stay alive, theft is permitted, even for eminent men, and it will not detract from their fame. It is certain that, to save his life, even a Brahmana can do it. One should steal first from a low person, failing which one can steal from one's equal, or from even an eminent Dharmatman. Therefore at this time, when my life itself is ebbing away, I will steal this haunch of dog's meat. I see nothing wrong in such theft."

Maharishi Viswamitra resolved to do so, and lay down to sleep where the Chandalas lived. When the night had advanced and the whole

Chandala village had fallen asleep, the holy Viswamitra stealthily got up and entered the hut. The Chandala who owned it, an ugly man with phlegm-covered eyes, was lying like one asleep. He called out in a hoarse and dissonant voice, "Who is undoing the latch? The village is asleep but I am awake. Whoever you are, you are about to die."

Filled with fear at these harsh words, his heart palpitating and his face crimson with shame at the attempted theft, the sage answered, "O you blessed with a long life, I am Viswamitra. I have come here oppressed by the pangs of hunger. Do not slay me, O you of righteous understanding, if your sight is clear."

Hearing these words of the Maharishi, the Chandala rose up in terror from his bed and approached him. Joining his palms reverently, his eyes bathed in tears, he asked Kusika's son, "What are you doing here in the night, Brahmana?"

To conciliate the Chandala, Viswamitra said, "Famished as I am and about to die of starvation, I want to take that haunch of dog's meat. It is hunger that is urging me to this misdeed and it has made me sinful and shameless. My life-breath is fading, and hunger has destroyed my Vedic learning. I have lost my senses through weakness and have no scruple left about clean or unclean food. Although I know it is sinful, I still wish to take away that haunch of dog's meat. I wandered from house to house in your hamlet, and when I failed to obtain any alms, I decided upon this misdeed. Fire is the mouth of the Devas and is also their priest, and should take nothing that is not pure and clean. At times, however, the great Agni Deva becomes a consumer of everything. Understand that I have now in that respect become just like him."

The Chandala answered, "O Maharishi, listen to my words of truth about your duty and act so that your punya is not destroyed. The wise say that a dog is less clean than a jackal, and that the haunch of a dog is a much worse part of his body than any other. You have not discerned this, Maharishi, for this theft of unclean food belonging to a Chandala is inconsistent with dharma. You are blessed, look for some other means for preserving your life and let not your tapasyas suffer destruction as a result of your craving for dog's meat. Knowing the duties that the shastras have laid down, you should not do something that will result in confusion in your dharma. Do not cast off dharma, for you are its greatest observer."

Thus addressed, O Bharatarishabha, the famished Maharishi Viswamitra once more said, "It has been a long time since I ate anything, and I do not see any other means of staying alive. When one is facing death, one should preserve one's life by any means in one's power, not enquire into their character. Later, when one is able, one should seek to acquire punya. Kshatriyas should observe the practices of Indra, while it is the duty of Brahmanas to behave like Agni.

The Vedas are fire and, since they constitute my strength, I will eat even this unclean food to appease my hunger. That which preserves life should certainly be done without scruple, for life is better than death and, as long as there is life, one can acquire dharma. I am ready to eat this to save my life, knowing that this food is impure. Give me your permission. If I survive, I will acquire dharma and, by penances and knowledge, wipe out the abomination of my present conduct, like the light of the firmament that can banish even the densest darkness."

The Chandala said, "By eating this food, someone like you cannot obtain long life, for it can neither give you strength nor the gratification offered by ambrosia. Pray seek some other kind of alms, and not this dog's meat which is defiled food for Munis."

Viswamitra replied, "During a famine like this, any other kind of meat cannot be easily obtained. Besides, O Chandala, I have no means to buy food, and I am ravenous. I can no longer move and am without any hope. I believe that in that piece of dog's meat I will find all the six kinds of taste."

The Chandala said, "The shastras prescribe only five kinds of five-clawed animals as clean food for Brahmanas, Kshatriyas and Vaisyas. Do not hunger for this unclean food."

Viswamitra said, "The great Rishi Agastya, when hungry, ate the Asura Vatapi. I am in distress, I am hungry, and I will therefore eat that haunch of dog's meat."

The Chandala said, "Ask for some other alms, as it does not become you ever to do such a thing. If, however, it pleases you, you can take this piece of dog's meat."

Viswamitra said, "Those whom you call good are authorities on matters of duty. I am following their example. I now regard this dog's haunch to be better food than anything that is highly pure."

The Chandala said, "One can never regard the action of an adharmic person as an eternal practice. What is improper can never become proper. Do not deceive yourself into committing a sinful deed."

Viswamitra replied, "A Rishi cannot do anything sinful. In the present case, the deer and the dog to me are the same, both animals. I will, therefore, eat this dog's haunch."

The Chandala said, "In the case of the Rishi Agastya, he did as the Brahmanas requested him. Under those circumstances it could not be a sin. That in which there is no sin is dharma. Besides, one should by all means protect and preserve Brahmanas, who are the gurus of three other varnas."

Viswamitra said, "I am a Brahmana and my body is a very dear friend, worthy of the highest reverence from me. It is to sustain this body that I wish to take away that dog's haunch. So eager have I become that I no longer have any fear of you or your fierce brethren."

The Chandala said, "Men lay down their lives rather than eat impure food. They realise all their desires by conquering hunger. You too must conquer your craving and obtain those rewards."

Viswamitra said, "I observe strict vows and my heart is set on peace. To preserve the root of all religious punya, I will eat food that is unclean. It is evident that one would regard such an action as righteous in a Rishi, while to someone of unclean soul the eating of dog's flesh would appear sacreligious. Even if the conclusion at which I have arrived is wrong, and if I eat this dog's meat I will not, as a result, become like you."

The Chandala said, "I have decided that I must try my best to restrain you from this offence. A Brahmana by evil karma falls from his high state. It is for this that I am reproving you."

Viswamitra retorted, "Cattle continue to drink, regardless of the croaking of the frogs. You can claim no knowledge about what is dharma and what is not, so don't think too highly of yourself."

The Chandala replied, "I am preaching to you only because I have become your friend. Do whatever is beneficial, do not be tempted into doing anything wicked."

Viswamitra said, "If you are a friend who wishes my happiness, help me from this misery. If you willingly give me this dog's haunch, I can consider myself saved by the aid of dharma and not by sin."

The Chandala said, 'I dare not gift you with this piece of meat, nor can I quietly suffer the theft of my own food. If I give you this meat and if you, a Brahmana, take it, both of us will sink into regions of sorrow in the next world."

Viswamitra said, "If I commit this sinful deed today, I will certainly save my life which is sacred. After I save my life, I will practice dharma and cleanse my soul. Tell me which of these two is preferable, to die without food, or save my life by taking this food that is impure."

The Chandala said: "In duties concerning one's varna or varnasrama, one is the best judge of propriety or impropriety. You know which of these two actions is sinful. I think that he who would regard dog's meat as clean food, would in matters of food abstain from nothing!"

Viswamitra replied, 'In accepting an unclean gift, or in eating unclean food, there is sin. When, however, one's life is in danger, there is no sin in accepting such a present or eating such food. Besides, the eating of impure food that is not accompanied by slaughter and deception, is not a matter of much consequence, and will provoke only mild censure."

The Chandala said, "If this is your argument for eating unclean food, it is clear that you do not respect the morality of the Vedas and Arya. You have taught me by your example, O greatest of Brahmanas, that it is not a sin to disregard the distinction between food that is clean and unclean."

Viswamitra said, "It is not that a man incurs a grave sin by eating forbidden food. The precept that one becomes degraded by drinking wine is only in order to restrain men. Other strictures of the same type, whatever they be, in fact every sin, cannot destroy one's punya."

The Chandala said, "The learned man who takes dog's meat from an unworthy place, from an unclean wretch, from one who leads an evil life, commits an action contrary to that one calls good. As a result, he is certain to suffer the pangs of repentance."

The Chandala, having said these words to Kusika's son, fell silent. The wise Viswamitra, to save his life, then took away that haunch of dog's meat to the woods to eat with his wife. He resolved that he would first gratify the deities according to due rites and then eat the meat at his pleasure.

Lighting a fire according to the Brahma rites, the Maharishi began to cook the meat into sacrificial Charu, as the Aindragneya rites prescribe. He then began the ceremonies in honour of the Devas and the Pitris, O Bhaarata, divided the Charu into as many portions as were necessary according to the injunctions of the shastras, and invoked the Devas, with Indra at their head, to accept their shares.

Meanwhile, the chief of the celestials caused heavy rain to fall. The showers revived all the creatures and caused plants and herbs to grow once more. Viswamitra completed the rites in honour of the Devas and the Pitris and, having duly gratified them, ate the meat. Burning away all his sins later by his penances, the sage, after a long time, acquired the most wonderful ascetic success.

Even so should a Mahatman proceed who is knowledgeable and can devise means to preserve his own life when in trouble. By using his understanding thus, a man should survive to win punya and enjoy happiness and prosperity. For this reason, O son of Kunti, a learned man of cleansed soul should live and work in this world, relying upon his own intelligence to discriminate between dharma and adharma.'"

CANTO 142

"Yudhishtira says, 'If something so horrible can be commended that, like falsehood, should be held in aversion, then from what deeds should I desist? Why then shouldn't robbers be respected? I am stunned, my heart is sore, all the ties that bind me to dharma are loosened! I cannot calm my mind and venture to act as you suggest.'

Bhishma says, 'I am not instructing you about duty that I have learned from the Vedas alone. What I have told you is the result of wisdom and experience, the honey that the learned have gathered. Kings should gather wisdom from various sources. One cannot make his course through the world with the aid of a dharma that is one-sided. Duty must spring from understanding and from discovering the practices of those who are good, O son of Kuru. Attend to my words. Only kings who have superior intelligence can rule and expect victory. A weak-minded king can never display wisdom if he has not drawn any from the examples before him.

Dharma sometimes takes the shape of adharma, and vice versa. He who does not know this is baffled when confronted by an actual instance of the kind. Before the occasion arises, O Bhaarata, one should understand the circumstances under which dharma and its reverse become confused. Having acquired this knowledge, a wise king should act according to his judgment when the occasion comes. Ordinary people misunderstand what he does at such a time. Some possess true knowledge. Some have false knowledge. Truly ascertaining the nature of each kind of knowledge, a wise king derives understanding from those who are good.

Those who are breakers of dharma find fault with the shastras. Those who have no wealth find inconsistencies in the treatises on gaining wealth. Those who seek knowledge only for their livelihood, Rajan, are sinful, enemies of dharma. Evil men of immature understanding can never truly comprehend things, just as men who do not know the shastras are unable to be guided in all their actions by reason. They can only see the faults of the shastras and criticize them. Even if they understand the true meaning of the shastras, they will still proclaim that scriptural injunctions are unsound. Such men proclaim the superiority of their own knowledge by decrying the knowledge of others. They use words as weapons and arrows and speak as if they were real masters of their sciences. They are traders in learning and Rakshasas among men. Through such pretexts they abandon the dharma that good and wise men have established.

We hear that the contents of dharma are not to be understood by either discussion or one's own intelligence. Indra himself says that this is the opinion of the sage Brihaspati. Some are of the opinion that no text in the shastras has been laid down without a reason. Many, even if they properly understand the shastras, never act according to them. A class of wise men declares that dharma is nothing else but the approved course of the world. The man of true knowledge should find out for himself the dharma laid down for the good. If even a wise man speaks of morality under the influence of anger, confusion of understanding or ignorance, his efforts are in vain.

Discourses on morality are worthy of praise when made with the aid of an intelligence derived from the true letter and spirit of the shastras, not those made with the help of anything else. Even words from an ignorant man, if they carry sense, can be considered pious and wise. In olden days, Usanas revealed this incontrovertible truth to the Daityas, that shastras are not shastras if they cannot stand the test of reason. The possession or absence of knowledge that is mixed with doubts is the same thing. You should get rid of such knowledge, tearing it up from the roots. You should regard one who does not listen to my words as someone who has allowed himself to be misled.

Do you not see that you were created for the accomplishment of bold deeds? Look at me, dear child, how by performing the dharma of my varna, I have dispatched innumerable Kshatriyas to Swarga! There are some who are not pleased with me for this. Brahma created the goat, the horse and the Kshatriya for the same purpose, to be useful. A Kshatriya therefore, should always seek the happiness of all creatures. The sin that attaches to killing a man who should not be killed is equal to that which is incurred by not killing one who deserves to be killed. This is the established order of things which a weak-minded king does not observes.

Therefore, a king should be severe in making all his subjects observe their respective duties. If this is not done, they will prowl like wolves, devouring one another. He is a wretch among Kshatriyas in whose territories robbers go about plundering the property of other people, like crows taking little fishes from water. Appoint high-born men who have Vedic knowledge as your ministers, govern the earth and protect your subjects righteously. The Kshatriya who is ignorant of customs and traditions and levies taxes upon his people improperly is a eunuch of his varna.

A king should be neither severe nor mild, and deserves praise if he rules righteously. He should be severe on occasions demanding severity, and mild when it is necessary to be so. Painful is the observance of Kshatriya dharma. Therefore, rule your kingdom as you are created for the accomplishment of great deeds and I have great love for you. The percipient Sakra has said that in times of distress the great duty of a king is to punish the evil and to protect the good.'

Yudhishtira says, 'Tell me, Pitamaha, if there is any rule regarding Rajadharma which should under no circumstances be violated.'

Bhishma replies, 'One should always worship the Brahmanas venerated for their learning, devoted to penances and rich in conduct conformable to the injunctions of the Vedas. This indeed, is a great and sacred duty. Let your conduct towards the Brahmanas always be that which you observe towards Devas. The Brahmanas, if enraged, can inflict diverse kinds of wrong, O Rajan. If they are gratified, great fame will be yours. Satisfied, the Brahmanas are like nectar, and enraged, they are like poison.'"

CANTO 143

"Yudhishtira asks, 'O wise Pitamaha who knows all the shastras, tell me, what is the punya earned by one who shelters a petitioner seeking protection?'

Bhishma replies, 'It is worthy of you to ask such a question, for great is the punya, O Rajan, in cherishing such supplicants. Protecting such people, mahatmas of old, king Sivi and others, attained great happiness in Swarga. One hears of a pigeon who, in accordance with due rites, even fed his own flesh to an enemy who came as a supplicant.'

Yudhishtira says, 'How did this pigeon of old feed a foe with his own flesh, and what did he win in the end by such conduct?'

Bhishma says, 'Listen then, Rajan, to this excellent story that cleanses the listener of every sin. This very question, O son of Pritha, had been humbly put to Bhrigu's son Rama by Muchkunda, and to him the sage narrated the tale of how a pigeon won prosperity.

The sage said, "O Mahabaho Rajan, I will narrate to you a story about the truth connected with dharma artha and kama. A wicked fowler who resembled Yama the Destroyer himself used to wander through the great vana in the olden days. He was black as a raven, with bloodshot eyes, long legs, short feet, a large mouth and bulging cheeks. He had no friend, relative or kinsman, since all had cast him off for the exceedingly cruel life he led. Indeed, the wise should renounce from a distance a man of evil conduct, for he who injures himself cannot be expected to do good to others. The heinous men who take the lives of other creatures are like poisonous snakes, a source of trouble to all creatures.

He went to the woods with his nets to trap birds and sell their meat, never understanding what a sinful life it was that he led. The evil wretch, stupefied by destiny, and preferring no other profession, lived in the forest for many long years in this manner with his wife, One day, as he was wandering through the vana intent on his business, a great storm arose that tossed the trees and seemed about to uproot them. In a moment dense clouds covered the sky, lit with flashes of lightning like a sea covered with merchants' boats and vessels. Then Indra Deva entered the cloud and in a moment the earth was flooded with torrential rain submerging all the forest paths.

The fowler, crazed with fear and trembling with cold, roved the vana looking for high ground but failed to find any. The force of the cloudburst had thrown down and killed many birds. Lions, bears and other animals, had taken shelter in whatever high ground they could find. Fear filled all the denizens of the forest because of that terrifying storm and, frightened and hungry, they roamed through the woods in packs small and large. The fowler, however, his limbs stiffened by cold, could neither stop where he was nor move on.

While in this state, he spied a she-pigeon lying on the ground, stiffened with cold. Though in the same predicament, the sinful wretch, through force of habit, picked her up and put her in a cage. Even when he himself was in trouble, he had no scruple in harming a fellow-creature. He then saw in the midst of that forest a lordly tree, blue as the clouds, the resort of a myriad birds seeking shade and shelter. It seemed that the Creator placed it there for the benefit of all creatures, like a good man in the world.

Soon the sky cleared and became spangled with hundreds of stars, like a magnificent lake smiling with blooming lilies. Turning his gaze up to the firmament rich with stars and clear of clouds, the fowler advanced, trembling with cold. Seeing that darkness had already fallen, and realizing that his home lay a great distance away, he resolved to pass the night under the shade of that tree. Bowing down to it with joined hands, he addressed that monarch of the forest, saying, 'I ask all the deities that have this tree for their resort to grant me shelter.' He then spread some leaves on the ground for a bed, and lay down, resting his head on a stone. Though overwhelmed with affliction, the man soon fell asleep.""

CANTO 144

"Bhishma says, 'In one of the branches of that tree, O Rajan, a pigeon with beautiful feathers lived for many years with his family. That morning his wife had gone out in search of food but had not returned. Disturbed that the night had come and his wife had not yet come back, the bird began to lament: "Ah, what a huge storm and harrowing downpour we have had today! Alas, you have not yet returned, dear wife! Why has she has not yet come back to us? Is everything right with my beloved spouse in the vana? Without her, my home seems empty! A house-holder's home, even if filled with sons and grandsons and daughters-in-law and servants, is empty without the housewife. One's house is not one's home; only one's wife is one's home. A house without the wife is a desolate wilderness.

If my dear wife of eyes fringed with red, of multicolored plumes and sweet voice, does not come back today, my life itself will become worthless. Of excellent vows, she never eats before I eat, never bathes before I bathe, never sits before I sit down, and never lies down before I lie down. She rejoices when I rejoice, and grieves when I am sad. When I am away she is downcast, and even when I am angry she continues to speak sweetly. Ever devoted to her lord and ever relying upon her husband, she always does what is agreeable and beneficial for him. Worthy of praise is he on earth who has such a spouse! That amiable creature knows that I am fatigued and hungry. Devoted to me and constant in her love, my celebrated spouse is surpassingly sweet-tempered and worships me ardently.

Even the foot of a tree is one's home if one lives there in the company of one's spouse; without her, even a palace is veritably a desolate wilderness. One's spouse is one's associate in all one's deeds of dharma, artha and kama. When one sets out for a strange land, one's wife is one's trusted companion. One says that the wife is the richest possession of her husband. In this world the wife is one's only associate in all the concerns of life, the best of medicines that one can have in sickness and sorrow. There is no friend like her. There is no refuge better than her. There is no better ally in the world than her in work undertaken for the acquisition of punya. He, who does not have in his home a wife who is chaste and of agreeable speech, should go to the vana. For such a man there is no difference between home and wilderness."'"

CANTO 145

"Bhishma says, 'Hearing these piteous lamentations of the pigeon on the tree, the she-pigeon that the fowler seized began to say to herself, "Whether I have any merit or not, truly there is no limit to my good fortune when my dear lord speaks thus of me. She is no wife with whom her lord is not content. In the case of women, if they gratify their lords, all the deities are also pleased. Since the marriage union takes place in the presence of fire, the husband is the wife's greatest deity. The wife with whom her husband is not pleased gets reduced to ashes, like a flowering creeper in a forest fire."

Having reflected thus, the kind she-pigeon, overcome with sorrow, and casting her eyes upon her lord from inside the cage where the fowler had imprisoned her, said to her grief-stricken husband, "Listen while I tell you how you can rescue me. This fowler lies here by your home, stricken with cold and hunger. Do him the duties of hospitality. The sin that one commits by Brahmahatya or by slaying a cow, the mother of the world, is equal to that which one incurs by allowing a supplicant to perish for want of help. You possess knowledge of self; therefore, follow the course that our swadharma has ordained for us. We have heard that the householder who practises dharma according to his abilities wins inexhaustible regions of bliss hereafter. You have sons and progeny; therefore do not be concerned about your own body and, for the sake of winning dharma and artha, offer worship to this fowler so that his heart will be pleased. Do not, O bird, indulge in any grief on my account. You may continue to live, taking other wives!" So said the amiable she-bird, overcome with sorrow, gazing at her husband from within the fowler's cage where she had been immured.'"

CANTO 146

"Bhishma says, 'Hearing his wife's words, full of morality and reason, the pigeon was thrilled, and his eyes filled with tears of joy. He then, according to the rites laid down in the shastras, scrupulously honoured the fowler whose avocation was the slaughter of birds.

He addressed the fowler, "You are welcome today. Tell me what I can do for you. This is your home, so tell me your pleasure and what I can do for you. Do not fret. I ask you out of regard, for you have solicited shelter at our hands, and hospitality should be shown even to one's foe. Like the tree, which does not withdraw its shade even from one who approaches to cut it down, one should faithfully carry out the duties of hospitality to those who need shelter. Indeed, one is especially bound to do so if one happens to be a grihasta, leading a life of domesticity consisting of the five sacrifices. According to the shastras, if one blunders in performing the five sacrifices, he loses both this world and the next. Tell me then clearly and confidently what your wishes are, and I will accomplish them all."

The fowler replied, "I am stiff with cold. Let provision be made to warm me."

The bird gathered together a number of dry leaves on the ground and, taking a single leaf in his beak, speedily went to a spot where fire was kept, and returned with a little cinder. He then set fire to the dry leaves and, when they leapt into vigorous flames, invited his guest, "Come and warm your limbs trustfully and without fear." The fowler said, "Tathaasthu," and set to warm himself. Recovering, he demanded of his winged host, "I am hungry. I want you to give me some food."

The bird said, "I have no means to appease your hunger. We denizens of the woods always live upon what we get every day. Like the Munis of the vana we never hoard for the morrow." Mentally deploring this method of living, the bird grew pale with shame and began to reflect silently on what he should do. Soon, however, his mind became clear. Addressing the slaughterer of his species, the bird said, "I will gratify you. Wait for a moment."

He stoked the fire with the some dry leaves and, filled with joy, said to the fowler, "I heard in former days from Maharishis, Devas and Pitris that there is great punya in honouring a guest. O amiable one, be kind to me. I tell you truly that my heart is set upon gratifying you, my guest." Having formed his resolution, the high-souled bird thrice circumambulated the fire with a smiling face and plunged into it directly. Seeing the bird enter the flames, the fowler began to upbraid himself, "Oh, what have I done! Alas, dark and terrible will be my sin, without doubt, as a result of my own deeds! I am exceedingly cruel and worthy of reproof!" Indeed, observing the bird lay down his life, the fowler, filled with remorse for his own actions, began to lament like you.'"

CANTO 147

"Bhishma says, 'The fowler, seeing the pigeon cast himself into the fire, was filled with compassion and began to reproach himself, "Alas, cruel and senseless that I am, what have I done! I am certainly a mean wretch! Great will be my sin for everlasting years!'

He went on repeating, "I am unworthy of any punya. My understanding is perverse, and I am sinful in all I do. Alas, I am a cruel wretch for discarding any kinds of honourable occupation and becoming a fowler. This high-souled pigeon, by laying down his own life, has taught me a grave lesson. Abandoning wives and sons, I will certainly give up this life that I held so dear. From this day, denying every comfort to my body, I will wear it out like a shallow tank in the season of summer. I will suffer hunger, thirst and penances and, reduced to emaciation, covered all over with visible veins, I will, by diverse methods practise such vows so as to be in touch with the other world. By giving up his body, the pigeon has shown the worship that one should pay to an atithi. From now on I will follow dharma—the highest refuge. Indeed, I will practise such dharma as the righteous pigeon, the greatest of all winged creatures, has shown me."

Having formed this resolution and said these words, the fowler, once a man of fierce deeds, proceeded to make a Mahaprasthana—a tour of the world from where there is no return, observing the most rigid vows. He threw away his stout staff, his sharp-pointed iron-stick, his nets, snares and his iron cage, and set at liberty the she-pigeon that he had captured.'"

CANTO 148

"Bhishma says, 'After the fowler had left, the she-pigeon, grieving for her husband, wept copiously and lamented, "I cannot, O dear lord, recollect a single instance of you having done me an injury! A widow, even if mother of many children, is still miserable without a husband, for she becomes helpless and an object of pity with her friends. You always cherished and honoured me with sweet, pleasant, charming and delightful words. I sported with you in valleys, in springs and on delightful tree-tops. You made me happy when we wandered through the skies but, dear lord, where are those joys now?

Limited are the gifts of a father, a brother and a son. The gifts that her husband alone makes to her are unlimited. Which woman would not, therefore, adore her lord? A woman has no protector like her lord, and no happiness like her lord. Abandoning all her wealth and possessions, a woman should take to her lord as her only refuge. Life here is of no use to me, now that I am separated from you. What chaste woman would venture to bear the burden of life when deprived of her lord?"

Filled with sorrow and lamenting piteously, the she-pigeon, devoted to her lord, threw herself onto the blazing fire. She saw her dead husband, adorned with bracelets, seated on a celestial carriage, adored by many Mahatmans and meritorious beings standing around him. Indeed, there he was in the firmament, decked with fine garlands, attired in splendid robes and adorned with every ornament. Around him were innumerable divine chariots ridden by beings who had acted meritoriously while in this world. Seated on his own carriage, the bird ascended to heaven and, obtaining honours for his deeds in this world, continued to sport joyfully in the company of his wife.'"

CANTO 149

"Bhishma says, 'The fowler, O Rajan, was filled with sorrow at the sight of that pair of pigeons seated on their heavenly chariot and at his own misfortune, and began to reflect on how he could achieve the same consummation. He resolved to himself, "By austerities like those of the pigeon, I must attain just such a high end!" The fowler, who had lived by the slaughter of birds, set out on a journey without return. Living upon air alone, without any exertion, he cast off all desires in order to acquire Swarga.

After he had walked for some distance, he saw an extensive and delightful lake full of cool and pure water, blooming with lotuses and teeming with diverse waterfowl. The very sight of such a lake would slake the thirst of a man. The fowler, emaciated with fasts, without even glancing at the lake, gladly entered a vana he saw to be large and inhabited by beasts of prey. He wandered lacerated by prickles and pointed thorns and covered all over with blood, in that forest devoid of men but abounding with animals of diverse species. Some time later, a powerful wind caused a forest fire to break out from friction between mighty trees. The raging element, splendid as if it had been the end of the Yuga, began to consume that large forest of tall trees, thick bushes and creepers. With flames fanned by the wind and myriads of sparks flying about in all directions, the all-consuming deity began to burn that dense forest abounding with birds and beasts. The fowler, ready to die, ran with glad heart into the spreading conflagration and, consumed by fire, was cleansed of all his sins. The fever of his heart dispelled, he beheld himself at last in heaven, shining in splendour like Indra in the midst of Yakshas, Gandharvas and men crowned with ascetic success.

Thus did the pigeon and his devoted spouse, along with the fowler, ascend to heaven for their meritorious deeds. The woman who follows her husband thus speedily ascends to heaven and shines there in splendour, like the she-pigeon of whom I have spoken.

This is the old story of the high-souled fowler and the pigeon and how they earned a highly meritorious end by their dharmic deeds. No evil befalls one who listens to this story or recites it daily, even if error invades his mind. O Yudhisthira, foremost of righteous persons, the protection of a supplicant is truly meritorious. Even the slayer of a cow, by practising this duty, maybe cleansed of sin, but one who slays a supplicant will never be purified. By listening to this sacred and sin-cleansing story, one becomes freed from distress and attains Swarga.'"

CANTO 150

"Yudhishtira says, 'Tell me, Bhaaratottama, when a man lacking judgment commits sin, how can he be purified?'

Bhishma replies, 'Let me narrate to you the old story, much-lauded by the Rishis, of what the Muni Indrota, the son of Sunaka, advised the valiant king Janamejaya. There was in days of yore a king of great energy called Janamejaya, the son of Parikshit. That lord of earth, Janamejaya, once from lack of judgment slew a Brahmana. At this, all the Brahmanas, together with his priests, abandoned him. Deserted by his subjects as well, and burning day and night with remorse, the king retired into the vana to undergo the most rigid tapasya in order to earn punya, to cleanse himself of the sin of Brahmahatya. He questioned many Brahmanas, and wandered from country to country over the whole earth.

One day, in course of his wanderings, he met Indrota, the son of Sunaka, of rigid vows and, approaching him, touched his feet in reverence. The sage, seeing the king before him, reproved him gravely, saying, "You have committed a great sin. You are guilty of foeticide. Why have you come here, and what is your business with us? Do not touch me at any cost! Go away, your presence does not give me any pleasure. You smell like blood and you look like a corpse. Though polluted, you seem to be pure, and though dead you move like a living man! Dead within, you are of defiled soul, for you are always intent upon sin. Though you sleep and wake, your life is miserable and useless, O Rajan. You have been created for ignoble and sinful deeds. Fathers wish for sons from a desire to obtain all kinds of blessings, and in the hope that their sons will perform tapasyas and yagnas, worship the Devas and practise vairagya. Behold, the whole varna of your ancestors has fallen into hell as a result of your actions. All the hopes your ancestors placed on you have become fruitless. You live in vain, for you have treated with hatred and malice the Brahmanas, whom other men worship to obtain long life, fame and Swarga. Leaving this world when the time comes, you will have to fall headlong into hell, as a result of your sinful deeds, and remain in that posture for innumerable years, tortured by iron-beaked vultures and peacocks. Returning to this world, you will have to take birth in a lowly order of creatures. If you think, O Rajan, that this world is nothing and that the next world is the shadow of a shadow, the legions of Yama in hell will dispel your disbelief!"'"

CANTO 151

"Bhishma continues, 'Janamejaya replied to the sage Indrota, "You rebuke one who deserves to be rebuked, you censure one deserving censure when you harangue me for my misdeeds. My actions have been sinful, but I implore you to be merciful towards me, since I burn with remorse as though in a blazing fire! Recalling my deeds makes me wretched. Truly, I am afraid of Yama. How can I bear to live without extracting that dart from my heart? O Saunaka, suppress your wrath, instruct me now.

I solemnly declare that I will once more show the same regard for Brahmanas as I did before. Let not my line become extinct and my race sink into the dust. Those who have wronged Brahmanas and thereby forfeited all claim to the respect of the world and to social interaction with their fellowmen, as decreed in the Vedas, should have no one to bear their names or continue their lineage. Utterly desolate, I reiterate my resolve. Protect me like sages who protect the poor without accepting gifts. Sinful men who abstain from sacrifices never attain heaven and have to pass their time in the pits of hell like the unclean Pullindas and Khasas. Ignorant that I am, grant me wisdom, like an Acharya to his shishya or a father to his son. Bless me, O Indrota, son of Sunaka!"

Saunaka replied, "It is no wonder that a man without wisdom does many improper deeds. Knowing this, a person of real understanding is never angry with mortals but grieves for others, being then beyond an object of others' regrets. One surveys all creatures in the world like a man on a mountain-top surveying people below.

He who becomes an object of censure, who dislikes good men and avoids them, will never obtain blessings and never understand the impropriety of his actions. You know the energy and the nobility of the Brahmanas, as the Vedas and other scriptures have laid down. Let your acts now gain you tranquillity of heart, and let Brahmanas be your refuge. If they cease to be angry with you, that will ensure your happiness in heaven. If you repent your sin, your vision will be clear and you will perceive dharma."

Janamejaya said, "I repent my sins, and I will never again seek to tarnish my dharma. I desire to be cleansed. Bless me."

Indrota said, "Drive out your arrogance and pride, Janamejaya, and show your regard for me! Employ yourself in the good of all creatures, and always remember the mandates of dharma. I do not reprove you from narrowness of mind or avarice. Listen now, with these Brahmanas here, to the words of truth that I speak. I ask for nothing but to instruct you in the ways of dharma. People will croak and bray and condemn me for what I am going to do. They will even call me sinful, and my kinsmen and friends will reject me. However, they will benefit from my utterance that will help them surmount the difficulties of life. Those possessed of wisdom will understand my motives.

These are my views, O child, regarding the Brahmanas. Listen to me, O Bhaarata, and act so that, through my efforts, they procure every blessing. Also pledge your word that you will never again injure the Brahmanas."

Janamejaya replied, "I swear, even touching your feet, that I will never again, in thought, word, or deed, injure the Brahmanas."'

CANTO 152

'Saunaka said, "As your heart has been greatly perturbed, I will speak to you about dharma. You are knowledgeable, powerful, and now, with a placid heart, of your own will in search of dharma. A king who is stern at first and compassionate later, and who acts for the good to all creatures, is certainly wonderful. People say that the king who commences with severity burns the whole world. You were earlier harsh, but now you turn your eyes to dharma. Forsaking luxurious food and articles that you have long enjoyed, you have taken to strict tapasya. All this, O Janamejaya, is certain to appear wonderful to kings who are sunk in sin.

That an affluent man should become liberal, or a wealthy one become an ascetic reluctant to spend wealth, is not a marvel. Such a man is little different from Agastya who was unwilling to create wealth in order to gratify his wife; the same cause that makes an affluent man charitable operates to make an ascetic careful of his wealth. An ill-judged action creates much misery, while one accomplished with the aid of discernment has beneficial results. Sacrifice, gift, compassion, the Vedas and truth: these five are purifying. The sixth is well-performed tapasya, salutary for kings. By conducting it properly, Janamejaya, you are certain to earn great merit and punya. It is said that visiting sacred places is also highly cleansing, as Yayati sang in the following verses: 'That mortal who would earn life and longevity should, after having performed sacrifices with devotion, renounce them and practise penances.'

The field of Kuru is held to be sacred, and the river Saraswati more so. The tirthas of the Saraswati are more sacred than Saraswati herself; and the tirtha called Prithudaka is more sacred than all the tirthas of the Saraswati. One who has bathed in Prithudaka and drunk its waters will not have a premature death to lament. You will regain life and acquire longevity if you go to Mahasaras, to all the tirthas designated by the name of Pushkara, to Prabhasa, to the northern lake Manasa and to Kalodaka. Lake Manasa is on the spot where the waters of the Saraswati and the Drisadwati mingle, and one with Vedic knowledge should bathe in these places.

Manu has said that charity is the best of all duties, and that renunciation is better than charity. In this connection there is a verse composed by Satyavat. One should act as a child, innocent, without either goodness or sin. In the true nature of all creatures in this world, there is neither misery nor happiness. That which is called misery and happiness is the result of a troubled imagination. This is also true of all living creatures. The lives are superior, of those who have taken to renunciation and abstained from action, both meritorious and sinful.

I will now tell you those actions best for a king. With your might and charity, conquer Swarga, O Rajan! He who possesses force and energy will attain dharma. Rule the earth for the Brahmanas and for happiness. You formerly used to condemn the Brahmanas, so gratify them now. Though they have denounced and deserted you, do still, guided by knowledge of self, solemnly pledge never to injure them. Engage in work that is suitable for you, and seek what is for your greatest good.

Amongst rulers, some are as cool as snow; some as fierce as fire; some become like a plough; and some like a thunder-bolt. He who wishes to prevent self-destruction should never mix with evil men for any reason, general or specific. For a sinful deed committed only once, one can cleanse oneself by repentance, and for one committed twice. by vowing never to commit it again. For such an action committed thrice, one can cleanse oneself by resolving to bear oneself righteously.

By committing such a deed repeatedly, one can cleanse oneself by a pilgrimage to sacred places.

One who wants to obtain prosperity should do all that results in punya. Those who live amid fragrant odours, smell sweet, while those who live in amid foul odours, smell disgusting. One devoted to the practice of tapasya gets soon cleansed of all one's sins. By worshipping the homa fire for a year, one stained by diverse sins becomes purified, and worshipping the fire for three years cleanses one guilty of foeticide. One guilty of foeticide becomes cleansed at even a hundred yojanas from Mahasaras, or by setting out on the tirthas called Pushkara, Prabhasa, or Manasa in the north.

A slayer can be purified by saving from danger as many creatures of a particular species as those he has killed. Manu has said that by diving in water after thrice reciting the Aghamarshana mantras, one reaps the fruits of the final bath in an Aswamedha. Such an action soon cleanses one of all one's sins, and causes one to regain the esteem of the world. All creatures become docile to such a man, like the feeble-minded to those around them.

Once, long ago, the Devas and Asuras approached the celestial guru Brihaspati and humbly asked him, 'You know, O Maharishi, the rewards of dharma, and of those other deeds that lead to hell. Does not he to whom good and bad are the same, liberate himself from both punya and paapa? Tell us, Maharishi, what the fruits of dharma are and how a dharmatman drives out his sins.'

Brihaspati answered, 'If having committed a sin by mistake, one understands its nature and performs meritorious acts, one will cleanse oneself like dirty cloth washed clean by some saline substance. If one does not boast after committing a sin, but through faith, frees oneself from malice, one will acquire punya. He who hides the faults of good men, even when exposed, earns punya despite committing faults himself. As the sun rising in the morning disperses darkness, one dispels all ones sins by acting righteously.'"

Indrota, the son of Sunaka, said these words to king Janamejaya and personally assisted him in the performance of the Aswamedha yagna. The king, cleansed of his sins, regained his punya, shone with splendour like a blazing fire, and then entered his kingdom like Soma in his full form entering Swarga.'"

CANTO 153

"Yudhishtira asks, 'Have you, O Pitamaha, ever seen or heard of any mortal who was restored to life after death?'

Bhishma says, 'Listen, O Rajan, to this story of the conversation between a vulture and a jackal which took place long ago in the forest of Naimisha. Once upon a time, a Brahmana, after great difficulties, obtained a son with beautiful, large eyes. The child died of infantile convulsions. Some of his grief-stricken kinsmen, lamenting aloud, picked up that boy of tender years, the sole wealth of his family, and took him to the crematorium. There they began to pass the child from one breast to another, clamouring more bitterly in grief as they recalled the beloved prattle of the child, heavy-hearted and unable to go leaving its body on the bare ground.

Hearing their cries, a vulture came there and told them: "Go away and do not tarry, you have to cast off but one child. Thousands of men and thousands of women are left here by relatives in the course of time. See, the whole universe is subject to happiness and sorrow. Union and disunion can be seen, turn by turn. Those who have come to the crematorium bringing the dead bodies of their kinsmen, and those who sit by those bodies from affection, themselves disappear from the world as a result of their own actions, when their allotted life-span run out. There is no need to linger in the crematorium, this horrible place full of vultures and jackals, abounding with skeletons and fearsome creatures.

No one, friend or foe, having once succumbed to the power of Time, ever comes back. This is the fate of all creatures. In this world of mortals, every one that is born is sure to die. Who will restore to life one who is dead and gone on the way, as ordained by the Yama? At this hour when men are about to close their daily toil, and the sun is retiring to the Asta hills, return to your homes and give up your attachment to the child."

Hearing these words of the vulture, the grief of the kinsmen seemed to abate and, placing the child on the bare ground, they prepared to go away. Assuring themselves of the fact that the child was indeed dead, and with no hope of seeing him again, they began to leave, with loud plaints. At this time a jackal, black as a raven, issued out of his hole and said to the departing kinsmen, "Surely you kinsmen of this dead child have no affection for him. The sun still shines in the sky, you fools! Indulge your feelings without fear. Many are the virtues of the hour, and this one may come back to life! Why do you spread a few blades of Kusa grass on the ground and with hearts of steel abandon this dear child to the crematorium? Surely you have no affection for this young child whose words, as soon as they left his lips, used to gladden you so greatly!

Look at the affection that even birds and beasts bear towards their offspring. They get no return for bringing up their young ones. Like the sacrifices of the Rishis that are never undertaken from a desire for recompense, the affection of animals, birds and insects does not result in any reward, either here or hereafter. Yet they cherish their young ones, who grow up and never cherish them in return in their old age. Are they not grieved when they do not see their little ones? Where, indeed, is affection to be seen in human beings, that they claim the influence of grief? Where would you go, leaving here this child who is the perpetuator of his race? Shed tears for him for awhile, and look at him lovingly a little longer, for objects so dear are difficult to abandon.

They are friends who wait by the side of one who is weak, of one who is prosecuted in a court of law, of one who is borne towards the crematorium. Life's breath is dear to all, and all feel the influence of affection. Behold the devotion exhibited by even those that belong to the intermediate species! How can you leave, casting off this boy with eyes large as the petals of the lotus, and handsome as a newly-married youth, washed clean and adorned with floral garlands?" Hearing these touching words of the jackal, the men turned back for the sake of the corpse.

The vulture now said, "Alas, you men of no strength of mind, why do you turn back at the bidding of a cruel and mean jackal of little intelligence? Why do you mourn for that compound of five elements deserted by their presiding deities, no longer tenanted, motionless, and stiff as a piece of wood? Why do you not grieve for your own selves? Do you practice austere tapasya to cleanse yourselves from sin? Everything may be had by tapasya, what will your lamentations do? Ill-luck is born with the body, because of which this boy has died, plunging you into infinite grief. Wealth, cattle, gold, precious gems, children, all have their root in tapasya. Tapasya is the result of yoga.

Among animate beings, the measure of sorrow or joy depends on the actions of a previous life. Indeed, everyone comes into the world bringing with him his own measure of happiness and suffering. The son is not bound by the actions of the father, nor the father by those of the son. Bound by their own deeds, good and bad, all have to travel by this common road. Duly practise all the duties, and abstain from adharmic acts. Wait reverentially upon the Devas and the Brahmanas according to the directions of the shastras. Give up sorrow and unhappiness, and abstain from parental affection. Leave the child on this exposed ground, and go away without delay.

The doer alone enjoys the fruit of his actions, good or bad. What have kinsmen to do with it? Relatives abandon their deceased kinsman, however dear. Eyes bathed in tears, they go away and cease to display affection for the dead. Wise or ignorant, rich or poor, everyone with their good and bad karma succumbs to Time. What will you do by mourning for one who is dead? Time is the lord of all and, in obedience to his very nature, casts an equal eye on all things. In pride of youth, or in helpless infancy, bearing the weight of years, or lying in the mother's womb, everyone is subject to be assailed by Death. Such, indeed, is the course of the world."

The jackal said, "Alas, that light-brained vulture has diminished the affection cherished by your weeping selves, overwhelmed with sorrow for your deceased child. This is obvious because, convinced by his calm and well-expressed words, you go back to town, abandoning an affection so entrenched. Alas, I had supposed that the grief felt by men who loudly lament the death of a child, like cattle who miss their calves, would be great. Today, however, I understand what the measure of bereavement is of human beings on earth. Witnessing their great attachment, I had shed tears. It now seems that their affection is frail!

One must always strive to succeed with the help of destiny. Hard work, hope and destiny, together produce rewards. How can happiness be had from despondency? Objects of desire can be won by resolution. Why, then, do you go back so heartlessly? Where do you go, abandoning in the wilderness your own son, this perpetuator of the race of his fathers? Stay here till the sun sets and the evening twilight comes. You may then take away this boy with yourselves, or stay with him."

The vulture now said, "I am a full thousand years old today, but I have never seen a dead creature, male or female, or of ambiguous sex, revive after death. Some die in the womb, some soon after birth, some in infancy, some in youth and some in old age. The fortunes of all creatures, including even beasts and birds, are unpredictable. The life-span of all creatures, mobile and immobile, is fixed beforehand. Men who have lost spouses, children and dear ones go back to their homes every day with hearts filled with sorrow, leaving on this spot their innumerable friends and foes.

This lifeless body no longer has any animal heat in it and is as stiff as a piece of wood! Why, then, do you not depart, leaving the body of this child whose life has entered a new body? This affection is meaningless, and hugging the child is useless. He does not see with his eyes, or hear with his ears. Leave him here and go away without delay to your respective homes. My words may appear cruel but are rational and bear directly on the high religion of Moksha."

Addressed thus by the sagacious vulture in words efficacious in awakening understanding, the men resolved to leave the spot and prepared to turn their backs upon the crematorium. Grief increases twofold at the sight of its object, remembering the actions of that object when alive.

Just at that time the jackal came with quick steps and looked at the child lying in the sleep of death. The jackal said, "Why do you, at the vulture's bidding, leave this child of golden complexion, adorned with ornaments, and capable of making offering to his pitris? If you abandon him, your affection will not come to an end, nor will your piteous lamentations. On the other hand, your grief will certainly increase. We have heard the story of how Rama killed a Sudra named Samvuka to uphold dharma, and restored to life a Brahmana child who had died prematurely. There is a similar story of the son of the Rajarishi Sweta who died too early, but the king, devoted to dharma, succeeded in reviving his dead child. In your case, also, some sage or deity may be willing to grant your desire and show compassion to you who are crying so piteously." The men, grief-stricken and full of affection for the child, retraced their steps and, placing the child's head on their laps, one after another, began to lament loudly.

Hearing their cries, the vulture, returned and said, "Why are you bathing this child with your tears? Why are you pressing him in this fashion with the touch of your palms? At the command of the grim king of justice the child has been sent to that sleep which knows no waking. Those who are endued with the punya of penances, who are wealthy and intelligent, in fact, all, succumb to death. This is the place intended for the dead. One sees relatives abandon thousands of kinsmen, young and old, and pass their nights and days in grief, rolling on the bare ground. Cease this fervor in exhibiting your sorrow. It is beyond belief that this child will come back to life. He will not get back his life at the jackal's bidding. If a person once dies and takes leave of his body, it can never come to life again. Hundreds of jackals, by laying down their own lives, will not succeed in reviving this child in hundreds of years. Only if Rudra, or Kumara, or Brahman, or Vishnu, grant him a boon, can this child come back to life. The jackal, you, and all the kinsmen of this one, and I, with all our merits and sins, are on the same road. For this reason, the wise should avoid behaviour that displeases others, harsh speeches, inflicting pain on others, adultery, sin and falsehood. Carefully seek dharma, truth, good of others, justice, compassion for all creatures, sincerity and honesty. They incur sin who do not look after their mothers, fathers, kinsmen and friends when alive. What will you do by weeping for him, who does not see with his eyes, nor stir in the least, after death?"

Thus addressed, the men, overwhelmed with sorrow and burning with grief on account of their affection for the child, departed for their homes, leaving the body.

The jackal said, "Alas, terrible is the world of mortals, where no creature can escape! Every creature's life-span is short, and beloved friends are always departing. It is full of vanity, falsehoods, accusations and evil reports. This dismal incident makes me dislike the world of men. Alas, shame on you, who thus turn back like foolish men at the vulture's bidding, though you are burning with grief for this child. Heartless ones, how can you go away, casting off parental affection, upon hearing the words of a sinful vulture of uncleansed soul? Happiness is followed by misery, and misery by happiness. In this world, enveloped by both, neither of these exists uninterruptedly. Men of little understanding, where do you go, casting off on the bare ground this child of such beauty, this son who is an ornament of your varna?

Truly, I cannot dispel the idea from my mind that this handsome child, blazing with beauty, is alive. He is not meant to die. I feel that you who are grief-stricken on his death will surely have good luck today. But you are concerned only for your own ease and trying to avoid possible inconvenience and discomfort. Where would you go, like fools, leaving this darling?"

Bhishma continued, 'Thus, O Rajan, the kinsmen of the deceased child, unable to decide upon what they should do, were persuaded to remain by the sinful and smooth-tongued jackal for his own purpose, the denizens of the crematorium who roamed there every night in quest of food.

The vulture said, "Dreadful is this spot, this wilderness resounding with the screech of owls and teeming with spirits, Yakshas and Rakshasas, terrible and ghastly like a mass of blue clouds. Give up the dead body and finish the funeral rites. Indeed, cast off the corpse and accomplish those rites before the sun sets and the points of the horizon are enveloped in gloom. Hawks are uttering their harsh cries, jackals are howling fiercely, lions are roaring. The sun is setting, the trees in the crematorium are turning dark from the blue smoke of the funeral pyres. The flesh-eating dwellers of this place are yelling in rage with hunger. Creatures of horrible forms that live in this frightful place, all those carnivorous animals of fearful visage that haunt this desert, will soon set upon you. This wilderness is terrifying. Danger will overpower you. Indeed, if you listen to these false and futile words of the jackal against your own good sense, all of you will surely be destroyed."

The jackal said, "Stay where you are! There is no fear, even in this desert, as long as the sun shines. Till the god of day sets, remain here with hope, engendered by your love. Lament as you please, unafraid, looking at this child with loving eyes. Frightful though this wilderness is, no danger will befall you. In reality it is an aspect of quiet and peace. It is here that the Pitris by their thousands took leave of the world. Wait as long as the sun shines. What are this vulture's words to you? If with benumbed intellect you accept the cruel vulture's harsh words, your child will never come back to life!"

The vulture then told those men that the sun had set. The jackal said it was not so. Both the vulture and the jackal felt the pangs of hunger, addressing the kinsmen of the dead child. Both of them had girded up their loins to accomplish their respective purposes. Exhausted with hunger and thirst, they thus disputed, taking recourse to the shastras. Moved by the words of the bird and the beast, sweet as nectar, wise and knowledgeable, the kinsmen at one moment wished to go away and at another to remain. Finally, moved by grief and sorrow, they waited, wailing bitterly, not knowing that the beast and the bird, skilled in accomplishing their own purposes, had only confused them by their words.

While the adroit bird and beast were thus disputing, and while the kinsmen of the dead child sat listening to them, the great god Sankara, urged by his divine spouse Uma, came there, his eyes moist with compassion. Addressing the kinsmen of the deceased child, the Deva said, "I am Sankara, giver of boons." With burdened hearts the men prostrated themselves before the great deity and said to him, "We have lost our only child, and all of us are at the point of death. We beg you to grant us life by granting life to this our son."

The Mahadeva, taking up a quantity of water in his hands granted to the dead child a life extending a hundred years. Then the ever-benevolent and illustrious wielder of the bow Pinaki granted a boon to both the jackal and the vulture which appeased their hunger. The men bowed to the Deva, filled with delight at their great good fortune, O Rajan, and left that spot in jubilation.

Through persistent hope, firm resolution and the grace of the great god, one can obtain the fruits of one's actions without delay. Witness the combination of circumstances and the resolve of those kinsmen: while they were crying with agonised hearts, their tears were wiped away. See, how within only a short time, through their persistence, they obtained the grace of Sankara and, their sorrows dispelled, were made happy. Indeed, O Bhaarata, those dejected kinsmen were filled with amazement and delight at the restoration of their child to life through Sankara's compassion. Casting off their grief, those Brahmanas, overjoyed, hastened back to their town with the restored child.

Behaviour like this has been ordained for all the four varnas. By listening to this auspicious story about dharma, artha, and mukti, a man obtains happiness both here and hereafter.'"

CANTO 154

"Yudhishtira says, 'What should a weak, worthless and light-brained man do, O Pitamaha, who from stupidity provokes, through insulting and boastful speeches, a powerful neighbour who can favour or punish, and is always ready for action, when the enemy advances against him in anger to exterminate him?'

Bhishma replies, 'Let me narrate, O Bhaarata, the old story of the discourse between Pavana and the lordly Salmali tree, growing on one of the heights of Himavat. Having grown for many centuries, the tree had stretched out his branches. His trunk was huge, its girth being four hundred cubits, and his myriad twigs and leaves cast a dense shade under which toil-worn elephants in rut used to rest, bathed in sweat, as did many animals of other species. Loaded with flowers and fruits, he was the abode of numberless parrots, male and female. Caravans of merchants and traders travelling along their routes, and munis living in the vana, used to rest under the shade of the delightful monarch of the forest.

One day, O Bharatarishabha, the sage Narada, seeing the wide-extending and innumerable branches of the tree and the circumference of his trunk, approached him and said, "You are delightful and charming, O Salmali, greatest of trees. I am always captivated by the sight of you, as enchanting birds of diverse kinds live on your branches, and elephants and other animals cheerfully dwell in your shade. Your limbs and trunk are gigantic, O wide-branched monarch of the forest. I never see any of them broken by the god of the wind. Is it the case, child, that Pavana is pleased with you and is your friend, that he always protects you in this vana?

The illustrious Pavana with great speed and force moves from their sites the tallest and strongest trees, even mountain summits. The sacred bearer of perfumes, blowing whither he wants, dries up rivers, tanks and seas, down to the very nether regions. Pavana protects you out of friendship, for certain. This is why, though having countless branches, you still bear leaves and flowers. O king of the forest, your verdure is delightful since these winged creatures sport joyfully on your twigs and branches. During the season when you break into bloom, the sweet notes of all these denizens of your branches are heard separately singing melodious songs. Then, O Salmali, these elephants that are the ornaments of their species, bathed in sweat, approach you with cries of delight, and are happy here. Diverse other species of animals living in the vana embellish you further. You are beautiful like the mountains of Meru inhabited by creatures of every kind. Frequented also by rishis and others engaged in tapasya, and by Yatis devoted to contemplation, this place, I think, must resemble Swarga itself."'

CANTO 155

'Narada said, "Without doubt, O Salmali, the terrible and irresistible Vayu Deva always protects you out of amity, and a close intimacy exists between you and the Wind. It is as if you have told him, 'I am yours,' and for that reason Vayu Deva shields you. I do not think there is tree or mountain or mansion in this world that the Wind has not broken. Assuredly, you stand here with all your branches, twigs and leaves intact, simply because, for some reason, that Deva shelters you."

The Salmali said, "The Wind is neither my friend, nor mate, nor well-wisher, nor my great Ordainer, O Narada Muni, that he should protect me. My fierce energy and might, O Narada, are greater than the Wind's. In truth, the strength of the Wind comes up to about only an eighteenth part of mine. When he advances in rage, tearing up trees and mountains in his path, I curb his strength by putting forth mine. Indeed, the Wind that breaks many things has himself been repeatedly broken by me. This is why, O Devarishi, I am not afraid of him even when he comes in anger."

Narada said, "O Salmali, your protection seems to be thoroughly perverse. There is no doubt that there is nothing equal to the Wind in strength. Even Indra, Yama, or Vaisravana, the lord of the waters, is not equal in might to Vayu Deva, whereas you are only a tree! The illustrious Wind god is at all times the cause of any act performed by the creatures in this world, since it is he that is the giver of life. When that god exerts himself with propriety, he makes it possible for all living creatures to live at their ease. When he moves with anger, calamities sweep over the creatures of the world. What can it be other than feeble understanding that induces you to not revere the Vayu Deva, the greatest in the universe, who deserves worship? You are worthless and of depraved perception. Indeed, you only indulge in meaningless bragging. You utter lies because your intellect is confused by anger and other evil passions.

O Salmali, I am certainly angry with you for speaking thus. I will myself report to Vayu Deva all your derogatory words. Chandanas, Syandanas, Salas, Saralas, Devadarus, Vetavas, Dhanwanas and other trees of good souls that are far stronger than you, have never uttered such invectives against the Deva as you of wicked understanding have done. All of them know the might of the Wind and their own, and these foremost of trees bow down their heads in respect to the deity. You, however, through folly, know not the infinite might of the Wind. I shall go to the Deva.""""

CANTO 156

"Bhishma continues, 'Narada, the greatest of all knowers of Brahma, reported to the Vayu Deva all that the Salmali had said about him.

Narada said, "There is a certain Salmali, a tree on the breast of Himavat, decked with branches and leaves spread wide around and with roots that extend deep into the earth. That tree has disparaged you and spoken many insulting words about you that are improper for me to repeat. I know that you, the foremost of all created things, are a superior and mighty entity, resembling in wrath the Destroyer himself."

Hearing these words of Narada, the Vayu Deva went to Salmali, and said to him in rage, "O Salmali, you have spoken spoken slightingly of me before Narada. Know that I am Vayu Deva, and I will certainly show you my power and might. You are no stranger to me, I know you well. It is only because the great Pitamaha, while he was creating the world, had for a time rested under you, that I have so far shown you grace. That is why you stand unharmed, O worst of trees, not because of your own might. You regard me lightly as if I were a common creature. I will show myself to you in such a way that you will not again affront me."

Bhishma continues, 'The Salmali laughed in derision and replied, "O Vayu Deva, you are angry with me! Do not hesitate to show me the extent of your might. Throw all your anger upon me. What will you do to me by giving way to wrath? Even if your strength had been your own,

I would not be afraid of you, as I am your superior in might. Those are not to be regarded as strong who possess physical strength alone."

The Vayu Deva left, saying, "Tomorrow I will test your strength."

When night fell, Salmali, calculating mentally the extent of the Wind's might, and realising his own self to be inferior to the Deva, said to himself, "All that I said to Narada is false. I am certainly inferior in might to the Wind, who is truly powerful. He is always mighty, as Narada said, and I am certainly weaker than other trees. But in astuteness no tree is my equal, so, relying upon my intelligence I will examine this fear that arises from the Wind. If all the other trees in the forest only relied upon the same kind of intelligence, surely no injury could result to them from Vayu Deva when he becomes angry. All of them, however, are devoid of understanding, and therefore do not know, as I do, why or how the Wind succeeds in shaking and tearing them up."''

CANTO 157

"Bhishma says, 'Having settled this in his mind, Salmali sadly caused all his branches, principal and subsidiary, to be cut off. He cast off his branches and leaves and flowers, and in the morning the tree looked steadily at the Wind, as he came towards him. Filled with rage and breathing hard, the Wind advanced, felling large trees, towards the spot where the Salmali stood. When he saw him divested of top and branches and leaves and flowers, the Wind smiled exultantly and addressed the lord of the forest who earlier had such a gigantic appearance.

"O Salmali, I would have done to you in my anger precisely what you have done to yourself by lopping off all your branches. You are now divested of your proud top and flowers, and without your shoots and leaves. In consequence of your own evil counsels, you have been brought under my power."

Salmali felt great shame. He remembered the words of Narada and began to repent his folly. Similarly, O Naravyaghra, a weak and foolish man, if he provokes the enmity of a powerful one, is obliged to repent like the Salmali of fable. Even when of equal might, men do not suddenly commence hostilities with those who have injured them. On the other hand, O Rajan, they display their might by degrees.

A foolish man should never provoke the hostility of an intelligent one. In such cases the intelligence of the astute man is like fire penetrating a heap of dry grass. Intelligence is the most precious possession that one can have. Similarly, Rajan, a man can have nothing here more valuable than might. One should therefore, overlook the wrongs which one of superior strength inflicts, just as one should would kindly overlook the actions of a child, an idiot, or a blind or deaf person.

The wisdom of this saying is witnessed in your case, O Parantapa. The eleven akshauhinis of Duryodhana, O you of great splendour, and the seven collected by you, were not in might equal to the single-handed mahatman, Arjuna. Therefore that illustrious Pandava, son of Paka's chastiser, routed and slew all the troops as he coursed the field of battle, relying on his own strength. I have told you of the duties of kings and the morality of duties in detail, Bhaarata. What else, Yudhishtira, do you wish to hear?'"

CANTO 158

"**Y**udhishtira says, 'I desire to hear in detail about the source of sin, O Bharatarishabha, and the foundation upon which it rests.'

Bhishma replies, 'Listen, Rajan: Lobha, greed alone, is the great destroyer. From lobha comes paapa and adharma, and they flow together and cause great misery. Covetousness is the source also of cunning and hypocrisy, which makes men sin in the world. Lobha causes anger, lust, loss of judgment, deception, pride, arrogance and malice, as well as vindictiveness, shamelessness, loss of prosperity, loss of virtue, anxiety, infamy, miserliness, cupidity, and partiality for every kind of impropriety. It causes conceit on account of birth, learning, beauty and wealth, as well as insensitivity, malevolence, mistrust, insincerity towards all, appropriation of other people's wealth, ravishment of other people's wives, harshness of speech, propensity to speak ill of others, ravening lust, gluttony, liability to premature death, malice, irresistible propensity for falsehood, unconquerable appetite for indulging in the passions, insatiable desire for gossip and slander, boastfulness, arrogance, neglect of duties, rashness, and perpetration of every kind of evil deed: all these proceed from lobha.

Men, whether infant, youth or adult, are unable to abandon covetousness. Such is the nature of greed that it never decays, even with the decay of life. Like the ocean that can never be filled, even by the constant discharge of innumerable rivers of immeasurable depth, covetousness is incapable of being gratified by any extent of acquisitions. However, a Muni should conquer this covetousness which is never gratified by acquisitions or satiated by the accomplishment of desires, which is not known in its real nature by the gods, the Gandharvas, the Asuras, the great snakes—in fact, by all classes of beings, this irresistible passion and folly which lures the heart to the unrealities of the world. Pride, malice, slander, crookedness, and incapacity to bear other people's good, are vices, O Kurusthama, that are seen in men of uncleansed soul in the grip of greed. Even great learned men who bear in their minds all the voluminous shastras, and who are competent to dispel the doubts of others, show themselves in this respect to be weak-minded and undergo great misery in consequence of this passion.

Greedy men are wedded to envy and anger and are outside the pale of good behaviour. With crooked hearts they utter sweet speeches, like dark pits with mouths covered with grass. Being of low minds, they rob the world wearing the hypocritical cloak of religion and virtue. They use equivocation to create diverse schisms in religion and destroy the ways of dharma. When evil men under the domination of lobha apparently practise the duties of dharma, the desecrations committed by them soon become acceptable among men. Pride, anger, arrogance, self-importance, insensibility, outbursts of joy and sorrow, all these can be seen in men swayed by greed. Understand, they who remain under the influence of covetousness are evil.

I shall now tell you about those who are designated good and whose practices are pure. One regards as virtuous, O Bhaarata, those who have no fear of an obligation to return to this world after death, and no fear of the next world; they who are not addicted to animal food; who cherish salutary behaviour and practise self-restraint; for whom pleasure and pain are equal, who have truth for their refuge, who are compassionate and give, rather than take; who worship Pitris, Devas and Atithis; who are universal benefactors, always ready to work for the good of others; whose minds are staunch and who observe all the duties laid down in the shastras, who are devoted to the good of all, who can give their all and lay down their very lives for others!

These advocates of dharma are incapable of being forced away from the path of virtue. Their conduct, conforming to the model set by the dharmatman of old, cannot be otherwise. They are fearless, tranquil, mild and always adhere to the right path. Full of compassion, they are always worshipped by the good. They are free from pride, lust and anger, and are not attached to any worldly object. They observe excellent vows and are always objects of regard. You should therefore, always wait upon them and seek instruction from them. They never aspire to virtue for the sake of wealth or fame, O Yudhishtira. They acquire it, rather, because it is a duty, like cherishing the body. Fear, wrath, restlessness and sorrow do not dwell in them. There is no mystery about them and they do not wear the outward garb of religion to mislead their fellowmen. They are perfectly contented, and make no error of judgment out of covetousness. They are devoted to truth and sincerity, and never fall from righteousness. You should always show regard for them, O son of Kunti!

They are neither delighted at any gain, nor pained at any loss. Free of attachment to anything, free of pride, they are wedded to goodness and look on everything equally. Gain and loss, happiness and sorrow, the agreeable and the disagreeable, life and death, are one in the eyes of these men of steady tread, engaged in the pursuit of divine knowledge, and devoted to the path of tranquillity and righteousness. Keep your senses under restraint, do not yield to imprudence, and always worship those Mahatmans who bear such love for dharma. Words cause good only through the favour of the Devas, O blessed one. Under different circumstances, they can produce evil consequences.'"

"Yudhishtira says, 'You have said, O Pitamaha, that the foundation of all evil is lobha. I wish, O sire, to hear of ignorance, avidya, in detail.'

Bhishma replies, 'The man who commits sin through avidya, who does not know that his end is near and who always hates the virtuous, soon incurs infamy. Avidya is the source of misery through which one suffers hardship, incurs great danger, and sinks into hell.'

Yudhishtira says, 'O Rajan, I desire to hear in full all the inseparable attributes of avidya: its origin, rise, place, growth, decay, root, course, time, cause and consequence. The misery that is felt in this world, is all born of ignorance.'

Bhishma replies, 'Attachment, hate, loss of judgment, joy, sorrow, vanity, lust, anger, pride, procrastination, idleness, desire, aversion, jealousy and all other sinful actions are known by their common name of avidya. Hear now, O Rajan, about its tendency, growth and other features about which you have enquired. These two, ignorance and covetousness, are the same. Both produce the same fruits and same faults, O Bhaarata! Avidya exists where lobha exists, and grows or shrinks along with lobha.

Manifold again is the course that it takes. Loss of judgment is the inseparable attribute and root of lobha. Eternity is ignorance's path and when avidya is apparent, the objects of covetousness are forfeited. From ignorance proceeds covetousness, and vice versa. Lobha should be shunned by all. Janaka, Yuvanaswa, Vrishadarbhi, Prasenajit and other kings attained Swarga because they repressed Lobha. Therefore let it be seen that you are resolute in avoiding covetousness, O Kurusthama. Thus will you obtain happiness, both here and in the next world.'"

CANTO 160

"Yudhishtira says, 'O Pitamaha, Mahatman, how can a person engaged in the study of the Vedas earn the highest happiness in heaven? According to the shastras, diverse kinds of action are considered in this world as productive of great punya. Tell me, what is regarded as great, both here and hereafter? The path of dharma is long and has innumerable branches, O Bhaarata! Amongst those, which are the few that should be preferred above others, according to you? Tell me about this, that is so inclusive and multifarious.'

Bhishma replies, 'I will tell you how you can attain great punya. Being wise, you will be as happy with the knowledge that I will impart to you as if you had drunk amrita. Each Maharishi has prescribed many rules of dharma, based upon his own wisdom, of which the highest is self-restraint. Among the ancients, those acquainted with truth have said that self-restraint leads to the highest punya, and that, for the Brahmana, it is his eternal duty, from which he obtains the rewards of his actions. In his case, the punya of self-restraint enhances tejas and surpasses charity, sacrifice and study of the Vedas.

Self-restraint is highly sacred; by it a man is cleansed of all his sins, is imbued with tejas and attains to the highest blessedness. Self-restraint, according to all dharmatman, is the highest of virtues in this world, O Narottama, and we have not heard of any other dharma that can equal it for acquiring the highest happiness both here and hereafter. The self-restrained man sleeps sweetly, wakes up happy, and moves through the world contentedly, his mind always cheerful. The man who is without self-restraint suffers misery and brings upon himself many calamities, all born of his own faults. It is said that for all the four varnas, self-restraint is the best of vows.

I will now tell you those attributes whose sum total is called self-restraint. Forgiveness, patience, abstention from injury, impartiality, truth, sincerity, conquest of the senses, cleverness, mildness, modesty, steadiness, liberality, freedom from wrath, contentment, sweetness of speech, benevolence, freedom from malice: the union of all these is called self-restraint. It also includes, O son of Kuru, veneration for the guru and universal compassion. The self-restrained man avoids adulation and slander, depravity, infamy, false speech, lust, covetousness, pride, arrogance, self-glorification, fear, envy and disrespect. He never incurs disgrace and is free from envy. He is not gratified with small acquisitions; he is just like the ocean that can never be filled.

The man of self-restraint is never bound by attachments that arise from earthly connections or sentiments like, "I am yours, you are mine, They are in me, and I am in them." Such a man, who adopts the practices of either cities or the vana, and who never indulges in slander or adulation, attains mukti. He is cheerful and of virtuous conduct, practises universal friendliness, has knowledge of the soul and, liberated from the diverse attachments of the earth, obtains great reward in the world. A man of excellent conduct, observant of duties, cheerful, learned and with knowledge of self, wins esteem here and attains to a high end hereafter.

All actions that one regards as good on earth, all those that dhartman practise, constitute the path of the Rishi possessed of knowledge. A good man never deviates from that path. Retiring from the world and taking to vanavasa, the learned man, having mastered his senses, who treads that path in quiet expectation of his death, is sure to attain to the state of Brahma. He who has no fear of any creature, and of whom no creature is afraid, has no fear to encounter after the dissolution of his body. He who exhausts his punya by actual enjoyment, rather than seeking to accumulate it, who views equally all creatures and practises a course of universal friendliness, attains Brahma. Just as the track of birds along the sky or of fowl over the surface of water cannot be discerned, the track of such a man does not attract notice.

For one who, abandoning home, adopts the dharma of moksha, many bright worlds wait to be enjoyed for eternity, O Rajan. By abandoning all actions, including in due course tapasya and the various branches of study, one becomes pure in one's desires and liberated from all restraints, a cheerful soul of pure heart, conversant with self, who then wins esteem in this world and at last attains Swarga. That eternal region of Brahman which springs from Vedic tapasya, and which is within hidden in a cave, can be won by only self-restraint. He who takes pleasure in true knowledge, who has become enlightened injures no creature, has no fear of coming back to this world, far less, any fear in respect of the others.

There is one fault in self-control, none other: that men regard one who has self-control as weak and unintelligent. Its merits are many, for by forgiveness, which is only another form of self-control, a man may easily acquire innumerable worlds. What need does he have for self-control who dwells in a forest? Similarly, O Bhaarata, of what use is vanavasa to one that has no self-control? Wherever a man of self-control dwells is a forest, even a sacred retreat.'"

Vaisampayana continued, "Hearing these words of Bhishma, Yudhishtira is highly gratified, as if he had imbibed amrita. He asks the greatest of Dharmatmans again to speak, and the perpetuator of Kuru's race once more begins to discourse cheerfully."

CANTO 161

"Bhishma says, 'The wise say that tapasya is the root of all things. The foolish man who has not undergone tapasya does not get the rewards of even his own actions. The mighty Brahma created the entire universe by tapasya. The Rishis acquired the Vedas through the power of tapasya. It was with the aid of tapasya that Pitamaha created food, fruit and roots. It is by tapasya that rishis and munis with rapt souls see the three worlds. It is through tapasya that medicines and antidotes to injurious substances, and diverse processes, produce their intended results. The accomplishment of all purposes depends upon tapasya. Things apparently unattainable are sure to be won by tapasya. Without doubt the Rishis obtained their six-fold divine attributes through tapasya.

Tapasya, when properly practiced, cleanses one who drinks alcoholic stimulants, one who robs others, one guilty of foeticide and one who violates his acharya's bed. Penances are of many kinds and can be seen in many different guises. However, of all the tapasyas that can be practised by refraining from pleasure and enjoyment, abstaining from food is supreme. It is superior, Rajan, to even compassion, truthfulness of speech, gifts, and restraining the senses. There is no action more difficult to accomplish than gift. There is no mode of life that is superior to serving one's mother. There is no creature superior to those who know the three Vedas. Similarly, sannyasa constitutes the greatest tapasya. People keep their senses under control for the sake of dharma and Swarga. In respect of such control over the senses, and in the acquisition of dharma, there is no tapasya greater than complete fasting. The Rishis, the Devas, humankind, beasts, birds, and all other creatures, mobile or inert, are all devoted to tapasyas, and whatever success they win is won through tapasya. Thus it was through tapasya that the Devas acquired their superiority The moon and stars too got their share of happiness through tapasya. Without doubt, the very status of godhead may be gained through tapasya.'"

CANTO 162

"Yudhishtira says, 'Brahmanas, Rishis, Pitris and the Devas all approve the dharma of truth. Tell me about truth, O Pitamaha! What are its characteristics, and how can it be acquired? How can one practice truth, and what can one gain by it?'

Bhishma replies, 'Confusion of duties of the four varnas is never approved. That which is called Truth always exists in a pure and pristine state in every one of the four varnas. With the righteous, Truth is always an eternal duty, and one should reverentially bow to it. Truth is the highest refuge of all, Truth is dharma; Truth is tapasya; Truth is Yoga; Truth is the eternal Brahman. Truth is said to be a yagna of a high order, upon which everything rests.

I will now tell you the forms of Truth and its characteristics, in due order, so that you may learn how it can be acquired. Truth, O Bhaarata, as it exists in the world, is of thirteen kinds. The forms that Truth assumes are impartiality, self-control, forgiveness, modesty, endurance, goodness, renunciation, contemplation, dignity, fortitude, compassion, and abstention from injury. These, O Rajan, are the thirteen forms of Truth.

Truth is immutable, eternal and permanent. It can be acquired through practices which do not militate against any of the other virtues, and through Yoga.

When desire, aversion, lust and wrath are shed, that trait which allows one to look upon oneself and one's foe, upon one's good and one's evil, with parity, is called impartiality.

Self-control consists in never coveting another man's possessions, in gravity and patience, a capacity to allay others' fears in respect to oneself, and immunity from maladies. One can acquire this through knowledge.

Devotion to the practice of charity and the observance of dharma constitutes goodwill, the sages say. One acquires universal goodwill by constant devotion to truth.

Forgiveness is that attribute which enables an esteemed and good man to endure both what is agreeable and disagreeable. One can acquire this virtue through the practice of truthfulness.

Modesty is that virtue by which an intelligent man, contented in mind and speech, achieves many good deeds and never incurs the censure of others. It can be acquired through the aid of dharma.

Endurance is that virtue which forgives for the sake of dharma and artha. It is a form of forgiveness which one acquires through patience, and its purpose is to attach people to oneself.

Sannyasa is the giving up of attachment and also of all earthly possessions. Only he who has given up anger and malice can achieve renunciation.

Goodness is that virtue by which one does what is beneficial to all creatures with alertness and care. It has no particular form and consists of divestment of all selfish attachments.

Fortitude is that virtue by which one remains tranquil in happiness and misery. The wise man, mindful of his own good, practises this virtue which teaches forgiveness and devotion to truth. He who casts off joy, fear and wrath, succeeds in acquiring fortitude. Abstention from injury to all creatures in thought, word and deed, kindness and charity, are the eternal duties of those who are good.

These thirteen attributes, though apparently distinct from one another, have but one and the same form, which is Truth. All these, O Bhaarata, support Truth and strengthen it. It is impossible, O Rajan, to enumerate the merits of Truth. It is for these reasons that the Brahmanas, the Pitris and the Devas acclaim Truth. There is no duty higher than Truth and no sin more heinous than untruth. Indeed, Truth is the very foundation of dharma. One should never destroy Truth. From Truth proceed gifts, and yagna with offerings, as well as the threefold Agnihotras, the Vedas, and everything else that leads to dharma. Once upon a time a thousand Awamedha yagnas and Truth were weighed against each other in the balance. Truth weighed more than the thousand Aswamedha yagnas.'"

CANTO 163

"Yudhishtira says, 'O you of great wisdom, tell me about the source of anger, lust, sorrow, loss of judgment, inclination to do evil, jealousy, malice, pride, envy, slander, incapacity to bear the good of others, unkindness and fear. Tell me everything truly and in detail, O Bharatarishabha.'

Bhishma says, 'These thirteen vices are considered powerful enemies of all beings. These, O Rajan, approach and tempt men from every side. They goad and trouble a reckless man or one who is not in his senses. Indeed, as soon as they see a man, they attack him fiercely, like wolves leaping upon their prey. From these proceed all kinds of grief, all kinds of sin. Every mortal, O Purushottama, should know this. I will now tell you of their origin, of the objects upon which they rest, and the means of their destruction. Listen with undivided attention, O Rajan, as I tell you precisely and in detail about the origin of wrath.

Anger springs from greed, which is strengthened by others' faults. Through forgiveness it remains dormant and disappears.

Lust springs from resolution. Indulgence strengthens it. When the wise man resolutely turns away from it, it disappears and dies.

Envy is caused by anger and covetousness. It disappears through compassion for all creatures, knowledge of self, and disregard for all worldly objects. Envy also arises from seeing the faults of other people, but in intelligent men it vanishes with true knowledge.

Loss of judgment has its origin in ignorance, and grows from sinfulness of habit. When one who suffers from this fault begins to take pleasure in the society of wise men, this vice at once and immediately hides its head.

Men perceive conflicting shastras, O scion of Kuru. From this circumstance springs the desire for diverse kinds of action. When one gains true knowledge, this desire is allayed.

Grief in a living being is caused by affection intensified by separation. When one comes to understand that the dead will not return, it subsides.

Incapacity to bear others' good fortune proceeds from anger and greed. Through compassion for every creature and a disregard for all earthly objects, it gets extinguished.

Malice proceeds from abandonment of Truth and indulgence in evil. This vice, O child, disappears if one serves the wise and the good.

Pride arises from conceit of birth, learning and prosperity. However, when one truly knows these three, it instantly disappears.

Jealousy springs from hankering and fellowship with ignoble and ill-bred people. Wisdom eradicates it.

Slander takes its rise from errors of conduct and through offensive and hateful speech. It disappears, O Rajan, upon seeing the world as it is.

Hate is born when one who causes affliction is powerful and the injured one unable to avenge the injury. It subsides through kindness.

Compassion proceeds from the sight of helpless and miserable creatures, with which the world abounds. The sentiment disappears when one understands the strength of dharma.

Covetousness in all creatures spring from ignorance. It dissolves once the impermanence of all objects of enjoyment is perceived.

One says that tranquillity of the soul alone can subdue all these faults. The sons of Dhritarashtra suffered from all these thirteen faults, while you, who were always in search of truth, have conquered all these vices because of your regard for your elders.'"

CANTO 164

"Yudhishtira says, 'From my observation of good men, I know what compassion is. However, O Bhaarata, I do not know evil men, or the nature of their actions. People avoid cruel men as they avoid thorns, pitfalls and fire. It is evident, O Bhaarata, that they will burn both here and hereafter. Therefore, O Kurusthama, tell me what, in truth, are the acts of such men.'

Bhishma says, 'Evil men are irresistibly inclined towards wicked acts. They slander others and incur infamy themselves. They always feel themselves to be cheated of their due. A spiteful man brags of his own deeds of charity, sees others with malicious eyes and is very mean, deceitful and full of cunning. He never gives others their due. He is arrogant, boastful and keeps evil company. He cannot distinguish the merits and faults of others, fears and suspects all with whom he comes into contact and praises only his associates. He detests all Munis who have taken to vanavasa. He is stupid, discontented, a miser, and a liar. He is cruel, takes delight in injuring others, and is exceedingly covetous.

Such a person regards a virtuous and accomplished man as a pest. Thinking everyone else to be like himself, he trusts nobody. He proclaims the faults of other people, however unjustified. As for his own faults, he does not glance at them because of the advantage he reaps from them. He regards someone who does him good as a simpleton whom he has cleverly deceived. He is filled with regret if he has at any time made any gift of wealth, even to a benefactor. Such a heartless person will calmly eat and drink all kinds of choice food by himself, in the presence of others who may be looking on longingly. He who dedicates the first portion of food to Brahmanas and shares what remains with friends and kinsmen, attains great happiness in the next world and infinite happiness here.

I have now, O chief of the Bhaaratas, told you the indications of an evil and malevolent man. Such a person should always be avoided by a wise man.'"

CANTO 165

"Bhishma says, 'O Bhaarata, wealth and knowledge should be given to poor Brahmanas who have been robbed of their wealth and who know all the Vedas and perform yagnas, in order to acquire the punya of dharma, so that they can discharge their obligations to Gurus and the Pitris, and pass their days in reciting and studying the shastras. To those Brahmanas who are not poor, only the dakshina need be given, while to those who have fallen from the status of Brahman due to their sinful deeds, uncooked food should be given outside the limits of the sacrificial altar.

The Brahmanas are the Vedas themselves and all yagnas with generous gifts. Their virtuous inclinations drive them to outdo one another in performing yagnas. The king should, therefore, make diverse costly gifts to them. The Brahmana who can provide for his family for three years or more deserves to drink the Soma. If despite the presence of a virtuous king on the throne, the yagna someone begins, especially a Brahmana, cannot be completed for want of only a fourth part of the estimated expenses, then the king should, to ensure the completion of that sacrifice, take away from his kinsmen the wealth of a Vaisya possessesing a large herd of cattle who is averse to sacrifices and abstains from quaffing Soma.

As the Sudra is not competent to perform a yagna, the king should take wealth away from him for this purpose. He should also, without any scruple, take away wealth from kinsmen who do not perform yagna though possessing a hundred head of cattle and also from him who abstains from yagna though possessing a thousand head of cattle. The king should publicly confiscate the wealth of men who do not practise charity, for by doing so he earns great punya.

The Brahmana forced by want to go without six meals, according to the rules, can take without permission what he requires for a single meal, from the husking tub or field or garden or any other place of a man who cares only for today, without any thought of the morrow, even a man of low pursuits. He should however, on his own, inform the king of his action. If the king knows his duty, he will not inflict any punishment upon such a Brahmana, remembering that a Brahmana faces want and hunger only through the fault of the Kshatriya. Having ascertained a Brahmana's learning and behaviour, the king should make provision for him, and protect him as a father protects a son of his own body. On the expiry of every year, one should perform the Vaisvanara sacrifice.

They who know religion say that the practice of a prescribed alternative does not destroy dharma. The Viswedevas, the Sadhyas, the Brahmanas and Maharishis, fearing death in times of trouble, have no scruple in following any alternative provisions laid down in the shastras. However, one who takes the alternative while able to live according to the primary provision is regarded as an evil man who will never succeed in winning any felicity in Swarga.

A Brahmana who knows the Vedas should never vaunt his power and knowledge to the king. The power of a Brahmana will always be superior to that of a king, which is why a king cannot bear or resist the power of the Brahmanas. The Brahmana is said to be the creator, ruler, lawmaker and god. No word of abuse or sarcasm should be addressed to a Brahmana. The Kshatriya should solve all his difficulties with the aid of the might of his arms, the Vaisya and the Sudra by wealth, and the Brahmana by mantras and homa. None, a maiden or young woman, one unacquainted with mantras, an ignorant person, or one who is impure, is competent to pour libations on the yagna fire. If any of these do so, he or she is sure to fall into hell, along with him for whom they officiate.

For this reason, none but a Brahmana with knowledge of the Vedas and skilled in all yagnas should pour sacrificial libations. They who know the shastras say that the man who, having kindled the yagna fire, does not give away the dedicated food as dakshina, is not the kindler of a yagna fire. One should, with his senses under control and with proper devotion, perform all the acts of punya. One should never worship the deities in yagnas in which dakshina is not given. A sacrifice not concluded with dakshina, rather than producing punya, brings about the destruction of one's children, animals and Swarga. Such a yagna destroys also one's senses, fame and achievements, one's very life-span.

Those Brahmanas who lie with women in their season, or who never perform yagnas, or whose families have no members who are educated in the Vedas, are veritable Sudras. The Brahmana who, having married a Sudra girl, resides for twelve continuous years in a village which is supplied only by a single well, becomes a Sudra in action. The Brahmana who summons to his bed an unmarried maiden, or suffers a Sudra to sit upon the same carpet with him, thinking him worthy of respect, can be cleansed only if he sits on a bed of dry grass behind some Kshatriya or Vaisya and gives him respect in that way. Listen, O Rajan, to my words on this subject. The sin that a Brahmana commits in a single night by serving a member of a lower varna, or by sporting with him in the same spot or on the same bed, can only by cleansed by sitting for three continuous years on a bed of grass behind a Kshatriya or Vaisya.

A falsehood, spoken in jest, or to a woman, is not sinful, O Rajan, nor one on the occasion of marriage, or for the benefit of one's guru, or to save one's own life; these five kinds of falsehood are said not to be sinful. One can acquire useful knowledge from even a man of low pursuits, with devotion and reverence. One can take up gold, without any scruple, from even an unclean place. A woman who is the ornament of her sex is acceptable from even a vile varna. Amrita, if extracted from poison, can be quaffed; water, women, jewels and other valuables can never be impure or unclean, according to the shastras. Even a Vaisya can take up weapons for his own safety, for the benefit of Brahmanas and cattle and on occasions of transfusion of varna.

Drinking alcohol, Brahmahatya, and the violation of the Acharya's bed are sins that, if committed consciously, have no reparation except death. The same can be said of stealing gold or a Brahmana's property. By drinking alcohol, having sexual congress with someone prohibited, mingling with a degraded person or, for a person of any of the other three varnas, having congress with a Brahmani, one becomes inevitably sullied. By mixing with such a person for one whole year in such matters as officiating in yagnas and teaching sexual congress, one too becomes corrupted. One, however, does not become so by mixing with a fallen person in such matters as riding on the same vehicle, sitting on the same seat, and eating in the same line.

Excluding the five grave sins mentioned above, all other sins have expiations prescribed for them by law, provided one does not indulge in them again. In the case of those who have been guilty of the first three of these five sins, drinking alcohol, Brahmahatya, and violation of the acharya's bed, there is no restriction on their surviving kinsmen about food and wearing ornaments, even if their funeral rites remain unperformed when they die. A Dharmatman should, in the observance of his dharma, discard his very friends and revered elders. In fact, until expiation is undertaken, the virtuous should not even talk with sinners.

A sinful man destroys his sin by acting virtuously afterwards and by tapasya. By calling a thief a thief, one incurs the sin of theft. By calling a man a thief who, however, is not a thief one incurs a sin twice the sin of theft. The maiden who suffers her virginity to be deflowered incurs three-fourths of the sin of killing a Brahmana, while the man who deflowers her incurs a sin equal to a fourth part of that of Brahmahatya.

By slandering or striking Brahmanas, one sinks in infamy for a hundred years, and by killing a Brahmana one sinks into hell for a thousand years. No one, therefore, should speak ill of a Brahmana or slay him. If a person strikes a Brahmana with a weapon, he will have to live in hell for as many years as the grains of dust that are soaked by the blood flowing from the wound. One guilty of foeticide becomes cleansed if he dies of wounds received in battle fought for the sake of cattle and Brahmanas. Casting himself on a blazing fire can also cleanse him.

A drinker of alcoholic liquors becomes cleansed by drinking hot alcohol. Burning his body with that hot drink, he gets cleansed through death in the other world. A Brahmana stained by such a sin obtains regions of felicity by such a course, not by any other. For violating the bed of a guru, the evil-souled and sinful wretch becomes cleansed by death from embracing a heated female figure of iron. Or, he could cut off his organ and testicles and, bearing them in his hands, he should go in a straight course towards the south-west and then end his life. He could also wash away his sin by dying in order to benefit a Brahmana, or by performing an Ashwamedha yagna or a cow-sacrifice or an Agnishtoma, and thus regain esteem both here and hereafter.

The slayer of a Brahmana should practise the vow of Brahmacharya for twelve years and devoting himself to tapasya and the life of a Muni, wander, holding all the while in his hands the skull of the slain, and proclaiming his sin to all. This is also the expiation provided for one who slays a pregnant woman, knowing her condition. The man who knowingly slays such a woman incurs double the sin that follows from Brahmanicide. A drinker of alcohol could regain his purity if he lived on frugal fare, practiced Brahmacharya vows, slept on the bare ground, performed for more than three years the sacrifice next to the Agnishtoma, and then gave away a thousand cattle with one bull.

For slaying a Vaisya one should perform such a sacrifice for two years and make a present of a hundred cattle with one bull, and for a Sudra, one should perform such a sacrifice for one year and make a present of a hundred cattle with one bull. For slaying a dog or bear or camel, one should perform the same penance laid down for the slaughter of a Sudra. For slaying a cat, a chasa, a frog, a crow, a reptile, or a rat, one says that, one incurs the sin of animal slaughter

O Rajan, I will now tell you of other kinds of expiations in their order. For all minor sins one should repent or practise some vow for one year. For congress with the wife of a Brahmana adept in the Vedas, one should for three years practise the vow of Brahmacharya, taking a little food at the fourth part of the day. For congress with any other woman who is not one's wife, one should undergo a similar penance for two years. For taking delight in a woman's company by sitting with her on the same spot or on the same seat, one should live only on water for three days to doing cleanse oneself. The same is laid down the same for one who defiles a blazing fire.

The shastras conclude that he who kills his father, mother or acharya, without adequate cause, is definitely disgraced, O Kurusthama. Only food and clothes should be given to a wife guilty of adultery or one confined in a prison. Indeed, the vows that the shastras lay down for a male guilty of adultery should also be applied to a woman. In the case of a woman who abandons her husband of a superior caste and has congress with a vile person of a lower varna, the king should cause her to be devoured by dogs in a public place, in the midst of a large concourse of spectators. A wise king should cause the male committing adultery under such circumstances to be placed upon a heated bed of iron and then, placing faggots underneath, burn the sinner. The same punishment, O Rajan, is provided for a woman guilty of adultery.

The sinner who does not perform expiation within a year of the commission of the sin incurs paapa that is double of what attaches to the original sin. One who associates with such a person for two years must wander over the earth, devoting himself to tapasya and living upon alms. One associating with a sinner for four years should adopt such a mode of life for five years.

If a younger brother weds before his elder brother, then all three, the elder brother, the younger brother and his wife, become tainted. To cleanse themselves, they should either observe the vows prescribed for one who has neglected his sacrificial fire, or practise the vow of Chandrayana for a month, or some other painful vow. The younger brother should give his wife to his unmarried elder brother and afterwards, with his permission, take her back. By such means all three can be cleansed of their sin.

By slaying animals except a cow, the slayer is not stained. The learned know that man has dominion over all the lower animals. A sinner, holding in his hand a yak-tail and an earthen pot, should go about proclaiming his sin. He should every day beg only from seven families and live upon what he thus obtains. By doing this for twelve days he can be cleansed of his sin. He who is unable to carry in his hand the yak-tail while practising the vow should observe the vow of the sannyasi for a whole year. Among men such expiation is the best.

For those who are able to practise charity, the shastras lay down the practice of in all such cases. By giving away only one cow, those who have faith and dharma can cleanse themselves. One who eats or drinks the flesh, ordure or urine, of a dog, a boar, a man, a cock, or a camel must have his investiture of the sacred thread re-performed. If a soma-drinking Brahmana inhales the scent of alcohol from the mouth of one who has drunk it, he should drink warm water for three days or warm milk for the same period. Alternatively, drinking warm water for three days, he should live for that period upon air alone. These are the eternal injunctions laid down for the expiation of sin, especially for a Brahmana who has committed these offences through ignorance and want of judgment.'"

CANTO 166

Vaisampayana said, "Upon the completion of this speech, Nakula, an accomplished swordsman, questions the Kuru Pitamaha lying on his bed of arrows.

Nakula says, 'The bow, O Pitamaha, is regarded in this world as the foremost of weapons. I, however, prefer the sword, O Rajan, for when the bow is cut off or broken, when horses are dead or weakened, a good warrior, well-trained in swordsmanship, can protect himself with his sword. He can single-handedly withstand many bowmen, or adversaries armed with maces and darts. I have this doubt, and I am curious to know the truth. O Rajan, which is really the greatest weapon in battle? How and for what purpose was the sword created? Who was the first guru of the weapon? Tell me all this, O Pitamaha.'"

Vaisampayana continued, "Hearing these words of the intelligent son of Madri, the virtuous Bhishma, the supreme master of the science of archery, as he lay stretched upon his bed of arrows, answers the high-souled adept Nakula, Drona's disciple, in profound and melodious words, displaying his considerable knowledge on the subject.

Bhishma says, 'Hear the truth, O son of Madri, about what you have asked me. Your question has caused my excited heart to send a flow of blood through my wounds like a hill of red chalk. In ancient times the universe was one vast expanse of water, motionless and sky-less, and without this earth occupying any space in it. Enveloped in darkness and intangible, its aspect was exceedingly awesome. In extent it was immeasurable, and utter silence reigned over all.

In his own proper time the Pitamaha of the universe took his birth. He then created the wind and fire, and the sun also of great energy. He also created the sky, the heavens, the nether regions, earth, the directions, the firmament with the moon and the stars, the constellations, the planets, the year, the seasons, the months, the two fortnights, lighted and dark, and the smaller divisions of time.

The divine Pitamaha, then, assuming a visible form, obtained by the power of his will some sons of great tejas. They are the sages Marichi, Atri, Pulastya, Pulaha, Kratu, Vasishtha, Angiras, the mighty and powerful lord Rudra and Prachetas. The last begot Daksha, who in his turn had sixty daughters. Maharishis took away all these daughters with the object of fathering children upon them. From them sprang all the creatures of the universe, including the Devas, Pitris, Gandharvas, Apsaras, diverse kinds of Rakshasas, birds and animals and fishes, monkeys, great snakes and diverse species of fowl that range the air or sport on the water, as well as vegetables, and all oviparous or viviparous beings or those born of filth. Thus the whole universe of animate and inanimate creatures sprang into existence.

The universal Pitamaha, having thus summoned into existence all mobile and immobile creatures, then promulgated the eternal religion laid down in the Vedas. That was accepted by the Devas, with their Gurus, priests, the Adityas, the Vasus, the Rudras, the Sadhyas, the Maruts, the Aswins, Bhrigu, Atri, Angiras, the Siddhas, Kasyapa rich in penances, Vasishtha, Gautama, Agastya, Narada, Parvata, the Valikhilya Rishis, those other Rishis known under the names of Prabhasas, the Sikatas, the Ghritapas, the Somavayavyas, the Vaiswanaras, Marichipas, the Akrishtas, the Hansas, those born of Fire, the Vanaprasthas, and the Prasnis. All of them obeyed Brahman.

The foremost of the Danavas, however, yielding to wrath and covetousness in the night, and against the Pitamaha's commands, began to cause the destruction of dharma. They were Hiranyakasipu, Hiranyaksha,

Virochana, Samvara, Viprachitti, Prahlada, Namuchi and Vali. These and many other Daityas and Danavas, transcending all restraints of duty and religion, sported and took delight in all kinds of evil deeds. Regarding themselves equal in point of birth with the Devas, they began to challenge them and the sages of pure behaviour. They never did any good to the other creatures of the universe or showed compassion for any of them. Disregarding the three well-known means, they began to persecute and afflict all, wielding the rod of chastisement. Indeed, the greatest of Asuras, filled with pride, abandoned every friendly interaction with other creatures.

The divine Brahman, accompanied by the sages, went to a delightful summit of Himavat a hundred yojanas in area, adorned with diverse kinds of jewels and gems, upon whose surface the stars seemed to rest like so many lotuses on a lake. On that prince of mountains, overgrown with forests of flowering trees, the greatest of the gods, Brahman, remained to carry out the business of the world. After the lapse of a thousand years, the powerful god made arrangements for a grand yagna, according to the forms laid down in the scriptures. The sacrificial altar was arrayed with Rishis adept in performing all yagnas, with faggots of sacrificial fuel and blazing fires, and embellished with beautiful sacrificial plates and vessels all made of gold. All the chief gods took their seats on the platform which further scintillated with the presence of high regenerate Rishis.

I have heard from the Rishis that soon something very awful occurred in that sacrifice. A creature appeared whose splendour equalled that of the Moon himself, when he rises in the star-studded firmament. Tall, lean, and dark with gleaming, sharp teeth, scattering the flames around him, he seemed irresistible and possessed of surpassing energy. Seeing him materialize, the earth trembled and the Ocean became agitated with tall waves and terrifying eddies. Meteors foreboding catastrophe shot through the sky. Inauspicious winds began to blow, branches of trees came crashing down, and all the points of the compass became unquiet. Creatures began to quake with dread. Seeing the fearful agitation of the universe at the entity which had sprung from the sacrificial fire, the

Pitamaha said to the great Rishis, the Devas, and the Gandharvas, "It was I who thought into existence this being of powerful tejas. His name is Asi, sword. I have created him for the protection of the world and the destruction of the enemies of the gods."

The being, abandoning the form he first assumed, then took the shape of a sword of great magnificence, highly polished and sharp-edged, which rose like the instrument of annihilation at the end of the Yuga. Then Brahma handed over that sharp weapon to the blue-throated Rudra, to enable him to put down irreligion and sin. At this, the divine Rudra of immeasurable soul, whose emblem on his banner is Nandi, the foremost of bulls, whom the Maharishis praised, took up the sword and assumed a different shape. Putting forth four arms, he grew so tall that, though standing on the earth, he touched the very sun with his head. With eyes turned upwards and with every limb extended, he began to vomit flames of fire from his mouth. Assuming diverse colours in his complexion, turning from blue to white to red, wearing a black deer-skin studded with stars of gold, he bore on his forehead a third eye resembling the sun in splendour. His other two eyes, one of which was black and the other tawny, glittered brightly. The divine Mahadeva, the bearer of the Sula, lacerater of the eyes of Bhaga, took up the sword whose splendour resembled that of the all-destructive Yuga fire. Wielding an immense shield with three high bosses which looked like a mass of dark clouds adorned with flashes of lightning, he began to perform diverse transformations. Mighty and powerful, he began to whirl the sword in the sky, hungry for an encounter. Loud were the roars he uttered, and terrifying the bellow of his laughter. Indeed, O Bhaarata, Rudra's form was exceedingly fearsome.

The Danavas, hearing that Rudra had assumed the form in order to undertake fierce deeds, began to advance upon him exultantly with great velocity, showering huge rocks upon him as they came, blazing brands of wood, and several terrible weapons made of iron, each as sharp as a razor. The Danava host, however, witnessing the swelling might of the indestructible Rudra, soon began to tremble with fear. Although

Rudra was alone and single-handed, he moved on the battle-field like quicksilver, sword in hand, so that the Asuras thought there were a thousand identical Rudras battling with them.

Tearing, piercing, afflicting, cutting, lopping off and grinding down, the Mahadeva moved among the masses of his foes like a forest fire raging through heaps of dry grass. The mighty Asuras, broken by the god whirling his sword, their arms, thighs and chests cut off and pierced, their heads severed from their trunks, began to fall down on the earth. Others among the Danavas, wounded by the strokes of the sword, broke and fled in all directions, inciting one another to escape. Some plunged into the bowels of the earth, others found cover under mountains, some went upwards and others dived into the depths of the sea.

As the dreadful and fierce battle progressed, the earth became mired with flesh and blood, and horrible sights were to be seen all around. Strewn with the fallen bodies of blood-drenched Danavas, the earth appeared overspread with mountains covered with Kinsukas, or like a beautiful woman attired in crimson robes, intoxicated with alcohol. After the Danavas had been slain and Dharma re-established on earth, the auspicious Rudra cast off his terrifying form and assumed his own benevolent shape.

All the Rishis and celestials then worshipped the Deva of gods with loud acclamations and hailed his conquest. The divine Rudra, gave the sword, the protector of religion, dyed with the blood of Danavas, with due worship to Vishnu. He presented it to the divine Marichi, who gave it to all the Maharishis, who in turn passed it on to Vasava. Vasava presented it to the Regents of the world, O Yudhishtara, who gave that large sword to Manu, the son of Surya.

At the time they gave it to Manu, they said, "You are the lord of all men. Protect all creatures with this sword that contains religion within its womb, meting out punishment to those who have transgressed dharma for the sake of the body or the mind. They should be protected in conformity with the law, never according to caprice. Some should be punished with oral rebukes, fines and forfeitures. Loss of limb or death should never be inflicted for slight reasons. These punishments should be regarded as diverse forms of the sword, of which verbal censure is the first. These are the shapes that the sword assumes as a result of the transgressions of men under protection."

In time, Manu installed his own son Kshupa as the sovereign of all creatures, and gave him the sword for their protection. From Kshupa, Ikshvaku took it, and Pururavas from Ikshvaku. From Pururavas, Ayus took it, and Nahusha from him. From Nahusha, Yayati took it, and Puru from Yayati. From Puru Amurtarya took it, and from him it descended to the royal Bhumisaya. From Bhumisaya to Dushmanta's son Bhaarata. From Bhaarata, O Rajan, to righteous Ailavila. From Ailavila king Dhundumara took it and from Dhundumara Kamvoja took it, and from Kamvoja, Muchukunda. From Muchukunda Marutta took it, and from Marutta Raivata. From Raivata Yuvanaswa took it, and from Yuvanaswa Raghu. From Raghu the valiant Harinaswa took it. From Harinaswa Sunaka took the sword and from him the Dharmatman Usinara. From the last the Bhojas and the Yadavas took it and Sivi from the Yadus. From Sivi it descended to Pratardana. From Pratardana Ashtaka received it, and from Ashtaka by Prishadaswa. From Prishadaswa Bharadwaja received it, and from the last Drona. After Drona Kripa took it. From Kripa, you and your brothers obtained that best of swords. The constellation under which the sword was born is Krittika. Agni is its deity, and Rohini is its Gotra. Rudra is its great acharya.

The sword has eight names, not generally known. Listen to me as I reveal them to you. If one mentions these, O son of Pandu, one can always win victory. The names then are Asi, Vaisasana, Khadga, Sharp-edged, Difficult of Acquisition, Sirgarbha, Victory, and Protector of Righteousness. Of all weapons, son of Madravati, the sword is the foremost. The Puranas truly declare that it was first wielded by Mahadeva. As regards the bow, again, Parantapa, it was Prithu who first created it. It was with the aid of this weapon that that son of Vena, while he governed the earth virtuously for many years, milked her of crops and grain in profusion. It becomes you, son of Madri, to regard what the Rishis have said, as conclusive proof. All men skilled in battle should worship the sword. I have now told you truly the first portion of your query, in detail, about the origin and creation of the sword, Bharatarishabha! One who listens to this excellent story of the origin of the sword will succeed in winning fame in this world and eternal felicity in the next.'"

CANTO 167

Vaisampayana said, "When Bhishma falls silent, Yudhishtira and the others return home. The king, addressing his brothers, with Vidura forming the fifth, says, 'The course of the world rests upon dharma, artha, and kama. Among these three, which is the greatest, the second, and the last, in point of importance? For subduing the triple aggregate, upon which of the first three should the mind concentrate? It becomes you all to answer this question truthfully and cheerfully.'

The highly intelligent Vidura, familiar with the science of artha, with the course of the world and with truth, first speaks, recollecting the contents of the shastras. Vidura says, 'Study of the various shastras, asceticism, gift, faith, performance of yagnas, forgiveness, sincerety of disposition, compassion, truth, self-restraint, these constitute benefits of dharma. Adopt dharma, never let your heart stray from it. Both dharma and artha have their roots in these, and all these are capable of being included in one term. It is by dharma that the Rishis have crossed sansara. It is upon dharma that the worlds depend for their existence, that the Devas attained their position of superiority. It is upon dharma that artha rests. The wise say that dharma, O Rajan, is highest in point of punya, artha is in the middle and kama is the lowest of the three. For this reason, one should live with restrained soul, paying attention primarily to dharma. One should also behave towards all creatures as towards oneself.'

After Vidura, Pritha's son Arjuna, well skilled in the science of Artha, and conversant with the truths of both dharma and artha, urged on by the drift of Yudhishtira's question, says, 'This world, O Rajan, is the field of action, and therefore one lauds action. Agriculture, trade, cattle-rearing and diverse arts constitute artha, which is the end of all such actions. The Srutis declare that without artha or dana, both dharma and moha cannot be won. Even men of uncleansed souls, if they have diverse kinds of Wealth, are able to perform the highest deeds of dharma and gratify desires apparently difficult to attain. The Sruti declares both dharma and moha to be the limbs of dana. Through artha, both dharma and objects of moha can be gained. Just as all creatures worship Brahman, even men of superior birth worship a wealthy man. Even those attired in deer-skins and bearing matted locks on their heads, self-restrained men who smear their bodies with mire, who have their senses under complete control, even shaven-headed Brahmacharins, and those who live separated from one another, cherish a need for wealth. The excellence of dana is attested by those attired in yellow robes, bearing long beards, graced with modesty, learned, contented, and freed from all attachments; those following the practices of their ancestors, and their respective duties and others desirous of heaven, believers and unbelievers, and rigid practitioners of the highest yoga. It is said that he who gives his dependants objects of enjoyment, and afflicts his foes with punishments truly possesses dana. Even this O best of intelligent men, is truly my opinion. However, listen now to these two speak.'

The two sons of Madri, Nakula and Sahadeva, then say, 'Sitting or lying, walking and standing, one should strive to acquire dana even by the most vigorous means. If one obtains dana, which is highly prized and difficult to acquire, one is certain to get all the objects of moha. The dana which is connected with dharma, and also the dharma which is connected with dana, is certainly like amrita. For this reason, our opinions are that one without wealth cannot gratify any moha; similarly, there can be no dana in one lacking dharma. He who is outside the pale of both dharma and dana, is therefore to the world an object of fear. For this reason, one should seek dana devotedly but without disregarding the requirements of dharma. They who believe this succeed in acquiring whatever they desire. One should first practise dharma; next acquire dana without sacrificing dharma; and then seek the gratification of moha, for this should be the last action of one who has been successful in acquiring wealth.'"

Vaisampayana continues, "The twin sons of the Aswins then fall silent, and Bhimasena begins to speak. 'One without moha never wishes for dana. One without moha never wishes for dharma. One without moha never feels any wish. For this reason, moha is the greatest of all the three. It is under the influence of moha that the very Rishis devote themselves to tapasyas, subsisting upon fruits or living only upon roots or air. Similarly, others who have Vedic knowledge study the Vedas and their branches, or rites of faith and sacrifice, or on making or accepting gifts. Traders, agriculturists, keepers of cattle, artists, artisans, and those who are employed in rites of propitiation, all work from moha. There are some who dive into the depths of the ocean, induced by moha. Indeed the principle of moha takes various forms and pervades everything. A man outside the pale of moha never is, was, or will be, seen in this world.

This is the truth, O Rajan. Both dharma and artha are based upon moha. Just as butter represents the essence of curds, moha is the essence of artha and dharma. Oil is better than oil-seeds, ghee is better than sour milk, and flowers and fruits are better than wood. Similarly, moha is better than dharma and artha. As honeyed juice is extracted from flowers, so moha is extracted from these two. It is the parent of dharma and artha, and the soul of both. Without moha the Brahmanas would never receive sweets or wealth, without moha the diverse kinds of action evident in the world would never occur. For these reasons, moha is the best of the triple aggregate.

Attired in excellent robes, adorned with every ornament, and exhilarated with sweet wines, you approach beautiful damsels to sport with them. Moha, O Rajan, should be for us the greatest of the three. Reflecting upon the question to its very roots, this is the conclusion to which I have come. Do not hesitate to accept it, O Dharmaputra! My words, not hollow but loaded with dharma, will be acceptable to all good men. Dharma, artha, and moha should all be minded equally. He who devotes himself to only one of them is certainly not a superior man. He who devotes himself to only two of them, is average, but he who attends to all the three is the best of his species.' Having said these words briefly and comprehensively to the heroes, the wise Bhima, smeared with sandal-paste, adorned with beautiful garlands and ornaments, and surrounded by friends, falls silent.

Then king Yudhishtira the Just, that most learned of virtuous men, duly reflecting for a while upon the words spoken by everyone and considering them all to be false philosophy, says, 'Without doubt, all of you have settled conclusions in respect of the shastras, and all of you know what the authorities say. I have heard the words you have spoken with such certainty, so listen now with concentrated attention to what I say. He who is not employed in punya or in paapa, he who does not attend to artha or dharma or moha, who is above all faults, who regards equally gold and a brickbat, becomes liberated from pleasure and pain and the need to accomplish his purposes. All creatures are subject to birth and death, and are liable to change and decay. Awakened repeatedly by the benefits and evils of existence, all of them applaud mukti. We do not know, however, what mukti is. The self-born and divine Brahma says that there is no mukti for one bound by ties of attachment and affection. The learned, however, seek Nirvana. For this reason, one should never regard anything as either agreeable or disagreeable. This view seems to be the best. No one in this world can do as he pleases. I work precisely as I am made to act. The great Ordainer, who makes all creatures proceed as He wills, is supreme. Understand that no one can, by his deeds, get what is unobtainable; whatever is to be, will be. And since he who has withdrawn himself from the triple aggregate can win mukti, it is clear that mukti produces the highest good.'"

Vaisampayana continued, "Having heard these significant, reasonable and persuasive words of Yudhishtira, Bhima and others are filled with delight and joining their hands, bow to the Kuru prince and applaud him. Indeed, O Rajan, hearing the beautifully turned speech of the king, so agreeable to the heart, so well adorned with sweet syllables and devoid of discordance and dissonance, those foremost of men begin to applaud Yudhishtira enthusiastically. The high-souled son of Dharma, of great tejas, in turn praises his auditors. Then, once more, the king addresses the great soul, Gangaputra, questioning him about dharma."

CANTO 168

"Yudhishtira says, 'O Pitamaha, you who are great in wisdom, I will ask you a question which I trust you will answer completely, O enhancer of the happiness of the Kurus. What kind of men are of gentle disposition? With whom can the most agreeable friendship exist? Tell us also who are always able to do good, now and later. I am of the opinion that neither immense wealth, nor relatives, nor kinsmen occupy the place of friends who wish us well. A friend who will listen to beneficial advice and will also do good, is exceedingly rare. O Mahatman, discourse fully on these topics.'

Bhishma replies, 'Listen to me, O Yudhishtira, as I tell you in detail of men with whom friendships may and may not be formed. You should avoid one who is covetous; one who is ruthless; one who has renounced the duties of his varna; one who is mean, cruel, or suspicious of all; one who is idle or procrastinates; one who is of a crooked disposition, who is an object of universal disgrace, who brings dishonour to his Guru; one of sinful practices, wedded to sin, addicted to the seven well-known vices; one of an evil soul, shameless, whose sight is always directed towards sin; one who is an atheist, a slanderer of the Vedas; one whose senses are not controlled, who transgresses all restraints, who gives free indulgence to lust; one who is untruthful, deceitful and a rogue; one who is foolish; one who is envious, whose conduct is bad, whose soul has not been cleansed; one who is a gambler, one who is deserted by all, and one who abandons or seeks to injure friends,

You should shun that wicked soul, O Bharatarishabha, who is never satisfied with what another may give him according to his means; who becomes angry on occasions that do not justify anger and wrangles without cause; who is restless of mind, a sinful person; who is never pleased with his friends, has no scruple in deserting well-meaning friends, and quarrels with friends when they do him a very slight injury or unintentionally inflict on him a wrong; one who speaks like a friend but acts like an enemy; a wretch of perverse perceptions who is always mindful of his self-interest but blind to his own good; one who never takes delight in what is good for himself or others.

Avoid one who drinks alcoholic liquors; one who is engaged in killing living creatures; one who hates others, is wrathful and without compassion; one who is pained at the sight of others' happiness; one who injures friends, is ungrateful and vile. Never form alliances of friendship with any of them, or with one who is always intent upon pointing out the faults of others.

Listen now to me as I specify those with whom alliances can be formed. Kings should accept those who are well-born, from good families, and perpetuators of their races; those possessed of agreeable qualities, eloquence and politeness of speech, varied knowledge and science; those who have accomplishments and merit, who have no faults; those who are free from covetousness and avarice; those who are never exhausted by hard work; those who are good to their friends, grateful, and firm in truth; those who have subdued their senses and are devoted to athletic and other exercises; those who are famous for forming alliances of friendship.

You should regard as persons worthy of friendship, O Rajan, those who are contented if one treats them according to the best of one's powers, who do not get angry on occasions that do not justify anger and are never displeased without sufficient cause; those who know well the science of Artha and who, even when annoyed, succeed in keeping their minds tranquil; those who devote themselves to the service of friends at personal sacrifice; those who are never estranged from friends but continue unchanged in their attachment like a blanket made of wool that retains its colour; those who never spurn anyone for being poor, who never dishonour young women by yielding to lust and loss of judgment; those who are trustworthy, who never point out the wrong way to friends; those who are devoted to the practice of dharma, who look equally on gold and brickbats; those who adhere with firmness to friends and well-wishers; and those who muster their own people to accomplish the business of friends, disregarding their own dignity and status. Indeed, the dominions of a king who befriends such superior men will spread in every direction like the light of the lord of the stars.

Alliances should be formed with men who are experts in weaponry, who have subdued their anger, who are always strong in battle and are of high birth, good behaviour and varied accomplishments. Among the vicious men that I have mentioned, O Rajan, the vilest are those who are ungrateful and who injure friends. Everyone should avoid these men of evil conduct. That much is certain.'

Yudhishtira says, 'I want to hear in detail a description of those who are injurers of friends and ungrateful persons.'

Bhishma replies, 'I will narrate to you an old story of what happened in the country of the Mlecchas to the north. There was a certain Brahmana belonging to the middle country, without any Vedic learning, who entered a prosperous village of hunters to beg for alms. In that village lived a wealthy robber, conversant with the distinctive features of all the varnas, who was devoted to the Brahmanas, firm in truth, and always engaged in charity. Going to the den of that robber, the Brahmana begged for alms, including a house to live in and such necessities of life as would last a year. The robber also bestowed on him a piece of new cloth and a young widowed woman. The Brahmana, Gautama, was filled with delight and began to live happily in the spacious house which the robber chief assigned to him, accommodating as well the relatives and kinsmen of the female slave he had been given. In this way he lived for many years in that prosperous village of hunters.

Gautama also began assiduously to practise archery and every day, like the other robbers living there, went into the vana and slaughtered wild cranes and other living creatures in great numbers. Through his intimacy with the robbers he soon forgot compassion, grew adept at killing creatures and became like one of the band. Living happily in that robber village for many months, he slew large numbers of wild cranes.

One day a Brahmana came to the village, clad in rags and deer-skins, with matted locks on his head. Pure of conduct, he was proficient in his study of the Vedas, humble in his disposition, frugal of habit, devoted to Brahmanas, and observant of Brahmacharya vows. The Brahmana belonged to Gautama's native area and had been his dear friend. In the course of his wanderings, he had come to the robber village where Gautama now lived. Since he never accepted food given by a Sudra, he began to search for the house of a Brahmana from where he could receive hospitality. Roving through the village infested with robber-families, he finally arrived at Gautama's house, just as he was returning home from the vana. Gautama was armed with bow and sword, carrying a load of slaughtered cranes, his body smeared with the blood that trickled down from the bag on his shoulders. The two friends met.

Recognising the man who had fallen away from the pure practices of the varna of his birth and now resembled a cannibal, the newly-arrived guest exploded: "What folly is this! You are a Brahmana, and the perpetuator of a Brahmana family. Born in a respectable family belonging to the middle country, how have you become a robber? Recollect, Muni, your famous kinsmen of earlier times, who were all well versed in the Vedas. Alas, born in their varna, you have become a stigma to it! Awaken yourself by your own exertions, O Muni, recollect the energy, the conduct, the learning, the self-restraint, the compassion that are yours, and abandon this present abode!"

Gautama answered him, great moved by the words of his well-meaning friend, "O Maharishi, I am poor and have no knowledge of the Vedas. Understand, O best of Brahmanas, that I abide here for the sake of wealth alone. However, today the sight of you is a blessing to me. We shall leave this place together tomorrow. Spend the night here with me."

The newly-arrived Brahmana, through compassion, passed the night there, but refrained from touching anything. Indeed, though hungry and invited repeatedly to eat, the guest refused to touch any food in that house.'"

CANTO 169

"Bhishma says, 'When the night had passed, O Bhaarata, and that best of Brahmanas had left, Gautama emerged from his house and walked towards the sea. On the way he fell in with some merchants setting out to voyage on the ocean, and with them he proceeded onwards. It so happened, O Rajan, that while the large merchant caravan was passing through a valley, an elephant in musth assailed it and killed almost everyone. Having escaped the peril somehow, the Brahmana fled northwards to save his life, not knowing where he was going. Parted from the caravan and far from where he started out, he began to wander alone in a forest like a Kimpurusha.

At last he came upon the road that led to the ocean, and on it he journeyed till he reached a forest abounding with flowering trees, inhabited by Yakshas and Kinnaras. Marvellous mango trees that put forth flowers and fruits throughout the year adorned that vana, in splendour like the very Nandana in Swarga. Salas, palmyras, tamalas with clusters of black aloes, and many venerable sandal trees also grew there. Upon that delightful tableland, fragrant with manifold perfumes, birds of various species poured forth their melodies. Winged creatures called Bharundas, with human faces, Bhulingas, and other birds belonging to mountainous regions and the sea, warbled sweetly.

Gautama made his way through the vana, absorbed in the mellifluous strains of birdsong. He came upon a level spot of land covered with golden sands, like Swarga itself in beauty. On the plot stood a towering and graceful nyagrodha with a spherical crown with many branches extending like a cupola over the plain, each branch like the parent tree in beauty and size. The area beneath the magnificent tree was drenched with water perfumed with heady sandal.

So enchanting was the place that it seemed to him a garden in the sabha of Brahma himself. Gautama was entranced by this auspicious glade, like the home of a Deva, and sat down with a contended heart. O son of Kunti, a delicious breeze, laden with the perfume of many kinds of flowers, began to blow softly, cooling his limbs and filling him with bliss. Fanned by that redolent breeze, the Brahmana was overcome by a fine languor and fell asleep.

Meanwhile the sun set behind the Asta hills in the west and, with the advance of twilight, a marvellous bird, the foremost of its kind, returned from the realm of Brahma to that magical glade which was his home. Nadijangha was his name and he was a prince of cranes, the wise son of sage Kasyapa, and a dear friend of the Creator. He was also well known on earth by the name of Rajadharman. Indeed, he surpassed all in fame and wisdom. The child of a celestial maiden, herself possessed of great beauty and learning, he was like a Deva in splendour. Adorned with many ornaments as brilliant as the sun, Rajadharman blazed with beauty. Seeing that amazing bird, Gautama was filled with wonder. But, exhausted and ravaged as he was by hunger and thirst, the Brahmana could only stare at the bird with the thought of killing it for food.

Rajadharman said affectionately, in exquisite human speech, "Welcome, O Brahmana! It is my great good fortune that has brought you to my home. The sun has set, and twilight is here. You are today my dear and precious guest. Let me worship you according to the rites laid down in the shastras, and you can go where you want tomorrow morning."""

CANTO 170

"Bhishma says, 'Hearing these sweet words, Gautama was astonished. Seized with great curiosity, he gazed fixedly at Rajadharman, who said, "O Brahmana, I am the son of Kasyapa by one of the daughters of the sage Daksha Prajapati. Welcome, O foremost of Brahmanas of great merit, you are my guest today."

After he offered him hospitality according to the rites laid down in the shastras, the crane made an excellent couch of the Sala flowers that lay all around. He also offered Gautama several large fish caught from the deep waters of the Bhagirathi, and offered his guest a blazing fire. After the Brahmana had eaten and was sated, the bird, possessed of tapodhana, the bounty of penances, began to fan him with his wings to drive away Gautama's fatigue.

Seeing his guest seated at his case, he questioned him about his ancestry. Gautama answered, "I am a Brahmana and my name is Gautama," and then fell silent. The bird made his guest a soft bed of tender leaves strewn with fragrant flowers. Gautama lay down on it, and was contented. The eloquent son of Kasyapa, who was like Yama himself in his knowledge of dharma, asked him about how and why he had come there. Gautama answered him, "I am very poor, O Mahatman. I want to go to the sea to earn wealth for myself."

The son of Kasyapa cheerfully told him: "Do not be anxious, you will succeed, O best of Brahmanas, and return home with much wealth. The sage Brihaspati has spoken of four means to acquire wealth: inheritance, sudden luck or the favour of the Devas, by labour, and through the aid or kindness of friends. I have become your friend. I cherish kind feelings towards you, and I will exert myself to help you acquire wealth."

The night faded and morning came. Seeing his guest rise refreshed from bed, the crane said to him, "Go, friend, follow this very route and you are sure to succeed. At the distance of about three yojanas from this place, there is a strong and mighty king of the Rakshasas. His name is Virupaksha, and he is a friend of mine. Go to him, O Brahmanottama. At my request, Virupaksha will surely give you as much wealth as you want."

Thus, Yudhishtira, Gautama cheerfully set out from that place, eating to his fill, on the way, fruits sweet as amrita. Gazing at the sandal, aloe and birch trees that stood along the road and enjoying their refreshing shade, the Brahmana went along quickly till he reached the city of Meruvraja. It had lofty archways and high walls of stone, and was surrounded by a deep moat. Large rocks and engines of defence were kept ready on the ramparts. Gautama was announced to the intelligent Rakshasa as a guest sent to him by his friend the crane, and received very gladly.

O Yudhishtira, the king of the Rakshasas ordered his attendants, "Let Gautama be fetched here immediately." At the king's command, his men, quick as hawks, went from his splendid palace to the gate and accosted Gautama, "You may have heard of our king Virupaksha, of boundless courage. He is impatient to see you. Make haste, do not tarry."

The Brahmana forgot his toil, in his surprise, and ran with the messengers. He was awestruck by the great affluence of the city and filled with wonder. Soon he entered the king's palace in the company of the messengers, agog for a sight of the king of the Rakshasas.'"

CANTO 171

"Bhishma says, 'Gautama was led into a spacious apartment, and introduced to the king of the Rakshasas. Virupaksha welcomed him with the customary offerings and gave him an opulent seat to make him comfortable. The king asked him about his antecedents and his practices, his study of the Vedas and his observance of the Brahmacharya vow. The Brahmana, however, only stated his name and vamsa, without answering his other queries.

The king, seeing that his visitor was destitute of Brahmanic splendour and Vedic knowledge, went on to ask about his country of residence. He asked, "Where do you live, O blessed one, and to what vamsa does your wife belong? Speak truly, do not fear. Trust us without anxiety."

Gautama said, "I belong by birth to the middle country. I live in a village of hunters. I married a Sudra woman, a widow. This is the truth."

Bhishma continues, 'The king then began to reflect as to what he should do, and how he might acquire punya. He thought to himself, "This man is by birth a Brahmana and a friend of the high-souled Rajadharman who has sent him to me. I must do what is agreeable to my beloved friend. He is is my brother, a dear relative and a true friend of my heart.

On this day of this month of Kartika, a thousand of the foremost Brahmanas are to be entertained in my house. This Gautama also shall be entertained with them, and I shall give wealth to him too. This is a sacred day and Gautama has come here to me as a guest. The wealth that is to be given away to the Brahmanas is ready. What is there, then, to think about?"

Even as Virupaksha was pondering this, a thousand learned Brahmanas came to the palace, purified by baths, anointed with sandalwood paste and flowers, attired in long robes of linen. The Rakshasa king received the guests according to the rites laid down in the shastras. At his command, O best of the Bhaaratas, skins were spread out for them for them to sit upon. The royal servants placed mats of kusa grass on the ground.

Those thousand Dvijottamas, having been duly honoured by the king sat down on those kusasanas. The Rakshasa chief ritually worshipped his guests, as decreed by the shastras, with sesame seeds, green blades of grass and water. Those among them who were selected to represent the Viswedevas, the Pitris and the deities of fire, were smeared with sandal-paste and received flowers as well as other kinds of costly offerings. After such worship, every one of them looked as effulgent as the moon in the heavens.

Then bright and polished plates of gold, adorned with engravings, and filled with excellent food prepared with ghee and honey, were laid before those Brahmanas. Every year on the days of full moon of the months of Ashadha and Magha, a large number of Brahmanas would be honoured thus by the Rakshasa chief and fed the rarest delicacies they could desire.

On the day of the full moon in the month of Kartika, after the end of autumn, the king used to give to the Brahmanas diverse wealth—gold, silver, priceless jewels and gems, pearls, magnificent diamonds, lapis lazuli, deer-skins, and hides of the Ranku deer. Indeed, O Bhaarata, having piled up a heap of wealth of many kinds to distribute as Dakshina to his blessed guests, the mighty Virupaksha would say to those Brahmanottamas, "Take from these jewels and gems as much as you wish and can carry away." He also used to urge them, "Take these plates of gold and vessels which you have used for your meal and go your way, O foremost of Brahmanas."

Invited by the high-souled Rakshasa king, those bulls among Brahmanas took as much wealth as each desired. Worshipped with treasures and clothed in excellent robes, those best of Brahmanas were elated. Meanwhile Virupaksha restrained the Rakshasas that had come to his palace from diverse lands and said again to the thousand Brahmanas, "This one day, regenerate ones, have no fear from the Rakshasas here. Sport as you wish, then leave us quickly when your hearts are full."

The Brahmanas then, having taken all they wanted, streamed out of Virupaksha's city with celerity. Losing no time, Gautama also took a sizeable quantity of gold and went his way. Carrying his burden with difficulty, he reached that same banyan under which he had met the crane. He sat himself down, exhausted and hungry.

While Gautama was resting there, O king, that best of birds Rajadharman came to him. Devoted to his friends, the marvellous krauncha gladdened Gautama by bidding him a warm welcome. Flapping his wings, he fanned his guest to dispel his fatigue. The wise crane worshipped Gautama, and made arrangements for his food.

Having eaten and refreshed himself, Gautama began to think, "Moved by greed and foolishness, I have taken this heavy load of bright gold. I have a long way to travel and no food to eat on my journey. How will I keep myself going?" He thought and thought, but could not devise how he would find any food to eat on his way home. Then, O Naravyaghra, a vile thought struck him, ungrateful as he was: "This prince of cranes, so large and amply fleshed, is here by my side. I will remain here quietly until I bag him, and then leave this spot and travel with great speed."'"

"Bhishma says, 'There, under that majestic banyan tree, the prince of birds had kindled and kept up a fire with high and blazing flames for the warmth and protection of his guest. On one side of the fire, the bird slept trustfully. The ungrateful and evil-souled wretch, with a flaming branch from that very fire, killed his sleeping host. He was delighted at having dispatched the crane, never thinking that he had committed a sin. Peeling off the feathers and skin, he roasted the flesh on the fire. Then, taking the cooked meat up with the gold he had brought, the Brahmana departed quickly from the glade of golden sand and the great nyagrodha tree.

The next day, the Rakshasa king Virupaksha, said to his son, "Alas, my son, I do not see Rajadharman, that best of birds, even today. Every morning he goes to the abode of Brahma to worship the Pitamaha, and never returns home without paying me a visit. Two mornings and two nights have passed without him visiting me and my mind is not at peace. Go and enquire after my friend.

Gautama, who came here, is without Vedic learning and Brahmanic tejas. He has found his way to the abode of my friend. I greatly fear that worst of Brahmanas has slain Rajadharman. I saw through him by the signs he showed of an evil mind and evil ways. Of cruel and grim visage, without compassion, that vile man is like a robber. This Gautama has gone to the abode of my friend, and my heart has grown very anxious.

Fly, my son, to Rajadharman's home and find out whether that pure-souled bird is still alive. Hurry!"

The prince, accompanied by other Rakshasas, set forth with great speed and, at the foot of the banyan, beheld the remains of Rajadharman. Sobbing with grief, the son of the Rakshasa king ran as fast as he could to seize Gautama. The Rakshasas did not have to go far before they caught the Brahmana and found on him the remains of Rajadharman, without wings, bones and feet. The Rakshasas hastened to Meruvraja with their captive. They showed the king the mutilated body of Rajadharman, and thrust the ungrateful sinner down at his feet.

Seeing the remains of his friend, the king, with his counsellors and priest, began to weep aloud. Indeed, the voices of lamentation were heard in his home and in the entire city of the Rakshasa king, as men, women, and children were plunged in grief. The king then said to his son, "Let this sinful wretch be slain, and let these Rakshasas here feast on his flesh. He is of sinful deeds, sinful habits, sinful soul, and inured to sin. You must kill this brute yourself."

Though commanded by their king, many fearsome Rakshasas of terrible prowess declared their unwillingness to eat the flesh of that sinner. Indeed, those wanderers of the night said to the king, "Let this vilest of men be given away to the cannibals of the forest." Bending their heads to their king, they told him, "It does not become you to give us this sinful wretch for our food." The king said, "Tathaastu! Let this ungrateful creature then be given to the man-eating brigands without delay."

The Rakshasas, armed with lances and battle-axes, hacked that vile wretch into pieces and gave his flesh away to the cannibals. However, even they refused to eat the flesh of that ungrateful man. For one who slays a Brahmana, drinks alcohol, who steals, or who has fallen away from a vow, there is expiation, O Rajan, but there is none for an ingrate. The cruel and heinous man who injures a friend will neither be eaten even by savage cannibals, nor even by the worms that feed on carrion.'"

CANTO 173

"Bhishma says, 'The Rakshasa king then had a funeral pyre made for the prince of cranes and adorned it with jewels, gems, perfumes and costly robes. Setting the body of the prince of birds upon it, the mighty chief of the Rakshasas had the obsequial rites of his friend performed according to the law.

Just then, the auspicious Devi Surabhi, the celestial cow and daughter of the sage Daksha, appeared in the sky above the place where the pyre had been set up. Her breasts were full of milk. From her mouth, O sinless king, froth mixed with milk fell upon Rajadharman's funeral pyre. At this, the prince of cranes revived and was whole again. Rising, he approached his friend, the king of the Rakshasas. The chief of the celestials himself also appeared in the city of Virupaksha. Indra said to the Rakshasa king, "How fortunate it is that you have revived the prince of cranes!" The lord of the Devas narrated to Virupaksha the story of the curse that Brahma had called upon Rajadharman, the best of birds.

Indra said, "Once upon a time, Rajan, this prince of cranes absented himself from Brahmaloka when his attendance was expected. In wrath the Pitamaha said, 'Since this vile krauncha has not presented himself today in my assembly, that wicked one will not die quickly so as to be able to leave the earth.' Because of the curse of Brahma, the prince of cranes, though slain by Gautama, has come back to life, through the virtue of the nectar with which his body was drenched."

After Indra had fallen silent, Rajadharman, bowing to the chief of the celestials, said, "O first of devas, if your heart is inclined graciously towards me, let my dear friend Gautama be restored to life!"

At this, O Narottama, Vasava sprinkled nectar over Gautama and restored him to life. Rajadharman, the prince of cranes, approached his friend Gautama, who still bore on his shoulders the load of gold that he had got from the king of the Rakshasas, embraced him joyfully and, dismissing the sinful Gautama, with his wealth, returned to his own home.

The next day, at the appointed time, he went to the Pitamaha, who honoured the high-souled bird with such attentions as are shown to a cherished guest. Gautama, too, returned to his home in the village of the hunters and sired many sinful children upon his Sudra wife. A dire curse was pronounced on him by the gods, that the ungrateful sinner should sink into a terrible hell for many years along with his children and wife.

This is the story that Narada once told me, Yudhishtira, and, recollecting the incidents of this weighty narrative, O Bharatarishabha, I have told you all its details. Whence can an ungrateful person derive repute? Where is his place? Whence can he derive happiness? An ingrate does not deserve to be trusted and can never escape a dire fate. He who injures a friend sinks into terrible and everlasting hell.

Everyone should be appreciative of friends and try to help them. Everything can be obtained from friends, honours and all kinds of objects of enjoyment. Through their efforts, one can escape from various kinds of danger and distress. A wise person should distinguish his friend with his best attentions. He should shun ungrateful men, for the shameless and sinful person who mistreats his friends is a wretch of his varna and the vilest of creatures.

I have thus told you, Yudhishtira, what the characteristics of that sinner are who is tainted by ingratitude and who harms his friend. What else do you want to hear?'"

Vaisampayana said, "O Janamejaya, hearing these words spoken by Bhishma, Yudhishtira is deeply gratified."

$$\frac{344}{16}$$
150 P